The Turgot Collection

Anne Robert Jacques Turgot
(1727–1781)

The Turgot Collection

Writings, Speeches, and Letters of
Anne Robert Jacques Turgot,
Baron de Laune

Edited by
David Gordon

© 2011 by the Ludwig von Mises Institute and published under the Creative Commons Attribution License 3.0.
http://creativecommons.org/licenses/by/3.0/

Ludwig von Mises Institute
518 West Magnolia Avenue
Auburn, Alabama 36832
mises.org

ISBN: 978-1-933550-94-7

Contents

Acknowledgements vii

Introduction by Murray N. Rothbard ix

PART I: ECONOMICS

1. Reflections on the Formation and Distribution of Wealth . . 5
2. Letter to l'Abbé de Cicé, since then Bishop of Auxerre, on the Replacing of Money by Paper. Also Known as the "Letter on Paper-Money" 69
3. Remarks on the Notes to the Translation of Josiah Child . . 81
4. Fairs and Markets 89
5. In Praise of Gournay 99
6. Observations on a Paper by Saint-Péravey 131
7. Observations on the Paper by Graslin 149
8. Value and Money 163
9. Plan for a Paper on Taxation 185
10. Extracts from "Paper on Lending at Interest" 205
11. Extracts from "Letters on the Grain Trade" 225
12. Letter to l'Abbé Terray on the "Marque des Fers" . . . 249
13. Six Projects of Edicts 261

    Which Suppresses the Corvée and Decrees the Construction of Highways for a Money Price 261

    Decreeing the Suppression of Craft-Guilds 274

    Which Repeals Certain Rules Concerning Grain Products 291

    Enacting the Suppression of the Exchange of Poissy . 303

    Enacting a Change and Modification of Taxes on Suet 308

    Enacting the Suppression of Offices Connected with the Ports, Quays, Stalls and Markets of Paris 311

PART II: PHILOSOPHY

14. A Philosophical Review of the Successive Advances of the Human Mind 321
15. On Universal History 347

PART III: SOCIAL QUESTIONS

16. On Some Social Questions, Including the Education of the Young 419
17. Local Government and National Education 431
18. Religious Liberty "Le conciliateur" 441
19. Religious Equality 451
20. Endowments 461

PART IV: CORRESPONDENCE

To Voltaire 475
To Condorcet 476
To David Hume 483
To Mlle. de Lespinasse 493
To Abbé Morellet 494
To Dr. Josiah Tucker 495
To Dr. Richard Price 498
To du Pont 506

Appendix: Miscellaneous Extracts 509
Sources 519
Index 523

Acknowledgements

The Mises Institute would like to thank the many people involved in preparing this manuscript for publication, most especially Peter Groenewegen, emeritus professor of economics at the University of Sydney. This book reprints many of his translations of Turgot's economics writings (sources are listed in the back) and we are very grateful for his permission for doing so. In addition, many have been involved in hunting for other resources, formatting, proofing, consulting and other editorial work over the years, including Theresa Heckman, Lauren Barlow, Jeffrey Tucker, Natalie Marcus, Eric Larsen, and Joseph Salerno. The inspiration for this volume comes from the work of Murray N. Rothbard.

Introduction

by Murray N. Rothbard

Anne Robert Jacques Turgot's career in economics was brief but brilliant, and in every way remarkable. In the first place, he died rather young, and second, the time and energy he devoted to economics was comparatively little. He was a busy man of affairs, born in Paris to a distinguished Norman family which had long served as important royal officials. Turgot's father, Michel-Étienne, was a Councillor of the Parliament of Paris, a master of requests, and top administrator of the city of Paris. His mother was the intellectual and aristocratic Dame Madeleine-Françoise Martineau.

Turgot had a sparkling career as a student, earning honors at the Seminary of Saint-Sulpice and then at the great theological faculty of the University of Paris, the Sorbonne. As a younger son of a distinguished but not wealthy family, Turgot was expected to enter the Church, the preferred path of advancement for someone in that position in eighteenth-century France. But although he became an Abbé, Turgot decided instead to become magistrate, master of requests, *intendant*, and, finally, a short-lived and controversial minister of finance (or "controller-general") in a heroic but ill-fated attempt to sweep away statist restrictions on the market economy in a virtual revolution from above.

Not only was Turgot a busy administrator, but his intellectual interests were wide-ranging, and most of his spare time was spent

---

This article is an edited version of a 1986 booklet, *The Brilliance of Turgot* (Auburn, Ala.: Ludwig von Mises Institute).

reading and writing, not in economics, but in history, literature, philology, and the natural sciences. His contributions to economics were brief, scattered, and hasty. His most famous work, "Reflections on the Formation and Distribution of Wealth" (1766), comprised only fifty-three pages. This brevity only highlights the great contributions to economics made by this remarkable man.

In the history of thought, the style is often the man, and Turgot's clarity and lucidity of style mirrors the virtues of his thought, and contrasts refreshingly to the prolix and turgid prose of the physiocrat school.

Laissez-faire and Free Trade

Turgot's mentor in economics and in administration was his great friend Jacques Claude Marie Vincent, Marquis de Gournay (1712–1759). It is fitting, then, that Turgot developed his laissez-faire views most fully in one of his early works, "In Praise of Gournay" ("Éloge de Gournay," or "Elegy to Gournay," 1759), a tribute offered when the Marquis died young after a long illness.[1] Turgot made it clear that the network of detailed mercantilist regulation of industry was not simply intellectual error, but a veritable system of coerced cartelization and special privilege conferred by the State. For Turgot, freedom of domestic and foreign trade followed equally from the enormous mutual benefits of free exchange. All the restrictions "forget that no commercial transaction can be anything other than reciprocal," and that it is absurd to try to sell everything to foreigners while buying nothing from them in return.

Turgot then goes on, in his "Elegy," to make a vital pre-Hayekian point about the uses of indispensable particular knowledge by individual actors and entrepreneurs in the free market. These committed, on-the-spot participants in the market process know far more about their situations than do intellectuals aloof from the fray.

---

[1] Turgot wrote the "Elegy" in a few days, as material for Gournay's official eulogist, writer Jean François Marmontel. Marmontel simply took extracts from Turgot's essay, and published them as the official eulogy.

In proceeding to a more detailed analysis of the market process, Turgot points out that self-interest is the prime mover of the process, and that in the free market, individual interest must *always* coincide with the general interest. The buyer will select the seller who will give him the lowest price for the most suitable product, and the seller will sell his best merchandise at the highest competitive price. Governmental restrictions and special privileges, on the other hand, compel consumers to buy poorer products at higher prices. Turgot concludes that "the general freedom of buying and selling is therefore the only means of assuring, on the one hand, the seller of a price sufficient to encourage production, and on the other hand, the consumer, of the best merchandise at the lowest price." Turgot concluded that government should be strictly limited to protecting individuals against "great injustice" and the nation against invasion. "The government should always protect the natural liberty of the buyer to buy, and of the seller to sell."

It is possible, Turgot conceded, that on the free market there will sometimes be "a cheating merchant and a duped consumer." But then the market will supply its own remedies: "the cheated consumer will learn by experience and will cease to frequent the cheating merchant, who will fall into discredit and thus will be punished for his fraudulence." Turgot, in fact, ridiculed attempts by government to insure against fraud or harm to consumers.

> To expect the government to prevent such fraud from ever occurring would be like wanting it to provide cushions for all the children who might fall. To assume it to be possible to prevent successfully, by regulation, all possible malpractices of this kind, is to sacrifice to a chimerical perfection the whole progress of industry.

Turgot added that all such regulations and inspections "always involve expenses, and that these expenses are always a tax on the merchandise, and as a result overcharge the domestic consumer and discourage the foreign buyer." Turgot concludes with a splendid flourish: "To suppose all consumers to be dupes, and all merchants and manufacturers to be cheats, has the effect of authorizing them to be so, and of degrading all the working members of the community."

Turgot goes on once more in the Hayekian theme of greater knowledge by the particular actors in the market. Gournay's entire laissez-faire doctrine, he points out, "was founded on the complete impossibility of directing, by invariant rules and by continuous inspection a multitude of transactions which by their immensity alone could not be fully known, and which, moreover, are continually dependent on a multitude of ever changing circumstances which cannot be managed or even foreseen." Turgot concludes his elegy to his friend and teacher by noting Gournay's belief that most people were "well disposed toward the sweet principles of commercial freedom," but prejudice and a search for special privilege often bar the way. Every person, Turgot pointed out, wants to make an exception to the general principle of freedom, and "this exception is generally based on their personal interest."

Turgot's final writings on economics were written while he was intendant at Limoges, in the years just before becoming Controller-General in 1774. They reflect his embroilment in a struggle for free trade within the royal bureaucracy. In his last work, the "Letter to l'Abbé Terray [the Controller-General] on the 'Marque des Fers'" (1773), Turgot trenchantly lashes out at the system of protective tariffs as a war of all against all using State monopoly privilege as a weapon, at the expense of the consumers.

Turgot indeed, in anticipation of Bastiat seventy-five years later, calls this system a "war of reciprocal oppression, in which the government lends its authority to all against all." He concludes that "Whatever sophisms are collected by the self-interest of a few merchants, the truth is that all branches of commerce ought to be free, equally free, and entirely free."[2]

Turgot was close to the physiocrats, not only in advocating freedom of trade, but also in calling for a single tax on the "net product" of land. Even more than in the case of the physiocrats, one gets the impression with Turgot that his real passion was in

---

[2] In the course of arguing in this letter for free trade in iron, Turgot anticipated the great Ricardian doctrine of comparative advantage, in which each region concentrates on producing that commodity which it can make efficiently relative to other regions.

getting rid of the stifling taxes on all other walks of life, rather than in imposing them on agricultural land. Turgot's views on taxes were most fully, if still briefly, worked out in his "Plan for a Paper on Taxation in General" (1763), an outline of an unfinished essay he had begun to write as *intendant* at Limoges for the benefit of the Controller-General. Turgot claimed that taxes on towns were shifted backward to agriculture, and showed how taxation crippled commerce, distorted the location of towns, and led to the illegal evasion of duties. Privileged monopolies, furthermore, raised prices severely and encouraged smuggling. Taxes on capital destroyed accumulated thrift and hobbled industry. Turgot's eloquence was confined to pillorying bad taxes rather than elaborating on the alleged virtues of the land tax. Turgot's summation of the tax system was trenchant and hard-hitting: "It seems that Public Finance, like a greedy monster, has been lying in wait for the entire wealth of the people."

Value, Exchange, and Price

One of the most remarkable contributions by Turgot was an unpublished and unfinished paper, "Value and Money," written around 1769. Turgot developed an Austrian-type theory first of Crusoe economics, then of an isolated two-person exchange, which he later expanded to four persons, and then to a complete market. By concentrating first on the economics of an isolated Crusoe figure, Turgot was able to work out economic laws that transcend exchange and apply to all individual actions.

First, Turgot examines an isolated man, and works out a sophisticated analysis of his value or utility scale. By valuing and forming preference scales of different objects, Crusoe confers value upon various economic goods, and compares and chooses between them on the basis of their relative worth to him, not only between various present uses of goods but also between consuming them now and accumulating them for "future needs." Like his French precursors, Turgot sees that the subjective utility of a good diminishes as its supply to a person increases; and like them, he lacks only the concept of the marginal unit to complete the theory. But he went far beyond his predecessors in the precision and clarity of his analysis. He also sees that the subjective values of goods will change rapidly on the market, and there is at least a hint in his discussion that he realized that this subjective value is strictly ordinal and not subject to measure.

Turgot saw that a "these *appraisals* are not permanent, they change continually with the need of the person." Turgot proceeds not only to diminishing utility, but to a strong anticipation of diminishing *marginal* utility, since he concentrates on the *unit* of the particular goods: "When the savage is hungry, he values a piece of game more than the best bearskin; but let his appetite be satisfied and let him be cold, and it will be the bearskin that becomes valuable to him."

After bringing the anticipation of future needs into his discussion, Turgot deals with diminishing utility as a function of abundance. Armed with this tool of analysis, he helps solve the value paradox:

> Water, in spite of its necessity and the multitude of pleasures which it provides for man, is not regarded as a precious thing in a well-watered country; that man does not seek to gain its possession, since the abundance of this element allows him to find it all around him.

Turgot then proceeds to a truly noteworthy discussion, anticipating the modern concentration on economics as the allocation of scarce resources to a large and far-less-limited number of alternative ends:

> To obtain the satisfaction of these wants, man has only an even more limited quantity of strength and resources. Each particular object of enjoyment costs him trouble, hardship, labor, and, at the very least, time. It is this use of his resources applied to the quest for each object which provides the offset to his enjoyment, and forms as it were the cost of the thing.

Although Turgot called the cost of a product its "fundamental value," he comes down generally to a rudimentary version of the later Austrian view that all costs are really "opportunity costs," sacrifices foregoing a certain amount of resources that would have been produced elsewhere. Thus, Turgot's actor (in this case an isolated one) appraises and evaluates objects on the basis of their significance to himself. First, Turgot says that this significance, or utility, is the importance of his "time and toil" expended, but then he treats this concept as equivalent to productive opportunity foregone: as "the portion of his resources which he can use to acquire an evaluated object without thereby sacrificing the quest for other objects of equal or greater importance."

Having analyzed the actions of an isolated Crusoe, Turgot brings in Friday, that is, he now assumes two men and sees how an exchange will develop. Here, in a perceptive analysis, he works out the Austrian theory of isolated two-person exchange, virtually as it would be arrived at by Carl Menger a century later. First, he has two savages on a desert island, each with valuable goods in his possession, but the goods being suited to different wants. One man has a surplus of fish, the other of hides, and the result will be that each will exchange part of his surplus for the others, so that both parties to the exchange will benefit. Commerce, or exchange, has developed.

Turgot then changes the conditions of his example, and supposes that the two goods are corn and wood, and that each commodity could therefore be stored for future needs, so that each would not be automatically eager to dispose of his surplus. Each man will then weigh the relative "esteem" to him of the two products, and supplies and demands until the two parties agree on a price at which each man will value what he obtains in exchange more highly than what he gives up. Both sides will then benefit from the exchange.

Turgot then unfortunately goes off the subjective value track by adding, unnecessarily, that the terms of exchange arrived at through this bargaining process will have "equal exchange value," since otherwise the person cooler to the exchange "would force the other to come closer to his price by a better offer." It is unclear here what Turgot means by saying that "each gives equal value to receive equal value"; there is perhaps an inchoate notion here that the price arrived at through bargaining will be halfway between the value-scales of each. He is, however, perfectly correct in pointing out that the exchange increases the wealth of both parties. He then brings in the competition of two sellers for each of the products and shows how the competition affects the value-scales of the participants.

A few years earlier in his most important work, "Reflections on the Formation and Distribution of Wealth,"[3] Turgot had pointed out the bargaining process, where each party wants to get as much as he can and give up as little as possible in exchange. The price of any good will vary in accordance with the urgency of need among the participants; there is no "true price" toward which the market tends.

Finally, in his repeated analysis of human action as the result of expectations, rather than in equilibrium or as possessing perfect knowledge, Turgot anticipates the Austrian emphasis on expectations as the key to actions on the market. Turgot's very emphasis on expectations, of course, implies that they can be and often are disappointed in the market.

The Theory of Production and Distribution

In one sense, Turgot's theory of production followed the physiocrats—only agriculture is productive, so there should be a single tax on land. But the major thrust of his theory of production was quite different from that of physiocracy. Even though only land was supposed to be productive, Turgot readily conceded that natural resources must be transformed by human labor, and that labor must enter into each stage of the production process. Here Turgot had worked out the rudiments of the crucial Austrian theory that production takes *time* and that it passes through various *stages*, each of which takes time, and that therefore the basic classes of factors of production are land, labor, and time.

One of Turgot's most remarkable contributions to economics, the significance of which was lost until the twentieth century, was

---

[3] The "Reflections" (1766), remarkably, were scribbled hastily in order to explain to two Chinese students in Paris questions that Turgot was preparing to ask them about the Chinese economy. Rarely has a work so important arisen from so trivial a cause.

his brilliant and almost off-hand development of the laws of diminishing returns. This gem arose out of a contest for essays on indirect taxation which he had inspired to be held by the Royal Agricultural Society of Limoges. Unhappiness with the wining physiocratic essay by Guérineau de Saint-Péravy led him to develop his own views in "Observations on a Paper by Saint-Péravy" (1767). Here, Turgot went to the heart of the physiocratic error of assuming a fixed proportion of the various expenditures of different classes of people. But, Turgot pointed out, not only are the proportions of factors to product variable, but also after a point, "all further expenditure would be useless, and that such increases could even become detrimental. In this case, the advances would be increased without increasing the product. There is therefore a *maximum* point of production which it is impossible to pass." Furthermore, it is "more than likely that as the advances are increased gradually past this point up to the point where they return nothing, each increase would be less and less productive." On the other hand, if the farmer reduces the factors from the point of maximum production, the same changes in proportion would be found.

In short, Turgot had worked out, in fully developed form, an analysis of the law of diminishing returns which would not be surpassed, or possibly equaled, until the twentieth century.[4] Increasing the quantity of factors raises the marginal productivity (the quantity produced by each increase of factors) until a maximum point is reached, after which the marginal productivity falls, eventually to zero, and then becomes negative.

The Theory of Capital, Entrepreneurship, Savings, and Interest

In the roster of Turgot's outstanding contributions to economic theory, the most remarkable was his theory of capital and interest, which, in contrast to such fields as utility, sprang up virtually full-blown, unrelated to preceding contributions. Not only that, but

---

[4] According to Schumpeter, not until a journal article by Edgeworth in 1911.

Turgot worked out almost completely the Austrian theory of capital and interest a century before it was set forth in definitive form by Eugen von Böhm-Bawerk.

Turgot's theory of capital proper was echoed in the British classical economists as well as the Austrians. In his great "Reflections," Turgot pointed out that wealth is accumulated by means of consumed and saved annual produce. Savings are accumulated in the form of money, and then invested in various kinds of capital goods. Furthermore, as Turgot pointed out, the "capitalist-entrepreneur" must first accumulate saved capital in order to "advance" their payment to laborers while the product is being worked on. In agriculture, the capitalist-entrepreneur must save funds to pay workers, buy cattle, pay for buildings and equipment, etc., until the harvest is reaped and sold and he can recoup his advances. And so it is in every field of production.

Some of this was picked up by Adam Smith and the later British classicists, but they failed to absorb two vital points. One was that Turgot's capitalist was a capitalist-*entrepreneur*. He not only advanced savings to workers and other factors of production, he also, as Cantillon had first pointed out, bore the risks of uncertainty of the market. Cantillon's theory of the entrepreneur as a pervasive risk-bearer facing uncertainty, thereby equilibrating market conditions, had lacked one key element: an analysis of capital and the realization that the major driving force of the market economy is not just any entrepreneur but the *capitalist*-entrepreneur, the man who combines both functions. Yet Turgot's memorable achievement in developing the theory of the capitalist-entrepreneur, has, as Professor Hoselitz pointed out, "been completely ignored" until the twentieth century.

If the British classicists totally neglected the entrepreneur, they also failed to absorb Turgot's proto-Austrian emphasis on the crucial role of *time* in production, and the fact that industries may require many stages of production and sale. Turgot anticipated the Austrian concept of opportunity cost, and pointed out that the capitalist will tend to earn his imputed wages and the opportunity that the capitalist sacrificed by not investing his money elsewhere. In short, the capitalist's accounting profits will tend to a long-run equilibrium plus the imputed wages of his own labor and skill. In agriculture, manufacturing, or any other field of production, there are two basic classes of producers in society: (a) the entrepreneurs/owners of capital, and (b) the workers.

At this point, Turgot incorporated a germ of valuable insight from the physiocrats—invested capital must continue to return a steady profit through continued circulation of expenditures, or dislocations in production and payments will occur. Integrating his analyses of money and capital, Turgot then pointed out that before the development of gold or silver as money, the scope for entrepreneurship had been very limited. For, to develop the division of labor and stages of production, it is necessary to accumulate large sums of capital, and to undertake extensive exchanges, none of which is possible without money.

Seeing that advances of savings to factors of production are a key to investment, and that this process is only developed in a money economy, Turgot then proceeded to a crucial Austrian point: since money and capital advances are indispensable to all enterprises, laborers are therefore willing to *pay* capitalists a discount out of production for the service of having money paid them in advance of future revenue. In short, that the interest return on investment is the payment by laborers to the capitalists for the function of advancing them present money so that they do not have to wait for years for their home.

The following year, in his scintillating comments on the paper by Saint-Péravy, Turgot expanded his analysis of savings and capital to set forth an excellent anticipation of Say's Law. Turgot rebutted pre-Keynesian fears of the physiocrats that money not spent on consumption would "leak" out of the circular flow and thereby wreck the economy. As a result, the physiocrats tended to oppose savings per se. Turgot, however, pointed out that advances of capital are vital in all enterprises, and where might the advances come from, if not out of savings? He also noted that it made no difference if such savings were supplied by landed proprietors or by entrepreneurs. For entrepreneurial savings to be large enough to accumulate capital and expand production, profits have to be higher than the amount required to merely maintain the current capital stock.

Turgot goes on to point out that the physiocrats assume without proof that savings simply leak out of circulation. Instead, he says, money will return to circulation immediately; savings will be used either (a) to buy land, (b) to be invested as advances to workers and other factors, or (c) to be loaned out at interest. All of these uses of savings return money to the circular flow. Advances of capital, for example, return to circulation in paying for equipment, buildings, raw materials, or wages. The purchase of land transfers money to the seller of land, who in turn will either buy something with the money, pay his debts, or re-lend the amount. In any case, the money returns promptly to circulation.

Turgot then engaged in a similar analysis of spending flows if savings are loaned at interest. If consumers borrow the money, they borrow in order to spend, and so the money expended returns to circulation. If they borrow to pay debts or buy land, the same thing occurs. And if entrepreneurs borrow the money, it will be poured into advances and investments, and the money will once again return to circulation. Money saved, therefore, is not lost; it returns to circulation. Furthermore, the value of savings invested in capital is far greater than that piled up in hoards, so that money will tend to return to circulation quickly. Furthermore, Turgot pointed out, even if increased savings actually withdrew a small amount of money from circulation for a considerable time, the lower price of the produce will be more than offset for the entrepreneur by the increased advances and the consequent greater output and lowering of the cost of production. Here, Turgot had the germ of the much later Mises-Hayek analysis of how savings narrows but lengthens the structure of production.

The acme of Turgot's contribution to economic theory was his sophisticated analysis of interest. We have already seen Turgot's remarkable insight in seeing interest return on investment as a price paid by laborers to capitalist-entrepreneurs for advances of savings in the form of present money. Turgot also demonstrated—far ahead of his time—the relationship between this natural rate of interest and the interest on money loans. He showed, for example, that the two must tend to be equal on the market, since the owners of capital will continually balance their expected returns in different channels of use, whether they be money loans or direct investment in production. The lender sells the use of his money now, and the borrower buys the use, and the "price" of those loans, i.e., the loan rate of interest, will be determined, as in the case of any commodity, by the higgling and haggling of supply and demand on the market. Increased demand for loans will raise interest rates; increased supply of loans will lower them. People borrow for many reasons—to try to make an entrepreneurial profit, to purchase land, pay debts, or consume—while lenders are concerned with just two matters—interest return and the safety of their capital.

While there will be a market tendency to equate loan rates of interest and interest returns on investment, loans tend to be a less risky form of channeling savings. So that investment in risky enterprises will only be made if entrepreneurs expect that their profit will be greater than the loan rate of interest. He also pointed out that government bonds will tend to be the least risky investment, so that they will earn the lowest interest return. Turgot went on to declare that the "true evil" of government debt is that it presents advantages to the public creditors but channels their savings into "sterile" and unproductive uses, and maintains a high interest rate in competition with productive uses.

Pressing on to an analysis of the nature and use of lending at interest, Turgot engaged in an incisive and hard-hitting critique of usury laws, which the physiocrats were still trying to defend. A loan, Turgot pointed out, "is a reciprocal contract, free between the two parties, which they make only because it is advantageous to them." Turgot moved in for the clincher: "Now on what principle can a crime be discovered in a contract advantageous to two parties, with which both parties are satisfied, and which certainly does no injury to anyone else?" There is no exploitation in charging interest just as there is none in the sale of any commodity. To attack a lender for "taking advantage" of the borrower's need for money by demanding interest "is as absurd an argument as saying that a baker who demands money for the bread he sells, takes advantage of the buyer's need for bread."

It is true, Turgot says to the anti-usury wing of the Scholastics, that money employed successfully in enterprises yields a profit, or invested in land yields revenue. The lender gives up, during the term of the loan, not only possession of the metal but also "the profit or the revenue he would have been able to procure by it, and the interest which indemnifies him for this loss cannot be looked upon as unjust." Thus, Turgot integrates his analysis and justification for interest with a generalized view of opportunity cost, that is, of income foregone from lending money. And then, above all, Turgot declares, there is the property right of the lender, a crucial point that must not be overlooked.

In the highly influential "Paper on Lending at Interest" (1770), Turgot focused on the crucial problem of interest: *why* are borrowers willing to pay the interest premium for the use of money? The opponents of usury, he noted, hold that the lender, in requiring more than the principal to be returned, is receiving a value in excess of the value of the loan, and that this excess is somehow deeply immoral. But then Turgot came to the critical point: "It is true that in repaying the principal, the borrower returns exactly the same weight of metal which the lender had given him." But why, he adds, should the weight of the money metal be the crucial consideration, and not "the value and the usefulness it has for the lender and the borrower?" Specifically, arriving at the vital Böhm-Bawerkian-Austrian concept of time preference, Turgot urges us to compare "the difference in usefulness which exists at the date of borrowing between a sum currently owned and an equal sum which is to be received at a distant date." The key is time preference—the discounting of the future and the concomitant placing of a premium upon the present. Turgot points to the well-known motto, "a bird in the hand is better than two in the bush." Since a sum of money actually owned now "is preferable to the assurance of receiving a similar sum in one or several years' time," the same sum of money paid and returned is scarcely an equivalent value, for the lender "gives the money and receives only an assurance." But cannot this loss in value "be compensated by the assurance of an increase in the sum proportioned to the delay?" Turgot concluded that "this compensation is precisely the rate of interest." He added that what has to be compared in a loan transaction is *not* the value of the money when it is loaned with the value of the money when it has been repaid, but the "value of the promise of a sum of money" compared to "the value of a sum of money available now." For a loan is precisely the transfer of a sum of money in the future. Hence, a maximum rate of interest imposed by law would deprive virtually all risky enterprises of credit.

In addition to developing the Austrian theory of time preference, Turgot was the first person, in his "Reflections," to point to the corollary concept of *capitalization*, that is, that the present capital value of land or other capital good on the market tends to equal the sum of its expected annual future rents, or returns, discounted by the market rate of time preference, or rate of interest.

As if this were not enough to contribute to economics, Turgot also pioneered a sophisticated analysis of the relation between the interest rate and the quantity of money. There is little connection, he pointed out, between the value of currency in terms of prices and the interest rate. The supply of money may be plentiful, and hence the value of money low in terms of commodities, but interest may at the same time be very high. Perhaps following David Hume's similar model, Turgot asks what would happen if the quantity of silver money in a country suddenly doubled, *and* that increase were magically distributed in equal proportions to every person. Turgot then points out that prices will rise, perhaps doubling, and that therefore the value of silver in terms of commodities will fall. But, he adds, it by no means follows that the interest rate will fall if people's expenditure proportions remain the same.

Indeed, Turgot points out that, depending on how the spending-saving proportions are affected, a rise in the quantity of money could *raise* interest rates. Suppose, he says, that all wealthy people decide to spend their incomes and annual profits on consumption and spend their capital on foolish expenditures. The increased consumption spending will raise the prices of consumer goods, and, there being far less money to lend or to spend on investments, interest rates will rise along with prices. In short, spending will accelerate and prices rise, while, at the same time, time-preference rates rise, people spend more and save less, and interest rates will increase. Thus, Turgot is over a century ahead of his time in working out the sophisticated Austrian relationship between what Mises would call the "money-relation"—the relation between the supply and demand for money, which determines prices or the price level—and the rates of time preference, which determine the spending-saving proportion and the rate of interest. Here, too, was the beginning of the rudiments of the Austrian theory of the business cycle, of the relationship between expansion of the money supply and the rate of interest.

As for the movements in the rate of time preference or interest, an increase in the spirit of thrift will lower interest rates and increase the amount of savings and the accumulation of capital; a rise in the spirit of luxury will do the opposite. The spirit of thrift, Turgot notes, has been steadily rising in Europe over several centuries, and hence interest rates have tended to fall. The various interest rates and rates of return on loans, investments, and land will tend to equilibrate throughout the market and tend toward a single rate of return. Capital, Turgot notes, will move out of lower-profit industries and regions and into higher-profit industries and regions.

Theory of Money

While Turgot did not devote a great deal of attention to the theory of money, he had some important contributions to make. In addition to continuing the Hume model and integrating it with his analysis of interest, Turgot was emphatic in his opposition to the now dominant idea that money is purely a conventional token. In contrast, Turgot declared, "it is not at all by virtue of a *convention* that money is exchanged for all the other values: it is because it is itself an object of commerce, a form of wealth, because it has a value, and because any value exchanges in trade for an equal value."

In his unfinished dictionary article on "Value and Money," Turgot develops his monetary theory further. Drawing on his knowledge of linguistics, he declares that money is a kind of language, bringing forms of various conventional things into a "common term or standard." The common term of all currencies is the actual value, or prices, or the objects they try to measure. These "measures," however, are hardly perfect, Turgot acknowledges, since the values of gold and silver always vary in relation to commodities as well as each other. All moneys are made of the same materials, largely gold and silver, and differ only on the units of currency. And all these units are reducible to each other, as are other measures of length or volume, by expressions of weight in each standard currency. There are two kinds of money, Turgot notes, *real* money—coins, pieces of metal marked by inscriptions—and *fictitious* money, serving as units of account or *numeraires*. When real money units are defined in terms of the units of account, the various units are then linked to each other and to specific weights of gold or silver.

Problems arise, Turgot shows, because the real moneys in the world are not just one metal but two—gold and silver. The relative values of gold and silver on the market will then vary in accordance with the relative scarcity of gold and silver in the various nations.

Influence

One of the striking examples of injustice in the historiography of economic thought is the treatment accorded to Turgot's brilliant analysis of capital and interest by the great founder of Austrian capital-and-interest theory, Eugen von Böhm-Bawerk. In the 1880s, Böhm-Bawerk set out, in the first volume of his *Capital and Interest*, to clear the path for his own theory of interest by studying and demolishing previous, competing theories. Unfortunately, instead of acknowledging Turgot as his forerunner in the pioneering Austrian theory, Böhm-Bawerk brusquely dismissed the Frenchman as a mere physiocratic land-productivity theorist. This unfairness to Turgot is all the more heightened by recent information that Böhm-Bawerk, in his first evaluation of Turgot's theory of interest in a still-unpublished seminar paper in 1876, reveals the enormous influence of Turgot's views on his later developed thought. Perhaps we must conclude that, in this case as in others, Böhm-Bawerk's need to claim originality and to demolish all of his predecessors took precedence over the requirements of truth and justice.

In the light of Böhm-Bawerk's mistreatment, it is heart-warming to see Schumpeter's appreciative summation of Turgot's great contributions to economics. Concentrating almost exclusively on Turgot's "Reflections," Schumpeter declares that his theory of price formation is "almost faultless, and, barring explicit formulation of the marginal principle, within measurable distance of that of Böhm-Bawerk." The theory of saving, investment, and capital is "the first serious analysis of these matters" and "proved almost unbelievably hardy. It is doubtful whether Alfred Marshall had advanced beyond it, certain that J.S. Mill had not. Böhm-Bawerk no doubt added a new branch to it, but substantially he subscribed to Turgot's propositions." Turgot's interest theory is "not only by far the greatest performance . . . the eighteenth century produced but it clearly foreshadowed much of the best thought of the last decades of the nineteenth."

Selected Readings

Böhm-Bawerk, Eugen von. 1959. *Capital and Interest*. Vol. 1. South Holland, Ill.: Libertarian Press. Pp. 39–45.

Fetter, Frank. 1977. *Capital, Interest, and Rent: Essays in the Theory of Distribution*. Edited by Murray N. Rothbard. Kansas City: Sheed Andrews and McMeel. Pp. 39–45.

Groenewegen, Peter D. 1983. "Turgot's Place in the History of Economic Thought: A Bicentenary Estimate." *History of Political Economy* 115 (Winter): 611–15.

_____. 1977. *The Economics of A.R.J. Turgot*. The Hague: Martinus Nijhoff. Pp. xxix–xxx.

_____. 1971. "A Reinterpretation of Turgot's *Theory of Capital and Interest*." *Economic Journal* 81: 327–28, 333, 339–40.

Rothbard, Murray N. 1995. *Economic Thought before Adam Smith*. Vol. 1. *An Austrian Perspective on the History of Economic Thought*. Cheltenham, U.K.: Edward Elgar. Pp. 383–463.

Schumpeter, Joseph. 1954. *History of Economic Analysis*. New York: Oxford Unversity Press.

Turgot, A.R.J. 1898. *Reflections on the Formation and the Distribution of Riches*. Translated by William J. Ashley. New York: Macmillan. Reprinted, New York: Augustus M. Kelley, 1921, 1963, and 1971.

PART I
Economics

Reflections on the Formation and Distribution of Wealth

Turgot first explains the need for a division of labor. If everyone had to produce whatever he needed, starting from an equal distribution of natural resources, almost no one would be able to secure his needs. The division of labor produces inequality, and this is a necessary price of progress. In the development of the division of labor and an expanding market, money is essential. As exchanges proliferate, a common price for a good, in exchange for another particular good, will establish itself. When each good has a price in terms of some other good, we can proceed to establish the price of any good in terms of any other good. In effect, every good functions as money. Nevertheless, it is practically necessary to have one or two goods singled out as money, and gold and silver have nearly universally been adopted for this function. Turgot first expounds the standard Physiocratic view that agricultural land is the sole source of productive activity, but he later emphasizes the importance of accumulation of money. This is essential for large-scale investment and a prosperous economy. The state should not restrict interest rates. The determination of the rate of interest should be left to the market. Without an adequate rate of return, accumulation of money will not take place.

CHAPTER 1

Reflections on the Formation and Distribution of Wealth

1. The impossibility of Commerce upon the supposition of an equal division of lands, where every man would possess only what is necessary for his own support.

If the land was divided among all the inhabitants of a country in such a way that each of them possessed precisely the quantity necessary for his support, and nothing more, it is evident that all being equal, no one would be willing to work for others. Neither would any of them possess the wherewithal to pay for the labor of others, for each person having only so much land as was necessary to produce a subsistence, would consume all he had gathered, and would have nothing which he could exchange for the labor of others.

2. The above hypothesis has never existed and could not have continued. The diversity of soils and the multiplicity of wants lead to an exchange of the products of the land for other products.

This hypothesis could never have existed, because the earth was cultivated before it was divided; cultivation itself having been the only reason for a division, and for that law which secures to every one his property. The first people who engaged in cultivation probably cultivated as much land as their resources permitted, and consequently, more than was necessary for their support.

Written 1766.

Even if this state of affairs could have existed, it could not possibly have endured; each man obtaining from his field only his subsistence, and not having the means wherewith to pay others for their labor, could only provide for his other wants of shelter, clothing etc. by his own labor, and this would be virtually impossible, *every type of soil by no means producing everything.*

The man whose land was fit only for grain, and would produce neither cotton nor hemp, would lack cloth to clothe himself. Another would have a piece of land suitable for cotton, which would not produce grain. A third would be without wood to keep himself warm, while a fourth would lack grain to feed himself. Experience would soon teach every one the kinds of products for which his land was most suitable and he would confine himself to the cultivation of that particular crop in order to obtain those things he required by means of exchange with his neighbors; who, having in turn reached the same conclusion, would have cultivated the crop best suited to their land, and given up the cultivation of all others.

3. The products of the earth require long and difficult preparations in order to make them suitable for the wants of man.

The crops which the earth yield to satisfy the different wants of man, cannot usually serve that purpose in the state in which nature gives them; they must undergo various changes and be prepared by art. Wheat must be converted into flour, then into bread; hides must be tanned or dressed; wool and cotton must be spun; silk must be drawn from the cocoon; hemp and flax must be soaked, peeled, spun, and next, different fabrics must be woven from them, and then they must be cut and sewn into garments, footwear, etc. If the same man who, on his own land, cultivates these different articles, and uses them to supply his own wants, was also forced to perform all the intermediate operations himself, it is certain that he would succeed very badly. The greater part of these preparations require care, attention and a long experience, such as are only to be acquired by working continuously and on a great quantity of materials. Take, for example, the preparation of hides: what laborer could attend to all the details necessary in this operation, which continues for several months, sometimes for several years? If he could, would he be able to, for a single hide? What a loss of time, space, materials which might have served either at the same time or successively, to tan a large quantity of hides! And even if he did succeed in tanning a single hide, he only needs one pair of shoes; what will he do with the rest? Shall he kill an ox to make this pair of shoes? Shall he cut down a tree to make a pair of wooden shoes? The same thing may be said concerning all the other wants of man, who, if he were reduced to his own field and his own labor, would waste much time and trouble in order to be very badly equipped in every respect, and would also cultivate his land very badly.

4. The necessity of these preparations brings about the exchange of products for labor.

The same motive which has established the exchange of various crops between the cultivators of different types of soil, must also have brought about the exchange of crops for labor, between the cultivators and another part of society which came to prefer the occupation of preparing and working up the produce of the land to that of growing it. Every one profited by this arrangement, for each, by devoting himself to a single kind of labor, succeeded much better in it. The husbandman obtained from his field the greatest possible quantity of produce and procured for himself by means of exchange all his other wants with much greater facility than he could have done by his own labor. The shoemaker, by making shoes for the husbandman, secured for himself a portion of the latter's harvest. Each workman labored to satisfy the wants of all other types of workmen, who in turn all worked for him.

5. Pre-eminence of the husbandman who produces, over the artisan who works up materials. The husbandman is the prime mover in the circulation of labor; it is he who causes the soil to produce the wages of every artisan.

It must, however, be observed that the husbandman, who furnishes everyone with the most important and the most considerable objects of their consumption (I mean their food, and moreover the materials of almost every manufacture) has the advantage of a greater degree of independence. His labor, among the various kinds of labor which are divided between the different members of society, retains the same primacy and pre-eminence, as the procuring of food did among the different works he was obliged, when in a solitary state, to employ himself in, in order to supply himself with his wants of all kinds. This is not a pre-eminence of honor or of dignity, but *of physical necessity*. The husbandman, generally, speaking, can get on without the labor of other workmen; but no workman can labor, if the husbandman does not provide his food. In this circulation, which, by a reciprocal exchange of wants, renders men necessary to one another, and constitutes the bond of society, it is therefore the labor of the husbandman which is the prime mover. What his labor causes the land to produce beyond his personal wants, is the sole fund for the payment of wages which the other members of society receive in exchange for their labor. The latter, by availing themselves of the price of this exchange to purchase in their turn the commodities of the husbandman, only return to him precisely what they have received. There is here a very basic difference between these two kinds of labor, which it is necessary to emphasise in order to be convinced of the evidence on which it rests, before dealing with the innumerable consequences which flow from it.

6. The wages of the workman are limited to his subsistence by the competition among the workmen. He gets only his livelihood.

The mere workman who depends only on his arms and his industry, has nothing except in so far as he succeeds in selling his labor to others. He sells it at a lower or higher price; but his low or high price does not depend on himself alone; it results from the agreement he makes with the buyer of his labor. The latter pays him as little as he can; because he has the choice among a great number of workmen, he prefers the one who works cheapest. The workmen are therefore compelled to lower their price in competition with one another. In every kind of work it must, and, in effect, it does happen, that the wages of the workman are limited to what is necessary to procure him a subsistence.

7. The husbandman is the only one whose industry produces more than the wages of his labor. He, therefore is the unique source of all wealth.

The position of the husbandman is materially different. The soil, independent of any other man, or of any agreement, pays him directly the price of his toil. Nature does not bargain with him to compel him to content himself with what is absolutely necessary. What she grants is neither related to his wants, nor a contractual valuation of the price of his days of work. It is the physical result of the fertility of the soil, and of the wisdom, far more than the laboriousness, of the means which he has employed to render it fruitful. As soon as the labor of the husbandman produces more than his wants, he can, with the surplus which nature accords him as a pure gift above the wages of his toil, purchase the labor of other members of society. The latter, in selling to him, only obtain a livelihood; but the husbandman, besides his subsistence, collects an independent and disposable wealth, which he has not purchased and which he sells. He is, therefore, the unique source of the wealth which, by its circulation, animates all the industry of society, because he is the only one whose labor produces more than the wages of his labor.

8. Primary division of society into two classes, the one productive or the cultivators, the other stipendiary, or the artisans.

Here then is the whole society divided, by a necessity founded on the nature of things, into two classes, both industrious, one of which, by its labor, produces or rather, draws from the soil, wealth which is continually regenerated, and which supplies the whole society with subsistence and with materials for all its needs; while the other is employed in giving to the said materials such preparations and forms as render them suitable for the use of man, and sells its labor to the first class, and receives its subsistence in exchange. The first may be called the *productive*, the latter the *stipendiary* class.

9. In Ancient times, the proprietor could not have been distinguished from the cultivator.

Hitherto no distinction has been made between the husbandman and the proprietor of the land, and in early times they were not in fact so distinguished. It is by the labor of those who were the first to cultivate the fields, and enclosed them to secure their harvest, that all the lands ceased to be common, and that landed proprieties were established. Until societies were consolidated and until public power, or the law, becoming predominant over individual power was able to guarantee to each man the tranquil possession of his property against all invasion from without, a man could retain the ownership of a field only in the way he had acquired it, and by continuing to cultivate it. It would not have been safe to get his field cultivated by another who, having taken all the trouble would not easily have understood that the whole harvest did not belong to him. Moreover, in this early time, as every industrious man would find as much land as he wished, he could not be tempted to till the soil for another. Every proprietor had to cultivate his fields himself or abandon them completely.

10. Progress of society; all lands have an owner.

But the land filled up and was cultivated to a greater extent. With the passage of time, the best lands all came to be occupied; there remained for those who came last nothing but the barren land, rejected by the first. But finally all land found an owner, and those who could not have properties had at first no other resources than that of exchanging the labor of their arms, in the occupations of the stipendiary class, for the surplus produce of the cultivating proprietor.

11. It begins to be possible for the proprietors to transfer the labor of cultivation to hired cultivators.

However, since the land returned to the owner who cultivated it not only his subsistence, not only that wherewith to procure himself, by way of exchange, the other things he needed, but also a considerable surplus, he could with this surplus pay other men to cultivate his land, and for men who live on wages it was as good to earn them in this occupation as in any other. Thus ownership could be separated from the labor of cultivation, and it soon was.

12. Inequality in the division of land: causes which make this inevitable.

The original proprietors at first occupied, as has already been said, as much land as their resources permitted them to cultivate with their families. A man of greater strength, more industrious, more concerned about the future, occupied more than a man of contrary character. He whose family was more numerous, as he had more needs and more hands at his disposal, extended his possessions further: here was already a first inequality. All pieces of ground are not equally fertile; two men with the same area of land and the same amount of labor, may reap a very different harvest: (this is a) second source of inequality. Property, in descending from fathers to their children, divided into greater or smaller portions, according to whether the descendants were more or less numerous; as one generation succeeds another, the inheritances are sometimes still further subdivided; sometimes they are reunited again by the extinction of some of the branches: (this is a) third source of inequality. The contrast between the intelligence, the activity, and above all, the thrift of some and the indolence, inaction, and dissipation of others, was a fourth principle of inequality, and the most powerful of all. The negligent and improvident proprietor, who cultivates badly, who in years of abundance consumes in frivolous things the whole of his surplus, finds himself reduced on the slightest accident to request assistance from his more provident neighbor, and to live by borrowing. If by a further accident, or by a continuation of his negligence, he finds himself not in a condition to repay his debt, if he is obliged to have recourse to new loans, he will at last have no other means at his disposal but to abandon part, or even the whole of his property to his creditor, who will take it as an equivalent, or assign it to another, in exchange for other assets with which he will discharge his obligation to his creditor.

13. Consequence of this inequality: the cultivator distinguished from the proprietor.

Thus is landed property made subject to purchase and sale. The portion of the dissipating or unfortunate proprietor serves to increase that of the proprietor who has been more fortunate or prudent, and in this infinitely varied inequality of possessions, it is inevitable that many proprietors must possess more than they can cultivate. Besides, it is very natural for a rich man to wish for a tranquil enjoyment of his wealth, and instead of employing his whole time in toilsome labor, to prefer to give part of his surplus to people who work for him.

14. Division of the produce between the cultivator and the proprietor. Net product, or revenue.

By this new arrangement, the product of the land is divided into two parts: the one includes the subsistence and the profits of the husbandman, which are the rewards for his labor, and the condition on which he agrees to cultivate the field of the proprietor; the other, which remains, is that independent and disposable part which the soil produces as a pure gift to him who cultivates it, over and above his advances and the wages of his trouble, and this is the portion of the proprietor or the *revenue*, with which the latter can live without labor, and which he takes wherever he wishes.

15. A new division of society into three classes: the cultivators, the artisans and the proprietors, or the productive, stipendiary and disposable classes.

We now behold society divided into three classes: the class of Husbandmen, for whom the name of *productive class* may be reserved; the class of artisans and others *receiving stipends* from the produce of the land; and the class of *proprietors*, the only one which, not being confined by the need of subsistence to a particular species of labor, may be employed for the general needs of the society, such as war, and the administration of justice, either by a personal service, or by the payment of a part of their revenue, with which the State, or society, may hire men to discharge these functions. The name which, for this reason, suits it best, is that of *disposable class*.

16. Resemblance between the two working, or non-disposable classes.

The two classes of cultivators and artisans resemble each other in many respects, and particularly in this, that those who compose them do not possess any revenue, and both equally live on the wages which are paid them out of the product of the soil. Both have also this in common, that they gain only the price of their labor and their advances, and that this price is nearly the same in the two classes. The proprietor bargains with those who cultivate in his land to pay them as small a part as possible of its product, in the same manner as he bargains with the shoemaker to buy his shoes as cheaply as possible. In short, neither the cultivator nor the artisan receives more than a bare recompense for his labor.

17. Essential differences between the two working classes.

But there is this difference between the two kinds of labor, that the work of the cultivator produces not only his own wages, but also that revenue which serves to pay the whole class of artisans and other stipendiaries, whereas the artisans receive simply their wages, that is, their share of the produce of the land in exchange for their labor, and do not produce any revenue. The proprietor has nothing but by the labor of the cultivator. He receives from him his subsistence, and the wherewithal to pay for the labor of the other stipendiaries. He has need of the cultivator because of a necessity arising from the physical order of things by virtue of which the soil produces nothing without labor; but the cultivator needs the proprietor only by virtue of human conventions, and of those civil laws which guaranteed, to the first cultivators and to their heirs, the ownership of the land they occupied, even when they ceased to cultivate it. But these laws can secure the man who does not work only that part of the produce which the land gives over and above the return due to the cultivators. The proprietor is obliged to give up the latter on pain of losing the whole. The cultivator, confined though he is to the recompense for his labor, thus preserves that natural and physical primacy which renders him the prime mover in the whole machinery of society, and which causes his own subsistence, as well as the wealth of the proprietor and the wages of all the other labors, to depend on his labor alone. The artisan, on the contrary, receives his wages either from the proprietor or from the cultivator, and gives them by the exchange of his labor, only the equivalent of these wages, and nothing more.

Thus, although neither the cultivator nor the artisan gains more than the recompense of his labor, the cultivator causes, over and above that recompense, the generation of the revenue of the proprietor; while the artisan generates no revenue, either for himself or for others.

18. This difference justifies their being distinguished as the productive class and barren class respectively.

We may then distinguish the two non-disposable classes as the *productive class*, which is that of the cultivators, and the *sterile class*, which includes all the other stipendiary members of society.

19. How the proprietors can draw the revenue from their lands.

The proprietors who do not till their lands themselves, may adopt different methods of having them cultivated, or make different arrangements with those who cultivate them.

20. First method: cultivation by wage laborers.

They may, in the first place, pay men, by the day or by the year, to till their fields, and reserve to themselves the whole of the produce, a method which assumes that the proprietor advances both the seed and the wages of the workmen until after the harvest. But this method has the drawback of requiring much labor and diligence on the part of the proprietor, who alone can direct the workmen in their labor, watch over the employment of their time and on their trustworthiness in not diverting any of the produce to their own use. It is true that he may also hire a man of more intelligence, whom he knows to be trustworthy, to direct the workmen and keep an account of the produce, as overseer or manager; but he will always be subject to fraud. Besides, this method is extremely expensive, unless a large population, and want of employment in other kinds of work, forces the workmen to be content with very low wages.

21. Second method: cultivation by slaves.

In times not very distant from the origin of society, it was almost impossible to find men willing to cultivate the land which belonged to others, because, all the land not as yet having been occupied, those who were willing to labor preferred the clearing of new lands, and cultivating them on their own account; this is more or less the case in all new Colonies.

Violent men have therefore conceived the idea of obliging other men by force to labor for them. They owned slaves. These latter had no justice to look for from the hands of people who could not have reduced them to slavery without violating all the rights of humanity. Yet, the physical law of nature still assures them their part of the products which they raised, for the master must necessarily feed them in order to profit by their labor. But wages of this kind are limited to the barest necessities and to their subsistence.

This abominable custom of slavery has formerly been universal, and is still spread over the greater part of the earth. The principal object of the wars carried on by the people of antiquity was to carry off slaves, whom the conquerors either compelled to labor for themselves, or sold to others. This brigandage and this trade still continue in all their horror on the coast of Guinea, where the Europeans encourage it by going thither to purchase Negroes for the cultivation of the American Colonies.

The excessive labor to which avaricious masters force their slaves, causes many of them to perish; and it becomes necessary, in order always to maintain the number requisite for cultivation, that this trade should annually supply a very large number of them. And as war is always the principal source which supplies this commerce, it is evident that it can exist only as long as men are divided into very small nations who are incessantly plundering each other, and as long as every district makes war upon its neighbors. Let England, France and Spain carry on the most cruel hostilities, only the frontiers of each State will be affected, and that in a few places only. All the rest of the country will be peaceful, and the small number of prisoners they could make on either side would be an inadequate resource for the agriculture of each of the three nations.

22. Cultivation by slaves cannot continue to exist in large societies.

Thus when men gather together into large societies, slave recruits are no longer numerous enough to take the place of those used up by agriculture. And although the labor of men is supplemented by that of beasts, there comes a time when the lands can no longer be worked by slaves. The employment of them is then retained only for domestic service, and in the end dies out; because as nations become more civilised, they enter into agreements for the exchange of prisoners of war. These conventions are the more readily made, as every individual is very much concerned to be free from the danger of falling into a state of slavery.

23. Bondage to the soil succeeds slavery proper.

The descendants of the first slaves, originally attached to the cultivation of the lands, experience a change in their condition. As internal peace within the several nations no longer leaves commerce the wherewithal to satisfy the excessive consumption of slaves, the masters are obliged to handle them with more consideration. Those who were born in the house, accustomed from infancy to their condition, are less revolted by it, and their masters have less need to employ severity in controlling them. By degrees the land they cultivate becomes their country; they have no language other than that of their masters; they become part of the same nation; good relations develop, followed by trust and humanity on the part of their masters.

24. Vassalage succeeds bondage to the soil, and the slave becomes proprietor. Third method: alienation of an estate in return for a fixed due.

The administration of an estate cultivated by slaves is an onerous task and a constraint on one's place of residence. The master secures for himself a freer, easier and safer enjoyment of his property by interesting his slaves in the cultivation of it, and by yielding to each of them a certain portion of the ground, on condition of their paying him a share of the produce. Some have made a temporary agreement, and have left their *serfs*, or slaves, only a precarious and revocable possession. Others have given up the estate in perpetuity, retaining an annual rent payable either in kind or in money, and exacting from the possessors certain duties. Those who received these lands, under the condition prescribed, became proprietors and freemen, under the name of *tenants* or *vassals*; and the former proprietors, under the title of *lords*, reserved only the right of exacting the payment of rent, and other stipulated dues. Thus things have come to pass in the greater part of Europe.

25. Fourth method: share cropping.

These estates, rendered free on the condition of payment of rent, may again change their proprietors, be divided and reunited in consequence of successions and sales, and such a *vassal* may in his turn have more land than he can cultivate himself. As a rule the rent to which those lands are subject is not so large but that, with good cultivation, there can still be procured, over and above the advances, the expenses and the subsistence of the cultivator, a surplus of produce which forms a revenue. Henceforth the *vassal* proprietor is also likely to desire to enjoy this revenue without labor, and to have his estate cultivated by others. Moreover, most of the lords alienated only those parts of their possessions, which are the least within their reach, and retain those which they can have cultivated with least expense. Cultivation by slaves being no longer practicable, the first method which offered itself, and the simplest to induce free men to cultivate estates which did not belong to them, was to give up to them a part of the produce; a plan which would induce them to cultivate the land better than laborers on fixed wages would be likely to do. The most common division has been that into two equal parts, one of which belonged to the cultivator and the other to the proprietor. This has given rise to the name of *métayer* (*medietarius*), or share cropping. In arrangements of this kind, which occur in the greater part of France, the proprietor pays all the advances of the cultivation, that is to say, he provides at his own expense the working cattle, the ploughs and other instruments of husbandry, seed, and the support of the cultivator and his family, from the time the latter enters into the *métairie* until the first harvest.

26. Fifth method: renting, or the letting-out of land.

Intelligent and rich cultivators, who suspected to what extent an active and well directed cultivation, for which neither labor nor expense was spared, would raise the fertility of the soil, rightly judged that they would gain more, if the proprietor should consent to give up to them, for a certain number of years, the whole of every harvest, on condition of paying him annually a fixed revenue, and making all the advances of cultivation. Thereby they would be assured that the increase in product obtained by their expenses and labor, would belong entirely to themselves. The proprietor, on the other hand, gained thereby a more tranquil enjoyment of his revenue, being freed from the care of making the advances and keeping an account of the product; a more steady enjoyment, since he received every year the same price of his lease; and a more certain enjoyment, because he never ran the risk of losing his advances, and the cattle and other effects with which the tenants had stocked his farm became a security for his payment. Besides, the lease being only for a small number of years, if his tenant had given him too low a price for his land, he could raise it at the end of the lease.

27. The last method is the most advantageous of all, but it assumes an already wealthy country.

This method of putting out lands to lease is the most advantageous of all both to the proprietors and to the cultivators. It is established everywhere where there are wealthy cultivators, capable of making the advances of cultivation; and as wealthy cultivators are able to bestow much more labor and manure upon the land, there results from it a prodigious increase in the productions and the revenue from estates.

In Picardy, Normandy, the neighborhood of Paris, and in most of the Provinces in the north of France, the lands are cultivated by tenant farmers; in the provinces of the South, by share-croppers.

Likewise the Northern provinces are incomparably richer and better cultivated than the Southern provinces.

28. Recapitulation of the several methods of making estates productive.

I have just enumerated five different methods by which the proprietors have been able to remove themselves of the labor of cultivation, and make their land productive by the hands of others.

Firstly, by workmen paid fixed wages.

Secondly, by slaves.

Thirdly, by giving up the estate in return for the payment of a rent.

Fourthly, by granting to the cultivator a fixed portion of the produce, usually half, the proprietor undertaking to make the advances of cultivation.

Fifthly, by letting their lands to farmers, who undertake to make all the advances of cultivation, and who engage to pay the proprietor a fixed revenue during the number of years agreed upon.

Of these five methods, the first is too expensive, and very seldom practised; the second can take place only in countries still ignorant and barbarous; the third is not so much a method of getting what one can out of a property as a surrender of the property in consideration of a lien upon the estate, so that the former proprietor is, properly speaking, no more than a creditor of the new proprietor.

The last two methods of cultivation are the most common, to wit: the cultivation by Share-croppers in the poor countries, and cultivation by farmers in the richer countries.

29. Of capitals in general, and of the revenue of money.

There is another way of being rich, without laboring and without possessing lands, of which I have not yet spoken. It is necessary to explain its origin and its connection with the rest of the system of the distribution of wealth in the society which I have just outlined. This way consists in living by what is called the revenue of one's money, or on the interest drawn from money placed on loan.

30. Of the use of gold and silver in commerce.

Silver and gold are two articles of commerce like any other, and less precious than many others, because they are of no use for the real needs of life. To explain how these metals have become the representative pledges of every kind of wealth, what influence they exercise in the progress of commerce, and how they enter into the composition of fortunes, it is necessary to go back a little and to retrace our steps.

31. Rise of commerce. Principle of valuation of exchangeable objects.

Reciprocal wants led to the introduction of exchange of what people owned for what they did not own. Commodities began to be exchanged for one another, and for labor. In exchanging, it is necessary that each party should agree to the quantity and quality of each of the things exchanged. In this agreement it is natural that each should desire to receive as much, and to give as little, as he can, both being equally masters of what they have to give in exchange, each has to balance the attachment he has for the commodity he gives, against the desire he has for the commodity he wishes to receive, and to fix accordingly the quantity of each of the things exchanged. If the two persons do not agree, they will have to approach one another by yielding a little on both sides, offering more and contenting themselves with less. I will assume that one needs corn and the other wine, and that they agree to exchange one bushel of corn for six pints of wine. It is evident that by both of them one bushel of corn and six pints of wine are looked upon as exactly equivalent, and that in this particular exchange, the price of a bushel of corn is six pints of wine, and the price of six pints of wine is one bushel of corn. But in another exchange between other men, this price will be different, according as one of them shall have a more or less urgent need for the commodity belonging to the other; and a bushel of corn may be exchanged against eight pints of wine, while another bushel shall be exchanged for four pints only. Now it is evident that not one of these three prices can be looked on as the true price of a bushel of corn, rather than the other; for, to each of the dealers, the wine he has received was equivalent to the corn he had given. In short, so long as we consider each exchange as isolated and standing by itself, the value of the thing exchanged has no other measure than the needs or desires of one party weighed with those of the other, and is fixed only by their agreement.

32. How current value is established in the exchange of commodities.

However, it happens that several Individuals have wine to offer to the man who has corn. If one is not willing to give more than four pints for one bushel, the owner of the corn will not give him his corn, when he comes to learn that someone else will give six or eight pints for the same bushel. If the former wishes to have corn, he will be obliged to raise his price equal to what is offered by others. The sellers of wine profit on their side by the competition among the sellers of corn. No one resolves to part with his commodity until he has compared the different offers that are made to him of the commodity he needs and he gives preference to the highest offer. The value of the corn and wine is no longer debated between two isolated individuals in relation to their respective wants and resources, but is fixed with those of all the sellers of wine. For he who would willingly give eight pints of wine for one bushel of corn, will give but four when he learns that an owner of corn is willing to give two bushels for eight pints. The price will become the current price to which all the buyers and sellers will conform in their exchanges; and it will be true to say that six pints of wine will be to everyone the equivalent of one bushel of corn, if that is the mean price, until a diminution of offer on the one side, or of demand, on the other, causes this valuation to change.

33. Commerce gives to all commodities a current value with respect to every other commodity; from which it follows that every commodity is the equivalent of a certain quantity of every other commodity, and may be looked on as a pledge which represents it.

Corn is not only exchanged for wine, but also for all other commodities which the owners of corn may need, such as wood, leather, wool, cotton, etc.; it is the same with wine and every other particular commodity. If one bushel of corn is equivalent to six pints of wine, and one sheep is equivalent to three bushels of corn, this same sheep will be equivalent to eighteen pints of wine. He, who, having corn, wants wine, may, without inconvenience, exchange his corn for a sheep, in order afterward to exchange the sheep for the wine which he needs.

34. Each commodity may serve as a scale or common measure, by which to compare the value of all others.

It follows from this, that in a country where commerce is brisk, where there is much production and much consumption, where there are many offers and demands for all sorts of commodities, each kind will have a current price relative to every other kind; that is a certain quantity of one will be of equal value with a certain quantity of each of the others. Thus the same quantity of corn which is worth eighteen pints of wine, will also be worth one sheep, a piece of dressed leather, or a certain quantity of iron, and all these things will have an equal value in commerce. To express or make known the value of any particular thing, it is evident that it is sufficient to state the quantity of any other known commodity which will be looked on as if equivalent. Thus, to make known what a piece of leather of a certain size is worth, we may say indifferently that it is worth three bushels of corn, or eighteen pints of wine. We may similarly express the value of a certain quantity of wine by the number of sheep, or bushels of corn which it is worth in commerce.

From this it can be seen that all the kinds of commodities which are exchangeable objects, measure one another, so to speak, and that each may serve as a common measure, or scale of comparison to which to refer the value of all the others; and in like manner each commodity becomes in the hands of its owner, a means to obtain all the others, a sort of universal pledge.

35. Every commodity does not present an equally convenient scale of values. The preference, therefore, has in practice necessarily been given to those which, not being susceptible to any great

The Formation and Distribution of Wealth

difference in quality, have a value principally related to the number and the quantity.

But although all commodities have essentially this property of representing all others, being able to serve as a common measure to express their value, and as a universal pledge to procure all of them by way of an exchange, all cannot be used with the same degree of facility for these two purposes. The more susceptible any commodity is to changing its value on account of its quality, the more difficult it is to use it as a scale to which to relate the value of other commodities. For example, if eighteen pints of wine of *Anjou* are the equivalent of one sheep, eighteen pints of *Cape* wine may be the equivalent of eighteen sheep. Thus the person who, to express the value of a sheep, would say that it is worth eighteen pints of wine, would be using ambiguous speech which would not communicate any precise idea, at least until he added a good many explanations, which would be very inconvenient. Men, therefore, have been obliged to prefer for their scale of comparison such commodities, which being more commonly in use and consequently of a better known value, were more like each other, and of which, consequently, the value had more relation to the number of the quantity than to the quality.

36. The want of an exact correspondence between the value and the number or quantity is supplied by average valuation, which becomes an ideal money.

In a country where there is only one race of sheep, the value of a fleece or of a sheep may easily be taken for the common measure of values, and it may be said that a barrel of wine, or a piece of stuff, is worth a certain number of fleeces or sheep. There is in reality some inequality among sheep, but when it is a question of selling sheep, care is taken to estimate that inequality, and to reckon, for example, two lambs as one sheep. When it is a question of valuing any other commodity, the common value of a sheep of medium age and condition is taken as the unit. In this way, the expression of values in terms of sheep becomes an agreed form of expression, and this word one sheep, in the language of commerce, simply signifies a certain value which, in the minds of those who hear it, carries not merely the idea of one sheep, but of a certain quantity of the more common types of commodities which are regarded as the equivalent of this value, and this expression will end by being so entirely applied to a fictitious and abstract value, rather than to a real sheep, and that [if by chance a pestilence occurs among the sheep, and in order][1] to purchase one of them, it becomes necessary to give double the quantity of corn or wine that was formerly given, people will rather say that *one sheep* is worth *two sheep* than change the expression they have been accustomed to for all the other values.

37. Examples of those mean valuations which become an ideal expression of value.

In the commerce of all nations, several examples are known of these fictitious valuations in terms of commodities which are, so to speak, only an agreed form of expression of their value. Thus the cooks of Paris, and the fishmongers who provide great houses, generally sell *by the piece*. A fat pullet is reckoned as one piece, a chicken as half a piece, more or less, according to the season, and so on. In the slave trade to the American Colonies, a cargo of Negroes is sold at the rate of so much per Negro head, *a piece of India*. The women and children are valued in such a way that, for example, three children, or one woman and one child, are reckoned as one head of Negro. The valuation is increased or diminished on account of the strength or other qualities of the slaves, so that certain slaves are reckoned as *two head of Negro*.

The *Mandingo* Negros, who carry on the gold dust trade with the Arabian merchants, relate all their commodities to a fictitious scale whose parts are called *macutes*, so that they tell the merchants that they will give so many *macutes* in gold. They value likewise in *macutes* the commodities they receive, and bargain with the merchants on this valuation.

In the same way in Holland people reckon by *bank florins*, which are only fictitious money, and which in commerce, have

---

[1] Line missing in Groenewegen translation. Taken from Ashley, *Reflections*, 1989. [Ed. note.]

sometimes a higher, sometimes a lower value than the coins called *florins*.

38. Every commodity is a pledge representing all other commodities, but it is more or less convenient in practice according to the ease with which it can be transported and stored without deterioration.

The variation in the quality of commodities, and in their prices in accordance with that quality, which renders them more or less suitable than others to serve as a common measure, is also more or less an impediment to their being a representative pledge of every other commodity of a like value. But with respect to this last property there is also a very great difference between the different types of commodities. For example, it is evident that a man who owns a piece of cloth, is far more certain of obtaining a certain quantity of corn for it, when he wants it, than if he had a barrel of wine of the same value, the wine being subject to an infinity of accidents which in an instant may cause it to lose its entire value.

39. Every commodity has the two essential properties of money, of measuring and representing all value; and in this sense all merchandise is money.

The two properties of serving as a common measure of all values, and of being a representative pledge of all other commodities of a like value, include everything that constitutes the essence and use of what is called money; and it follows from the details which I have just given, that all merchandise is, in some respect, *money*, and shares more or less, according to the nature of each, in these two essential properties. All are more or less suitable to serve as a common measure in proportion as they are in more general use, of more similar quality, and easier to divide into parts of equal value. All are more or less suitable to be a universal pledge of exchanges in proportion as they are less susceptible to deterioration or alteration in quantity or quality.

40. Reciprocally, all money is essentially merchandise.

We can take only what itself has a value as a common measure of value, that which is received in commerce in exchange for other values; and there is no universal, representative pledge of value, except something of equal value. Purely conventional money is therefore an impossibility.

41. Different substances have been able to serve, and have served, as ordinary money.

Many nations have adopted in their language and in their trade, as a common measure of value, different substances, more or less precious; there are even at this day some barbaric peoples who make use of a species of little shells called *Cowries*. I remember having seen, when at College, apricot stones exchanged and passed as a type of money among the Scholars, who used them to play certain games. I have already spoken of the reckoning by head of cattle; traces of this can be found in the Laws of the ancient Germanic nations who broke up the Roman Empire. The early Romans, or at least the Latins, their ancestors, made use of it also. It is claimed that the first coins they struck in copper, represented the value of a sheep, and bore the image of that animal, and that the name of *pecunia*, has come from *pecus*. This conjecture has a great deal of probability.

42. Metals, and particularly gold and silver, are the most suitable for this purpose: and why.

We have now come to the introduction of the precious metals into commerce. All the metals, as they have been discovered, have been admitted into exchange, on account of their real usefulness: their splendor has caused them to be sought after, to serve as ornaments; their malleability and their solidity have rendered them suitable for making utensils, more durable and lighter than those of clay. But these substances could not be brought into commerce without almost immediately becoming a universal Money. A piece of any metal, of whatever sort, has the same qualities as another piece of the same metal, provided they are both equally pure. Now, the ease with which we can separate, by different chemical operations, a metal from other metals with which it is incorporated, enables us always to bring it to the degree of purity, or, as it is called, the *standard*, which is desired, and the value of metal can only vary then according to its weight. In expressing, therefore, the value of all commodities by the weight of metal which may be had in exchange, we shall have the clearest, the most convenient, and the most precise expression of value; and hence it is impossible that it should not, in practice, be preferred to every other. Nor are the metals less suitable than other commodities for becoming the universal pledge of all the values that they can measure; as they are susceptible for all imaginable divisions, there is no commodity whose value, great or small, cannot be exactly paid for by a certain quantity of metal. To this advantage of lending themselves to every kind of division, they join that of being unalterable, and those which are scarce, like gold and silver, have a very great value in a very inconsiderable weight and bulk.

These two metals then, are, of all commodities, the most easy to verify as to their quality, to divide as to their quantity, to keep for a long time without deterioration, and to convey to all places at the least expense. Every one who has a surplus commodity and who does not need, at the time, any other commodity for use, will hasten to exchange it for money, with which he is more certain than with anything else, to procure himself the commodity he wants at the moment he needs it.

43. By the nature of things, gold and silver are constituted money and universal money, independently of any convention and of any law.

Here then are gold and silver constituted money, and universal money, and that without any arbitrary agreement among men, without the intervention of any law, but only by the nature of things. They are not, as people imagine, signs of value; they have a value themselves. If they are capable of being the measure and pledge of other values, they have this property in common with all other commodities which have a value in commerce. They differ from them only because, being at the same time more divisible, more unchangeable, and of more easy conveyance than other commodities, it is more convenient to use them to measure and represent value.

44. The employment of other metals for these purposes is only subsidiary.

All metals would be capable of being used as money. But those which are very common have too little value in too large a bulk to be used in the everyday exchanges in trade. Copper, silver, and gold are the only ones which have been brought into constant use. And even copper, except among some peoples to whom neither mines nor commerce have supplied a sufficient quantity of gold or silver, has never been used except in exchanges of the smallest values.

45. The use of gold and silver as money has augmented their value as substances.

It is impossible but that the eagerness with which every one has sought to exchange his superfluous commodities for gold and silver, rather than for any other commodity, must have greatly augmented the value of these two materials in commerce. They are thereby rendered more suitable for their employment as pledge, or common measure.

46. Variations in the value of gold and of silver, compared with the other commodities, and with one another.

This value is susceptible to change, and in fact does continually change so that the same quantity of metal which answered to a certain quantity of such or such a commodity, ceases to correspond to it, and more or less money is required to represent the same commodity. When it requires more, the commodity is said to be dearer; when it requires less, it is said to be cheaper; but it might just as well be said that it is the money which is cheaper in the first case, and dearer in the latter. Silver and gold vary in price not only as compared with all other commodities, but they also vary in price among themselves, according as they are more or less abundant. It is well known that in Europe at the present time from fourteen to fifteen ounces of silver are given for one ounce of gold, and that in former times only ten to eleven ounces of silver were given for one ounce of gold. In China, even at present only about twelve ounces of silver are given to get one ounce of gold, so that there is a very great advantage in carrying silver to China, to exchange for gold to bring back to Europe. It is evident that, in the long run, this commerce will make gold more common in Europe and less common in China, and that the value of these two metals must finally come to the same proportion everywhere.

A thousand different causes compete to determine at any moment the value of commodities when compared either with each other, or with silver, and cause them to change incessantly. The same causes determine the value (of money), and cause it to vary, when compared either with the value of each particular commodity, or with all the other values which are in commerce at the time. It is not possible to disentangle these different causes, and to unfold their effects, without entering into very extensive and very difficult details, and I shall abstain from entering upon this discussion.

47. The practice of making payment in money has given rise to the distinction between seller and buyer.

In proportion as people have become accustomed to the practice of valuing everything in money, of exchanging all their superfluous commodities for money, and of not parting with that money but for the things which are useful or agreeable to them at the moment, they have become accustomed to consider the exchanges of commerce from a new point of view. They have distinguished two persons, the seller and the buyer: the seller was the one who gave commodities for money, and the buyer was the one who gave money for commodities.

48. The use of money has greatly facilitated the separation of the different labors among the different members of society.

The more money came to stand for everything else, the more did it become possible for everyone, by devoting himself entirely to the kind of cultivation and industry he had chosen, to relieve himself completely of all care of supplying his other wants, and to think only of obtaining as much money as possible, by the sale of his fruits or his labor, very sure that by means of this money he could get all the rest: in this way the use of money has prodigiously hastened the progress of society.

49. Of the reserve of annual produce, accumulated to form capitals.

As soon as men were found whose property in land assured them an annual revenue more than sufficient to satisfy all their requirements, there were sure to be found men who, anxious about the future, or merely prudent, put aside part of what they gathered every year, either to meet contingencies, or to increase their comforts. When the produce they gathered was difficult to preserve, they must have sought to obtain, by exchange, articles of a more durable nature, whose value would not be destroyed by time, or which could be employed in such a manner, as to procure profits which would more than make up for their deterioration.

50. Moveable wealth;[2] accumulation of money.

Possessions of this kind, resulting from the accumulation of annual produce not consumed, are known by the name of *moveable wealth*. Furniture, houses, plate, commodities in warehouses, the tools of each trade, and cattle, belong to this kind of wealth. It is evident that men toiled hard to procure themselves as much as they could of this kind of wealth, before they became acquainted with money; but it is no less clear that, as soon as it was known, as soon as it was proved to be the most changeable of all commodities, and the easiest to keep without trouble, it could not fail to be sought after by whoever wished to accumulate. It was not only the proprietors of landed estates who thus accumulated their surplus produce. Although the profits of industry are not, like the revenue of the soil, a gift of nature, and the working man draws from his labor only the price which is given him by the persons who pay him his wages;

---

[2] The French, *richesses mobilières,* translated here as "moveable wealth," has a wider connotation in that it is also the antonym of real property. In this sense, Turgot's division of wealth into *bien-fonds* and *richesses mobilières* also implies the legal distinction between real and personal property.

although the latter economises as much as possible in the payment of these wages, and competition obliges the working man to content himself with a price less than he would like, it is nevertheless certain that this competition has never been numerous or keen enough in any kind of labor, to prevent, at any time, a man who is more expert, more active, and above all, more thrifty than others in his personal consumption, from earning a little more than was necessary for the subsistence of himself and his family, and from setting aside this surplus to create therewith a little store.

51. Moveable wealth is an indispensable prerequisite for all lucrative work.

It is also necessary that in every trade the workmen or the entrepreneur who set them to work have a certain fund of moveable wealth, accumulated beforehand. Here we are again obliged to retrace our steps and to recall several matters which at first were only hinted at in passing, when the division of the several professions was discussed, and the different methods by which proprietors could make their estates productive; because this could not be explained at that time without breaking the line of argument.

52. Necessity of advances in agriculture.

Every type of labor, in agriculture, in industry or in commerce, requires advances. Even if the soil were cultivated by hand, it would be necessary to sow before reaping; it would be necessary to live until after the harvest. The more agriculture is brought to perfection, and the more energetic it becomes, the more considerable these advances are. There is need of cattle, implements of husbandry, buildings to house the cattle and store the produce; it is necessary to pay a number of people proportioned to the extent of the enterprise, and to enable them to subsist until the harvest. It is only by means of considerable advances that a large return is obtained, and that the lands yield a large revenue. In any craft whatsoever, it is necessary that the workman has tools in advance, that he has a sufficient quantity of materials on which to work; and he has to subsist while waiting for the sale of his finished goods.

53. First advances furnished by the land while still uncultivated.

It is the land which is always the first and unique source of all wealth; it is the land which by cultivation produces all the revenue; it is the land also which provided the first fund of advances, prior to cultivation. The first cultivator took the seed which he sowed from the plants which the earth had of itself produced; while waiting for the harvest, he lived by hunting, by fishing, and upon wild fruits; his tools have been the branches of trees, torn down in the forest, and shaped with stones sharpened against other stones; the animals wandering in the woods he took himself in the chase, or caught in his traps; he brought them into subjection and tamed them; he used them at first for food, afterward to help him in his labor. The first fund grew gradually; cattle were in early times the most sought after of all moveable wealth, and also the easiest to accumulate; they die, but they reproduce themselves, and the wealth of which they consist is in a way indestructible: this fund itself grows by the mere process of generation, and gives an annual product, either in dairy produce, or in wool, in hides or other materials, which, with the wood obtained in the forest, was the first fund for the works of industry.

54. Cattle, moveable wealth even before the cultivation of the soil.

In times when there was still a large quantity of uncultivated land which did not belong to anyone, cattle could be maintained without there being a proprietor of land. It is even probable that mankind has almost everywhere begun to collect herds and to live on their produce before devoting themselves to the more toilsome labor of cultivation. It seems that the nations which cultivated the earth in the earliest times, were those which found in their country types of animals more susceptible of being tamed, and which were led in this way from the wandering and restless life of hunters and fishermen to the more tranquil enjoyment of pastoral pursuits. Pastoral life requires a longer residence in the same place, affords more leisure, more opportunities to study the difference between lands, to observe the way of nature in the production of plants which serve for the support of cattle. Perhaps it is for this reason, that the Asiatic nations were the first to cultivate the earth, and that the peoples of America have remained so long in a Savage State.

55. Another kind of moveable wealth, and of advances of agriculture: slaves.

Slaves were another kind of moveable wealth, procured at first by violence, and afterward by way of commerce and exchange. Those who had many slaves employed them not only in the cultivation of the land, but also in different works of industry. The ease with which these two kinds of wealth could be accumulated almost without limit, and used independently from the land, made it possible to value the lands themselves, and to compare their value to that of moveable wealth.

56. Moveable wealth has an exchangeable value relative to the land itself.

A man who happened to have a good many pieces of land, but no cattle or slaves, would certainly make an advantageous bargain by surrendering a part of his land to a person who gave him in exchange cattle and slaves to cultivate the rest. It is principally in this way that landed estates themselves entered into commerce, and had a value comparable with that of all other commodities. If four bushels of corn, the net product of an acre of land, were worth six sheep, the acre itself which produced them, could be transferred for a certain value, larger of course, but always easily determined in the same manner as the price of other commodities; i.e., first by the chaffering between the dealers, and afterward by the current price established by the competition of those who wish to exchange land for cattle, and those who wish to give up cattle for land. It is in accordance with this current price that lands are valued when a debtor is sued by his creditor, and is compelled to surrender his estate to him.

57. Valuation of lands in accordance with the proportion of the revenue to the amount of moveable wealth, or the value for which

they are exchanged: this proportion is what is called the penny of the price of land.[3]

It is evident that if a piece of land which produces a revenue equivalent to six sheep, can be sold for a certain value which may always be expressed by a number of sheep equivalent to that value, this number will bear a definite proportion with that of six, and will contain it a certain number of times. Thus the price of an estate will be simply so many times its revenue; twenty times if the price is one hundred and twenty sheep; thirty times, if it is one hundred and eighty sheep. And so the current price of land regulates itself in accordance with the relation between the value of the estate and the value of the revenue; and the number of times that the price of the estate contains the revenue is called so many years purchase of land. It is sold at the price of twenty, thirty, or forty years purchase, when twenty, thirty, or forty times the revenue is paid to obtain it. It is also no less evident that this price or this rate must vary according to the number of purchasers or sellers of land, in the same manner as the price of all other commodities varies in accordance with the varying proportion between the offer and the demand.

58. Every money capital, or every sum of value, whatever it may be, is the equivalent of a piece of land producing a revenue equal to some definite fraction of this sum. First employment of capitals. Purchase of a landed estate.

Let us now go back to the time after the introduction of money. The ease with which it can be accumulated made it the most sought after form of moveable wealth, and furnished the means of accumulation unceasingly by the simple means of thrift. Whoever, either from the revenue of his land, or from the wages of his labor or industry, receives each year more value than he needs to spend, may set aside this surplus and accumulate it: these accumulated values are what is called *a capital*. The timid miser who accumulates money with the objective of preventing worries about lacking the

---

[3] This phrase, "the penny of the price of land" is synonymous with the English expression, "the number of years' purchase of the annual rent." The "penny" was also another expression for a rate per cent, the twentieth penny, for example, being 5 per cent.

necessaries of life in an uncertain future, keeps his money in a hoard. If the dangers which he foresaw should eventuate, and he in his poverty should be reduced to live each year upon his treasure, or if a prodigal heir should spend it by degrees, this treasure would soon be exhausted, and the capital entirely lost to the owner. The latter can draw a far greater advantage from it. Since a landed estate of a certain revenue is only the equivalent of a sum of value equal to this revenue multiplied a certain number of times, it follows that any sum whatsoever of value is equivalent to a landed estate producing a revenue equal to a definite fraction of this sum: it is perfectly the same whether this sum of value, or this capital consists of a mass of metal, or of any other matter, since money represents every kind of value, just as every kind of value represents money. In the first place, therefore, the owner of *a capital* can use it to purchase lands, but he has other possibilities as well.

59. Another employment of money in advances for enterprises of manufacture or industry.

I have already observed that all labors, whether of cultivation or industry, require advances, and I have shown how the earth, by the fruits and herbs which it produces of itself for the nourishment of man and beast, and by the trees of which men have formed their first tools, had furnished the first advances of cultivation, and even of the first handmade articles that each man might fashion for his own use. For instance, it is the earth that provided the first stone, clay and wood of which the first houses were built; and, before the separation of occupations when the same man that cultivated the earth provided also for his other wants by his own labor, there was no need of other advances: but when a large part of society had only their arms to maintain themselves, it was necessary that those who thus lived on wages, should have something in advance to begin with, either to procure the materials upon which they worked, or to maintain them while waiting for their wages.

60. Further explanations of the use of the advance of capitals in enterprises of industry, on their return and on the profits which they ought to yield.

In early times, he who set men to work, supplied the materials himself, and paid the wages of the workmen from day to day. It was the cultivator or the proprietor himself that gave the Spinner the hemp he had gathered, and he maintained her during the time of her working; then he passed the yarn to a Weaver, to whom he gave, every day, the wage agreed upon; but those slight daily advances could be sufficient only for works of the simplest and roughest kind. A vast number of crafts, and even of those crafts engaged in by the poorest members of society, require that the same materials should pass through a multitude of different hands, and undergo, for a very long time exceedingly difficult and varied operations. I have already mentioned the preparation of leather, of which shoes are made: whoever has seen the workshop of a tanner, cannot help feeling the absolute impossibility of one, or even several poor persons providing themselves with hides, lime, tan, utensils, etc., and causing the buildings necessary for establishing a tannery to be erected, and of their living for several months until their leather was sold. In this craft, and in many others, must not those that work at it have learnt the trade before they venture to touch the materials, lest they should spoil them in their first attempts? Here then is another indispensable advance. Who then will collect the materials for the work, the ingredients, the tools necessary for the process? Who is to construct canals, markets, and buildings of every kind? Who will enable that great number of workmen to live until their leather is sold, of whom none individually would be able to prepare a single hide, considering moreover that the profits of the sale of a single tanned hide could not furnish subsistence for any one of them? Who will defray the expenses for the instruction of pupils and apprentices? Who will maintain them until they are sufficiently instructed, guiding them gradually from an easy labor proportionate to their age, to works that demand the utmost strength and ability? It will be one of those owners of *capitals*, or moveable accumulated values, who will employ them partly in advance for the construction of the establishment and the purchase of materials, partly for the daily wages of the workmen who labor in the preparation of them. It is he who will wait for the sale of the leather to return him not only all his advances, but also a profit sufficient to compensate him for what his money would have been worth to him, had he turned it to the acquisition of an estate, and moreover, the wages due to his labor and care, to his risk, and even to his skill; for surely, if the profits were the same, he would have preferred living without any exertion on the revenue of the land which he could have purchased with the same capital. As fast as this capital returns to him by the sale of his products, he uses it for new purchases to furnish and maintain his manufactory by this continual circulation; he lives on his profits, and lays aside what he can spare to increase his capital, and to direct it to his business, thereby increasing the amount of his advances, in order to increase his profits even more.

61. Subdivision of the industrial stipendiary class into capitalist entrepreneurs and simple workmen.

Thus the whole class employed in supplying the different wants of society with an immense variety of industrial products is, so to speak, subdivided into two orders: that of the entrepreneurs, manufacturers and mastercraftsmen, all owners of large capitals, which they invest profitably as advances for setting men at work; the second order, composed of simple artisans, who have no other property than their arms, who advance only their daily labor, and receive no profit but their wages.

62. Another employment of capitals, in advances for agricultural enterprises. Explanations as to the use, the return and indispensable profits of capitals in agricultural enterprises.

In speaking first of the employment of capitals in manufacturing enterprises, I had in view to present a more striking example of the necessity and effect of large advances, and of the course of their circulation; but I have slightly reversed the natural order, which would have required that I should rather begin to speak of enterprises of agriculture, which also can neither be performed, nor extended, nor afford any profit, but by means of considerable advances. It is the owners of large capitals who, in order to make them productive in agricultural enterprises, take leases of land, and pay the proprietors large rents, taking on themselves the whole burden of advances. Their position is essentially the same as that of entrepreneurs of manufacturing industry: Like them, they are obliged to make the first advances of the enterprise, to provide themselves with cattle, horses, tools of husbandry, to purchase the first seeds; like them, they must maintain and nourish their carters, reapers, threshers, servants and laborers of every kind, who have nothing but their arms, who advance only their labor, and earn only their wages; like them, they have to obtain from the harvest, apart from the return of their capital, i.e., their original and annual advances, firstly, a profit equal to the revenue they would be able to acquire with their capital without any labor; secondly, the wages and the price of their labor, of their risk and their industry; thirdly, the wherewithal to replace annually the wear and tear of their property, the cattle that die and the tools that wear out, etc. All this must be first deducted from the price of the produce of the earth; the surplus serves the cultivator to pay the proprietor for the permission he has given to use his field for establishing his enterprise. This is the price of the lease, the revenue of the proprietor, the *net product*, for all that the earth produces up to the amount of the advances, and the profits of every kind due to him who made these advances, cannot be regarded as a *revenue*, but only as the *return of the expenses of cultivation*, considering that if the cultivator did not get them back, he would be loath to risk his wealth and trouble in cultivating the field of another.

63. The competition between the capitalist entrepreneurs establishes the current price of lands and farming on a large scale.

The competition between rich entrepreneurs in agriculture fixes the current price of leases, in proportion to the fertility of the soil, and the price at which its produce is sold, always according to the calculations which the farmers make both of their expenditures, and of the profits they ought to draw from their advances. They cannot give the proprietors more than the surplus. But when the competition among them is very keen, they give him the whole of this surplus, the proprietor only leasing his land to him who offers the highest rent.

64. The lack of capitalist entrepreneurs in agriculture restricts cultivation to small scale farming.

When, on the contrary, there are no rich men who have large capitals to put into agricultural enterprises, when, through the low price of the products of the land, or for any other reason, the crops are not sufficient to assure the entrepreneurs, besides the return of their funds, profits at least equal to those they would derive from their money by employing it in some other way, then farmers cannot be found who are willing to lease lands. The proprietors are forced to hire *colons* or *métayers*, who are unable to make any advances, or to cultivate properly. The proprietor himself makes some small advances, which produce him a very small revenue: if the land happens to belong to a proprietor who is poor, in debt, or neglectful, to a widow, or a Minor, it stays out of cultivation. Such is the true origin of the difference, I have already noticed, between Provinces where the lands are cultivated by wealthy farmers, as in Normandy and the Ile de France, and those where they are cultivated only by poor *métayers*, as in Limousin, Angoumois, Bourbonnais and many others.

65. Subdivision of the class of cultivators into entrepreneurs or farmers, and mere wage farmers, whether servants or day laborers.

Hence it follows, that the class of cultivators, like that of the manufacturers, may be divided into two orders of men, that of the entrepreneurs or capitalists, who make all the advances, and that of the mere wage earning workmen. It is also evident, that capitals alone can form and support great enterprises of agriculture which give the estates an invariable rental value, so to speak, and which assure the proprietor a revenue which is always constant and as large as possible.

66. Fourth employment of capitals, in advances for commercial enterprises. Necessity of the interposition of merchants, properly

so called, between the producers of the commodity and the consumers.

The entrepreneurs, either in agriculture or in manufacturing, draw their advances and their profits only from the sale of the fruits of the earth, or of the manufactured commodities. It is always the wants and the *means* of the consumer that sets the price of the sale; but the consumer does not always need the good at the moment of harvest or at the completion of manufacture. Yet the entrepreneurs require that their funds should return to them immediately and regularly, in order that they may put them back into their enterprises. The harvest must be followed without interruption by the ploughings and the sowing of the seed. The workmen of a manufactory must be kept at work continuously, a fresh set of articles must be begun as soon as the first are finished, materials must be replaced as they are being consumed. It would not be safe to interrupt the workings of a going enterprise, and they could not be taken up again just when desired. The entrepreneur, therefore, has the greatest possible interest in having his funds returned promptly by the sale of his crops or commodities. On the other hand, it is in the consumer's interest to find the things he needs when and where he wants them; it would be extremely inconvenient for him to be obliged to purchase, at the time of the harvest, his provisions for a whole year. Among the articles that are commonly consumed there are many that require long and expensive labors, labors that cannot be undertaken with profit except on a large quantity of materials, so large that the consumption of a small number of men, or of a limited district, cannot suffice as a market for the products of a single manufactory even. Enterprises of this kind must then necessarily be few in number, at a considerable distance from each other, and consequently very far from the homes of the great majority of consumers. There is no man above extreme poverty who is not in a position to consume several things, which are neither gathered nor fabricated, except in places considerably distant from his home, and no less distant from each other. A man who could only obtain the objects of his consumption by buying them directly from the hand of the person who gathers or manufactures them, would either go without a good many things, or spend his life in travel.

This double interest on the part of both the producer and the consumer, of the first to find an opportunity to sell, of the other, to find an opportunity to buy, and yet not to lose precious time in waiting for the purchaser, or in seeking the seller, must have suggested to a third party to act as intermediaries between the two. This is the purpose of the profession of merchants, who purchase goods from the hands of the producer, to store them in warehouses, wither the consumer goes to get what he needs. In this way, the entrepreneur, assured of the sale and the return of his funds, devotes himself undisturbedly and continuously to further production, and the consumer finds within his reach, and at any moment the things which he needs.

67. **Different orders of merchants. They all have this in common, that they purchase to sell again; and that their business depends upon advances which must return with profit in order to be once more put into the enterprise.**

From the Huckster who displays her herbs on the market place, to the shipowner of Nantes or Cadiz who carries on his sales and purchases even to India and America, the profession of a merchant, or, more correctly, of commerce, is divided into an infinity of branches, and, as it were, levels. One trader confines himself to stocking up several types of commodities which he sells in his shop to all those who present themselves; another goes with certain commodities to a place where they are in demand, to bring from thence in exchange such things as are produced there, and are wanting in the place from whence he departed; one makes his exchanges in his own neighborhood, and by himself, another by means of correspondents, and with the services of carriers whom he pays, and whom he sends and brings from one Province to another, from one kingdom to another, from Europe to Asia, and from Asia to Europe. One sells his merchandise in small quantities to the several individuals who consume them; another sells only in large quantities at the time to other merchants who retail them to the consumers; but all have this in common that they *buy to sell again*, and that their first purchases are an advance which returns to them only in course of time. It must return to them, like those of the cultivators and manufacturers, not only within a certain period, to be employed again in new purchases, but also firstly, with a profit equal to the revenue they would be able to acquire with their capital without any labor; secondly, with the wages and the price of their labor, their risk, and their industry. Without the assurance of this return, and of these indispensable profits, no merchant would engage in commerce, nor could anyone possibly continue therein: it is from this point of view that he guides himself in his purchases, when he calculates the quantity and the price of the things which he can hope to sell in a certain period. The retailer learns by experience, and by the outcome of limited trials made cautiously, what are the approximate wants of the consumers whom he is in a position to supply. The trader learns from his correspondents about the abundance or scarcity, and the price of merchandise in those different countries to which his commerce extends; he directs his speculations accordingly, he sends his goods from the country where they bear a low price to those where they are sold for a higher price, it being understood that the expenses of carriage enter into the calculation of the advances that have to return to him.

Since commerce is necessary, and it is impossible to undertake any commerce without advances proportionate to its extent, we see here another method of employing moveable wealth, a new use to which the owner of a mass of values saved and accumulated, of a sum of money, *of a capital*, in short, can put it to obtain his subsistence, and to increase, if he can, his wealth.

68. The true idea of the circulation of money.

From what has just been said it can be seen that the cultivation of estates, manufactures of all kinds, and all the branches of trade, depend upon the mass of capitals, or of moveable, accumulated wealth, which, having been first advanced by the entrepreneurs in each of these different classes of work, must return to them again every year with a steady profit; that is, the capital to be again invested and advanced in the continuation of the same enterprises, and the profits for the more or less comfortable living of the entrepreneurs. It is this advance and this continual return which constitutes *what ought to be called the circulation of money*; this useful and fruitful circulation, which gives life to all the labor of society, which maintains all the movement and life of the body politic, and which is correctly compared to the circulation of the blood in the animal body. For if, by any disorder whatsoever in the sequence of expenditure of the different classes of society, the entrepreneurs cease to get back their advances with such profit as they have a right to expect, it is evident that they will be obliged to reduce their enterprises; that the amount of labor, of the consumption of the fruits of the earth, of the production and of the revenue would be equally diminished; that poverty will take the place of wealth, and that the common workman, ceasing to find employment, will fall into the deepest misery.

69. All enterprises, especially those of manufactures and of commerce, could not fail to have been very limited before the introduction of gold and silver in trade.

It is hardly necessary to remark that enterprises of all kinds, but especially those of manufactures and still more those of commerce, must have been very limited before the introduction of gold and silver in trade; since it was almost impossible to accumulate large capitals, and even more difficult to multiply and divide payments as much as is necessary to facilitate and increase the exchanges to the extent which a spirited commerce and circulation require. The cultivation of the land alone may support itself to a certain degree, because cattle are the principal object of the advances required therein; moreover, it is probable that there was no other entrepreneur in agriculture than the proprietor. As to crafts of all kinds, they must necessarily have languished greatly before the introduction of money; they were limited to the rudest types of occupation, for which the proprietors furnished the advances by feeding the workmen and by providing them with materials, or which they caused to be carried on at home by their Domestics.

70. Capitals being as necessary to all enterprises as labor and industry, the industrious man shares voluntarily the profit of his

enterprise with the capitalist who furnishes him with the funds he needs.

Since capitals are the indispensable foundation of all lucrative enterprises; since with money we can furnish means for cultivation, establish manufactures, and set up trade, the profits of which accumulated and frugally saved, will become a new capital; since in short, money is the principal means of begetting money, those who, with their industry and love of labor, have no capitals, or do not have sufficient for the enterprise they wish to embark on, have no difficulty in deciding to give up to the owners of such capital or money who are willing to trust it to them, a portion of the profits they expect to receive over and above the return of their advances.

71. Fifth employment of capitals, lending at interest. Nature of the loan.

The owners of money balance the risk their capital may run, if the enterprise does not succeed, with the advantage of enjoying a definite profit without labor, and regulate themselves thereby to require more or less profit or interest for their money, or to consent to lend it for such interest as the borrower offers. Here another opportunity is open to the owner of money; lending at interest, or the trade in money. Let no one mistake me here, lending at interest is nothing but a commercial transaction, in which the Lender is the man who sells the use of his money, and the borrower is a man who buys; precisely as the proprietor of an estate and a farmer sell and buy, respectively the use of a piece of land which is let out. The Latin term for a loan of money at interest expresses it exactly, *usura pecuniae*, a word which, translated into French has become hateful by consequence of false ideas being formed as to the interest of money.

72. False ideas about the lending at interest.

The price of the loan is by no means founded, as might be imagined, on the profit the borrower hopes to make with the capital of which he purchases the use. This price, like the price of every commodity, is determined by the chaffering of seller and buyer; by the balance between the offer and the demand. People borrow for all kinds of purposes, and with all sorts of motives. One borrows to undertake an enterprise which will make his fortune, another to buy an estate, another to pay a gaming debt, another to make up for the loss of his revenue, of which some accident has deprived him, another to keep himself alive, while waiting for what he can get by his labor; but all these motives which influence the borrower are quite immaterial to the lender. The latter is only concerned with two things: the interest he is to receive, and the safety of his capital. He does not trouble himself about the use the borrower will make of it, any more than the merchant concerns himself with the use the buyer makes of the commodity he sells him.

73. Errors of the schoolmen refuted.

It is for want of having examined the lending at interest in its true light, that moralists, more dogmatic than enlightened, have endeavored to have it looked upon as a crime. The scholastic theologians have concluded from the fact that money does not produce anything by itself that it was unjust to exact interest from money placed on loan. Full of their prejudices, they have believed their doctrine was sanctioned by this passage from the Gospel, *mutuum date nihil inde sperantes*.[4] Those theologians who have adopted more reasonable principles on the subject of interest, have endured the harshest reproaches from Writers of the opposite party.

Nevertheless, it needs but a little reflection to realise the lack of depth in the pretexts which have been used to condemn the taking of interest. A loan is a reciprocal contract, free between the two parties, which they make only because it is advantageous to them. It is evident that, if the lender finds it to his advantage to receive something as the hire for his money, the borrower is no less interested in finding the money he needs, since he decides to borrow and to pay the hire of this money. Now on what principle can a crime be discovered in a contract advantageous to two parties, with which both parties are satisfied, and which certainly does no injury to anyone else? To say that the lender takes advantage of the borrower's need

---

[4] I.e., Luke 6: 35, which in the American Standard Version reads as follows: "and lend, hoping for nothing again."

of money to demand interest, is as absurd an argument as saying that a baker who demands money for the bread he sells, takes advantage of the buyer's need for bread. If in this latter case, the money is an equivalent for the bread the buyer receives, the money which the borrower receives today is equally an equivalent of the capital and interest he promises to return at the end of a certain time; for, in short, it is an advantage for the borrower to have, during the interval, the use of the money he needs, and it is a disadvantage to the lender to be deprived of it. This disadvantage is capable of being estimated, and is estimated: the *interest* is the price of it. This price ought to be higher if the lender runs the risk of losing his capital by the insolvency of the borrower. The bargain therefore is perfectly equal on both sides, and consequently just and honest. Money considered as a physical substance, as a mass of metal, does not produce anything; but money employed in advances in enterprises of agriculture, manufactures, commerce, procures a definite profit; with money an estate can be purchased, and a revenue procured thereby; the person, therefore, who lends his money, does not only give up the barren possession of such money, but deprives himself of the profit or the revenue he would have been able to procure by it, and the interest which indemnifies him for this loss cannot be looked upon as unjust. The schoolmen, compelled to acknowledge the justice of these considerations, have allowed that interest may be taken, provided the capital is alienated, that is, provided the lender renounced his right to demand the repayment of his money in a certain time, and leave the borrower free to keep it as long as he wished while paying only interest. The reason for this toleration was that then it is no longer a loan, for which an interest is taken, but a rent which is purchased with a sum of money, just as an estate is purchased. This was a petty subterfuge to which they had recourse in order to concede the absolute necessity of loans in the course of transactions of society, without clearly acknowledging the falsity of the principles upon which they had condemned it. But this condition of the alienation of capital is not an advantage to the borrower, who remains no less burdened with the debt until he has repaid this capital, and whose property is always destined as security for this capital. It is even a disadvantage, as he finds it more difficult to borrow money when he needs it; for persons who would willingly consent to lend for a year or two a sum of money which they had destined for the purchase of an estate, would not lend it for an indefinite period. Moreover, if it is permissible to sell money for a perpetual rent, why would it not be permissible to let it for some years in return for a rent which only continues for that number of years? If a rent of a thousand francs per year is equivalent to the sum of twenty thousand francs in the case of a man who keeps this sum in perpetuity, a thousand francs will be the amount for the possession of that sum for one year.

74. True foundation of the interest of money.

A man then may let out his money as lawfully as he may sell it; and the owner of money may do either one or the other, not only because money is equivalent to a revenue, and a means of procuring a revenue, not only because the lender loses, during the time of the loan, the revenue he might have procured by it, not only because he risks his capital, not only because the borrower can employ it in advantageous acquisition, or in enterprises from which he may draw large profits; the owner of money may lawfully draw the interest of it by a more general and decisive principle. Even if all the foregoing were not the case, he would none the less have the right to require an interest for his loan simply because the money is his property. Since it is his property he is free to keep it, nothing obliges him to lend; if then he does lend, he may attach conditions to the loan as he sees fit. In this he does no injury to the borrower, since the latter agrees to the conditions, and has no right of any kind over the sum lent. The profit that may be procured by the use of money is doubtlessly one of the commonest motives influencing the borrower to borrow on interest; it is one of the means which facilitates his payment of the interest, but this is by no means what gives the lender the right to require it; it is enough for him that his money is his own, and this right is inseparable from property. He who buys bread does it for his support, but the right the baker has to ask a price is quite independent of the use of the bread; it is the same right he would have to sell him stones, a right founded on this principle alone, that the bread is his own, and no one has any right to force him to give it for nothing.

75. Reply to an objection.

This reflection makes us realise how false and how distant from the meaning of the Gospel, is the application which the dogmatists made of the passage *mutuum date nihil inde sperantes* (lend without expecting gain). The passage is clear, as interpreted by moderate and reasonable theologians, as a precept of charity. All mankind are bound to assist one another; a rich man who would see his fellow creature in distress, and who instead of providing for his wants, would sell him what he needed would be equally deficient in the duties of Christianity and those of humanity. In such circumstances, charity does not only require us to lend without interest, she orders us to lend, and even to give if necessary. To convert the precept of charity into a precept of rigorous justice, is equally repugnant to reason, and to the sense of the text. Those whom I attack here do not claim that it is a duty of (Christian) justice to lend their money; they must then agree that the first words of the passage, *mutuum date*, contain only a precept of charity; now I ask why they seek to extend the close of the passage into an obligation of (Christian) justice.[5] What, shall the lending itself not be a strict precept, and shall only its accessory, the condition of the loan, be made one! This is in effect what men would have been told: "You are free to lend or not to lend, but if you do lend, take care you do not require any interest for your money, and even when a merchant shall require a loan of you for an enterprise from which he hopes to make large profits, it will be a crime for you to accept the interest he offers you; you must absolutely either lend him gratuitously, or not lend to him at all. You have indeed one method of making interest lawful, that is to lend your capital for an indefinite term, and to give up the right of demanding its repayment allowing your debtor to do so when he pleases or when he can. If you find any inconvenience on the score of security, or if you foresee you will need your money in a certain number of years, you have no other course to take but not to lend:

---

[5] Turgot here contrasts the loose interpretation of Christian charity of the first part of the Gospel quotation, with the strict prohibition of charging interest as an interpretation of the second part.

it will be better to cause this merchant to miss a precious opportunity, than to commit a sin in helping him to take advantage of it." This is what has been seen in these five words; *mutuum date nihil inde sperantes*, when they have been read with the prejudices created by a false metaphysics. Everyone who reads this text without prejudice, will soon find its real meaning; that is, "*as men, as Christians, you are all brothers, all friends: act toward each other as brethren and friends; help each other in your necessities; let your purses be open to one another, and do not sell the assistance which you owe each other by requiring interest on a loan which charity commands you to make.*" This is the true sense of the passage in question. The obligation to lend without interest, and that to lend, are evidently connected together; they are of the same order, and both inculcate a duty of charity, and not a precept of rigorous justice, applicable to all cases of lending.

76. The rate of interest ought to be determined just like that of all commodities, by nothing but the course of trade.

I have already said that the price of money is regulated like that of all other commodities, by the balance of offer and demand: thus, when there are many borrowers who need money, the interest of money becomes higher; when there are many owners who are ready to lend, it falls. It is therefore a further mistake to believe that the interest of money in trade ought to be fixed by the laws of princes. It is a current price, determined like that of all other commodities. This price varies a little according to the greater or less security which the lender has of not losing his capital; but on equal security, it ought to rise and fall in proportion to the abundance and the need, and the law no more ought to fix the rate of interest than it ought to regulate the price of any other commodity which circulates in commerce.

77. Money has two different valuations in commerce. One expresses the quantity of money we give to procure different sorts of commodities; the other expresses the relation a sum of money

has to the interest it will procure in accordance with the course of trade.

It appears from this explanation of the manner in which money is either sold or let out for an annual interest, that there are two ways of valuing money in commerce. In buying and selling, a certain weight of silver represents a certain quantity of value, or of commodities of every kind; for example, one ounce of silver is the equivalent of a certain quantity of corn, or of a certain number of days' labor. In lending, and in the trade in money, a capital is the equivalent of a rent equal to a fixed portion of that capital; and conversely, an annual rent represents a capital equal to the amount of that rent repeated a certain number of times, according as the interest is at a higher or lower rate.[6]

78. These two valuations are independent of each other, and are governed by quite different principles.

These two different evaluations have much less connection, and depend much less on each other than one would be tempted to believe at first sight. Money may be very common in ordinary commerce, may have a very low value, answer to a very small quantity of commodities, and the interest of money may at the same time be very high.

Assume that there are one million ounces of silver in currency circulating in commerce, and that an ounce of silver is given in the market for a bushel of corn; suppose that there is brought into the State, in some manner or other, a second million ounces of silver, and that this increase is distributed to every purse in the same proportion as the first million, so that he who had two ounces before, now has four. The silver considered as a quantity of metal will certainly diminish in price, or, which is the same thing, commodities will be paid for more dearly, and it becomes necessary, in order to procure the same measure of corn which was obtained with one ounce of silver, to give a good deal more silver, and perhaps *two*

---

[6] Turgot here seems to indicate the relationship between capital and income, capital value being income capitalized by the current rate of interest.

ounces instead of *one*. But it does not by any means follow from this that the interest of money falls, if all this money is carried to the market and employed in the current expenses of those who possess it, as by supposition the first million ounces were; for the interest of money falls only when there is more money to be lent, in proportion to the wants of the borrowers, than there was before. Now the money which is carried to market is not for lending; it is the money which is placed in reserve, the accumulated capitals, that are lent, and so far from the increase of the money in the market, or the diminution of its price in relation to commodities in the ordinary course of trade infallibly, and as an immediate consequence, bringing about a decrease in the interest of money, it may, on the contrary, happen that the very cause which increases the money in the market, and which increases the price of other commodities by lowering the price of money, is precisely that which increases the hire of money, or the rate of interest.

Indeed, suppose for a moment that all the wealthy people in a nation, instead of saving from their revenues or from their annual profits, spend the whole of it; suppose that, not satisfied with spending their revenue, they spend their capital; suppose that a man who has a hundred thousand francs in money, instead of employing them in a profitable manner, or lending them, consumes them piecemeal in foolish expenses; it is evident that on the one hand there will be more money employed in current purchases, in satisfying the wants and humors of every individual, and that consequently its price will fall; on the other hand there will certainly be much less money to lend, and, as many people will ruin themselves, there will probably also be more borrowers. The interest of money will consequently increase, while money itself will become common in circulation, and fall in price, and precisely for the same reason.

We shall cease to be surprised at this apparently peculiar result, if we consider that the money brought into the market for the purchase of corn, is that which is daily spent to satisfy one's needs, and that which is offered on loan, is precisely that which is saved from one's daily expenditure to be laid by and formed into capitals.

79. **In the valuation of money with regard to commodities, it is the money considered as metal that is the subject of the estimate. In the evaluation of the penny of money, it is the use of the money for a definite time that is the subject of the estimate.**

In the market a measure of corn is equivalent to a certain weight of silver; it is a quantity of silver that is purchased with the commodity; it is this quantity which is valued and compared with other different values. In a loan on interest, the object of the valuation is the use of a certain quantity of value during a certain time. It is no longer the comparison of a quantity of silver with a quantity of corn; it is now a quantity of values which is compared with a definite portion of itself, which becomes the price of the use of this quantity for a certain time. Let twenty thousand ounces of silver be equivalent in the market to twenty thousand measures of corn, or only to ten thousand, the use of those twenty thousand ounces of silver for a year will none the less be worth in the money market the twentieth part of the principal sum, or one thousand ounces of silver, if interest is at the twentieth penny.[7]

80. The price of interest depends directly on the relation between the demand of the borrowers and the offer of the lenders, and this relation depends chiefly on the quantity of moveable wealth accumulated by the saving of revenues and of annual products to form capitals, whether these capitals exist in money or in any other kind of effects having a value in commerce.

The price of silver in the market is relative only to the quantity of this metal used in current exchanges; but the rate of interest is relative to the quantity of values accumulated and laid by to form capitals. It does not matter whether these values are in metal or other effects, provided these effects are easily convertible into money. It is far from being the case, that the mass of metal existing in a State is as large as the amount of the values lent on interest in the course of a year; but all the capitals, in furniture, merchandise, tools and cattle, take the place of silver and represent it. A paper signed by a man who is known to be

---

[7] I.e., 5 per cent.

worth a hundred thousand francs, and who promises to pay a hundred thousand francs at a certain date, is worth a hundred thousand francs until that date: all the capitals of the man who has signed this note are answerable for the payment of it, whatever the nature of the effects he has in his possession, provided they have a value of a hundred thousand francs. It is not therefore the quantity of silver existing as metal which causes the rate of interest to rise or fall, or which brings more money into the market to be lent; it is simply the sum of capitals to be found in commerce, that is to say, the current sum of moveable values of every kind, accumulated, saved gradually out of the revenues and profits, to be employed by the owner to procure himself new profits and new revenues. It is these accumulated savings which are offered to the borrowers, and the more there are of them, the lower the interest of money will be, at least if the number of borrowers is not augmented in proportion.

81. The spirit of thrift in a nation continually increases the amount of capitals, luxury continually tends to destroy them.

The spirit of thrift in a nation continually tends to increase the amount of the capitals, to increase the number of lenders, and to diminish that of borrowers. The habit of luxury has precisely the opposite effect, and by what has already been remarked on the use of capitals in all enterprises, whether of agriculture, manufacture, or commerce, we may judge if luxury enriches a nation, or impoverishes it.

82. The fall in the rate of interest proves that thrift generally has prevailed over luxury in Europe.

Since the interest of money has been constantly diminishing in Europe for several centuries, we must conclude that the spirit of thrift has been more general than the spirit of luxury. It is only people already rich who give themselves up to luxury, and among the rich, those who are sensible confine their expenses to their revenues, and are very careful not to touch their capitals. Those who wish to become rich are far more numerous in a nation than those who are already so. Now, in the present state of things, as all land is occupied, there is but one way to become rich, it is either to possess, or to procure in some way, a revenue or an annual profit above what is absolutely necessary for subsistence, and to reserve this surplus every year so as to form a capital, by means of which a person may obtain an increase in revenue or annual profit, which may again be saved and converted into capital. There are consequently a great many people interested and occupied in accumulating capitals.

83. Recapitulation of the five different methods of employing capitals.

I have reckoned five different methods of employing capitals, or of profitably investing them.

The first is to buy a landed estate, which brings in a definite revenue.

The second is to invest money in agricultural enterprises by taking a lease of land, the produce of which ought to yield, over and above the price of the lease, the interest on the advances, and the price of the labor of the man who devotes both his wealth and his toil to its cultivation.

The third is to invest a capital in industrial and manufacturing enterprises.

The fourth is to invest it in commercial enterprises.

And the fifth method is to lend it to those who need it, in return for an annual interest.

84. The influence which the different methods of employing capitals have on each other.

It is evident that the annual product which can be drawn from capitals invested in these different employments, are influenced by each other, and are all related to the current rate of the interest of money.

85. Money invested in land is bound to bring the least.

The person who invests his money in the purchase of an estate, leased to a solvent Tenant, procures himself a revenue which entails very little trouble, and which he can spend in the most agreeable manner, by giving free play to all his tastes. There is the additional advantage in the purchase of this kind of property over that of any other, that the possession of it is more secure against all kinds of accidents. We must therefore purchase an equal revenue in land at a higher price, or content ourselves with a less revenue for an equal capital.

86. Money placed on loan ought to bring a little more than the revenue of landed estates acquired with an equal capital.

The person who lends money on interest, enjoys it even more peaceably and freely than the possessor of land, but the insolvency of his debtor may cause him to lose his capital. He will not therefore content himself with an interest equal to the revenue of the land which he might buy with the same capital. The investment of money lent must consequently be larger than the revenue of an estate purchased with the same capital; for if the lender found an estate for sale with a revenue equal to the interest, he would prefer this way of using it.

87. Money invested in agricultural, manufacturing or commercial enterprises, is bound to bring more than the interest of money on loan.

For a like reason, money employed in agriculture, in industry or in commerce, ought to produce a more considerable profit than the revenue of the same capital employed in the purchase of estates, or the interest of money placed on loan; for since these employments require, in addition to the capital advanced, much care and labor, if they were not more lucrative, it would be more advantageous to secure an equal revenue which might be enjoyed without having to do anything. It is necessary then, that, besides the interest of the capital, the entrepreneur should draw every year a profit to recompense him for his care, his labor, his talents and his risks, and to furnish him in addition that with which he may replace the annual wear and tear of his advances, which he is obliged from the very first to convert into effects which are liable to deterioration and which are, moreover, exposed to all kinds of accidents.

88. However, the products of these different employments are limited by each other, and notwithstanding their inequality, preserve a kind of equilibrium.

The different uses of the capitals produce, therefore, very unequal products; but this inequality does not prevent them from having a reciprocal influence on each other, nor from establishing a kind of equilibrium amongst themselves, like that between two liquids of unequal gravity, which come into contact with each other at the base of an inverted siphon, of which they fill the two branches; they will not be on a level, but the height of the one cannot increase without the other also rising in the opposite branch.

Suppose that suddenly, a very great number of proprietors of estates wish to sell them: it is obvious that the price of estates will fall, and that with a less sum a larger revenue may be acquired; this cannot happen without the interest of money rising, for the owners of money would choose rather to buy estates, than to lend at an interest which was no higher than the revenues of the lands they could purchase. If, then, the borrowers want to have money, they will be forced to pay a greater rate. If the interest of money becomes higher, people will prefer lending it to using it in a more toilsome and hazardous fashion in enterprises of agriculture, industry and commerce, and they will only enter those enterprises which will produce, besides the wages of their labor, a profit much greater than the rate of interest on money placed on loan. In short, as soon as the profits resulting from an employment of money, whatever it may be, increase or diminish, capitals turn in that direction or withdraw from other employments, or withdraw and turn toward other employments; and this necessarily alters in each of these employments, the relation between the capital and the annual product. Generally, money invested in landed property does not bring in as much as money placed on loan; and money placed on loan brings less than money employed in enterprises involving labor; but whatever be the way in which money is employed, its product cannot increase or decrease without all the other employments experiencing a proportionate increase or decrease.

89. The current interest of money is the thermometer by which the abundance or scarcity of capitals may be judged; it is the measure of the extent to which a nation can expand its enterprises of agriculture, manufacture and commerce.

Thus the current interest of money placed on loan may be considered as a kind of thermometer of the abundance or scarcity of capitals in a nation, and of the extent of the enterprises of every kind on which she may embark: it is evident that the lower the interest of money is, the higher is the value of landed estates. A man that has fifty thousand livres in rent, has a property worth only one million, if estates are sold at the twentieth penny; he has two million, if land is sold at the fortieth penny. If the interest is at 5 per cent all uncleared land whose produce would not yield 5 per cent over and above the replacement of the advances, and the recompense of the care of the cultivator, would remain uncultivated. No manufacture, no commerce will exist if they will not bring in 5 per cent over and above the wages of the entrepreneur's exertions and risks. If there is a neighboring nation in which the interest stands only at 2 per cent, it will not only carry on all the branches of commerce, from which the nation where interest is at 5 per cent finds itself excluded, but moreover, as its manufacturers and merchants can content themselves with a lower profit, they will place their goods on all markets at a much lower price, and will draw to themselves the almost exclusive trade in all those commodities of which the trade is not retained (by exceptional circumstances or by the excessive cost of carriage), for the commerce of the nation where money is worth 5 per cent.

90. Influence of the rate of interest of money on all lucrative enterprises.

The price of interest may be looked upon as a kind of level, beneath which all labor, agriculture, industry and commerce come to an end. It is like a sea spread over a vast area; the summits of the mounts rise above the waters, and form fertile and cultivated islands. If this sea happens to flow back, in proportion as it descends, first the slopes, then the plains and valleys appear, and are covered with productions of every kind. It is enough that the water rises or falls a foot to inundate immense tracts, or throw them open to cultivation. It is the abundance of capitals which animates all enterprises, and the low interest of money is at the same time the effect and the index of the abundance of capitals.

91. The total wealth of a nation consists: firstly, in the net revenue of all landed estates, multiplied by the rate at which land is sold; secondly, in the sum of all moveable wealth existing in the nation.

Landed estates are equivalent to a capital equal to their revenue multiplied by the current penny at which lands are sold. Thus if we add the revenue of all lands, that is, the net revenue they render to the proprietors, and to all those that share in the property, such as the Lord that levies a rent, the curate that levies the tithe, the sovereign that levies the tax; if, I say, we should add all these sums, and multiply them by the rate at which lands are sold, we would have the sum of all the wealth of a nation in landed estates. To obtain the whole of a nation's wealth, the moveable wealth ought to be added, which consist in the sum of capitals employed in enterprises of agriculture, industry, and commerce, which never come out of them (because) all advances, in any kind of enterprise, must continually return to the entrepreneurs, to be reinvested in the enterprises, which could not continue without them. It would be a very gross error to confound the immense mass of moveable wealth with the mass of money that exists in a State; the latter is but a very small thing in comparison. To be convinced of this, we need only remember the immense quantity of cattle, utensils and seed which constitute the advances of agriculture; of raw materials, tools, furniture and merchandise of every kind which fill the workhouses, shops, and warehouses of all manufacturers, merchants and traders, and it will be plain that in the totality of wealth, both landed or moveable, of a nation, the specie makes but a very small part. But all wealth and money are continually exchangeable, they all represent money, and money represents them all.

92. The sum of capitals on loan cannot be included in this without double counting.

The amount of capitals which are placed on loan must not be included in the calculation of the wealth of the nation; for these capitals can only have been lent either to proprietors of estates, or to entrepreneurs who invest them in their enterprises, since only these two kinds of people can answer for that capital, and pay the interest; a sum of money lent to people who have neither estate nor industry, would be a dead capital, and not an active one. If the proprietor of an estate of four hundred thousand francs borrows a hundred thousand, his land is charged with a rent that diminishes his revenue in a like proportion, and if he should sell his property, out of the four hundred thousand francs he would receive, a hundred thousand would belong to the creditor. The capital of the lender would, therefore, in the calculation of existing wealth, be a repetition of an equal part of the value of the land. The land is always worth four hundred thousand francs: when the proprietor borrows a hundred thousand francs, this does not make it five hundred thousand francs; it only brings about that out of the four hundred thousand francs, a hundred thousand belong to the lender and that there remains no more than three hundred thousand francs for the borrower.

The same double counting would take place if the total sum of capitals were to include the money lent to an entrepreneur to be employed in the advances of his enterprise; for this loan does not increase the total sum of advances necessary for that enterprise. It only brings about that that sum, and the part of the profits which represent its interest, belong to the lender. Whether a merchant employs ten thousand francs of his own property in his trade and takes the whole profit, or whether he has borrowed these ten thousand francs from another to whom he pays interest, contenting himself with the surplus of the profit, and the wages of his industry, there are never more than ten thousand francs.

But if we cannot include in the calculation of the wealth of a nation the capital which corresponds to the interest of money placed on loan without counting it twice over, we ought to include the other kinds of moveable property, which, though they were originally an object of expenditure, and do not bear any profit, become, however, by their durability, a true capital which is continually accumulated, and which, when required, may be exchanged for money, making, as it were, a reserve fund which may return into commerce and, when desired, make up for the loss of other capitals. This includes the furniture of every kind, jewels, plate, paintings, statues, ready money shut up in the chests of misers: all these things have a value, and the sum of all these values may reach a considerable amount in rich nations. Yet be it considerable or not, it is still true that it must be added to the sum of the prices of landed estates, and to that of the advances circulating in enterprises of every kind in order to make up the sum total of the wealth of a nation. Besides it is superfluous to say that, though it is easy to define, as has just been done, of what consists the sum of the wealth of a nation, it is probably impossible to discover to how much it amounts, unless some rule be found to determine the proportion of the total commerce of a nation, to the revenue of its land: a thing perhaps feasible, but which has not yet been executed in such a manner as to dispel all doubts.

93. In which of the three classes of society the capitalists who are lenders of money are to be included.

Let us now see how what we have just discussed about the different ways of employing capitals, agrees with what we have established before about the division of all the members of society into three classes, the productive class or that of cultivators, the industrial or commercial class, and the disposable class, or that of proprietors.

94. The capitalist lender of money belongs to the disposable class as far as his person is concerned.

We have seen that every rich man is necessarily owner either of a capital in moveable wealth, or of an estate in land equivalent to a capital. Every landed estate is the equivalent of a capital; consequently every proprietor is a capitalist, but not every capitalist is a proprietor of a landed estate; and the owner of a moveable capital may choose whether to use it in acquiring a landed estate, or to invest it in the enterprises of the agricultural class, or the industrial class. The capitalist who has become an entrepreneur in agriculture or industry, is no more of the disposable class either as regards himself or his profits, than the mere workmen in those two classes; they are both set aside for the carrying on of their enterprises. The capitalist who confines himself to lending money, lends it either to a proprietor, or to an entrepreneur. If he lends it to a proprietor, he seems to belong to the class of proprietors, and he becomes part-owner of the property; the revenue of the land is assigned to the payment of the interest of his loan, the value of the estate is pledged to provide security for his capital to its full amount. If the lender of money has lent to an entrepreneur, it is certain that his person belongs to the disposable class; but his capital is sunk in the advances of the enterprise, and cannot be withdrawn without injuring the enterprise, unless it is replaced by a capital of equal value.

95. The interest drawn by the lender of money is disposable so far as the use he can make of it is concerned.

Indeed, the interest he draws from that capital seems to be disposable, since the entrepreneur and the enterprise can do without it; and it seems also that we may conclude from this, that in the profits of the two working classes, there is a disposable portion, namely, that which corresponds to the interest of the advances, calculated at the current rate of interest of money placed on loan. It appears also that this conclusion is in conflict with what we have said before, that only the class of proprietors had a revenue properly so called, a disposable revenue, and every member of the two other classes had only wages and profits. This deserves some explanation. If we consider the thousand *écus* received annually by a man who has lent sixty thousand francs to a merchant, in relation to the use he may make of them, it cannot be doubted that they are absolutely disposable, since the enterprise can do without them.

96. The interest of the money is not disposable in this sense, that the State can, without harm, appropriate part of it for its wants.

But it does not follow that they are disposable in the sense that the State can, with impunity, appropriate part of them for the public wants. Those thousand *écus* are not a return which agriculture or commerce bestows gratuitously on the person who has made the advances, it is the price and the condition of these advances, without which the enterprise could not be carried on. If this return is diminished, the capitalist will withdraw his money, and the enterprise will come to an end. This return ought then to be inviolable, and enjoy an entire immunity, because it is the price of an advance made for an enterprise, without which the enterprise could not go on. To encroach upon it, would cause an augmentation in the price of advances in all enterprises, and consequently, diminish the enterprises themselves, that is, agriculture, industry and commerce.

This answer should lead us to conclude, that if we said that the capitalist who had lent money to a proprietor, *appeared* to belong to the class of proprietors, this *appearance* had something equivocal about it which needed to be unraveled. In fact, the strict truth is that the interest of his money is no more disposable, that is, is no more capable of being encroached upon, than the money lent to the entrepreneurs in agriculture, and commerce. This interest is equally the price of a free agreement, and cannot be encroached upon without altering or changing the price of the loan; now, it matters little to whom the loan has been made; if the price changes or increases for the proprietor of lands, it will also change or increase for the cultivator, the manufacturer, and the merchant. In short, the capitalist lender of money ought to be considered as a dealer in a commodity absolutely necessary for the production of wealth, which cannot be at too low a price. It is as unreasonable to burden this commerce with a tax as it would be to lay a tax on a dunghill which serves to manure the land. Let us conclude from this, that the person who lends money belongs properly to the disposable class as to his person, because he has nothing to do, but not as to the nature of his wealth, whether the interest of his money is paid by the proprietor of land, out of a portion of his revenue, or whether it is paid by an entrepreneur, out of the part of his profits designed to pay the interest of his advances.

97. Objection.

It will undoubtedly be replied, that the capitalist may indifferently either lend his money, or employ it in the purchase of an estate; that in either case he draws only an equal price for his money, and that, whichever way he has employed it, he ought none the less to contribute to the public charges.

98. Answer to the objection.

In the first place, I answer that in fact, when the capitalist has purchased an estate, the revenue is the equivalent to him of what he would have drawn from his money by lending it; but there is this essential difference with respect to the State, that the price which he gives for his land does not contribute in any respect to the revenue it produces. It would not have yielded a smaller revenue, if he had not purchased it. The revenue, as we have already explained, consists in what the land produces, beyond the wages of the cultivators, their profits, and the interest of their advances. It is not the same with the interest of a loan; it is the very condition of the loan, the price of the advance, without which neither the revenue nor the profits which serve to pay it, would exist.

I answer, in the second place, that if the lands alone were burdened with the contribution to the public charges, as soon as that contribution would be regulated, the capitalist who purchased these lands would not reckon in the interest of his money that part of the revenue which is set aside for this contribution; just as a man who now buys an estate, does not buy the tithe which the curate receives, but only the revenue which remains after the tithe is deducted.

99. There exists no truly disposable revenue in a state except the net product of land.

We see by what has been said, that the interest of money lent is taken from the revenue of lands, or from the profits of agricultural, industrial and commercial enterprises. But we have already shown that these profits themselves were only a part of the produce of lands; that the produce of land is divided into two portions; that the one was designed for the wages of the cultivator, for his profits, for the return and interest of his advances; and that the other was the share of the proprietor, or the revenue which the proprietor expended at his pleasure, and from which he contributed to the general expenses of the State. We have demonstrated, that what the other classes of society received, was merely the wages and profits paid either by the proprietor from his revenue, or by the agents of the productive class from the part destined for their needs, and which they are obliged to purchase from the industrial class. Whether these profits be distributed in wages to the workmen, in profits to entrepreneurs, or in interest on advances, they do not change in their nature, and do not increase the sum of the revenue produced by the productive class over and above the price of its labor, in which the industrial class shares only to the extent of the price of its labor.

It therefore remains true that there is no revenue save the net product of land, and that all other annual profit is paid, either by that revenue, or forms part of the expenditure that serves to produce the revenue.

100. The land has also furnished the whole amount of moveable wealth, or capitals in existence, which are formed only by part of its produce being saved every year.

Not only is it true that there does not exist, nor can exist, any other revenue than the net product of land, but it is also the earth that has furnished all capitals that form the total of all the advances of agriculture and commerce. It has produced, without cultivation, the first rude advances indispensable to the earliest labors; all the rest are the accumulated fruits of the thrift of successive ages since men began to cultivate the earth. This thrift undoubtedly takes place not only out of the revenues of proprietors, but also out of the profits of all the members of the working classes. It is even generally true, that, although the proprietors have a greater surplus, they save less; for, as they have more leisure, they have more wants, and more passions; they regard themselves as more assured of their fortune; and think more about enjoying it contentedly, than about increasing it: luxury is their lot. The wage-receivers, and especially the entrepreneurs of the other classes, receiving profits proportionate to their advances, talents and activity, have, though they do not possess a revenue properly so called, a surplus beyond their subsistence; and almost all of them, devoted as they are to their enterprises, and occupied with increasing their fortune, removed by their labor from amusements and expensive passions, save all their surplus, to invest it again in their enterprise, and to increase it. Most of the entrepreneurs in agriculture borrow little, and they almost all invest only their own funds. The entrepreneurs of other employments, who want to consolidate their fortunes, strive to attain the same position, and, unless they have great ability, those who carry on their enterprises on borrowed funds, run great risk of failing. But, although capitals are formed in part by saving from the profits of the working classes, yet, as those profits always come from the earth, since they are all paid, either from the revenue, or from the expenses that are used to produce the revenue, it is evident that the capitals are derived from the earth just like the revenue, or rather, that they are but an accumulation of a part of the values produced by the earth, which the proprietors of the revenue, or those who share it, are able to accumulate every year, without using it for the satisfaction of their wants.

101. Although money is the immediate object of saving, and is, so to speak, the first material of capitals when they are being formed, yet specie forms an almost inappreciable part of the sum total of capitals.

We have seen that money forms scarcely any part of the sum total of existing capitals, but plays a great part in the creation of capitals. In fact, almost all savings are made only in money; it is in money that the revenues return to the proprietors, that the advances and profits return to the entrepreneurs of every kind; it is therefore from money that they save, and the annual increase in capitals takes place in money; but all the entrepreneurs make no other use of it than to convert it immediately into the different kinds of effects on which their enterprises depend; thus, this money returns to the circulation, and the greater part of capitals exist only in effects of different kinds, as we have already explained above.

Letter to l'Abbé de Cicé, since then Bishop of Auxerre, on the Replacing of Money by Paper.

Also Known as the "Letter on Paper-Money"

Turgot responds to a defense of John Law's system against the argument that it is all right for the state to go into debt, because merchants' expenses very often exceed their capital, Turgot responds that merchants earn a profit on their expenses; from this profit, they are able to repay their debt. The state, by contrast, engages in no productive activities and its debt is a drain on the population. When the state goes into debt, it will often issue paper money. This serves no purpose. Any amount of gold or silver is adequate for all the transactions in the economy, because prices adjust in accord with the total amount of the monetary commodity. If the state tries to introduce paper money de novo to replace a commodity standard, it will be unsuccessful, because there will be no means for people to know how goods should be priced in the new money. Paper money can only be successful if it can be compared with existing commodity money.

CHAPTER 2

Letter to l'Abbé de Cicé, since then Bishop of Auxerre, on the Replacing of Money by Paper.

Also Known as the "Letter on Paper-Money"

Paris, 7 April 1749

I avail myself of the first free time which has come along to write to you.[1]

You are well aware that the seminary is not a place of comfort, and you know also that it is not one which can compensate me for the pleasure of seeing you.

Here we are already reduced to conversing from a distance. I have by no means forgotten my promises, and, to start immediately on some matters which merit our attention, I shall tell you that I have read the three letters, published by l'Abbé Terrasson

---

[1] This passage was apparently changed by du Pont de Nemours, and should read as follows: "The duties with which we are burdened have prevented me to write until today, my dear friend, and I avail myself of the first free time available. Undoubtedly, you yourself are also very busy, as much with the duties of holy week as with your visits to town. At least, I've seen a letter from l'Abbé Véri where he indicated that his company at Bourges was good as well as numerous; I request you to give my regards to all, but especially to him; that could alleviate the boredom caused by being away from Paris and refresh you after the hardships of study and the important matters you would like to discuss. As for me, my dear friend, you fancy that the seminary isn't a place of comfort, but you know also that there is nothing which can compensate me for the pleasure of seeing you, and of embracing you as frequently as my affection desires."

in favor of Law's system, some days before the famous decree of the 21st of May, 1720, which, as you know, covered it with ridicule.[2]

Part of these writings deals with "*rentes constituées*,"[3] which, he maintains, are usurious. His reasoning contains some truth, some falsity, and nothing profound. He knows nothing of the origin of interest on money, nor of the way in which this is produced through labor and circulation, but he shows quite clearly that the Parliament, in its remonstrances about the falling value of the funds, was even more ignorant than he himself.

The remainder of the work deals with credit and its nature, and as this is the foundation of the *system*, or rather, is *the whole* system,[4] I will give you an account of the reflections that occurred to me while reading it. I believe that the principles which he expounds are those of Law himself, since he was undoubtedly writing in harmony with him; and consequently I cannot help thinking that Law had neither a sufficiently certain nor a sufficiently extensive insight for the work which he had undertaken.

"Firstly," says l'Abbé Terrasson at the beginning of his second letter, "it is an accepted commercial axiom that the credit of a well-managed merchant amounts to ten times his capital." But this credit is not a credit of banknotes as that of Law's bank. A merchant who desires to purchase merchandise worth ten times his capital, and who pays in bills payable to the bearer, would soon be ruined. The true meaning of this statement is as follows. A merchant borrows a sum of money in order to invest it to good account, and not only does he derive from this sum enough to pay the agreed interest and to repay the principal at the end of a certain period, but

---

[2] L'Abbé Jean Terrasson (1670–1750) in 1720 published three letters in the *Mercury* in which he defended John Law's financial system against the criticism of D'Aguesseau. Two of these letters were later published in pamphlet form under the title, *Lettres sur le nouveau système des finances*, (Paris: 1720).

[3] *Rentes constituées*: annuities in the National Debt. As Turgot pointed out, nearly the whole of Terrasson's first letter is devoted to this subject.

[4] I.e., Law's system of banking, credit and public finance which operated in France from 1716–1720. Law described the theory behind his system of credit in his *Money and Trade Considered with a Proposal for Supplying the Nation with Money* (1705).

also considerable profits for himself. This credit is not founded on the property of this merchant, but on his integrity and industry, and it necessarily assumes an exchange for a fixed term, arranged in advance; for if these bills were payable at sight, the merchant would never be able to invest the money which he borrowed. It is therefore inconsistent that a bill payable at sight should bear interest, and a credit of this nature could not exceed the capital of the borrower. Thus the profit which the merchant makes through his credit, and which is claimed to be ten times what he would make with his own funds, comes solely from his industry; it is a profit which he draws from the money which passes through his hands by means of the confidence caused by his punctuality in repaying it, and it is ridiculous to conclude from this, as I believe I read in Du Tot, that he is able to draw bills for ten times the money or assets he owns.

Observe, that the king derives no interest from the money he borrows: he needs it either to pay his debts, or for the expenses of the kingdom; consequently he is able to refund it only by taking from his domain, and it follows that he ruins himself if he borrows more than he owns. His credit resembles that of the clergy. In short, all credit is a loan and has a necessary relationship to its repayment. The merchant can borrow more than he owns, because it is not from what he owns that he pays both interest and principal, but from the merchandise which he buys with the borrowed money, and which, instead of dwindling in his hands, increases in price through his industry.

The state, the king, the clergy, the provincial estates, whose needs consume their loans, necessarily ruin themselves if, every year, their revenue is not sufficient to pay, besides their current expenses, the interest and part of the principal of what they have borrowed in times of exceptional needs.

L'Abbé Terrasson thinks very differently. According to him *"the king can greatly exceed the proportion of tenfold to which merchants and private persons are bound."* "The bill of a merchant," he says, "since it can be refused in commerce, does not circulate like money and consequently returns quickly to its source; its drawer finds himself obliged to honor it, and is deprived of the benefit of the credit.

It is different with the king: since everybody is obliged to accept his bill, and since it circulates like money, *he validly pays with his own promise.*" This doctrine is obviously an illusion.

If the bill is worth money, why promise to pay? If the bill takes the place of money, it is no longer credit. Law was conscious of this, and he states that his circulating paper is really a type of money; he maintains that it is as good as that of gold and silver. "These two metals," says l'Abbé Terrasson, "are only the tokens which stand for real wealth, i.e., commodities. *An écu is a bill conceived in these terms: Any seller will give the bearer the produce or commodity which he needs to the amount of three livres, for that same value of another commodity which has been given up to me, and the effigy of the prince takes the place of a signature.* Now what does it matter whether the token is silver or paper? Wouldn't it be better to choose a material which costs nothing, which does not have to be taken out of commerce where it is used as merchandise, which is indeed manufactured in the kingdom and which does not necessarily make us dependent on the foreigners and proprietors of mines *who profit greedily from the enticement which the glitter of gold and silver holds for the other nations*; a material which one can increase according to need, without ever fearing its deficiency, which, indeed, one would never be tempted to put to any use other than circulation? Paper has all these advantages, which make it preferable to silver." If all these reasonings were correct, this would be as good as the philosophers' stone; for there would never be any shortage of either gold or silver to buy all sorts of goods. But was it permissible for Law to ignore that gold, like everything else, lowers its price by its increase? If he had read and studied Locke,[5] who had written twenty years before him, he would have known that all the commodities of a State are always balanced among themselves and with gold and silver, in accordance with the proportion of their quantity and their vent; he would have learned that gold has no intrinsic value which always corresponds to a fixed quantity of merchandise; but that, when there is more gold, it is

---

[5] I.e., John Locke, *Some Considerations on the Consequences of the Lowering of Interest and Raising the Value of Money* which was first published in London in 1691.

cheaper, and more of it is given for a fixed quantity of merchandise; that gold, therefore, when it circulates freely, is always sufficient to meet the needs of the State, and that it matters little whether there are 100 million marks or one million, if all commodities are purchased more dearly in the same proportion. It would, be ridiculous to imagine that money is only token wealth, the repute of which is based on the stamp of a prince.

This stamp is only there to certify its weight and standard. In their respective relation with commodities, uncoined silver is at the same price as coined silver, the legal value is purely a name. This is what Law ignored when he established the bank.

It is thus as merchandise that silver is, not the token, but the common measure of other commodities, and this is not by an arbitrary convention based on the glitter of this metal, but because its value may always be ascertained, since it can be used in various shapes as merchandise, since it has, on account of this property, an exchange value, which is slightly raised by its use as money as well, and since it is, moreover, convertible to the same standard, and accurately divisible.

Thus gold draws its value from its scarcity, and far from it being an evil that it is used both as ordinary merchandise and as a measure at the same time, these two uses maintain its price.

I assume that the king can establish a system of paper money, although this would not be easy in spite of all his authority: let us examine what will be gained thereby. Firstly, if he increases its quantity he will debase it thereby; and as he reserves the power to increase it, it is impossible that the people would consent to give their wares at a nominal price, for a bill which a stroke of the pen can lower in value. "But," says l'Abbé Terrasson, "the king, in order to keep his credit, has an interest in restricting the paper within just bounds, and this interest of the prince is sufficient to build up confidence." What will these just bounds be, and how are they to be determined? Let us follow the system in all the different assumptions which can be made, and see what will be its soundness relative to its usefulness in each case.

At first I observe that it is absolutely impossible that the king should substitute the use of paper for that of gold and silver. The actual gold and silver, to consider them simply as tokens, are in fact distributed among the people by their very circulation, according to the proportion of commodities, industry, land and real wealth of each private person, or rather of the income derived from his wealth compared with his expenditure. Now this proportion can never be known, as it is hidden, and varies continually through new circulation. The king is not going to distribute his paper-money to each according to his possessions of gold money simply by prohibiting the use of the latter in commerce; it is essential that he draws the gold and silver from his subjects to himself, giving them his paper in place of it, and he is able to do this only by giving them his paper as representative of money. To make this clear, you only have to substitute a commodity for money, and see if the prince would be able to give paper for grain, if it would be accepted if he were never obliged to give anything else. Certainly not, then the people would not take it; and if attempts were made to force them, they would justly say that their grain is taken without payment. Thus the bank-notes used to announce their value in terms of silver; by their nature they were subject to repayment; and all credit is repayable, because people are loath to give silver for paper. That would be to put their fortune at the mercy of the prince as I will show below.

It is a point of theory and experience alike that the people will never receive paper other than as representative of, and therefore, convertible into, silver.

One of the ways, and perhaps the only one, in which the king would be able to draw the silver to himself through exchange, would be to receive his bills conjointly with silver, and to give out only bills while keeping the silver. Then he would choose between these two things: either to have this silver melted for use as merchandise and to reduce his subjects to the use of paper; or to allow silver and paper to circulate conjointly, both representative of one another.

I begin by examining this last hypothesis. Well then, I assume that the king puts a certain quantity of paper into commerce, equal to that of silver (Law wanted to put in ten times more): as the total quantity of tokens must always balance with the total quantity of commodities, which is always the same, it is evident that the tokens would halve in value; or, what is the same thing, that the commodities would double. But independently of their capacity as tokens of value, gold and silver have a real value as merchandise; a value which is also balanced with the other commodities proportionally to the quantity of these metals, and which, on the contrary, they do not lose through their capacity as money. That is to say, their value, as metals, will balance with more merchandise than the paper with which they are balanced as money. And since, as I will show below, the king is continually obliged to increase the number of his bills, if he does not wish to render them useless, this disproportion will increase to the point where the specie will no longer be reciprocally convertible with paper, which will be discredited daily, while silver maintains its value always, and will balance itself with the same quantity of goods. Now, as soon as the bills are no longer reciprocally convertible into silver, they have no longer any value, and this is what I am going to prove by examining the other assumption, which is that the king completely reduces his subjects to the use of paper-money.

I have already remarked that this has a general inconvenience, which is, that, since the quantity is arbitrary, there can never be any sure basis for its balance with commodities. While the legal value of money changes with its weight, it is always in the same proportion. But in the case of paper as sole legal tender, nothing is fixed, nothing ensures that the bills are of the same legal sum, neither greater nor smaller, as all the silver which used to be in the kingdom. And even if, by assumption, they were given all the confidence imaginable, if the bills were doubled, the commodities would rise proportionately, etc.

Firstly, it is therefore not true that the system is, as l'Abbé Terrasson puts forward, a means of always having enough tokens of the commodities for the expenses which are made, since it is equally contradictory that there should not be enough silver to counterbalance the commodities, and that it should be possible to have too much of it, since the price of the commodities is related to the relative scarcity of silver, and is simply the expression of that scarcity.

In the second place, the benefit which the king will derive from the system will be only a transient one during the creation of the bills, or rather, during their increase, but it will vanish very quickly, since the commodities will increase in price in proportion to the number of bills.

I can see what the retort will be: "There is," it will be said, "a difference with the pure increase of legal values by which specie increases in the hands of all the private persons among whom it circulates, and which affects nothing but the debts fixed in legal value. But when it is a question of the bills of the State, the increase is left entirely in the hands of the king who thereby creates wealth for himself according to his needs, and who, by putting the bills into circulation only while depreciating them, has already drawn from them all the profit when, through their circulation, these bills begin to raise the price of commodities."

What happens next? The king will be able, by thus creating bills for his needs, to exempt his people entirely from taxes, and to incur much more considerable expenses. It will be enough simply to know (and this is easily calculated) in what progression the number of bills must be increased each year; for it is evident that since those of the preceding year will have increased the price of commodities and balanced themselves with them, it will be necessary, in order to incur the same expenses, to make many more of them in the second year, following a progression which will again increase as the expenses take on a higher nominal value. In general, it is necessary always to keep the same proportion between the total sum of old bills and that of new bills, a quarter, for example.

Let us follow this hypothesis and consider its advantages and disadvantages. We will then draw some conclusions.

1. I acknowledge that, by this means, the king, while giving bills to his subjects for their commodities, bills which are not equivalent to goods, which would in any case be making use of their welfare,

Letter on Paper-Money

would at least save them the charges and vexations which increase the quantity and burden of taxation.

2. I am not very sure how one would be able to know if this aid which the king draws from his subjects would be paid by all in proportion to their wealth. It is evident that if the merchant, who has received the king's bill, obtains for it only the price which it must have in its circulation with the total of bills whose number it has increased, then in this case, those with whom the king deals directly would alone carry the burden of the tax.

The answer to this question depends on a fairly complicated problem, which is as follows: *when and how, through circulation, does a new sum of silver come to balance itself with the total mass of commodities?*—It is clear that it is only through being successively offered for the purchase of various commodities, that it comes to raise the price for the public and to lower its own price. When those who have received the silver of the king, spend it, it has not yet circulated and thus the commodities are not yet raised in price; it is only by passing through several hands that it succeeds in raising the price of all of them. It appears from this, that although nothing very precise can be said about this, it is, all the same, likely that the loss would spread itself fairly uniformly over all private persons, i.e., that they would all be discontented, and not unreasonably so.

It is known, through the money registers, that since the general recoinage[6] of 1726, 1,200 million worth of coin has been manufactured in France; what the foreigners have manufactured balances itself with what has left the kingdom due to the needs of the State. 1,200 million may thus be taken as a rough estimate. The revenue of the king is approximately 300, or a quarter. The king, therefore in order to provide for his necessary expenditure, needs a quarter of the total mass of legal value existing in the state and distributed in the circulation. In the case where the king creates all his revenue for himself, as in the case of the philosophers' stone or of the bills

---

[6] A declaration of 15 June 1726 stabilized the coinage of France by making 1 marc in gold the equivalent of 740 livres, 9 sols, 1 denier, and 1 marc in silver the equivalent of 51 livres, 3 sols, 3 deniers. This value lasted till 1785 when the coinage was further debased.

which are increased arbitrarily, since at the moment of multiplication the commodities have not yet increased in price, he would not be forced to make a greater increase. In the first year the total of bills will then be:

$$a + \frac{a}{4} = 1200 + 300 = 1500$$

The second year:

$$a + \frac{a}{4} + \frac{a + \frac{a}{4}}{4} = 1500 + \frac{1500}{4} = 1975$$

and so on. ...

(It is unfortunate that the remainder of this letter has been lost, but what has just been read of its shows that the young seminarist, at less than 22 years of age, had some very sound ideas on political economy in 1749. [Note by du Pont de Nemours.])

Remarks on the Notes to the Translation of Josiah Child

Turgot suggests that high interest rates encourage lending; but if this process is used to build up a large fortune, people who have accumulated it will after a while tend to dissipate it in spending on luxuries. Efforts by the state to regulate interest reflect an undue partiality to consumers. In general, regulation of the economy is unnecessary. The fear of loss of reputation will operate as an incentive to manufacturers to fulfill what they promise. Large amounts of military spending by a state are undesirable. If it is argued that small states such as Genoa and Venice need heavy spending on the military to defend themselves, the answer is that such expenditures would not be sufficient to prevent invasion by a larger state. These expenditures are thus useless.

CHAPTER 3

Remarks on the Notes to the Translation of Josiah Child

1. (Effects of High Interest.) I am not sure whether it is correct to say that a high rate of interest impedes the circulation of money and that by making it liable to a charge, it compels us as it were to bury it by converting it into hoards or into plate. On the contrary, it appears at first glance that the higher is the rate of interest on money, the less of an encumbrance it should be for people, because it is a good's low price that renders it troublesome to the owner. Thus if the opulent rentier invests his money in plate and jewels, it is not because opportunities for lending are wanting, but rather because they are on too easy terms, because people grow rich in too little time, because they soon prefer the pleasure of spending what they have acquired to that of increasing their wealth. Thrift lasting for some years is sufficient to restore a family's fortune; this is followed by dissipation and by the enormous extension of luxury. Luxury is the fruit of the excessive inequality of wealth and idleness. Now, the high rate of interest of money causes the inequality of wealth because money attracts money and absorbs all the profits

---

Written 1753–1754. This translation is the one that was published with the title: Traité sur le commerce et les avantages qui résultent de la réduction de l'intérêt de l'argent, by Josiah Child, bart., Avec un petit traité contre l'usure by Sir Thomas Culpeper (the Elder), translated from the English, Amsterdam and Berlin, 1754. This translation was the work of Vincent de Gournay and Butel-Dumont, and was to be accompanied by extensive notes of which Gournay, in the autumn of 1752, had already edited the greater part, but the Contrôleur-général did not permit their publication. These notes have unfortunately been lost.

of industry. It produces idleness because it offers an easy means of growing rich without working.

The high rate of interest of money therefore increases the opportunities for lending, but it produces luxury and luxury causes these opportunities to be scorned.

2. The Grain Trade.

The examples of Holland, Genoa, and Venice, where the State is without power and poor, even though the private citizens are rich, are not at all applicable to the question of the interest of money, since it is lower in these republics than in any other state of Europe.

Genoa and Venice are weak states relative to the more powerful states which surround them. I do not know whether the proportion between public revenue and military power and the extent of their territory and the state of their commerce is the same as in the majority of other states in Europe. If this proportion is smaller, I believe that it is proper to praise their governments for it; for apart from the fact that it has not been decided that it is too considerable in many of the more powerful states, no matter how much these republics would burden their subjects with taxes, they would be no more capable of resisting their neighbors because of it, and the people would be unhappy to no purpose.

With regard to Holland, it is far from true that the State is poor or weak relative to its size; it is true that the resilience of the government is weakened at present by the enormity of the public debt and by the changes which have occurred in the constitution of the State, but the Dutch have only their own imprudence to blame, and the wars in which they have involved themselves when blinded by their prosperity. The weakening of Holland is, moreover, a necessary consequence of the increase in the commerce of other states.

I should be sorry if the difference in the rate of interest between France and England is the cause of the difference in thinking on the subject of the grain trade; for it would be certain to be made into an argument against the freedom of this trade, on the pretext that the foreigners would profit from this difference by taking all our grain in times of abundance in order to sell it back to us in times of famine, with a profit of which the nation would be deprived.

3. The Rate of Interest.

I. In truth, I believe that our prejudices in this matter have a different origin. In the setting up of all the legislation dealing with corn, the cries of the consumers have been heeded to the exclusion of the needs of the cultivators. This manner of thinking has arisen in the republics where the sovereignty resides with the people of the cities, because the city dwellers are consumers only. The fear of sedition and the influence of the people's clamoring on timid magistrates who always observe the towns more intimately than the country side, has perpetuated it in nearly all the cities of Italy: corporations have the exclusive charter in corn and oil, which they supply to the people at a price fixed by the government and invariable. Our legislators have adopted the dispositions of Roman Law in this matter, and conform in this to popular demands. The same prejudices have held sway in all of Europe and even in England. The latter country had abandoned these ways sooner than we, not so much because the rate of interest is lower there than it is among us, but rather because they have been enlightened by the principles of commerce before us.

II. When the English changed their manner of thinking about the regulation of corn, they were as much at a disadvantage relative to the Dutch through the difference in interest rates as they are at present at an advantage relative to us. The Dutch did not find sufficient profit in removing their grain in order to discourage the English from establishing warehouses for themselves, and the latter have found a sufficiently strong interest to destroy all their prejudices.

III. I believe that it would be the same with us. It is true that in England the dispositions of the Act of Navigation were able to avert the competition of the Dutch and to counterbalance the effects of the different prices of money. But are we not capable of making up for this in part? Government inspection of the importation and exportation of corn, attention to lowering or raising duties at the right moment, would these not be adequate to avert the competition of foreigners and to assure our storehouse keepers a fair profit? But I doubt whether even these would be necessary.

IV. To prohibit interest as Moses did, is to prohibit lending, for people will not lend for nothing, above all when it is possible to borrow from foreigners. It is giving a monopoly of usury to the latter and to the evaders of the law, and consequently raising interest. The agrarian laws among the Jews compensated for what might be hurtful to the cultivation of the soil in the laws dealing with lending.

The Frenchman who is willing to lend to me on my bill, does not compel me to make my property over to him, but he makes his over to me; he gives up his right to demand reimbursement, but I do not renounce my duty to repay him. Besides, neither the French nor the Dutch practice usury; the price of money, like that of any other thing, must be settled by the relation between the supply and the demand and not by laws.

V. I do not know if 5 per cent at present is so very disadvantageous for us with respect to the English and the Dutch. The difference in the interest of money has some absolute and some relative aspects.

VI. I shall not dwell on the exceedingly vast subject of public credit, but I should wish to examine the usefulness of the transfer of debts in itself, and the advantages which result therefrom, and the means of making it more favorable.

VII. If all the sums paid by apprentices and at receptions[1] were used to repay the debts of the corporations and not for feasts, edifices, and law suits, the evil, if it were left to exist for a while, would perhaps bring with it its own remedy. Would there be no means of setting up a bureau of administration to deal with this?

VIII. This regulation which Child proposes to be imposed on the manufacturer is not unjust, but what purpose does it serve? It would give facilities for selling by the piece, but is not the declaration of the manufacturer enough? If he is dishonest, would he not

---

[1] I.e., into the guilds.

be equally punished by the loss of his reputation, whether he had marked his piece or not.

IX. I doubt strongly that the regulations would be useful even for the original establishment of manufactures. Some examples and some prices would be more useful.

X. On the gain of the State when the merchant loses.

XI. It is not the lack of opportunities, but the too large quantity on the one hand, and the kind of discredit attached to commerce on the other, which draw the money away from it, and raise interest.

XII. If the Kings had truly desired it, the nobility would enter commerce; it was necessary to set examples and worthy examples at that.

Fairs and Markets

Great fairs were common in Europe in Turgot's time and earlier, and he here considers the economic principles that underlie these institutions. In order for a fair to be able to maintain itself, the sellers must be able to recover the transportation costs of getting their goods to the fair. Likewise, buyers must think the trip worth enough to them to justify their expenses of traveling to the fair. Once a fair is established, the fact that a large number of deals can be made there becomes self-reinforcing. More people will travel to the fair, and this will permit more deals to be made. Many fairs have risen to prominence because they offer freedom from burdensome economic regulations by the state. The gains from this freedom do not offset the losses caused by unneeded regulation.

CHAPTER 4

Fairs and Markets

The word *fair*, which is derived from *forum*, a public square, was originally synonymous with that of *market*, and is still so in certain respects. Both signify a gathering of *sellers* and *buyers* at a set time and place, but the word *fair* seems to present the idea of a more numerous, more solemn, and consequently, less common gathering. The use of these two words in ordinary language appears to be determined by this distinction, which is immediately perceptible, but which itself arises from a less obvious, and as it were, more radical difference between these two things. This will be developed further.

It stands to reason that sellers and buyers cannot gather together at certain times and places without an attraction or an interest which compensates for, or which even exceeds the expenses of the journey and of the transportation of the produce and merchandise. Without this attraction, each would remain at home. The stronger it is, the longer the transportation which the produce can support, the more numerous and solemn the gathering of merchants and customers will be, and the more the district which has this gathering as its centre, can be extended. The natural course of trade in itself is enough to fashion this gathering and to increase it up to a certain point. The competition of the sellers limits the price of the produce, and the price of the

---

Written 1757. The article in the Encyclopédie on which this paper is based was titled simply "Foire."

produce in turn limits the number of sellers. Indeed, since all trade must support the person who undertakes it, it is essential that the number of sales compensates the merchant for the low profit which he makes on each sale, and that, consequently, the number of merchants is proportioned to the current number of consumers, so that each merchant is matched by a certain number of the latter. Recognizing this, I assume that the price of a commodity is such that in order to support the trade in it, it has to be sold in a market of three hundred families. It is obvious that three villages, each containing only one hundred families, will be able to support only a single merchant of this commodity. This merchant will probably live in that village of the three where the largest number can gather most conveniently and at the least expense, because this curtailment of expenses will give the merchant who is established in this village an advantage over those who would be tempted to set up business in any of the others. But several types of commodities would probably be in the same category and the merchant of each of these commodities would set up in the same place because of the curtailment of the expenses and because someone who needs two types of commodities prefers making one journey to making two; it is really as if he were paying less for each piece of merchandise. Once a place has become notable because of this self-same gathering together of different trades, it becomes more and more important, because all artisans who are not confined to the country side by the nature of their work, and all those whose wealth permits them to be idle, assemble there to obtain the conveniences of life. The competition of buyers draws the merchants in the hope of sales, and several of them set up business to deal in the same commodities. The competition of the merchants draws buyers in the hope of a good bargain, and both of them continue to increase in turn up to the point where for the remote buyers, the disadvantage of the distance offsets the cheapness of the commodities caused by competition, and even what custom and force of habit add to the attraction of a good bargain. In this manner different centers of commerce, or *markets*, are naturally formed, to which correspond an equal number of districts or departments of various sizes, according to the nature of the commodities, the

Fairs and Markets

relative ease of communications and the condition and relative size of the population. And such is, by the way, the most important and the most common origin of *small market towns* and *cities*.

The same reason of convenience which settles the gathering of buyers and sellers at certain places, also confines it to certain days, when the commodities are too paltry to support long transportation and when the district is not sufficiently populous to provide an adequate, daily market. These days are settled on through a form of silent agreement, for which the smallest circumstances provide a reason. The number of days' journey between the most important places in the neighborhood, together with certain dates which give rise to the departure of travelers, such as the proximity of certain feast days, certain days hallowed by usage for the payments of rents, all types of recurring solemnities, in short, all the types of occasions which bring together a group of people on specific days, become the principle for the establishment of a market on these same days, because traders have an interest in searching out buyers and vice versa.

But it takes only a fairly short distance for this interest, and the low prices resulting from competition, to be offset by the expenses of travel and of the transportation of the produce. Therefore it is not to the natural course of a commerce animated by freedom that one should attribute these splendid fairs, where the products of part of Europe are assembled at great expense and which appear to be the rendezvous of nations. The gain which must compensate for these exorbitant expenses does not arise from the natural order of things but results from the privileges and franchises granted to trade at certain times and places while everywhere else it is overburdened with taxes and duties. It is not surprising that the lack of freedom and the customary obstructions with which commerce has been burdened for so long in all of Europe, has forcibly directed it to those places where it was granted a little more freedom. This is how princes, by granting exemptions from duty, have created so many fairs in the various parts of Europe, and it stands to reason that these fairs are all the more important as the trade is more overburdened with duties in normal times.

A fair and a market are therefore both a gathering of merchants and customers at a set time and place; but in the case of markets the merchants and buyers are brought together by the mutual interest they have in seeking each other; while in the case of fairs it is the desire to enjoy certain privileges: from which it follows that this gathering is inevitably much more numerous and solemn at fairs. Although the natural course of commerce is sufficient to establish markets, as a result of the unfortunate principle which in nearly all governments has infected the administration of commerce, I mean, the mania of directing all, regulating all, and of never relying on the self-interest of man, it has happened, that in order to establish markets, the police[1] has been made to interfere; that the number of markets has been limited on the pretext of preventing them from becoming harmful to each other; that the sale of certain goods has been prohibited except at certain appointed places, either for the convenience of the clerks charged with receiving the duty with which they are burdened, or because the goods were required to be subjected to the formalities of testing and marking, while offices cannot be established everywhere. The opportunity cannot be grasped too often to attack this system so fatal to industry; it can be found more than once in the *Encyclopédie*. The most celebrated fairs in France are those of Lyons, Bordeaux, Beaucaire, etc.; in Germany, those of Leipzig, Frankfurt, etc. My objective here is neither to list them nor to give a detailed exposition of the privileges granted by various sovereigns either to fairs in general or to any one fair in particular. I shall limit myself to some reflection against the common enough illusion which makes some people cite the importance and the extent of the trade at certain fairs as a proof of the greatness of the commerce of a State.

Undoubtedly, a fair must enrich the place where it is held, and bring about the importance of a particular town; and when the whole of Europe was groaning under the manifold shackles of feudal government, when each village was, as it were, an independent and sovereign state, when the lords enclosed in their castles

---

[1] "Police" is used here in the sense of a branch of civil government.

envisaged commerce only as an opportunity of increasing their revenue by subjecting all those who were forced of necessity to cross their territory to a tax or to an exorbitant toll, there is no doubt that those who were the first to be sufficiently enlightened to feel that in slightly relaxing the severity of their duties, they would be more than compensated by the increase of commerce and consumption, soon observed the enrichment, the growth, and the improvement of their places of residence. It is certain that when kings and emperors had sufficiently increased their authority to remove the taxes levied by their vassals from the merchandise destined for the fairs of certain towns which they wished to favor, these towns necessarily became the centers of an exceedingly large commerce and saw the increase of their power as well as of their wealth. But since all these small sovereign states have been united into a single State, under a single prince, is it not strange that, if negligence, force of habit, the difficulty of redressing abuses even if desired, and the difficulty of desiring it, if these things have combined to keep the constraints in existence, namely these local duties and privileges which were established when each province and each village owed allegiance to a different sovereign, is it not strange, I repeat, that this haphazard result has not only been praised, but even imitated as if it were the act of rational policy? Is it not strange that with very good intentions, and with a view to making trade flourishing, new fairs have again been established, the privileges and exemptions of certain towns have yet again been increased, that certain branches of commerce have even been prevented from settling in the midst of the poor provinces for fear of hurting some other towns which for a long time have been enriched by these same branches of commerce? And what does it matter whether Peter or Jack, Maine or Brittany manufacture this or that commodity, provided that the state is enriched and Frenchmen are earning their living? What does it matter whether a piece of cloth is sold at Beaucaire or in its place of manufacture, provided that the laborer receives the value of his work? An enormous mass of trade, gathered together in one place and lumped closely together, will attract the attention of shallow politicians in a much more obvious manner. Water artificially brought together in lakes and canals amuses the traveler as a display of frivolous luxury, but the water which the rain uniformly diffuses over the fields, and which is only guided by the incline of the terrain and distributed through all the valleys, forming pools there, carries wealth and fecundity everywhere. What does it signify that a great deal of trading takes place in a certain spot on certain occasions, if this momentary trade is large only through the same causes which obstruct trade and which tend to decrease it at all other times and over the whole extent of the State? "Is it necessary," said the civic magistrate to whom we owe the translation of Child (M. de Gournay) and to whom France will one day perhaps owe the destruction of the obstacles which have been placed in the way of commerce in the desire to promote it—"is it necessary to fast all year in order to live sumptuously on certain days? In Holland there are no fairs at all, but the whole extent of the State and the whole year are, as it were, a continuous fair, because commerce in that country is always and everywhere equally flourishing."

It is said:

> The State cannot do without the revenue; in order to provide for its needs it must burden commodities with various taxes. However, it is no less necessary to facilitate the sale of our products, above all abroad, which cannot be done without lowering their prices as much as possible. Now these two objectives are reconciled by appointing places and times of immunity from duty, where the low price of the commodity attracts the foreigner and causes an extraordinary consumption, while the everyday consumption of necessaries sufficiently supplies the public revenue. The very desire to profit from these occasions of grace gives sellers and buyers an eagerness which the solemnity of these *great* fairs enhances even more by a type of enticement, from which an increase in the whole of commerce results.

Such are the pretexts which are alleged to uphold the usefulness of the great *fairs*. But it is not difficult to be convinced that it is possible, by general agreement, and while favoring equally all members of the State, to reconcile much more advantageously the two objectives which the government may have in view. Indeed, since the prince agrees to lose part of his duties and consents to sacrifice them in the interest of commerce, nothing prevents him, in making the duties uniform, from diminishing the total of what he agrees to forego. The objective of exempting the sales abroad from duty while letting them survive only on domestic consumption would be even more easily carried out by exempting from duty all the goods which leave the country, for after all, it cannot be denied that our *fairs* supply a large part of our domestic consumption. Under this arrangement, the extraordinary consumption which occurs at the time of fairs would greatly diminish; but it stands to reason that the reduction of the duties in ordinary times, would make the general consumption a great deal more abundant; with this difference that in the case of a uniform but moderate duty, commerce would gain all that the prince is willing to sacrifice to it; whereas in the case of a general and heavier duty, with local and temporary exemptions, the king may sacrifice much, and commerce gain almost nothing; or, what is the same thing, the commodities and merchandise can be lowered in price to a much lesser extent than the duties are lowered, and this because it is necessary to subtract from the advantages which this decrease yields, the costs of transportation of the produce and merchandise to the place designated for the *fair*, the change of abode, the rents of the marketplace increased yet again through the monopoly of the proprietors, and finally the risk of not selling in a rather short time, and of having made a long journey to no avail. Now, it is always necessary that the merchandise pay for all these expenses and these risks. It is far from true, therefore, that the sacrifice of duties by the prince is as useful to commerce in the form of temporary and local exemptions as it would be in the form of a slight reduction over the whole of the duties; it is far from true therefore, that the extraordinary consumption increases by special exemptions as much as the daily consumption is diminished through customary overtaxing. Add to this that there are no special exemptions which do not give rise to frauds in order to profit by them, to new constraints, to increases in the number of clerks and inspectors to prevent these frauds, and to the trouble of punishing them. This is another loss of men and money to the State.

Let us conclude that the *great* fairs are never as useful as the constraints which they imply are harmful; and that far from being the proof of the flourishing condition of commerce, they can only exist, on the contrary, in States where commerce is restricted, burdened with duties, and consequently, indifferent.

In Praise of Gournay

Turgot here gives an account of the life and views of his mentor, the Marquis de Gournay, who early came to see that commerce was burdened by unnecessary regulations. Why should one assume that the state needs to control commerce in a detailed way? To the contrary, Gournay argued that each person is the best judge of his own interest. When his interest coincides with the general interest, he should be allowed to pursue it without restriction. This raises the question, what is the general interest? As Gournay saw matters, this simply consisted of the interests of individuals voluntarily engaging in exchanges to better achieve their preferences. Individuals should be protected from fraud, but even here little reason exists to think that detailed government regulation can in fact protect persons. Far better that they learn by experience from their own mistakes. The interest of the state in increasing national wealth can be achieved by leaving individuals to make free exchanges. Further, general prosperity will insure that the state is not lacking in essential materials, a common fear of those who preach restrictions on trade.

CHAPTER 5

In Praise of Gournay

LETTER FROM TURGOT TO MARMONTEL

Paris, 22 July 1759

I have certainly not forgotten, sir, the note on the late M. de Gournay, which I promised you. I even counted on giving it to you last Monday, at Mme. Geoffrin's, but, not having found you there, and believing you to be in no great hurry, moreover, I took it back home, with the idea that perhaps I would have the time to complete the draft of the eulogy which I would like to make of this excellent citizen.

Since you can wait no longer, I am sending you an outline of it, sketched in great haste, which may yet be able to help you write it, and which you will undoubtedly use in a manner which does much greater justice to his glory than my efforts.

You are aware of my affection.

* * *

Jean Claude Marie Vincent, Seigneur de Gournay, honorary councilor of the Grand Council, and honorary Intendant of Commerce, died at Paris, June 27 (1759) at the age of forty-seven.[1]

Written 1759, "Éloge de Gournay." Jean-François Marmontel (1723–1799), French writer and contributor to the Encyclopédie. prepared the official eulogy of Gournay by having extracts of Turgot's eulogy printed in Le Mercuré, no. 8 (August, 1759).

[1] Turgot made two errors in this official description. Gournay's name was Jacques Claude Marie and not Jean Claude Marie, and his title was M. le Marquis de Gournay and not simply Sieur de Gournay.

He was born in St. Malo in May 1712. His father was Claude Vincent, one of the most important merchants of that town, and Secretary Royal.

His parents destined him for a commercial life, and sent him to Cadiz in 1729, when he was only just seventeen.

Left to his own devices at this early age, he was yet able to avoid the perils and frivolity which are but too common at that age, and, during his entire stay in Cadiz, his life was divided between study, the work of his business, and the numerous connections which his business required and which his personal merit soon procured him.

Through diligence and alertness he found time to enrich his mind with a mass of useful knowledge, without yet neglecting that higher literature, but it was, above all, to the science of commerce that he felt himself drawn and to which he directed his mind in all its vigor. To compare the products of nature and those of the arts in man in different climes, to arrive at the value of these different products, or, in other words, their relationship with the needs and wealth of people at home and abroad, the costs of transport which vary according to the nature of the commodities and the diversity of the routes, the many duties to which they are subject, etc., etc.; in short, to comprehend in its full scope, and to follow in its continual upheavals, the condition of natural production, of industry, of population, of wealth, of finance, of the needs and even the vagaries of fashion in all the nations that are united by commerce, in order to theorize profitably on the basis of a thorough study of all these details—this is to be concerned with the science of trade, as a merchant and constitutes only a part of the science of commerce. But to discover the causes and effects of that multitude of upheavals in all their diversity, to search out the elemental forces whose action, always in combination with, and sometimes disguised by, local circumstances, directs all the transactions of commerce; to recognize those special and basic laws, founded in Nature itself, by which all the values existent in commerce are balanced against each other and settle at a certain value, just as bodies left to themselves take their place, unaided, according to their specific gravity; to discern those complicated relations which link commerce with all the branches of political economy; to perceive the interdependence of commerce and agriculture, the influence of the one and the other on the wealth, the population, and the strength of states, their intimate connection with the laws and customs, and with all the processes of the government, especially with the distribution of its finances; to weigh the assistance which commerce receives from the Navy and that which it renders to it in return, the changes it produces in the respective interests of States, and the weight it places in the political balance of nations; in fine, to select, from among chance events and principles of administration adopted by the different nations of Europe, the true causes of their progress or of their decline in commerce—this is to approach the subject as a philosopher and a statesman.

If his position in life caused M. Vincent to concern himself with the science of commerce as under the first of these two points of view, his vast and penetrating intellect did not allow him to confine himself to this.

To the enlightenment which he drew from his own experience and his reflections, he added a reading of the best works on this subject produced by the different nations of Europe, and particularly by the English nation—the richest of all in such works, and with whose language he familiarized himself for this reason. The works which he read with most pleasure, and whose doctrine he most appreciated, were the Treatises of the famous Josiah Child[2] (which he afterward translated into French) and the Memoirs of the Grand Pensionary, Johan de Witt.[3] We know that these two great men are considered (the one in England, the other in Holland) as the legislators of commerce; that their principles have become national principles, and that the observance of these principles is regarded as one of the sources of the vast superiority in commerce which these two nations have acquired over all the other powers. M. Vincent constantly

---

[2] Sir Josiah Child (1630–1699), English merchant and economist. The treatise to which Turgot refers is his *Discourse Upon Trade* (1690) which Gournay had translated into French.

[3] Johan de Witt (1623–1672), prominent Dutch statesman. The treatise to which Turgot refers is the *Political Maxims of the State of Holland*, by John de Witt, pensionary of Holland (1662).

found verification of these simple and enlightened principles in the practice of an extensive business. He made them his own, without foreseeing that he was destined one day to spread their light through France, and to merit from his own country the same tribute of gratitude which England and Holland pay to those two benefactors of their nation and humanity. His talents and knowledge, together with the most perfect integrity, assured M. Vincent the admiration and the confidence of that multitude of merchants that commerce brings together at Cadiz from all parts of Europe, while at the same time his charming manners procured him their friendship. He soon enjoyed there an esteem unusual for his age, and which the natives of the country, his own compatriots, and the foreigners there, were equally eager to bestow upon him.

During his stay in Cadiz he had paid several visits to the Court of Spain, and to the various provinces of that kingdom.

In 1744, some commercial enterprises which had to be arranged with the Government brought him to France, and in contact with the Comte de Maurepas, then Minister of Navy, who soon discovered M. Vincent's worth.

After leaving Spain, M. Vincent resolved to spend some years traveling through the different parts of Europe in order to increase his knowledge, as well as to extend his correspondences and to form connections favorable to the business he intended to pursue. He visited Hamburg and traveled through Holland and England. Everywhere he made observations and collected notes on the state of commerce and shipping, and on the principles of administration adopted by the different nations in respect to those great objects. During his travels, he maintained an uninterrupted correspondence with M. de Maurepas, whom he acquainted with the knowledge which he was gathering. Everywhere, he made a favorable impression, and attracted the goodwill of the most considerable merchants, of men of great distinction in all walks of life, and of the ministers of foreign powers who were resident in the places through which he traveled. The Court of Vienna, as well as that of Berlin sought to procure his services, and made him very enticing proposals, but he rejected them. He had no other intention than to continue in business and to return to Spain, after having again seen Germany and Italy, when an unforeseen event interrupted his projects and brought him back to his own country.

M. Jametz de Villebarre, his business partner and friend, died in 1746, and being without children, made M. Vincent his sole heir. The latter was in England when he received this news; he returned to France. The amount of his fortune was sufficient for his modest needs; he felt he should settle in his own country and he gave up commerce in 1748. He then took his name from his estate of Gournay, which was included in the legacy he received from M. de Villebarre. The minister was aware how useful his knowledge of commerce might prove to the administration of that important sector. The court had planned to send him to the general peace discussions being held at Breda,[4] not unlike M. Ménager, who in 1711, had been sent to the conferences which preceded the Treaty of Utrecht, in order to discuss the commercial aspects of our interests. The changes which occurred in the conferences did not permit this wise project to be executed, but M. de Maurepas adhered to his original desire to make the talents of M. de Gournay useful to the government; he advised him to consider the prospects of a position as Intendant of Commerce, and to enter, in the meantime, one of the higher Courts. Consequently, in 1749, M. de Gournay purchased the office of councillor in the Grand Council. When an Intendancy of Commerce fell vacant in 1751, M. de Machault, who was also most familiar with the merits of M. de Gournay, had that office conferred on him. From this time onwards, his life was devoted to public affairs: his entry into the Ministry of Commerce appears to have marked the beginning of a period of profound change. During twenty years of experience in a wide and varied trade, in his frequent visits to the most competent merchants of Holland and England, in the reading of the most highly esteemed authors of these two nations, in his careful observation of the causes of their prosperity, M. de Gournay had formulated principles which appeared to be new to some of

---

[4] In 1748, at the end of the War of Austrian Succession. The peace treaty itself was signed at Aix-la-Chapelle in the same year.

the magistrates of whom the Ministry of Commerce was composed—M. de Gournay was of the opinion that every man who works deserves the gratitude of the public. He was astonished to find that a citizen could neither manufacture nor sell anything without having bought the right to do so by entering a corporation or guild at great expense, and that, after having bought this right, it was still sometimes necessary to have a law suit, to determine whether by entering this or that corporation he had acquired the right to manufacture precisely this or that article. He thought that a workman who had manufactured a piece of cloth had made a real addition to the stock of wealth in the State; that if this cloth happened to be inferior to others, there might yet be found among his customers somebody to whom this inferiority would be more suitable than a more expensive perfection. He could not see why this piece of cloth, for failing to conform to certain regulations, should be cut up into fragments of three ells in length, and why the unfortunate man who had made it should be ordered to pay a penalty, enough to reduce him and his family to poverty. He could not conceive why a workman, when making a piece of cloth, should be exposed to risks and expenses from which an idle man was exempt. He could not see of what use it might be that a manufactured piece of cloth should involve legal procedures and tedious discussions in order to establish whether it conformed to an extensive system of regulation, often difficult to understand, nor did he think that such discussions ought to be held between a manufacturer who cannot read and an inspector who cannot manufacture, nor that that inspector should yet be the final judge of the fortune of the unlucky man, etc.

M. de Gournay found it equally strange that, in a kingdom in which the order of succession was determined simply by custom, and in which the question of applying the death sentence to certain crimes was still left to the discretion of the courts, the government should have deigned to regulate by special legislation the length and breadth of each piece of cloth, the number of threads it was to contain, and to hallow with the seal of the legislature four volumes in quarto filled with these important details, and in addition innumerable statutes, dictated by the spirit of monopoly, the whole purpose of which were to discourage industry, to concentrate trade within the hands of a few people by multiplying formalities and charges, by subjecting industry to apprenticeships and journeymanships (*compagnonnages*) often years in some trades which can be learned in ten days, by excluding those who were not sons of masters, or those born outside a certain class, and by prohibiting the employment of women in the manufacture of cloth, etc., etc.

He had not imagined that in a kingdom subject to the same prince, all towns looked on each other as enemies, that they would assume the right to prohibit work within their precincts to other Frenchmen, classifying them as *foreigners*, to oppose the sale or the free transit of commodities of a neighboring province—and thereby for the sake of some fleeting interest, to contend against the general interest of the State, etc., etc.

He was no less astonished to see the government concern itself in regulating the circulation of each commodity, in prescribing one kind of industry in order to encourage another, in subjecting to special constraints the sale of the provisions most necessary to life, in forbidding the setting up of stores of a product whose crop varies from year to year and whose consumption is nearly always the same, in forbidding the exportation of an article subject to depreciation, and to see the government expect to secure the abundance of corn by making the condition of the farm laborer more uncertain and more unhappy than that of all other men, etc.

M. de Gournay was well aware that several of the abuses to which he was opposed had existed in former times in a large part of Europe, and that vestiges of them still remained even in England; but he also knew that the English government had abolished part of them; that, if some still remained, far from adopting them as useful institutions, that government tried to restrict them, and to prevent them from spreading, and continued to tolerate them only because the republican constitution sometimes places obstacles in the path of reform of certain abuses when these abuses can be corrected only by an authority which is always mistrusted by the people, even if it is used to their own advantage. Finally, he knew that for more than a century, all enlightened minds, whether in Holland or in England, had regarded these abuses as remnants of mediaeval barbarism and of the weakness of all the governments which had known neither the importance of public liberty, nor how to protect it against the invasions of the spirit of monopoly and of particular interests.

For twenty years, M. de Gournay had himself carried out, and had seen carried out, the greatest commerce on earth without having had occasion to learn, other than from books, of the existence of all those laws to which he saw so much importance attached, and therefore he did not believe that he would be taken for an *innovator* and a *man of systems*, when all he did was to develop those principles which experience had taught him, and which he saw unanimously recognized by the most enlightened merchants with whom he was associated.

These principles, which others styled as a new system, to him appeared to be no more than the maxims of the plainest common sense. This whole so-called *system* was founded on this maxim, that in general every man knows his own interest better than another to whom it is of no concern.

Hence he concluded that when the interest of individuals is precisely the same as the general interest, every man ought best to be left at liberty to do what he likes. Now, in the case of unrestrained commerce, M. de Gournay thought it impossible for the individual interest not to concur with the general interest.

Commerce can be connected with the general interest, or, what is the same thing, the State can interest itself in commerce, in two respects only. As protector of the individuals who compose it, it is in its interest that no one should be able to inflict any great injustice on another, against which the latter has no protection. Next in its capacity as a political unit forced to defend itself against foreign invasions, it is in the interest of the State that the stock of its wealth and the annual product of the soil and of industry should be as great as possible. In both respects, the State has a special interest in protecting the value of the necessities of life from those sudden shocks which, by plunging the people into the horrors of famine, may endanger public tranquility and the safety of citizens and magistrates. Now, it is clear that the interest of all the individuals, kept free from restraint of any kind, necessarily fulfils all these conditions of general usefulness.

As for the first object, that in trade no one should injure another, it is evidently sufficient that the government should always protect the natural liberty of the buyer to buy, and of the seller to sell. For if the buyer is always the one who decides whether to buy or not, it is certain that he will select among all the sellers the man who will give him at the best price the merchandise that suits him best. It is no less certain that every seller, it being his chief interest to gain preference over his competitors, will sell in general the best merchandise at the lowest possible price, in order to attract customers. It is not true therefore that a merchant may be interested in deception—unless he has some exclusive privilege.

But if the government limits the number of sellers by exclusive privileges or otherwise, it is certain that the consumer will be wronged and that the seller, certain of selling, will compel him to buy bad articles at a high price.

If, on the contrary, it is the number of buyers which is diminished, by the exclusion of foreigners or of certain other persons, then the seller is wronged, and, if the injury is carried to the point where the price does not compensate him, with profit, for the costs and risk, he will cease to produce the commodity in such abundance, and scarcity will result.

The general freedom of buying and selling is therefore the only means of assuring, on the one hand, the seller of a price sufficient to encourage production, and on the other hand, the consumer, of the best merchandise at the lowest price. This is not to say that in particular instances we may not find a cheating merchant and a duped consumer; but the cheated consumer will learn by experience and will cease to frequent the cheating merchant, who will fall into discredit and thus will be punished for his fraudulence; and this will never happen very often, because generally men will be enlightened upon their evident self-interest.

To expect the government to prevent such fraud from ever occurring would be like wanting it to provide cushions for all the children who might fall. To assume it to be possible to prevent successfully, by regulation, all possible malpractices of this kind, is to sacrifice to a chimerical perfection the whole progress of industry; it is to restrict the imagination of artificers to the narrow limits of the familiar; it is to forbid them all new experiments; to renounce even the hope of competing with the foreigners in the making of the new products which they invent daily, since, as they do not conform to our regulations, our workmen cannot imitate these articles without first having obtained permission from the government, that is to say, often after the foreign factories, having profited by the first eagerness of the consumer for this novelty, have already replaced it with something else. It means forgetting that the execution of these regulations is always entrusted to men who may have all the more interest in fraud or in conniving at fraud since the fraud which they might commit would be covered in some way by the seal of public authority and by the confidence which this seal inspires, in the consumers. It is also to forget that these regulations, these inspectors, these offices for inspection and marking, always involve expenses, and that these expenses are always a tax on the merchandise, and as a result overcharge the domestic consumer and discourage the foreign buyer. Thus, with obvious injustice, commerce, and consequently the nation, are charged with a heavy burden to save a few idle people the trouble of instructing themselves or of making enquiries to avoid being cheated. To suppose all consumers to be dupes, and all merchants and manufacturers to be cheats, has the effect of authorizing them to be so, and of degrading all the working members of the community.

As for the second object for the Government in this connection, which is to procure for the nation the greatest possible stock of wealth, is it not evident that since the only real wealth of the State is the annual output of its land and of the industry of its inhabitants, its wealth will be at its greatest when the produce of each acre of land, and of the industry of each individual is carried to the highest possible level? And is it not evident that each proprietor has more interest than any other person in drawing from his land the greatest possible return? That every individual has the same interest in gaining by his work as much money as possible? It is equally obvious that the employment of the soil or of industry which yields the greatest revenue to each proprietor or to each inhabitant will always be the one that is of the greatest advantage to the State, because the sum which the State can use annually for its needs is always an aliquot part of the total revenue which is annually produced in the State, and because the sum of these revenues is composed of the net revenue of each estate and of the product of the industry of each individual—if then, instead of leaving all this to private interests, the government takes it upon itself to prescribe to each what he must do, clearly all the benefits individuals lose because of the constraints imposed upon them, will represent an equal deduction from the total net revenue produced in the State each year.

To imagine that the State should encourage the earth to bring forth one kind of produce rather than another, that it ought to establish certain types of manufactures rather than some others; that consequently it ought to prohibit the production of some goods and order that of others; to forbid certain kinds of industry for fear of injuring other kinds; to claim to sustain manufacturing, when it is at the expense of agriculture by forcibly maintaining the price of provisions below their natural level; to establish certain manufactures at the expense of the Treasury; to heap privileges on them, favors, exclusions of all manufactures of the same kind for the purpose of procuring for the manufacturers a profit which it is assumed they could not obtain by the natural sale of their products: all this is to misunderstand greatly the true advantages of commerce; it is to forget that no commercial transaction can be anything other than reciprocal, and that, therefore, the desire to sell everything to the foreigners and to buy nothing from them, is absurd.

There is no need to prove that each individual is the only competent judge of this most advantageous use of his lands and of his labor. He alone has the particular knowledge without which the most enlightened man could only argue blindly. He alone has an experience which is all the more reliable since it is limited to a single object. He learns by repeated trials, by his successes, by his losses, and he acquires a feeling for it which is much more ingenious than the theoretical knowledge of the indifferent observer because it is stimulated by want.

If the objection is raised that apart from exchange value, the State may also be interested in being as little dependent as possible on other states for the commodities of prime necessity; firstly, all that this proves is that, although both freedom of industry and freedom of trade in the produce of the soil, are very precious, freedom of trade in the produce of the soil is yet the more essential; secondly, it will always be true that greater wealth and a larger population will give the State in question the means of ensuring its independence in a much more reliable manner. Besides, that suggestion is purely speculative; a large State always produces everything and with regard to a smaller one, a bad harvest would soon wreck this fine scheme of independence.

As for the third object, which may interest the State in two respects, both as protector of the individuals whom it must put in the way of earning a comfortable living by their own labor, and as a political body interested in preventing the domestic troubles which a famine could cause, this matter has been developed so clearly in the work of M. Herbert,[5] and in the article "Corn" by M. Quesnay,[6] that I refrain from discussing it here, since M. Marmontel knows these two works thoroughly.

It follows from this discussion that, in all respects in which commerce may interest the State, unrestrained individual interest will always produce the public welfare more surely than the operations of government, which are always faulty and of necessity directed by a hazy and dubious theory.

M. de Gournay concluded that the only aim the administration should set for itself was: firstly, to restore to all branches of commerce that precious liberty they had lost through the prejudices of ages of ignorance, through the ease with which the Government fell in with particular interests, and the desire for a misplaced perfection;

---

[5] Claude-Jacques Herbert, *Essai sur la police des grains, sur leur prix, et sur les effets de l'agriculture*, Londres, 1753.

[6] Francois Quesnay, "Grains," first published in the *Encyclopédie* in 1757.

secondly to grant the right to work to all members of the State, for the purpose of exciting the greatest competition in the market, which will infallibly produce the greatest perfection in manufacture, and the most advantageous price to the buyers; thirdly, to give at the same time as many competitors as possible to the buyer by opening for the seller all the outlets for his commodity, which is the only means of assuring labor its reward, and of perpetuating production, which has this reward as its sole object.

Besides this, the government should plan to remove those obstacles which retard the progress of industry by diminishing the extent and the certainty of its profits. M. de Gournay considered the chief of these obstacles to be the high interest of money, which, by offering to all owners of capital the means of spending their lives without working, encourages luxury and idleness and withdraws from commerce the riches and industry of a multitude of citizens, rendering them unproductive to the State; which excludes the nation from all branches of commerce not yielding one or 2 per cent more than the current rate of interest; which consequently gives foreigners the exclusive privilege of all these branches of commerce, and enables them to gain preference over us in almost all other countries by lowering the price more than we would afford to do; which gives the inhabitants of our colonies a powerful reason to engage in smuggling, and in this way weakens the natural affection they ought to have for the mother country; which alone would secure for the Dutch and the Hanse towns the carrying trade of all of Europe including even France itself; which, every year, makes us tributaries to the foreigners by the high rates we pay on their loans to us; which, finally, withdraws from cultivation all those lands which would not yield more than 5 per cent, since it is possible, to obtain the same return with the same capital, without working. But similarly, he believed that the dealings in capital itself, which have this rate of interest as their price, can be made to regulate this price equitably and with all necessary economy only, as in the case of all commerce, by competition and by mutual liberty, and that the government could best bring this about by, on the one hand abstaining from making laws whenever agreements can serve this purpose, and on the other hand, by not swelling the number of debtors and consumers of capital whether by borrowing or by not repaying punctually.

Another kind of obstacle to the progress of industry which M. de Gournay considered could not be cleared away too soon was that multiplicity of taxes which, owing to the necessity of meeting the requirements of the State, had been imposed upon labor of every kind, entailing vexatious modes of collection which were often more onerous than the taxes themselves; the arbitrary nature of the *taille*, the multiplicity of dues on every sort of merchandise, the complexity of tariffs, the inequality of these dues in the different provinces, the innumerable customs houses at the frontier of these provinces, the frequency of inspections and the importunity of enquiries necessary to provide against fraud, the necessity of relying on the solitary testimony of mercenary men of low character for proof of these frauds; the interminable disputes, so fatal to commerce that almost any merchant would prefer, in this respect, a disadvantageous arrangement to a law suit, no matter how obvious the justice of his case. Finally, he condemned the impenetrable obscurity and mystery resulting from this complexity of local dues and regulations published at different dates, an obscurity which is always interpreted in favor of revenue and against commerce. He condemned the excessive duties, the evils of smuggling, the loss of a multitude of citizens which this entails, etc., etc., etc.

Public finance is necessary, since the State needs revenue; but agriculture and commerce, or rather agriculture animated by commerce, is the ultimate source of these revenues. Thus public finance should not be prejudicial to commerce, since it would at the same time harm itself. These two interests are of necessity united, and if a conflict of interests seems to exist, it is perhaps because we have confused the interests of finance as related to the State and the monarchy, which are eternal, with the interests of the financiers, who, being charged with the collection of the revenues for a certain period only, prefer to increase present revenue rather than to conserve the source which produces this revenue. Add to this the dubious and fortuitous way in which this hydra of all types of duties has taken shape, i.e., by the successive gathering together of a multitude of fiefs and sovereignties, and the conservation of the taxes which each individual sovereign used to enjoy, while the urgency of the kingdom's needs has never left time to reform this chaos by establishing a uniform system of duties. Finally, there are the facilities which public finance has had at all times of making its voice heard, to the prejudice of commerce.

The fiscal authority consists of a body of accredited men, whose prestige varies with the urgency of the needs of the State. They are always occupied with a single object, never distracted nor negligent, resident in the capital and in constant touch with the government. The merchants, on the other hand, occupied each with his individual objective, dispersed in the provinces, without fame or protection, without a central meeting place, are only able to raise a feeble and solitary voice in any given case, a voice that is inevitably stifled both by the number and the prestige of their adversaries, and by the opportunities the latter have of engaging skilled writers in the defense of their interests. If the merchant agrees to abandon the care of his affairs in order to hold a litigation rather than to surrender his rights, the odds are high against him, and even if he wins, he still remains at the mercy of a powerful body which has, through the rigor of the laws which it has suggested to the ministry, an easy means of crushing the merchant; for (and this is not one of the least abuses), there exist several laws of this type which are impossible to execute and which the tax farmers only use to ensure the submission of individuals, by threatening a rigorous application of them.

M. de Gournay thought that the Board of Trade would be of much greater use if, rather than managing commerce, which ought to go its own way, it protected commerce against the activities of the public revenue. He would have liked the needs of the State to be such that they would allow commerce to be delivered from all kinds of duties. He believed that a nation fortunate enough to have reached this point would necessarily draw to itself the greater part of the commerce of Europe. He believed that all taxes, of whatever kind they may be, are, in the final analysis, paid by the landowner, who sells by so much the less the produce of his land, and that if all the taxes were assessed on landed property, the proprietors and the kingdom would thereby gain all that was now absorbed in the cost of administration, the unproductive employment of men now wasted in tax collection, in smuggling, or in preventing it, without even counting the immense gain from the increase in riches and value that would result from the increase in commerce.

There exist also some obstacles to the progress of industry that arise from our customs, from our prejudices, from some of our civil laws, but the two which are most disastrous I have already discussed, and the others would entail too much detail. Besides, M. de Gournay did not pretend to limit the duties of the government toward commerce strictly to that of maintaining its free course and removing the obstacles that oppose the improvement of industry. He was also quite convinced of the usefulness of the encouragements that could be given to industry either by recompensing the authors of useful inventions, or by encouraging, by prizes or gratuities, a competition among artisans to attain perfection. He knew that even when industry enjoyed the most complete freedom, these measures are often useful in hastening its natural progress, and that they are essential above all when the fear of constraints has not been completely dispelled and still slows down its development. But he could not give his approval when these encouragements could conceivably stand in the way of new progress through prohibitions and exclusive advantages. It was only with great reservations that he supported loans by the government, and he preferred other encouragements: rewards in proportion to production, and prizes designed to attain perfection in work, in short, marks of distinction and all measures which encourage competition among a greater number of men.

This, more or less, expresses M. de Gournay's attitude toward the administration of commerce; these are the principles which he constantly applied to all the matters discussed at the Board of Trade from the moment he entered it. As he had no idea of creating a new system, he was satisfied to develop only what was necessary to support his opinions in regard to each particular affair; but it was not long before the consistency and fruitfulness of his principles were recognized, and soon he had to countenance a mass of challenges.

He gave himself with pleasure to these discussions which could only elucidate the subject and in one way or another produce a knowledge of the truth. Free from all selfish interest, from all personal ambition, he lacked even that slavery to his opinions which self-love might have induced. All he lived for, and aspired to, was the public welfare; thus his opinions were expressed with as much modesty as courage. Equally incapable of taking an overbearing tone, and of speaking against his opinion, he delivered his sentiments in a straightforward manner which derived all its power from the strength of his reasoning. He skillfully put his ideas within the grasp of all minds, stating his principles with a kind of luminous precision, and emphasizing them by a sensible use of some well chosen examples. When he was contradicted, he listened with patience; however sharp the attack might be, he never discarded his customary politeness and gentleness, nor did he lose anything of the presence of mind and composure necessary to fathom completely the artful reasoning advanced against him.

His simple eloquence, animated by that engaging earnestness which pervades the discourse of a virtuous man who is deeply persuaded that he is upholding the cause of the public welfare, never detracted from the soundness of the discussion; sometimes it was seasoned with a harmless jest which was all the more pleasant since it was never pointless.

His zeal was gentle because it was purged of all self-esteem; but it was not therefore any the less earnest, for love of the public welfare gripped him.

He was convincing without being excessively attached to his opinions; his mind, always without bias, was constantly ready to receive fresh enlightenment; sometimes he did change his mind on important matters, and there was nothing to suggest that his previous opinion had in the least delayed that sudden impression which the proffered truth makes on one as fair-minded as he.

He had the good fortune to find in M. Trudaine, who was even then at the head of the administration of commerce, the same love of truth and of the public welfare that motivated himself. Since at that stage he had developed his ideas only as occasion arose during business discussion or in conversation, M. Trudaine urged him to give as it were an outline of his doctrine. It was with this in mind that he translated in 1752 the treatises on trade and the interest of money by Sir Josiah Child and Sir Thomas Culpeper. He added a great many interesting remarks in which he thoroughly examined and discussed the principles of the text, and clarified them by applying them to the most important questions of commerce. These remarks formed a work as considerable as that of the English authors, and M. de Gournay counted on having them printed together. He printed only the text however, in 1754: reasons, which no longer exist, then prevented the printing of the commentary.

His reputation became well established, and his zeal communicated itself to others. It is to the ardor with which he sought to direct all men of talent with whom he was acquainted to the study of commerce and political economy, and to the ease with which he communicated all the knowledge he acquired, that we owe that propitious fermentation of thought on these important questions that has taken place these last few years, and which sprang up two or three years after M. de Gournay had been Intendant of Commerce. Since then, it has already presented us with several works filled with laborious research and profound views, works that have cleared our nation of the charge of frivolity which it had not failed to incur by its indifference to those studies which are the most truly useful.

In spite of the opposition which he had to endure, M. de Gournay often tasted the satisfaction of succeeding in eradicating part of the abuses which he was attacking, and above all, of weakening the authority of those archaic principles which even then had to be relaxed as to the rigor and the extent of their application in order to withstand his attacks. However difficult people may have found it to embrace his principles to their full extent, his insight, his experience, the general esteem of the merchants for him personally, the unimpeachable purity of his views, these things inevitably earned him the confidence of the minister and the respect even of those who yet fought against his ideas.

His zeal induced him to make plans to tour the kingdom in order to see for himself the state of commerce and of manufactures, and to discover the reason for the rise or decay of each branch of trade, the abuses, the needs, the resources of each type. He started the execution of his plan in 1753 and departed in July. From that time up to December he traversed Bourgogne, Lyonnais, Dauphiné, Provence, upper and lower Languedoc, and returned finally by way of Lyon.

In 1754, he was unable to travel because of a tumor situated on his back, which he had cut out twice, and which had to be burned out the third time with the help of caustics, at the beginning of 1755. He resumed his travels in 1755 and made a tour of inspection of La Rochelle, Bordeaux, Montauban, the remainder of Guyenne and Bayonne. In 1756 he followed the course of the Loire from Orléans to Nantes, traveled through Maine, Anjou, the coast of Bretagne from Nantes to Saint-Malo, and returned to Rennes for the sitting of the States in 1756. The deterioration of his health did not permit him to make any further journeys.

At each step he found further reasons to confirm him in his principles, and new arguments against the restriction of commerce against which he was fighting. He took up the complaints of the friendless, poor manufacturer who, unable to write and to present his claims in plausible arguments, and having no representative at the Court, has always been the victim of a government misguided by interested men to whom he was forced to appeal. M. de Gournay applied himself to uncovering the hidden interests which had called for those allegedly useful rules whose sole object it was to put the poor more and more at the mercy of the rich. The fruits of his travels were the reform of an infinite number of abuses of this kind; a knowledge of the true state of the provinces giving more certainty and better direction to the operations of the Ministry; a more exact appreciation of complaints and requests; the facility which was afforded to the people and to the simple artisans of making known their own complaints; finally, a fresh spirit of emulation in all branches of commerce which M. de Gournay was able to spread by his persuasive eloquence, by the exactness with which he stated his ideas and by the happy contagion of his patriotic zeal.

He sought to inspire in the magistrates and notable persons in the places he visited a zeal for the prosperity of their town or their district; he interviewed men of letters, suggested subjects for treatment, and urged them to direct their studies toward questions of commerce, agriculture and all economic matters.

It is partly to his suggestions and to the zeal which he had inspired at the sittings of the States of Bretagne during his stay at Rennes in 1756 that the society[7] for the Perfection of agriculture, commerce and industry, established in Bretagne under the protection of the States and the auspices of the Duke d'Auguillon, owes its existence. This society was the first of its kind to be formed in France. Its program, which is connected with the municipal administration of the province, was drawn up by M. de Montaudouin, a merchant from Nantes.

M. de Gournay knew how to adapt himself to the degree of intelligence of his audience, and he answered the absurd objections—dictated by ignorance—with the same suavity and exactness with which he answered the bitter opposition, dictated by quite different principles, in Paris.

Full of respect for all those persons charged with the administration of the provinces which he visited, he gave them no occasion to think that his mission could cast the least shadow on their authority. Always forgetting himself, sacrificing himself without effort for the benefit of the objective, it was as far as possible through them and with them that he acted; he seemed only to supplement their zeal, and he often credited them in the presence of the minister with his own ideas. By this conduct, if he did not always succeed in convincing them of his principles, he at least always won their friendship.

The life of M. de Gournay does not offer any other outstanding event during the time that he continued as Intendant of Commerce. Ever occupied with the functions of his office, never missing any opportunity to put forward some useful ideas, or to spread

---

[7] *Société d'Agriculture de Bretagne.*

light among the public, there is hardly an important question on commerce or political economy on which he has not written several notes or reasoned letters. He devoted himself to this sort of work with a type of prodigality, producing nearly always, on every occasion, new papers, without referring his audience to the earlier ones he had written. He did not try to evade the trouble of rediscovering ideas which he had already expressed, or the unpleasantness of repeating himself. The reason for this manner of working was the small value which he attached to what he had composed, and his total unawareness of any literary repute. Overflowing with his salutary and fruitful principles, he applied them to every question with the greatest ease. Completely preoccupied with propagating some useful idea, he did not think of himself as a writer. Free from personal attachment to what he had written, he gave it over, without reservations, to all those who wished to instruct themselves, or to write, on these matters, and more often than not he did not even keep copies of what he had written. These fragments, jotted down in haste and forgotten by him, are nevertheless precious, even if regarded purely from the point of view of composition: his writings, like his conversation, was characterized by a natural eloquence, a lucid precision when expounding his principles, a remarkable art of presenting them from all types of viewpoints, of adapting them for all minds and of having them appreciated by examples which were always just right, and whose very rightness was often striking; a politeness which never failed, and a shrewd logic in the discussion of objections; finally, a patriotic and humane tone, which was unintentional and therefore all the more genuine.

M. de Gournay did not content himself with advocating his ideas through writing or speech: to command respect for the ideas he thought useful he applied the same activity, the same warmth and the same perseverance which an ambitious man puts into the pursuit of his own interests. Incapable of losing heart when the cause was a worthy one, he did not hesitate to push his efforts to the point of obtrusiveness. No proprietor of our isles has clamored with as much zeal for the freedom of trade for neutral vessels in our colonies during the war.[8] His solicitations were all the more animated and pressing because he demanded nothing for himself, even to the extent that he died without receiving any favor from the court.

Meanwhile, as he occupied himself solely with public work, his own fortune, as well as his health, had wasted away. He had sustained losses on the funds which he had left in Spain, and the state of his affairs forced him to leave his position as Intendant of Commerce in 1758. Some important people who knew how useful he was suggested that he ask the Court for some favors for himself which would compensate him for the losses he had sustained. He replied, "that he did not esteem himself sufficiently to believe that the State had to buy his services, that he had always looked upon similar favors as a dangerous practice, especially in the circumstances in which the State was situated, and that he did not desire to be reproached for being a party to exceptions to his own principles in his own interest." He added, "that he did not believe himself to be excused by his retirement from occupying himself with objectives useful for the well-being of trade." For this reason, he requested to keep his seat at the Board of Trade, with the title *honorary*, which was accorded to him.

Some time previously, he had similarly sold his Office of Councillor at the Grand Council, but had kept the title of *honorary councillor*.

Retirement did not deprive M. de Gournay of his importance. His zeal was not lessened because of it, his insight could still be as useful as ever. M. de Silhouette, whose regard for M. de Gournay speaks in praise of both of them, resolved, as soon as he had become Contrôleur-Général, to remove from retirement a man whose talents and zeal were so fitted to furthering his own designs. He began by inviting him to be present at the conference which the Intendants of Commerce held every week with the Contrôleur-Général, and at which M. de Gournay had ceased to be present. He also intended him to take up one of the positions of Royal Commissioner to the

---

[8] I.e., the Seven Years' War (1756–1763) in which France supported Austria against Prussia and England.

General-Farm.⁹ In this office, M. de Gournay would have been in a position to appraise the reciprocal complaints of commerce and finance, and to search for a means of reconciling these two interests of the State as far as possible, but he was not able to profit from this token of esteem of M. de Silhouette. When this proposition was put to him he had already been stricken by the illness of which he died.

His health had been deteriorating for a long time. After spending carnival time at his estate of Gournay, he returned with a pain in the hip he at first took for sciatica. For a time the pain gradually grew worse, and at the end of two months a tumor was discovered which appeared to be the source of the trouble, but several different attempted cures could not dissipate it. Weakness and emaciation increased. The waters had been suggested, but he was not strong enough to undertake the journey; a slow fever was consuming him. A last effort was made with the use of a resolvent which was regarded as more potent, but no sooner was it applied, than M. de Gournay lapsed into a violent fever accompanied by delirium. This state of affairs lasted for three days; at the end of this time, he regained consciousness, of which he made use to make his will and to receive the last rites of the church. He died that same evening.

In the year . . .¹⁰ he married Clothilde Verduc, and he lived in great harmony with her. No children resulted from this marriage.

M. de Gournay would merit the gratitude of the nation even if it would have been obliged to him only for having contributed more than any other person to the directing of minds toward economic knowledge. This glory would be secured for him even if his principles were still liable to opposition; and truth would always have profited from the discussion of matters to which he had given occasion for debate. Posterity will decide between him and his adversaries. But until the nation delivers its judgment, the honor of being the first to

---

⁹ I.e., the agency for collecting indirect taxation on behalf of the crown on a commission basis.

¹⁰ This is left blank in the French text. The date of marriage between Gournay and Clothilde Verduc was apparently not known to Turgot. In fact, Gournay was married in 1748, on his retirement from trade.

diffuse the principles of Child and of Johan de Witt may be confidently claimed in his memory. And, if one day these principles are adopted for commerce by our administration, if they will ever be for France what they have been for Holland and England, that is, a source of abundance and prosperity, our descendants will know that gratitude for it is due to M. de Gournay.

The opposition which his principles encountered has led some people to portray M. de Gournay as a fanatic and a *man of systems*. This phrase, *a man of systems*, has become a type of weapon in use by all those who are biased or interested in maintaining some abuse, and directed against all those who propose changes in the *status quo*.

The philosophers of recent times have indeed, with as much strength as reason, striven against the spirit of *systems*. They understood by this term those arbitrary suppositions with the help of which it is attempted to explain all phenomena and which actually explain them all equally, because they do not explain any; that lack of observation, that overhasty reliance on obscure analogies by which a particular fact is rashly transformed into a general principle, and the whole is judged by a superficial glance at a part; that blind presumption which relates all it does not know to the little it knows; which, dazzled by an idea or a principle, sees it everywhere, like the eye, fatigued by an intense look at the sun, casts its image on all the objects to which it directs itself; which wants to know all, explain all, arrange all, and which, ignorant of the inexhaustible variety of nature, claims to subjugate it to its arbitrary and limited methods, and tries to circumscribe the infinite in order to embrace it.

But when men of the world in their turn condemn *systems*, it is not in the philosophic sense. These men, accustomed to receive all opinions, one after the other, like a mirror reflects all images without retaining them, accustomed to find everything probable without ever being convinced, to ignore the intimate connection of effects with their causes, to contradict themselves constantly without being aware of it or placing any importance on it, these men cannot help but be astonished when they meet with a man who is inwardly convinced of a truth, and deduces consequences from it with the rigor of exact logic. Today they will listen to him, tomorrow they will listen to entirely contrary propositions, and they will be surprised not to see in him the same flexibility. They do not hesitate to call him a fanatic and a *man of systems*. Thus, although in their language the word *system* applies to an opinion adopted after mature consideration, supported by proofs and consistent in its consequences, they none the less take it amiss because the little attention of which they are capable does not enable them to judge the reasons, and does not offer them any opinion to which they can refer constantly or which is clearly related to a particular principle.

Yet it is true that all thinkers have a *system*, that a man who has no system or logical connection between his ideas must either be an imbecile or a madman.[11] Never mind. The two senses of the word system are confused, and he who has a system in the sense of the men of the world, that is, a settled opinion resulting from a chain of observations, will incur the reproaches made by the philosophers to the spirit of systems taken in quite a different sense, that of an opinion not founded on sufficient observation.

Taking the word system in the popular sense, M. de Gournay, undoubtedly, was a man of systems, since he had a viewpoint to which he was strongly attached. His adversaries were all men *of systems*, as much as he was, since they held an opinion contrary to his.

But if the word *system* is taken in the philosophical sense, which I first developed, nobody was further removed from that than he. On the contrary, he would rather have had the right to lay this reproach at the door of the principles against which he fought, since his whole doctrine was founded on the complete impossibility of directing, by invariant rules and by continuous inspection a multitude of transactions which by their immensity alone could not be fully known, and which, moreover, are continually dependent on a multitude of ever changing circumstances which cannot be managed or even foreseen; and since he therefore wanted the adminis-

---

[11] This sentence was changed by du Pont in his edition of Turgot's works. It should apparently read as follows: "In this last sense, it is however true that everybody who thinks has a system and that a system cannot be a matter for reproach, seeing that a system can only be confounded by an opposite system." (Note by Gustave Schelle.)

tration not to attempt to lead everybody by the hand, and not to claim the ability to do so, but rather to let them go their way and rely more on the natural motive of self-interest, than on the external and artificial restraints of regulations which were always arbitrary in spirit and often so in application. If arbitrariness and a mania for fitting facts to ideas rather than ideas to the facts are the distinguishing marks of the spirit of *systems*, then assuredly M. de Gournay was not a *man of systems*.

He was even less so as far as an obstinate attachment to his ideas was concerned. The humility with which he held them proved strongly that he was not conceited about them and that he upheld them only as a citizen. It can be said that few men have been as perfectly free as he was from that type of vanity which shuts the door on new ideas. He searched for new information as if he knew nothing, and was ready to examine every assertion as if he had never held any opinion to the contrary.

It must also be said that this so-called system of M. de Gournay had this peculiarity that its general principles have been adopted by nearly the whole world; that at all times the desire of commerce among all the nations has been expressed by those two words: *freedom* and *protection*, but above all freedom. M. le Gendre's phrase to M. Golbert is well known: *laissez-nous faire*. Often M. de Gournay differed from the men who treated him as a man of systems only in this: that he objected with the strictness of a just and righteous heart, to the exceptions which they allowed in favor of their own interests.

For example, the world is full of people who condemn exclusive privileges, but who believe that there are certain commodities for which they are necessary. This exception is generally based on their personal interest, or on that of individuals with whom these people are connected. Thus the majority of people is by nature well disposed toward the sweet principles of commercial freedom. But nearly all, either through interest, or through habit, or through subordination, insert some small modifications or exceptions.

M. de Gournay, in objecting to any exception in particular, had the majority with him, but by objecting to all exceptions at the same time, he ranged against him all the people who each wanted one exception, even though they were not united on the type of exception they desired. The result of this was a misleading unanimity of feeling against his principles, and an almost universal imputation of the title of *man of systems* against him personally.

This imputation was seized upon as a rallying cry by those who were turned into his adversaries because of envy or an excessive zeal for their own opinion, and gave them the excuse to oppose him as a solid body, instead of the empty shadow they really were, of which any man less zealous for the public welfare and less indifferent to his own interests, would have been terrified.

Opposition only served to stimulate his courage. He knew that by declaring the universality of his principles less candidly, and by failing to acknowledge all the remote consequences which derived therefrom, by being a party to some slight modifications, he would have evaded this dreaded title of a *man of systems* and would have escaped the bias which people endeavored to propagate against him. But he believed in the usefulness of developing principles to their fullest extent, and he wanted the nation to instruct herself; and only the clearest exposition of the truth could instruct her. He thought that such circumspection would be useful only to himself, and he held himself of no account.

It is not true that he believed, as several people alleged he did, that there was no need for any moderation in the reform of abuses; he knew how necessary it was to prepare all improvements, how dangerous too sudden shocks are; but he thought that the necessary moderation should be in the action and not in the thought. He did not desire to have the whole old edifice knocked down before the foundations of the new one had been molded, but he wanted an extensive plan to be drawn up before this task was started, to avoid acting blindly either in destroying, or conserving, or in reconstructing.

Finally, to M. de Gournay's very personal glory, there was his virtue, which was so well known that in spite of all the opposition which he had to endure, not the least shadow of suspicion ever tarnished the brightness of his reputation even for a moment. This virtue did not falter all through his life. Based on a deep feeling of justice and philanthropy, it made him a kindly and modest man, forbearing in society, irreproachable and even austere in his conduct and principles, but austere only for himself; even tempered at home, busy in his family circle to make all those around him happy, always ready to sacrifice, obligingly, all that he did not regard as duty. In public life he showed himself free from all self-interest, ambition, and almost entirely free from love of glory, and yet, none the less active for it, nor less indefatigable, nor less ingenious in the pursuit of the fulfillment of his designs, whose sole objective was the general welfare. He was a citizen completely occupied with the prosperity and glory of his country and the happiness of mankind. Humanity was one of the motives which tied him most to what was called his *system*. He most vigorously reproached his opponents for the principle of always favoring the rich and idle part of society at the expense of the poor and industrious part.

It is unfortunate in a way that men commendable for the most deserving virtues, and who are most truly useful to the world, are most unfavorably endowed in the distribution of fame. Posterity considers almost exclusively those actions which take place in public and which are dazzling, and it is perhaps more sensitive to their brilliance than to their usefulness. But, even if we assume its judgment to be always equitable in this respect, the motives and the spirit which produce these actions and which alone can lend them the mark of virtue, are ignored. The finer details are lost in the narrative of history, like the glow of a complexion and the delicacy of features vanish under the painter's colors. Only lifeless brush strokes remain, and actions whose character is misjudged. Sometimes spite and sometimes flattery interpret them at their pleasure, and only too often succeed in making posterity's verdict fluctuate between the purest virtue, and clever vice masked as virtue.

This misjudgment never occurs while these people are still living, and there is an interval of time when spite in vain attempts to tarnish a well-known virtue and when flattery that would offer undeserved honors can be repelled. This moment passes with the life of the person. Therefore the only means of ensuring, for that small number of men whose virtue is generally recognized, the continuation of the general esteem which they deserve, and of catching the fragrance of virtue which surrounds them, is to call forth the testimony of the present generation, and to call recent events to bear witness. In rendering this deserved public homage to the virtue of M. de Gournay, we feel sure that no voice will be lifted against us.

Observations on a Paper by Saint-Péravey on the Subject of Indirect Taxation

Turgot returns to a familiar theme, the view that taxation must ultimately fall on land. He makes points of value to later economists who abandoned this doctrine, derived from the Phsyiocrats. Continual changes in economic data make it impossible to arrive at constant numerical relationships among prices, a fact that Turgot uses to throw into question some calculations in the paper on which he is commenting. He goes on criticize attempts to regulate interest. A return on capital is essential: without it, lenders would not lend and economic progress could not occur. It is also incorrect to think that the accumulation of capital withdraws money from circulation; but even if it did, this would not be a bad thing.

CHAPTER 6

Observations on a Paper by Saint-Péravey on the Subject of Indirect Taxation

The author assumes firstly, that the proprietors spend half their income on purchases from the productive class and the other half on purchases from the industrial class; secondly, that the productive class spends only a quarter[1] of its income on manufactured goods.

These two propositions are to be regarded as hypotheses only, which contain some degree of realism, and which may be used in mathematical formulae, but from which completely precise conclusions can never be drawn. The proportion between the various expenditures of each class is too variable to permit of accurate calculation. Assumptions of this type may only be usefully employed to give a clearer idea of the circulation.

The author argues and calculates later on the basis of an assumption which he has already put forward as a principle, that the proportion between the annual advances in agricultural production, and its total product is as two is to five. The dubiousness of this assumption does not weaken what has previously been said to demonstrate that the indirect tax falls entirely on the proprietors, because this truth results purely from the impossibility of encroaching upon the advances and the wages of the agricultural and the industrial classes without ruining them. These classes can only pay

---

Written 1767 in discussion of Mémoire sur les effets de l'impôt indirect, by Saint Péravy.

[1] Turgot's "quarter" should be "a third."

at the expense of the proprietors, who are the only ones to receive the disposable portion of the crop, that gratuitous portion which the soil yields over and above the cost of working it. But since, in the subsequent estimation of the excess burden of the indirect tax by the effect which the decrease of the advances must cause, the starting point of the calculations is this assumed proportion between the annual advances and the total product of two to five, it is necessary to examine this assumption.

I would grant that this proportion has been established on the basis of exact calculations of the advances and the products of some farms *en grande culture* in a fertile region, which the author, or those who furnished him with the facts, visited in order to reassure themselves. But this procedure does not confer the right to draw from this particular calculation any general results; it takes little thought to realize that there can be no constant proportion between the advances and the product. Advances, which are only a form of expenditure, are not in themselves productive; they do not even have the productivity which the current rate of interest gives to loan money. If 20,000 livres put to interest return 1,000 francs, it can be concluded that 40,000 will return 2,000 francs. But from the fact that 2,000 livres of annual advances applied to a farm will return 5,000 francs worth of product, it cannot be concluded that another 2,000 livres employed on another plot of ground would also yield 5,000 francs, nor that 4,000 employed on the same land would yield 10,000. The expenses of agriculture consist in giving the soil such preparation as is most likely to make it fruitful. Now, the outcome of these preparations, which determines the product, is by no means proportioned to the expenditure: the knowledge of the cultivator renders the same amount of expenditure more or less productive, depending on the extent to which his method of applying it is appropriate to the nature of the soil and all the seasonal factors. If as much ploughing is bestowed on a light soil as on a heavy soil, the cost may be higher while the return may be lower. If Tull's system contains some truth,[2] production may be increased while economizing on the seed. Then the annual advances will diminish and the total product will increase. Production implies advances, but equal advances on soils of different fertility would yield very different total products, and this in itself would be sufficient to prove that product is not entirely proportional to advances. Even if applied to the same field it is not proportional, and it can never be assumed that double the advances will yield double the product. The earth certainly has a limited fertility, and assuming it to have been ploughed, manured, marled, ditched, watered, weeded, as far as it can be, it is obvious that all further expenditure would be useless, and that such increases could even become detrimental. In this case, the advances would be increased without increasing the product. There is therefore a *maximum* point of production which it is impossible to pass, and when this point has been reached, advances will not only cease producing 250 for 100, but will produce absolutely nothing.

While it may be granted to the author that, in the case of ordinary good cultivation, the annual advances return 250 for 100, it is more than likely that as the advances are increased gradually past this point up to the point where they return nothing, each increase would be less and less productive. The fruitfulness of the soil may be compared in this case with a spring which is compressed by loading it successively with equal weights. If the weights are light and the spring is rather stiff, the effect of the first few weights may be almost negligible. When the total weight is heavy enough to overcome the initial resistance, the spring will yield visibly and will compress; but when it has been compressed to a certain point, it will offer more resistance to the force which compresses it, and such weights as would have compressed it an inch, can compress it no more than a fraction of an inch. The effect will thus diminish increasingly. This comparison is not entirely accurate, but it is sufficient to show how,

---

[2] Presumably a reference to Tull's *The New Horse-Houghing Husbandry, or, an Essay on the Principles of Tillage and Vegetation*, Dublin, 1731.

as the soil approaches the point where it yields as much as it can produce, a very large outlay can only increase the product slightly.

If, instead of increasing the advances by equal degrees beyond the point at which they yield most, the farmer diminishes them, the same change in the proportion would be found. It is not just conceivable, but it is certain that very small advances yield a smaller profit than very large ones, and that the ratio between the profits is higher than that between the advances. If 2,000 livres yield 5,000, 1,000 may not even yield 1,500, and 500 will not yield 600.

Seed thrown on a soil which is naturally fertile, but has not been prepared at all, would be virtually a waste of expenditure. If the soil were tilled once, the produce would be greater; tilling it a second or a third time would not just double or triple, but quadruple or decuple the produce, which will thus increase in a much larger proportion than the expenditure, and this would be the case up to a certain point, at which the produce would be as large as possible relative to the advances.

Past this point, if the advances are still further increased, the product will still increase, but less so, and continuously less and less until an addition to the advances would add nothing further to the produce, because the fertility of the soil is exhausted and art cannot increase the product any further.

I will mention that it would be mistaken to imagine that the point at which the advances yield the most is the most advantageous one which the cultivator can attain, for, although further increments in advances do not yield as much as the preceding increments, if they yield enough to increase the *net product* of the soil, there is an advantage in making them, and it will still be a good investment. If it is assumed, for example, as it is by the author, that the annual advances in good cultivation yield 250 per cent, an increment which yields 225 per cent would still be exceedingly profitable. For, since the interest on fixed capital and the return of the first dose of annual advances has already been deducted from the 250 per cent, and since this deduction still leaves a very adequate *net product*, if from the product of the next dose of annual advances 100 is deducted for its replacement and 10 for the interest on the first dose, which becomes an addition to the fixed capital, of which the advances of the first year are always a part; if then, 110 per cent is deducted from the 225 produced by the new advances, a net product of 115 per cent would be obtained from the new advances, which would be added to the 250 per cent from the first advances, etc.

I have dwelt extensively on this point, because it is important not to surrender too easily to the hope of estimating with complete accuracy the decrease in total product caused by a decrease in annual advances when indirect taxation has broken into the latter. Here the author's calculations seem to be based on a fallacy, since he assumes that production is always in a proportion of five to two to the annual advances, and calculates the diminutions in the total product at this rate. It is evident from the above that the harmful effect of the diminution of the annual advances would be less when cultivation is already beyond the point at which the advances yield as much as possible. If, on the contrary, this diminution begins only when the annual advances yield the greatest product, the decrease must be greater; but below this, there must also be a point where the decrease in annual advances diminishes production in a still smaller proportion. In short, the decrease of advances must diminish the production in the same proportion as the gradual increase of advances had augmented it.

The fundamental principle of the paper, that the renewal of the cultivator's capital may not be impaired, and that he cannot decrease his advances without decreasing production, is beyond doubt; but the exact extent of this decrease does not appear to be susceptible to precise determination.

* * *

The rentier is a merchant of money. Interest is the price of capital. Since the capital yields nothing by itself, but only by virtue of the agreement of the contracting parties, a tax on interest is exactly like any other tax on commodities. If part of the price of any commodity whatsoever is taken away, obviously this price is prevented from falling to the buyer's advantage by the whole of what is demanded from the seller. It is thus the buyer, who in the final analysis in this case is the proprietor of the property, who pays the tax on interest. This reasoning appears at first glance to be contradicted at times when applied to the facts, through the influence which the authority of the law regulating interest exerts in this matter. But it must be noted that the effect of the law on interest is always to maintain it at a higher rate than would be the case in the absence of a law. This law, just like all other legal fixation of commodities, always raises the price, or interrupts commerce.

When the sovereign taxes interest, the whole impact of the law falls on the existing arrangements, and as the lender cannot demand reimbursement, he has no means at all of recouping his loss. As for new contracts, made after the passing of the Edict, if the lenders submit to the law of the tax, it is proof that the legal rate of interest was above the natural rate, for if the legal rate was too low, the lenders would evade the law by private arrangements, or else they would cease to lend.

If natural order, complete liberty and the competition which results from these existed in the trade in money, the reasoning put forward by the author would be as true in practice as it is in theory.

* * *

It is certain that houses do not produce any revenue which may be regarded as additional revenue for the State. Their rent is obviously a pure expense which, like all others, is paid from the produce of the soil. I believe, however, that houses should be taxed, not because of the value of the building, but because of the value of the land which they occupy and which is only used for building because in this way it yields more than in any other way.

* * *

It is physically impossible for the taxes on consumption to be graded on the basis of the disproportion between luxuries and necessities. The tax on consumption goods has a *maximum* which cannot be exceeded, and this maximum is determined by the relative ease of smuggling. The risks of smuggling are estimated like those of the sea, and it is a known fact that contraband can be insured. If the tax on a commodity is 15 per cent, and if the risk of smuggling is only 10 per cent, obviously nearly all supplies would be smuggled in, and the tax would produce so much the less for the government. Now the more precious the commodities are, the more value they have for their bulk, the easier it is to smuggle them. It is easier to hide 20,000 livres worth of lace work than twenty francs worth of corn; the duty must thus be diminished in proportion to the value of the commodities, and the expenditures of the rich are exactly those that are charged least. All excessive duties can be levied only by way of state monopoly; but the evils of this type of tax are innumerable, and the effects it produces, by disturbing trade and reversing all moral values in the minds of the people, are even more fatal than those it produces in its quality as an indirect tax, and which it has in common with all other taxes on consumption.[3]

* * *

It is certainly an evil that a very great part of private expenditure is made in the capital, but this disadvantage is not peculiar to the profit from the General-Farm. That of the Receiver-General, which arises out of direct taxation, that of the creditors, and pensioners of the government, the revenue of all great proprietors, are all spent in the capital. It is a great evil, but it derives from the general system of government rather than from the nature of the indirect tax.

It seems that the author here envisages as an evil that part of the profits of the Farmers-General are set apart to create capitals, and that the money which they have gathered is not immediately returned to the circulation. We may leave the Farmers-General, for the advantage, and what the author believes to be the disadvantage, of saving from profits, holds as much for any other profits as for theirs. Consider the question in general.

---

[3] A paragraph has been omitted at this point by du Pont. This paragraph reads in translation: "I am not sure if it is absolutely impossible for a government to ascertain the product of a farm exactly. In a vast, and consequently complicated administration, where so many interested parties are entitled to have an account of the profits in which they share rendered to them, it is impossible that the farmers do not have their account books very much in order so that the government can always have them produced."

The author, and the majority of economic writers, seem to assume that the whole of the revenue must necessarily be returned directly to the circulation, without any part of it being set aside for the formation of a monetary capital, and that, if it were otherwise, the reproduction would suffer by it. This assumption is far from true; it is sufficient, in order to see its falsity, to reflect on the importance of capitals in all the profitable enterprises of agriculture, of industry and of trade, and on the utter necessity of advances for all these enterprises.

What are these advances, and where lies their origin, if not in the savings from the revenue? The only true wealth is the produce of the soil; the advances can thus grow only by the setting aside of part of what the soil produces, and part of what is not absolutely necessary for the reproduction. It makes no difference whether this part is put aside by the entrepreneurs of the industrious classes, or by the proprietors. In the first case, the entrepreneurs retain part of their profits and accumulate capitals which they use to expand their enterprises; but for this it is necessary that their profits are a little higher than what is strictly required for the reproduction on the following year. This may occur in two ways; firstly, because besides the current return and replacement of their advances, besides the salary for their work and subsistence, they have a right to an interest on their advances equal to what the same capital would yield them in any other way without effort on their part, be it in the acquisition of landed property, or in lending at interest. Thus they need only a certain amount of capital to start with for the interest on this capital, accumulating with it, to swell it at quite a rapid rate, because their right to a subsistence in return for their work is independent of their right to profits from their capital. Secondly, because the absence of competition for some enterprises puts the entrepreneurs in the position of making profits which are higher than what is required for the continuation of those enterprises, and from which they can save a great deal each year. These profits are a portion of the net product which the entrepreneur appropriates over and above the returns which are necessarily due to him, and at the expense of the proprietors. The immediate result of this thrift is the accumulation of movable capitals, and these capitals are only accumulated for the purpose of obtaining a revenue or annual profit, which can only be done by employing this capital. The effect of this accumulation is to lower the interest of loan money; to increase the exchange value of landed property; to diminish the necessary returns of the entrepreneurs in all industry and the costs of all enterprises; to make profitable, and consequently possible, enterprises which were not so previously; to increase proportionately the total number of enterprises and the total output.

Of all the employments of money, that which requires the least effort on the part of the capitalists, is lending at interest; the second in order of ease is the acquisition of land; but the latter is first in order of security. Only the expectation of making a greater profit could urge the owner of a money capital to employ it in uncertain and laborious enterprises. The rate of interest of money is thus the first established standard, the parameter (if I may call it this) on the basis of which the exchange value of landed property and the profits of the advances in agricultural, industrial and commercial enterprises are established. It is useless to declaim against the public stocks and their useless owners; as long as this use of money, that is to say, as long as this need for borrowing money, will exist, it will be preferred, because it is in the nature of things that it should be. Only what is left over can be used to call into existence, by way of advances, enterprises which take trouble. It is like the bed of the Nile, which must necessarily be filled before the flood is diffused over the fields to fertilize them. There should be no complaining over the water flowing into this bed, for the law of gravity inevitably directs it there. There is even less call for complaint about the fact that the water accumulates, for without this accumulation the fields would not be irrigated. The true evil is that the bed is hollowed out so much that it absorbs the greater part of the water; the evil is that the government, through its numerous borrowings, continually presents money with a use which the owner finds advantageous and which is sterile as far as the State is concerned; the evil is that by this ruinous transaction it competes with the luxuries of private citizens to maintain the rate of interest at a level which is high in itself, and higher than that in foreign nations. But once this evil exists, it is no less beneficial that the owners of, or those who share in, the revenue of the State do not spend it in its entirety, and put part of it aside each year to convert it into capitals, since a low interest of money, and all its advantageous consequences result from the quantity of capitals offered by the lenders relative to the quantity demanded by the borrowers. If the whole of the net product had been spent each year without any accumulation, the stock of advances, of, I won't say *la grande culture*, but of the poorest cultivation, could never have been formed, and never could these advances grow. The whole thing is quite obvious.

But it is said, since the money does not return to the circulation, it diminishes the exchange values, and consequently the returns of the farmers who, when they sell more cheaply than they expected, pay the price of their lease by encroaching upon the renewal of their advances.

Four things may be said in reply to this.

Firstly, this argument would prove too much, for it would prove that the whole of the money collected by the proprietors as revenue must always return immediately into the hands of the cultivators, and that is completely untrue. The followers of the *Philosophie rurale*[4] themselves agree to this when they maintain so strongly the utter unimportance of what is called the balance of trade settled in money. For certainly, if, by the settlement of the balance of trade, part of of the specie circulating as money in the State flows abroad, the whole of this specie will not come back to match the commodities produced by the cultivator in the circulation; and, according to the thinking of the author, goods will fall in price. Yet, the author is persuaded that nothing is of less importance than the manner in which this monetary settlement takes place.

Secondly, each year the mass of gold and silver circulating in the world increases by the continual working of the mines. The silver which the mines yield is spread first through the State where

---

[4] I.e., Quesnay and the other leading Physiocrats.

Indirect Taxation 141

the mines are situated. It must either remain there in circulation, or be accumulated by the entrepreneurs, or leave the country to be exchanged for commodities. In fact the silver which is accumulated does not take long to return to circulation, and it is in the nature of things that the silver from the mines should leave the countries of origin in order to be exchanged for foreign commodities; for if it remained in the home countries, commodities would increase in price so stupendously, and silver would depreciate so strongly, that, on the one hand, part of the mines would cease to yield a profit to their entrepreneurs sufficient to meet the costs of exploitation, and the national production, being worthless, would cease; while, on the other hand, the difference in price between foreign goods and domestic goods would soon be so large that, in spite of all prohibitions by the government, the interest of all citizen-consumers would combine with that of the foreign sellers to break all the barriers with which the prejudiced administration would oppose the exportation of silver.

The silver which the States with mines draw from the bowels of the earth enters, through the monetary settlement of the balance of trade, into the States which sell their commodities to the owners of the mines. This silver, carried into the trading nation through commerce, has similar effects as that drawn directly from the mines in the State in which they are situated. Silver, having become plentiful, raises the price of commodities; soon they can no longer be given at the same price to the nation which settles (its balance) in silver, and nations in which silver is scarcer obtain the preference. The nation which had acquired the surplus of silver is itself compelled to draw part of its consumption goods from nations by virtue of their greater or smaller proximity to the country with mines, and by virtue of the stage in history during which they began to enter the system, or, if you wish, the great society of civilized and commercial nations; finally, by virtue of the extent to which their constitution and their domestic laws are favorable to the growth of production and to commercial activity. From Peru and Brazil, gold and silver pass into Spain and Portugal, from there to France, England and Holland, then to Germany and the Scandinavian countries. It is well known that gold and silver are still sufficiently scarce in Sweden for copper to be used as money there, as in the early days of the Roman Republic, when the word *aes* signified what the word silver money signifies today in the common usage of commerce and civil life.

As the mines do not cease to furnish a new increase of the stock of precious metals each year, the result is that, from the countries where these mines are exploited down to the last regions which share at the final stage and to the least extent in their annual distribution through trade, there is not one which, in the natural order of things, and disregarding the disturbances which may be occasioned by excessive expenditures abroad, war, and defaulting governments, does not experience every year an increase in the stock of its circulating medium.

In the type of scale which ranks these States by their relative wealth of silver, those which are the most fortunate and which approach most nearly a state of complete prosperity, are those where the abundance and the value of money are at the intermediate level to which perfect equilibrium would bring them if it were possible, over time, for the silver to be distributed over the earth in proportion to the total annual output of each district. The natural circulation of money in trade approaches this universal level; but it can never be reached as long as the mines are not exhausted, that is to say, as long as they yield in sufficient abundance to cover the expenses of production with a sufficient profit to encourage the entrepreneurs to make advances; for this determines the limit of their exploitation, and not their physical exhaustion.

This state of affairs would reduce the trade between all nations to the exchange of commodities, and there would be no real balance. The nations which are at present in this intermediate stage which have neither an abundance nor a deficiency of gold or silver, are almost in the same position, and they have no settlement in bullion of the balance of trade because they deliver as much of it to nations which have less bullion as they receive from those nations that have more.

Let us return to the question of the need to restore to the cultivator all the money he has paid out: I say that, if the quantity of money withdrawn from immediate circulation by saving is less, or even, if it is no more than the quantity of money introduced each year into the circulation by way of trade, the commodities will maintain their exchange value, the cultivators will use as much money for the reproduction as in the preceding year, and there will be no decline in wealth; the saving, therefore, will not be prejudicial to either the reproduction, or the revenue. Not only will it not be prejudicial, but in fact it will increase them, since in the final analysis its effect is always to increase the stock of capitals and the total advances, and to lower the rate of interest. If it really withdrew from the circulation the money put aside, it would prevent the increase in the price of commodities which results from the increase in money, it would maintain the nation's ability to sell her superfluous commodities to foreign owners of silver, it would reduce the need to buy from less wealthy foreigners things necessary for her consumption, which her own artisans could no longer furnish at such a low price. Even when the effect of saving is not to withdraw money from the circulation, it would make up, through the low price of labor caused by the increase in the exchange value of commodities. It removes all disadvantages from the superfluity of money and leaves only the advantages. Is there any one who does not know that in Holland wages are so high that they could destroy commerce if the low interest of money, and the resultant activity, did not compensate for this factor?

Thirdly, I assume for the moment that the immediate effect of saving is to withdraw money from circulation, and to lower the exchange value, to the detriment of the cultivator. I say that if the consequence of this saving is an increase in the advances, it will also cause a greater production, or, if you like, a decrease in the costs; so that the decrease in the exchange value resulting from the small amount of money withdrawn from circulation, is more than compensated by the number of articles sold, or by a smaller fundamental value[5] of each article sold; thus there is a real advantage in putting money aside. Now, it is most likely that the increase in the advances does more good than the harm done by the small decrease in the exchange value caused by saving. For this decrease will always be extremely small if unrestricted exportation continues to let our output share in the prices of the general market. Perhaps the increase in output caused by the introduction of new advances would bring about even more efficiently the decrease in exchange values. But the remedy for this disadvantage lies in this same communication with the general market; in the variety of output which the soil can produce, from amongst which the cultivator can choose those whose sale yields the highest profits, and prefer thistles to wheat if he finds this to his advantage; finally, in the increase of the population which follows naturally from the abundance of output.

Fourthly, it is assumed without any grounds that savings decrease the exchange values by withdrawing the sums put aside from the circulation. They almost all return to it immediately, and to be convinced of this, it is but necessary to reflect on the use which is made of the money saved; either it is used in the purchase of land, or it is lent at interest, or used as advances in agricultural, industrial, or commercial enterprises. It is obvious that this third type of use returns the capitals immediately to the circulation and exchanges them for equipment, beasts of burden, raw materials, wages of labor, and the purchase of goods which are the object of commerce. The

---

[5] Two types of value may be distinguished: fundamental value and exchange value. The fundamental value is what the thing costs to him who sells it, that is, the raw material cost, the interest of the advances, the wages of labor and industry. The exchange value is the price which the buyer agrees upon with the seller. The fundamental value is fairly stable and changes less frequently than the exchange value. The latter is ruled by supply and demand, it varies with needs, and often a single event suffices to produce very considerable and very sudden fluctuations. It is not in any essential proportion to the fundamental value, but it has a tendency to approach it continually, and can never move far away from it permanently. It is obvious that it cannot remain below it for a long time; for, as soon as a commodity can be sold only at a loss, its production is discontinued until the resulting scarcity has again raised it to a price above its fundamental value. The price can similarly not be much above the fundamental value for any length of time, for this high price, implying high profits, would call forth the commodity and generate lively competition among the sellers. Now the natural effect of this competition would be to lower the price until it again approaches the fundamental value. (Note by Turgot.)

same is true of the other two uses. The money of the acquirer of landed property goes to the seller; the latter usually sells in order to obtain a more useful acquisition, or to pay debts, and it is always to this last object that the price of the sale goes; for if the first seller buys other land, it will be the seller of this land, or if you wish, a third, who sells only to redeem his debts; and if the debts are pressing, the money is spent again immediately and put back into circulation. If the debts bear interest, the reimbursed creditor has nothing more urgent to do than to lend his money once again. Let us therefore see what happens to the money lent, what the borrower does with it.

Dissipating young gentlemen, and governments, borrow in order to spend, and what they spend returns immediately to the circulation. When they are wiser, they borrow to put their affairs in order, to pay outstanding debts and redeem debts which carry an excessive rate of interest. Some people borrow in order to make up the purchase price of land which they wish to acquire; and to this type of borrowing applies what I said above about the acquisition of land, to wit, that the money, at second or third hand, returns to the circulation, redistributing itself through trade. As for the loans of entrepreneurs, manufacturers, and merchants, it is well known that they are immediately poured into their enterprises and spent on advances of all sorts.

It follows of course from this analysis that money which is saved, accumulated, put aside for the formation of capitals, is not lost to the circulation, and that the sum of monetary values which are counterbalanced in the transactions of commerce with the other values to settle their price, neither decreases nor increases by it.

In a nation where agriculture, industry and commerce flourish, and where the interest of money is low, the stock of capitals is immense, and yet it is well known that the quantity of money placed in hoards is quite negligible; almost all the existing capitals are represented by paper which is equivalent to money because the assets which are responsible for their soundness are equivalent to money. But there really is no money in the tills other than what is required to meet the daily payments necessary for the flow of trade. Sometimes transfers involving several millions take place without a single *sou* in silver changing hands. The quantity of this money, which so to speak circulates in large stocks, is thus very limited, always proportioned to the intensity of commercial activity, and to the fluctuations which it gives to money, which are always about the same.

I believe to have shown two things: the one, that if saving withdrew money from circulation, it would not for this alone be a bad thing; the other, that in fact saving does not really withdraw from circulation the money it puts aside.

The outcome of this long note is that the reserves and the stock of money accumulated by the farmers of the indirect tax, are not a bad thing in themselves, and should not be counted among the drawbacks of this type of taxation. The excessive profits are undoubtedly an evil, because they are grasped from the people and because, as they never enter the coffers of the prince, they force the latter to raise the tax. It is an evil that these profits are spent in Paris, just as it is an evil that the large landowners spend their revenue in Paris. But it is a good thing that the Farmers-General spend only gradually part of them.

Observations on the Paper by Graslin in Favour of the Indirect Tax, to which the Royal Agricultural Society of Limoges has Given an Honorable Mention

Turgot defends the view, derived from the Physiocrats, that taxes must ultimately fall on the proprietors of agricultural land. In doing so, he anticipates important arguments by later arguments in defense of economic freedom. Against those who fear that free trade will lead to foreign countries' gaining control of all raw materials and ruining French industry, Turgot is dismissive. He compares this fear to the fear that freedom to export grain will lead to starvation of the exporting country. He also defends free competition as essential to just wages. Competition among workers prevents workers from taking advantage of a small labor supply; likewise, competition among employers impedes them from taking advantage of workers.

CHAPTER 7

Observations on the Paper by Graslin in Favour of the Indirect Tax, to which the Royal Agricultural Society of Limoges has Given an Honorable Mention

The author inappropriately charges the writers whom he attacks with considering the net product of the soil only, that is, the revenue as wealth. All that the earth produces is wealth. But these writers maintain correctly that the total of the *renascent wealth* of a State is confined to the total *annual output* of the soil. This output is divided into two parts, one of which is destined for the subsistence and the satisfaction of the wants of the cultivator, for the interest on and the replacement of the advances, in short, for all that is necessary, directly and indirectly, for the reproduction of the following year. But once this part is deducted, the surplus, which the cultivator gives to the proprietor of the soil forms the latter's revenue, which not being in any way necessary for the reproduction of the following year, is completely free, disposable, and susceptible to division among the titular owner, the recipient of the tithe, the *seigneur censier*,[1] the State, etc.

Written 1767. Graslin's paper entitled, Essai analytique sur la richesse et sur l'impôt, was written for a competition organized by the Royal Agricultural Society of Limoges on the subject of indirect taxation.

[1] I.e., the feudal lord to whom the commoners owed their *cens* or dues.

* * *

The author does not understand either the real distinction between the two working classes, one of which, applied directly to the work of the soil, produces, or, to remove all ambiguity, gathers directly all the wealth which the earth yields; the other, receiving nothing directly except by way of those who have gathered the fruits of the earth, earns its subsistence and receives it in exchange for its work, but does not add any new wealth to the total wealth produced by the earth alone.

* * *

It is not, as the author believes, all real wealth which can pay the tax; it must also be disposable, i.e., it must not be essential for the reproduction of the following year, be it immediately or a little later. Any wealth can be seized by a superior power, but no wealth which is essential for the work of reproduction can be diverted from it without harming this production, the national wealth, and by consequence, the source of power of the government. This comprises the whole of the theory of taxation.

The three primary consequences of this doctrine of the economic writers are summarized in unlimited freedom of trade. The usefulness of this liberty as declaimed by the principles which the author attacks, is based, moreover, on so many other incontestable propositions that its certainty does not depend by any means on the system adopted as regards the nature of wealth and of the revenue. It should not be believed either that in permitting the selling and buying of what and to whom one pleases, the whole of industry is abandoned for this, as the author and the other partisans of protection imagine or argue: the argument of those who, to create fear of freedom, assume that the foreigners will buy all our raw materials, will get hold of all of our industry, and will carry on the whole of our commerce, this argument is of the same type as that of the people who fear that the freedom of selling our grain abroad will cause us to die of hunger, although this freedom, of necessity, will increase our production and our stores, which will never seek an outlet in foreign parts when they find a profitable one at home.

* * *

I define as goods (*bona*) all objects of enjoyment, of property, of desire and of need. I define as value (*merae*) all things susceptible to exchange and evaluation. I define as wealth (*opes*) all goods which may be traded, all objects of enjoyment which have a value. The revenue is the wealth which the earth yields over and above the expenses and the returns to those who cultivate it. Water is a good which has no value at all. Work has a value, and is not in itself a good. Corn and cloth are wealth. What the farmer renders to the proprietor of an estate is a revenue.

It follows from these definitions that the output of the land, when it is only equal to the expenses, is wealth, but *non disposable* wealth; wealth and not revenue. In the example cited of a field planted with flax, which costs the cultivator *one hundred francs* and returns him only *one hundred francs*, this flax is *wealth* and has undoubtedly, like all other forms of wealth, its *usefulness*; but it is obvious that it does not yield any revenue either to the proprietor or to the State. The cultivator would not give a *sou* to the proprietor of such a field for permission to cultivate it; for what he gives could only be taken from his bodily needs. By the same argument, the State can draw nothing from this field, nor ask anything from the cultivator, without depriving him of his subsistence and consequently making it impossible for him to work. If all the fields of a kingdom were cultivated in this manner, it is obvious that the State could not levy any taxes, not because there would be no *wealth*, but because there would be no *revenue*, no disposable wealth; because, the whole annual output being set aside for the bodily needs of those who produce it, anything that might be taken from it would destroy the cultivation and the reproduction of the following year.

* * *

It is quite true, considering things vaguely, that as the subsistence of the cultivator makes up part of the expenses, the less the cultivator consumes for himself, the more remains for the net product. It is certain that if a farmer wore clothes of velvet, and his wife wore lace, this expense would have to be recovered from the product of the earth by diminishing the portion of the proprietor. But it does by no means follow that the misery of the cultivator increases the net product. On the contrary, it has been shown that the wealth of agricultural entrepreneurs is no less necessary than work itself to obtain a plentiful output from the soil. Since the fertility of the soil is limited, there is undoubtedly a point at which the augmentation of the advances would not increase the output in proportion to the increase of expenses; but at present this limit is far from being attained, and experience proves that in those places where the advances are largest, that is, where the cultivators are most wealthy, there is not only the greatest output, but also the greatest *net product*.

Assuming the output to remain the same, the smaller the share of the cultivator, the larger that of the proprietor or the other partakers of the net product. But, if the cultivator would not receive a fair amount in proportion to his advances, if he were not sufficiently wealthy to have a right to a large profit from large advances, the output would no longer be the same at all, and it would become even more scanty as the cultivator grows even poorer, up to the point when, at a certain level of poverty, there would no longer be any net product. Thus it is very far from true that the principles attacked by the author contradict the resolution which humanity dictated to Henry IV.

Moreover, the author does not appear to have distinguished here between the agricultural entrepreneur and the rural wage laborer, the ploughman, the day laborer, who works the soil with his arms. Yet these are two very different types of men who cooperate in quite different ways in the great work of the annual reproduction of wealth. The agricultural entrepreneur contributes to the reproduction through his advances; the man of toil contributes through his labor, for which the agricultural entrepreneur pays him his wages. It must, moreover, be admitted that the more the entrepreneur pays in wages to his carters, the more dearly he pays for the time of the reapers and other day laborers whom he employs, the more he lays out in costs, and that this outlay is always a deduction from the net product. What can be concluded from this? Is this not true in all systems? Is there any type of work in which profits are not diminished by the dearness of the labor? And is there any inhumanity in admitting a truth which only has to be expressed in words to become obvious? Moreover, there exists a natural proportion between the wealth produced, the revenue, and the wages, a proportion which establishes itself, and which causes that neither the entrepreneurs nor the proprietors have an interest in lowering the wages below this proportion. Apart from the fact that, in any kind of work, an ill paid man, who does not earn a plentiful livelihood by his work, works less well, the exchange value of the rural output is less. Now, if, when the cultivator pays his laborers less, he sells his grain for less, it is obvious that he is none the wealthier from this. The exchange value of the output of the soil is, normally, the measure of the wealth gathered each year by the cultivator, who shares it with the proprietor. A high exchange value of the produce of the soil and a large revenue enable the cultivator and the proprietor to pay high wages to men who live by their manual labor. High wages, on the one hand enable wage earners to consume more, and to increase their well-being: on the other hand, this well-being and these high wages offered, encourage population; the fruitfulness of the earth attracts foreigners, multiplies the people; and the increase in people in turn lowers wages through competition, while the number maintains the consumption and its exchange value. The exchange value of the produce, the revenue, the wage rate, the population, are things related to each other by a mutual dependence, which spontaneously reach their equilibrium according to a natural proportion; and this proportion is always maintained when commerce and competition are completely free.

The single practical conclusion that can be drawn from this, is that wage laborers must be *completely free* to work for whom they desire, in order that the employers, by contending for them when they need them, may place a just price on their labor; and that, on the other hand, the employers must be *completely free* to use such men as they deem proper, in order that the local workers may not, by taking advantage of their small number, force them to increase wages above the natural proportion which depends on the stock of wealth, the value of subsistence goods, the amount of work available and the number of workers, but which can never be settled by anything other than competition and freedom.

* * *

Although the expenses of agriculture are spent in the State, it does not follow that, as the author believes, the State will be just as wealthy when the costs increase at the expense of the *net product*. The State has not, and cannot have, any strength except for the *net product*, because all that is necessary for the reproduction is assigned to the needs of the individuals who work to create it, in such a way that nothing of it can be seized for the public expenditure. Now, if there can be no public expenditure, if there is no communal power to be used in the common interest, there is no State properly speaking; there is only a country peopled by inhabitants who are born, who live, and who die near each other. The expenses of agriculture remain in the State in the sense that they are expended between the Rhine, the Alps, the Pyrenees and the sea; but they neither are, nor can be, the property of the State considered as the body politic formed by the union of communal forces directed toward a common interest. The comparison with the silver mine, which costs one hundred marcs to exploit and which produces one hundred marcs, is fallacious. This silver mine obviously returns nothing to its proprietor, nor to the entrepreneur who would exploit it at his pleasure, but it is true that it leaves a value of one hundred marcs which, not being consumed, increases the sum of value existing in the State until this money flows abroad by means of the exchanges. In this respect, the renascent wealth of the soil which is consumed and reproduced annually, is very different from the non-consumable values which circulate continually without ever being destroyed. Certainly, the sum of values spent each year on the expenses of agriculture is consumed and destroyed entirely as subsistence for the agents of the reproduction. As for the values which circulate without being destroyed, such as the products of mines, the expenditure of the costs of extraction does not completely annihilate them, and only causes them to change hands. It may therefore be said that the State has gained one hundred marcs, in the sense that one hundred marcs exist in the country. But what increase in the wealth of the State, considered as the body politic, results from this? None, except in so far as the existence of this new circulating value can increase the sum of the revenue or the net product of the earth, be it in augmenting the advances allocated to the reproduction or to commerce, if the money is set aside to form a capital which is directed to a profitable use; or be it in increasing the exchange value of the output, if this money, carried immediately to the circulation, is presented in the market in current purchases and causes their price to rise. This proposition is capable of proof, but in order to demonstrate it fully it would be necessary to develop the true use of money in trade and the result of its introduction into a State in greater or lesser quantity, by considering this State as if it were isolated, and then as if it were surrounded by other States with which it has different commercial and political relations. These questions, which have never been fully developed, are too lengthy to be treated here. I shall say only that the author is very much mistaken by regarding money purely as a *conventional token of wealth*. It is not at all by virtue of a *convention* that money is exchanged for all the other values: it is because it is itself an object of commerce, a form of wealth, because it has a value, and because any value exchanges in trade for an equal value.

* * *

The author puts forward an objection to the principles of his adversaries which may be reduced to these questions: "If industry and trade do not produce any wealth, how do purely industrial and commercial nations live? How do they enrich themselves? If taxation can only be levied on the net product of the estates, how can these nations pay taxes? Would industry be a source of wealth in a commercial State but not in an agricultural State?"

There are no nations which are industrial and commercial as opposed to agricultural; and neither are there any nations which are agricultural to the exclusion of all industry and trade. The word *nation* has not as yet been defined very exactly, because nations have often been confused with bodies politic or States.

A *nation* is a collection of people who speak the same language. Thus all Greeks belonged to the same nation, even though they were divided into a host of States. Nowadays the Italians form a nation, and the Germans another, even though Italy and Germany are divided into several independent sovereign States. In former times the French nation was not united into a single monarchy; several provinces obeyed various sovereigns, and all those who speak French are not even united into the Kingdom of France.

A *State* is a collection of men united under a single government. In this connection, this distinction is neither as strictly grammatical nor as irrelevant as it appears.

The term nation can only be applied to a large populace distributed over a vast stretch of country which yields the inhabitants enough to satisfy their needs. The soil, through the work of agriculture, gives them food and raw materials for their clothes, industry fashions these raw materials and makes them suitable for various uses. Commerce brings consumers and producers together, saving them the trouble of searching for each other, and assuring them that they will find the commodity in the place and at the time they need it. Commerce, as the author of this paper says so well, is responsible for transportation, warehouses, stocks, and for waiting. The mutual needs of buyers and sellers encourage them to come together and they must naturally gather in those places in every province which are the most conveniently located, most densely populated, at which the course which each follows for his own affairs cross in the greatest number. Those points naturally become the commercial meeting places, the dwellings of the middle-men are gathered there, they develop into boroughs and towns where the gathering of buyers and sellers increases all the more as they are more certain of finding the opportunity to buy and sell there. Therefore, everywhere different centers of commerce spring up, more or less closely together and corresponding to districts of different sizes by reason of the abundance of the country's production, the size of the population, and the relative ease of transporting the commodities. The markets established in the principal places of each province for the retail trade and for the objects of daily consumption constitute as it were the first order of these centers of commerce, each of them corresponding to a very limited district only. There are also commodities with a less general and less frequent use, which are not consumed in sufficient quantity to allow the profitable establishment of their cultivation of manufacture in every individual place. The value of these commodities is normally high enough for a small volume to be able to bear the costs of long transport. The commerce in these goods is carried on in larger lots which are afterward distributed to the retailers. The same principle which established markets for the trade in the most common commodities in the places with the most frequented gatherings, establishes markets of a higher order for the wholesale trade. These correspond to a more extensive district, and merchandise gathers there from further afield to be distributed to more remote places. These large markets (*emporia*) are exactly what are called *ports* of commerce, entrepôts. They were towns of the kind which, in the centuries of feudal barbarism, having joined together for the general defense, formed the Hanseatic league. These ports of commerce are always large towns, and in any case they would become so by the gathering of citizens drawn to them by the commercial activity. It is the advantageous situation of towns at the crossroads, if I may be so bold to speak like this, of large commercial routes, or at the mouth of navigable rivers, the good quality of the harbors, and sometimes the industry of the inhabitants and the flourishing state of certain manufactures which causes the great entrepôts of commerce to be established there. Thus Nantes is the outlet of the Loire, Rouen that of the Seine, Bordeaux of the provinces through which the Garonne and Dordogne flow, the towns of Holland and Zealand of the Rhine, the Maas and the Scheldt, Hamburg of the Elbe, Venice of the Po. Tyre, Carthage, Messina, Genoa, and Cadiz have had an advantageous maritime location as their only advantage. Lyon, Geneva, Strasbourg, Orleans, Limoges, are entrepôts of a slightly lower order. In all these towns, commerce and trade are the principal occupations of the inhabitants, and each town corresponds to a more or less extensive area of several districts or provinces of which it is the entrepot, from which it gathers the products, and to which it distributes their needs. The territory and commerce of these entrepot towns are two correlated things necessary to each other, and the distinction between the commerce in the produce of the soil and the entrepôts or retail trade does not exist with respect to nations or regions. The fact is that certain towns and maritime coasts which served as entrepôts to an extensive commerce, have been able, through chance of circumstances, to form little political States separated from the territory of which they are the entrepot; but this chance has changed nothing in the nature of things. Holland, whatever be its government, will still be the outlet of the Rhine, the Maas and the Scheldt, and of the canals of prolific Belgium; she will still be a favorable place of commerce and entrepot for all the harbors of England, France and the Baltic States, and consequently also for most of the other countries which wish to keep up relations and exchange with these different States, for which Holland is particularly necessary.

Therefore to have advantage of location is to have a type of exclusive privilege in comparison with less happily situated places. Because of this privilege, which is a natural one and therefore not unjust, wages may be received which exceed the needs of those who earn them, even with economy for those who pay them, above all if the former are wise enough to live thriftily, as the Dutch do.

Consequently, from the excess of their wages over their needs, which they are well able to curtail, people in this situation easily accumulate capitals which lower the interest of money among them. This assures them a further claim to preference, a further increase in wages. It is from the excess of these wages over their needs that the Dutch are able to discharge their public expenditure and continue to enrich themselves.

They have not produced these wages, nor the wealth which pays them; they have earned them legitimately by their work which their location has made both lucrative for them and useful to those who employ them; they have earned their wages like the commission agents of our cities earn theirs.

In wealthy, civilized countries, illustrious scholars, great doctors, artists, poets, and even great comedians, may also earn respectable salaries, live in ease, afford considerable expenditure, practice charity, accumulate capitals. No one thinks that they have produced any of this wealth which they acquire, which they can dispose of, and which is transmitted to them, by whom? by the proprietors of the estates; who obtain it—from whom? from the cultivators, from the advances and from the work of agriculture: advances, work of which the process can neither be constrained nor interrupted without ruin; and it is of this last maxim that the theory of taxation consists, as I have already said.

The author, and those who share his opinions, persist by saying: "Since there are people who earn high salaries, they are therefore able to pay the tax: you agree that the Dutch pay taxes which sustain their republic. In order that the tax may not be arbitrary and be proportioned approximately to resources, is it not proper to levy it on consumer goods?

To this I reply:

Firstly, that the Dutch add the need to pay tax to their other needs, which must be provided for by their wages which other nations pay them; so that, apart from the portion which burdens the Dutch territory directly, the other nations pay the tax of that republic.

Secondly, that it is impossible to make consumers who are not proprietors pay tax on their consumption, because as soon as it is imposed, they are compelled either to curtail their consumption, or to lower the price which they are able to offer for the products which they consume, and because the one or the other measure throws this tax back on the producers and the sellers of these products.

Thirdly, that the price of high wages, like that of moderate ones, is regulated by competition and therefore cannot be impaired without the wage-earner recouping himself for it, for otherwise he would withdraw his labor and take it elsewhere.

To this must be added, fourthly, that if it is desired to place the tax on the more expensive consumption of the wealthier wage-earners, it will yield almost nothing, because the number of these rich wage-earners is always very small. And that, if, in order to increase the receipts, common consumption goods are made to bear the burden, it becomes very disproportionate to wages, almost nothing on those of the wage earners who earn a lot, and crushing, at least temporarily and until they have been able to reimburse themselves, on those of the poor wage-earners who carry out the most laborious and most useful work, to whom belong naturally all the specifically agricultural wage earners, who make up the greatest part of the population. This inevitably raises the costs of cultivation, and this is the most onerous manner of shifting the tax back onto the proprietors; the most ruinous for the capitals set aside for the cultivation in countries where estates are leased; the manner which causes the speediest abandonment of mediocre land, which, therefore, most inevitably decreases the subsistence of the population and most rapidly leads a nation to misery.

Value and Money

Turgot distinguishes between money as a commodity ("actual money") and money of account. The former can be measured. In contemporary European countries, commodity money consists of gold and silver, so the monies of different countries can be directly compared with one another as units of weight. Monies of account must first be given a value in terms of actual money before they can be compared with the money of another country. Turgot then proceeds to a general account of value, starting with the values of an isolated individual. A person will value goods according to the satisfaction they provide him: his opinion of these satisfactions is subject to change over time. In considering the value of a good, the person will take account of its scarcity. Exchanging goods with another person is an important way a person can increase his satisfaction. In an exchange, each person prefers the good he will acquire to the good he gives up. Turgot gives a complicated account of how this difference in valuation is consistent with equality in exchange. He extends his analysis to markets with more than two participants.

CHAPTER 8

Value and Money

Money has this in common with measures in general, that it is a type of language, differing among different peoples in everything that is arbitrary and conventional, but of which the forms are brought closer and made identical, in some respects, by their relation to a common term or standard.

This common term which brings all languages together and which gives all tongues a basic similarity in spite of the diversity of the sounds employed, is none other than the very ideas which these words express, that is, the objects of nature represented by the senses to the human mind and the notions man has formed by distinguishing the different aspects of these objects and by combining them in a thousand ways.

It is this common foundation, essential to all languages independently of all conventions, which allows each language, each system of convention adopted as the symbols of ideas, to be used as a basis of comparison for all the other systems of convention, as one would compare to the actual system of ideas which can be interpreted by each language, that which was originally expressed in any other language, that which can, in short, be translated.

The common term of all measures of length, area or volume is only the actual size, of which the different measures adopted by

---

Written 1769. This paper is presumed to have been written for Morellet's venture of a Dictionnaire de commerce in five volumes, a project which never materialized, though a prospectus was issued in 1769.

different peoples are but arbitrary divisions which can in like manner be compared and reduced to one another.

One language is translated into another, one measure is reduced to another. These different expressions indicate two very different operations.

Languages designate ideas through sounds which are in themselves extraneous to those ideas. These sounds, from one language to another, are entirely different, and to explain them, it is necessary to substitute one sound for another; for the sound of the foreign language, the sound which corresponds to it in the language into which it is being translated. Measures on the contrary, measure size only by size itself. Only the choice of the size taken by agreement for the unit of measurement, and the divisions adopted to indicate the different measures are arbitrary and subject to variation. Thus there are no substitutions to make from one thing to another, only quantities to be compared, and proportions to be substituted for other proportions.

The common term to which the *currencies* of all nations are related is the actual *value* of all objects of commerce which they serve to measure. But since this value can only be expressed by the quantity of money to which it corresponds, it follows that *money* can only be *valued* in terms of other *money*, just as sounds from one language can only be interpreted by means of the sounds of another.

Since the moneys of all civilized nations are made of the same materials, and since they, like measures, differ among themselves only with regard to the divisions of these materials and the arbitrary determination of what is regarded as the unit, they are susceptible, in this respect, to being reduced the one to the other, just as the measures employed by the divers nations are.

We shall see below, that this reduction is made in a very convenient manner, by the expression of their weight and their standard.

But this manner of valuing currencies by the statement of their weight and standard is not adequate for an understanding of the language of commerce in relation to money. All the nations of Europe know two types of money. In addition to the real coins, such as the écu, the louis, the crown and the guinea, which are pieces of metal, marked with a known inscription and negotiable under this denomination, each nation has created a kind of fictitious money which is called money of account or numéraire, whose denominations and divisions, without corresponding to any actual coin, form a common scale, to which actual money is related, by being valued in terms of the number of parts of this scale to which they correspond. In France, this is the livre of account or numéraire, composed of 20 sous, which in turn is subdivided into twelve deniers. There is no coin which corresponds to a livre, but an écu is worth three livres, a louis is worth twenty-four livres, and thus this expression of the values of the two coins in terms of the unit of account, establishes the relation between the écu and a louis as one to eight.

Since these moneys of account, as we have seen, are only arbitrary denominations, they vary from nation to nation, and, in the same nation, they may vary from one period to the other.

The English thus have their pound sterling, divided into 20 sous or shillings, which again divide into twelve deniers or pennies. The Dutch calculate in florins, whose divisions do not correspond to those of our livre.

We have therefore to show, in commercial geography, not only the real currencies of each nation, and their evaluation by weight and standard, but also the money of account employed by each nation, and furthermore, their relation to the real money negotiable in the nation, and the relations between the moneys of account of different nations. The relation of the money of account to the actual money of each nation is determined by expressing the value of the actual money in terms of the unit of account of the same country; that of ducats in terms of florins, that of the guinea in shillings and pence sterling, of the louis and écu in livres tournois.[1]

As for the mutual relations of the units of account customary among the different nations, the idea which first presents itself

---

[1] The *livre tournois*, as Turgot explains, was the French money of account, and takes its name from the French town of Tours. It has to be differentiated from the *livre Paris*, which was used for circulation.

is that of deducing them from the relations between the money of account of each nation and the actual money, and from the knowledge of the weight and standard of the latter. Indeed, knowing the weight and standard of an English crown and the weight and standard of a French écu, the relation between a crown and a French écu is known, and knowing how much an écu is worth in terms of deniers tournois, the value of a crown in terms of deniers tournois may be deduced; and as the value of a crown in terms of pence sterling is also known, the equivalent of pence sterling in deniers tournois is known, and hence the relation between the pound sterling and the livre tournois.

This method of valuing the moneys of account of different nations by comparing them with the actual money of each nation, and by the knowledge of the weight and standard of the latter, would not give rise to any difficulty if all the money was made of a single metal, silver for example, or if the relative value of different metals used for this purpose, gold and silver for example, was the same among all commercial nations, that is if a certain weight of pure gold, a marc[2] for example, was worth exactly the same number of grains of pure silver in all nations. But this relative value of gold and silver varies according to the abundance or relative scarcity of these two metals in the different nations.

If in one nation there is thirteen times more silver than gold, and thus in consequence thirteen marcs of silver exchange for one marc of gold, fourteen marcs of silver will exchange for one marc of gold in another nation where there is fourteen times more silver than gold. It follows from this, that if, in order to determine the value of the money of account of two nations where gold and silver do not have the same relative value, to value, for example, the pound sterling in terms of the livre tournois, gold coin is used as the term of comparison, a different result would be obtained than if silver coin had been used. It is clear that the true measure lies between these two results, but in order to determine it with complete and rigorous precision, it would be necessary to bring into the solution of this

---

[2] The marc was a weight of silver or gold, about 8 oz. troy.

problem a multitude of extremely delicate considerations. Meanwhile, the silver trade among nations, all the negotiations pertaining to that trade, the use of paper credit for money, the operations of the exchanges and of the banks all assume that this problem has been solved.

The word *money*, in its first, original and proper sense, which corresponds exactly to the Latin *moneta*, denotes a piece of metal of a specified weight and standard, and guaranteed by the inscription placed on it by the public authority. Stating the name, the inscription, the weight and the standard of each coin of different nations, while converting this weight to marcs, is all that has to be done in order to give a clear idea of money considered from this first point of view.

But usage has given a wider and more abstract meaning to this word *money*. Metals are divided into pieces of a certain weight; the authority guarantees their standard by an inscription, only in order that they may be used in commerce in a satisfactory and safe manner, so that they may serve there both as a measure of value and as a store representing the value of produce; moreover, the idea of dividing and marking the metals in this way, or, in short, of coining money, has been conceived only because these metals were already serving as a measure and a common pledge of all value.

Since money has no other use, this name has come to be regarded as designating that very use, and as it is true to say that money is the measure and pledge of value, because everything which acts as measure and pledge of value can take the place of money, the name money in this wide sense has been given to everything used in this way. It is in this sense that cowries are the *currency* of the Maldivian islands, that livestock was the *currency* of the Germanic tribes and the ancient inhabitants of Latium, that gold, silver and copper are the *currency* of civilized people; that these metals were *currency* before the idea of showing their weight and standard by a legal stamp was conceived. It is in this sense that the name *paper currency* is given to letters of credit, which represent money. It is, finally, in this sense that the name of money fits the purely abstract denominations which serve as a basis of mutual comparison for all values, even those of actual moneys, and which are called *money of account*, *bank money*, etc.

The word money in this sense, is not to be translated by the Latin word, *moneta*, but by that of *pecunia*, to which it corresponds very exactly.

It is in this last sense, that is, as a measure of value and a pledge of value, that we are going to look at *money* when we follow the course of its introduction in commerce and the progress which the art of *measuring* value has made among mankind.

First of all, it is essential to get a clear idea of what ought to be understood here by this word, *value*.

This abstract noun, which corresponds to the verb "*to be worth*" (*valoir*), in Latin *valere*, has in everyday language several meanings, which it is important to distinguish.

The original meaning of this word, in the Latin language, denoted strength, vigor, *valere* also meant *to be in good health*, and we keep this original meaning in French in the derivations *valide* (healthy), *invalide* (invalid), and *convalescence*. From this use of the word *valour* (*valeur*) as denoting strength, its meaning has been diverted to signify military courage, a virtue which the ancients have nearly always designated by the same word meaning physical strength. The word "*valoir*" in French has taken another frequently used meaning, and one which, although different from the sense given in commerce to this word and to the word *value*, forms, however, its original foundation.

It expresses the suitability relative to our needs by which the gifts and the goods of nature are regarded as fit for our enjoyment and for the satisfaction of our desires. It is said that a stew is *worthless* if its flavor is bad, that a food is *bad* for the health, that one material is *better* than another, an expression which has no relation to its *commercial value*, and which only signifies that it is more suitable to the use for which it is intended.

The adjectives *bad, mediocre, good, excellent*, describe the different degrees of this type of value. It must be observed, however, that the noun *value* is not nearly as much used in this sense as the verb

Value and Money

to be worth (*valoir*). But if it is used, it can only be understood to mean the suitability of an object for our enjoyment. Although this suitability is always relative to ourselves, yet we have in view, when explaining the word *value*, a real quality which is intrinsic to the object and through which it is suitable for our use.

This sense of the word *value* would be appropriate to a man in isolation, without any communication with other men.

Let us consider this man as exerting his abilities on a single object only; he will seek after it, avoid it, or treat it with indifference. In the first case, he would undoubtedly have a motive for seeking after this object; he would judge it to be suitable for his enjoyment, he will find it *good*, and this relative goodness could generally speaking be called *value*, it would not be susceptible to measurement, and the thing which has *value* would not be *evaluated*.

If the same man can choose between several objects suitable to his use, he will be able to prefer one to the other, find an orange more agreeable than chestnuts, a fur better for keeping out the cold than a cotton garment; he will regard one as *worth more* than another; he will compare them in his mind, he will appraise their *worth*. He will consequently decide to undertake those things which he prefers, and leave the others.

The savage has killed a calf, which he takes to his hut; on his way he finds a roe; he kills it and takes it instead of the calf in the expectation of eating a more delicious meat. In the same way a child, who had first filled his pockets with chestnuts, empties them in order to make room for some sugared almonds which have been given to him.

This, then, is a comparison of *value*, an evaluation of the different objects in the judgments of this savage and this child; but these *appraisals* are not permanent, they change continually with the need of the person. When the savage is hungry, he values a piece of game more than the best bearskin; but let his appetite be satisfied and let him be cold, and it will be the bearskin that becomes valuable to him.

As often as not, the savage confined his desires to the satisfaction of his immediate needs, and no matter what the quantity is of the objects for which he has no use, as soon as he has taken what he needs, he leaves the remainder, which is of no use to him.

Experience, however, teaches our savage that among the objects suitable for his enjoyment, there are some whose nature makes them capable of being kept for some time, and which he may accumulate for future needs: these keep their value even when the immediate need has been satisfied. He seeks to appropriate them, i.e., to put them in a safe place where he can hide or guard them. It may be seen that the number of considerations which enter into the estimation of this *value*, *relative* solely *to the man* who enjoys and desires, increases greatly through this new perspective which foresight adds to the original feeling of need. When this feeling, which at first was only transitory, assumes the character of permanence, the man begins to compare his needs, to adapt his quest for objects no longer to the swift impulse of the immediate need alone, but in accordance to the necessity and usefulness (*utilité*) of the different needs.

As for the other considerations by which this ranking of more or less pressing usefulness is weighed up or modified, one of the first which suggests itself is the suitability of the object, or its relative capacity to satisfy the type of need for which it is sought. It must be admitted that this degree of suitability, with regard to the estimation which results from it, falls to some extent within the order of usefulness since the pleasure of the keener enjoyment produced by this degree of suitability is itself an advantage which a man compares with the more urgent necessity of those objects whose abundance he prefers to the suitability of a single one.

A third consideration is the degree of difficulty which a man meets in procuring the object of his desires; for it is quite clear that of two things of equal usefulness and quality, he would regard that which cost him more toil to obtain as the more precious, and he will take much more care and effort to obtain it. It is for this reason that water, in spite of its necessity and the multitude of pleasures which it provides for man, is not regarded as a precious thing in a well-watered country; that man does not seek to gain its possession, since the abundance of this element allows him to find it all around him. But in the sandy deserts it would command an infinite price.[3]

We have not yet begun to discuss exchange, and already we have touched upon scarcity, one of the elements in the process of *valuation*. It must be pointed out, that the esteem attached to scarcity is still founded on a particular type of usefulness, for it is because it is more useful to accumulate a thing difficult to find, that it is more sought after and that a man puts more effort into acquiring it.

It is possible to deduce from these three considerations all those that enter into the determination of the type of *value* relating to man in isolation; they are the three elements which combine to determine it. To give it an appropriate name we shall call it *esteem value* (*valeur estimative*), because it is in fact the expression of the degree of esteem which a man attaches to the different objects of his desire.

It seems useful to stress this notion and to analyze what is meant by this degree of esteem which man attaches to his different wants; what is the essence of this valuation, or the expression of the unit to which the value of each particular object is compared, what is the notation of this scale of comparison and what is its unit of measurement.

Reflecting upon this, we find that the totality of things necessary for the subsistence and well-being of man form, if I may use the expression, a *sum of needs* which is fairly limited in spite of all their range and variety.

To obtain the satisfaction of these wants, man has only an even more limited quantity of strength and resources. Each particular object of enjoyment costs him trouble, hardship, labor, and, at the very least, time. It is this use of his resources applied to the quest for each object which provides the offset to his enjoyment, and forms as it were the cost of the thing. The man is still isolated, nature alone supplies his wants, and already he has made a first *bargain* with her, in which she supplies nothing unless he pays for it by his labor, the use of his resources and his time.

---

[3] This last sentence was added by du Pont.

His capital, in this kind of exchange is confined within narrow limits; he must adjust the sum of his enjoyments to it. He must make a choice in the tremendous store house of nature, and he must divide this *cost* of which he can dispose among the different objects which are agreeable to him, he must *appraise* them on the basis of their *importance* to his subsistence and well being. And what is this appraisal, other than the account he renders to himself of the portion of his toil and time, or, to express these two things in a single word, the portion of his resources which he can use to acquire an evaluated object without thereby sacrificing the quest for other objects of equal or greater importance?

What then is his measure of value here? What is his scale of comparison? It is clear that he has no other than his actual resources. The total sum of these resources is the only unit of this scale, the only fixed point of departure, and the values which he attributes to each object are the proportional parts of this scale. It follows from this that the *esteem value* (*valeur estimative*) of an object, for the man in isolation, is precisely that portion of his total resources which corresponds to the desire he has for this object, or what he is willing to use to satisfy this desire. It might be said, in other words, that it is the relation of this proportional part to the total of the man's resources, a relation expressed by a fraction, whose numerator was the unit and whose denominator the number of values or equal proportional parts which the total of the man's resources contained.

We cannot but pause for a further reflection. We have not yet seen the emergence of exchange, we have not yet brought together two individuals, and already from this first step in our enquiries we touch on one of the newest and most profound truths which the general theory of value contains. It is this truth which l'Abbé Galiani stated twenty years ago in his treatise *Della Moneta* with so much clarity and vigor, but almost without further development, when he said that the *common measure of all value is man*. It is plausible that this same truth, half grasped by the author of a work which has just appeared under the title *Essai analytique sur la richesse et l'impôt* has given rise to the doctrine of a constant and unique value which is always expressed by this unit and of which all individual values are only proportional parts, a doctrine which in that book is a blending of truth and falsity, and which for this reason has appeared rather obscure to the majority of its readers.

This is not the place in which to develop for our readers the obscurities in the short statement we have just made of a proposition which merits being discussed at a length commensurate with its importance; even less should we enumerate its numerous consequences at this moment.

Let us take up the thread of the argument which has guided us so far; let us extend our original assumptions. Instead of considering only one man, let us take two; let each one have in his possession something suitable for his use, but let these things be different and suited to different wants. Suppose, for example, that on a desert island, in the middle of the northern seas, two savages land on different sides, one bringing fish with him in his boat, more than he can consume himself, the other carrying hides beyond what he can use to clothe himself and to make himself a tent. The one bringing fish is cold, the one bringing hides is hungry. It will eventuate that the latter will ask the owner of the fish for part of his provisions, and will offer to give him in return some of his hides: the other will accept. Here is exchange, here is commerce.

Let us pause for a while to consider what happens in this exchange. It is obvious from the first that the man, who, having taken from his catch enough to feed himself for a few days beyond which time those fishes would decay, would have to throw away the remainder as useless, begins to value them when he sees that these fish may be used (by means of exchange) to obtain for him hides which he needs to clothe himself. This superfluous fish acquires in his eyes a value which it did not have before. The owner of the hides will reason likewise and will himself learn to *value* those hides for which personally he has no need. It is likely that in this first case, where we assume that our two men are each provided more than abundantly with the thing they possess, and are accustomed to attach no price to the surplus, the discussion on the conditions of exchange will not be very animated; each would let the other take, one all the fish, the other all the hides, which he himself does not need. But let us vary the assumptions a little: let us give each of these two men an interest in keeping their surplus, a motive to attach some value to it. Let us suppose that instead of fish, one had brought corn, which may be preserved for a very long time; that the other, instead of hides, had brought firewood, and that the island produced neither grain nor wood. One of our two savages has his subsistence, the other his firing for several months; they can only replenish their provisions by going back to the continent, from which they were perhaps driven away by the fear of wild beasts or a hostile nation; they can only do so in the stormy season by exposing themselves to the almost inevitable dangers of the sea. It stands to reason that the stock of corn and wood becomes very precious to the two owners, that it has great value for them; but the wood which the one can consume in a month will become quite useless to him, if in the meantime he dies of hunger for want of corn, and the owner of the corn will be no better off if he is in danger of perishing for want of wood. They will thus make an exchange, in order that each of them may have both wood and corn until the time when the season will permit them to put to sea in order to get more corn and wood on the continent. In these circumstances both would obviously be less generous; each will scrupulously weigh all the considerations which may council him to prefer a certain amount of the commodity which he does not have to a certain amount of that which he has; that is, he will calculate the intensity of the two needs, of the two interests which he balances, one against the other, to wit, the interest of keeping corn and that of acquiring wood, or of keeping wood and acquiring corn. In short, he will very precisely determine their esteem value relative to himself. This esteem value is proportional to the interest he has in obtaining the two things; and the comparison of the two *values* is obviously only the comparison of the two *interests*. But each makes his own calculations, and the results may be different: the one would exchange three measures of corn for six armfuls of wood, the other would give him six armfuls of wood only for nine measures of corn. Independently of this kind of mental evaluation by which each of them compares the interest he has of keeping to that of acquiring, both are also animated by a general interest independent of all comparisons, that is the interest of keeping as much of their own commodity as they can, and of acquiring as much as they can of that of the other. With this in mind, each will keep secret the mental comparison which he has made of his two interests, of the two values which he attached to the commodities for exchange, and he will sound out the owner of the commodity he desires by lower offers and higher demands. Since the other will follow the same procedure, they will discuss the conditions of the exchange, and as they both have a great interest in coming to an agreement, they will finally do so. Slowly each of them will increase his offers and reduce his demands, until they finally agree to give a certain quantity of corn for a certain quantity of wood. At the moment of exchange the one who, for example, gives four measures of corn for five armfuls of wood, without doubt prefers these five armfuls of wood to the four measures of corn; he will give them a higher esteem value. But for his part, the one who receives the four measures of corn also prefers them to the five armfuls of wood. This superiority of the esteem value attributed by the acquirer to the thing he acquires over the thing he gives up is essential to the exchange, for it is the sole motive for it. Each would remain as he was, if he did not find an interest, a personal profit, in exchange; if, in his own mind, he did not consider what he receives worth more than what he gives.

But this difference in esteem value is reciprocal and precisely equal on each side; for if it was not equal, one of them would be less desirous of the exchange and he would force the other to come closer to his price by a better offer. It is thus always exactly true that each gives equal value to *receive equal value*. If four measures of corn are given for five armfuls of wood, five armfuls of wood are also given for four measures of corn, and consequently, four measures of corn are equivalent to five armfuls of wood in this particular exchange. These things thus have equal exchange value.

Let us pause again. Let us see exactly what is meant by this *exchange value*, whose equality is the necessary condition of free exchange; let us not depart from the simplicity of our assumptions, where we have only two contracting parties and only two objects of exchange to consider. This *exchange value* is not exactly the same as the *esteem value*, or, in other words, the interest which each of the two separately attached to the two desired objects, whose possession he compares in order to determine what he must give up of the one to acquire some of the other, since the result of the comparison might not be the same in the minds of the two contracting parties. This first value, to which we have given the name *esteem value*, is arrived at through the comparison which each separately makes between the two interests that contend with one another in his case; it exists only in the interest of each of the two taken separately. *Exchange* value on the contrary, is adopted by both the contracting parties, who recognize its equality and who make it the condition of the exchange. In the determination of *esteem* value, each man, taken separately, has compared only two interests, attached by him to the object he has and to the one he desires to have. In the determination of *exchange* value, there are two men who compare, and four interests (which are) compared by them; but the two individual interests of each of the two contracting parties have first been compared between themselves separately, and it is the two results which are then compared together, or rather, discussed by the two contracting parties, in order to form one *average esteem value*, which becomes precisely the *exchange value*, to which we believe we must give the name of *appreciative value* (*valeur appréciative*) because it determines the *price* or the condition of exchange.

It can be seen from what we have just said, that the *appreciative value*, this value which is equal for the two objects exchanged, is essentially of the same nature as the *esteem value*. It differs from it only in so far as it is the *average* esteem value. We have seen, above, that for each of the contracting parties the esteem value of the thing received is higher than that of the thing given up, and that this difference is exactly equal on each side; by taking half of this difference in order to subtract it from the higher value and to add it to the lower value, they are made *equal*. We have seen that this perfect equality is precisely the characteristic of appreciative value in the exchange. Thus the appreciative value is evidently none other than the *average* of the esteem values which the two contracting parties attach to each object.

We have proved that the esteem value of an object, for the man in isolation, is none other than the relation between that part of his resources which a man can devote to the quest for this object and the totality of his resources; thus the appreciative value in the exchange between two men is the relation between the sum of the parts of their resources which they would be prepared to devote to the quest for each of the objects exchanged and the sum of the resources of those two men. It is worth noting here that the introduction of exchange between our two men increases the wealth of both of them, that is, it gives them both a greater quantity of satisfaction in return for the same resources. I assume in the example of our two savages that the shore which produces corn and the shore which produces wood, are remote from each other; a single savage would be obliged to make two journeys to obtain his provisions of corn and wood; he would consequently lose much time and hard work in navigating. If on the contrary there are two of them, they would use the time and effort that would have been put into the second journey, the one to cut wood, the other to obtain corn. The total sum of corn and wood gathered would be much bigger and so consequently, the share of each man.

Let us retrace our steps. It follows from our definition of *appreciative value* that it is not the relation between two things exchanged or between the *price* and the thing sold, as some people have been tempted to think. This expression would be absolutely inappropriate in the comparison of the two values, of the two terms of exchange. It implies a relation of equality, and this relation of equality assumes two things already equal; now, those two equal things are not the two things compared, but rather the value of the things exchanged. Thus, the *values* which have a relation of equality may not be confused with this relation of equality which assumes that two values have been compared. There is without doubt a sense in which the *values* have a relation, and we have explained it above in a careful study of esteem value; we have even said that this relation, like all relations, could be expressed as a fraction. It is precisely the equality of these two fractions that constitutes the essential condition of the exchange, an equality which is achieved by fixing the *appreciative* value at half the difference between the two esteem values.

In commercial language, *price* is often confused with *value* without causing inconvenience, because in effect the stating of a price always involves the stating of a value. They are, however, different concepts which it is important to distinguish. The price is the thing which is given in exchange for an object. From this definition it follows that this other object is also the price of the first. When exchange is under discussion, it is almost superfluous to make this remark, and as all commerce consists of exchange, it is obvious that this expression (*price*) always fits both things traded, which are equally each other's price. The price and the thing bought or, if you like the two prices, are of equal value: the price is worth as much as the purchase, and the purchase as much as the price. But the name value, strictly speaking, is no more applicable to one of these two terms of exchange than to the other. Why then do we use these terms for one another? Here is the reason; and its explanation will enable us to take a further step in the theory of *value*.

This reason is the impossibility of expressing value in terms of itself. It is easy to be convinced of this impossibility if only one reflects on what we have just said and demonstrated about the nature of value.

Indeed, how do we find the expression of a fraction whose first term, the numerator, the fundamental unit, is an inestimable object, which is defined in the vaguest possible manner? How can the value of an object be expressed as corresponding to the two-hundredth part of a man's resources, and of what resources are we talking? It is essential to introduce the consideration of time in the calculation of these resources, but what interval will be chosen? Will it be a life time, or a year, a month, a day? Nothing of the sort to be sure; for man, with respect to each object he needs, must, in order to obtain it, inevitably employ his resources for periods of vastly different duration. How to estimate these intervals of time which, passing at one and the same time for all types of man's needs, must yet only enter in unequal lengths into the calculation relative to each particular type of need. How to evaluate these imaginary parts of one continuous span of time, which flows, if I may put it in this way, along an indivisible line. And what thread could be a guide in such a labyrinth of calculations, of which all the elements are indeterminate? It is thus impossible to express *value* in itself; and all that human language can express in this regard is that the value of one thing equals the *value* of another. The benefit evaluated, or rather, felt by two men, establishes this equation in each particular case, without any one ever thinking of *summing* the resources of man in order to compare its total to each needed object. Interest always determines the result of this comparison, but it has never actually made the comparison, nor could it do so.

The only means of expressing value is then, as we have said, to express that one thing is equal in value to another; or, if you like, in other words to present one value as equal to a required value. Value, like size, has no other measure than itself, and if values are measured by comparison with other values, as length is measured by comparison with other lengths, then, in both means of comparison, there is no *fundamental unit* given by nature, there is only an *arbitrary unit* given by convention. Since in all exchange there are two equal values and since the measure of one can be given in terms of the other, there must be agreement about the arbitrary unit which is taken for the foundation of this measure, or, if you like, for the unit of notation of the parts which are to compose the scale of comparison for value. Suppose that one of the two contracting parties in the exchange wishes to express the value of the thing he acquires, he will take for the unit of his scale of value a constant part of what he gives, and he will express in whole numbers and in fractions of this unit the quantity he will give for a fixed quantity of the thing he receives. This quantity expresses the *value* for him, and will be the *price* of what he receives; from whence it can be seen that the price is always the expression of the value, and that thus, for the acquirer, to express the value is to give the price of the thing acquired in terms of the quantity he gives to acquire it. He will thus say indifferently that this quantity is *the value*, or *the price* of what he buys. In employing these two forms of speech he will have the same meaning in mind, and he will put the same meaning into the minds of those who hear him; which explains how the two words *value* and *price*, although expressing fundamentally different ideas, can, without causing inconvenience, be substituted for each other in daily speech, when rigorous precision is not required.

It is rather obvious that if one of the two contracting parties has taken a certain arbitrary part of the thing he gives up, in order to measure the value of the thing he acquires, the other party will have the same right in his turn to take that same thing acquired by his opponent, but given up by himself, in order to measure the value of the thing his opponent has given him, and which served as a measure for the latter. In our example, the one who has given four bags of corn for five armfuls of wood will take a bag of corn for the unit of his scale, and will say: the armful of wood is worth four-fifths of a bag of corn. The one who has given the wood for the corn, on the contrary, will take the armful of wood for his unit and will say: the bag of corn is worth one and a quarter armfuls of wood. This operation is exactly the same as that which takes place between two men who might wish to value reciprocally, the one French ells in terms of Spanish vares, the other Spanish vares in terms of French ells.[4]

In both cases, an aliquot part of the most familiar thing, which serves to evaluate the other, is taken as a fixed and indivisible unit, and the second is evaluated by comparing it with the part arbitrarily taken as the unit. But just as Spanish vares no more measure French ells than French ells measure Spanish vares, the bag of corn does not measure the value of an armful of wood any more than an armful of wood measures the value of a bag of corn.

From this general proposition the inference must be drawn that in all exchanges both terms of exchanges are equally the measure of the value of the other term; for the same reason, in all exchanges, the two terms are both equally representative scales, that is, whosoever has corn can obtain for that corn a quantity of wood equal in value with that corn, just as the person who has wood, can, with that wood, obtain a quantity of corn of equal value.

This is an extremely simple truth, but one that is very fundamental to the theory of value, money and commerce. Obvious as

---

[4] The Spanish *vare* and the French *ell* were both measures of length; the *vare* was about 92 cm., the Paris *ell* about 118 cm.

it may be, it is yet frequently misunderstood by the best of minds, and ignorance of its most immediate consequences has often led the administration into the most disastrous delusions. It suffices to quote the famous system of Law.

We have dwelt for a very long time on the first hypotheses of the man in isolation, and of the two men exchanging two objects; but we wished to draw from them all the ideas of the theory of value which do not entail more complications. By thus always utilizing the simplest possible hypothesis, the ideas which result from it necessarily present themselves to the mind in a neater and more straightforward fashion.

We have only to extend our assumptions, to multiply the number of traders and things traded, in order to see the birth of commerce and to complete the sequence of ideas attached to the word "to be worth" (*valoir*).

Even for this last objective, it will suffice to multiply the number of men, while still considering only two single objects of exchange.

If we assume there are four men instead of two, to wit, two owners of wood and two owners of corn, it may at first be imagined that two traders meet on the one hand, and two on the other, without any communication between the four; then each exchange will be made separately, as if the two contracting parties were alone in the world. But, the very fact that the exchanges are made separately is no reason why they should be made on the same conditions. In each exchange taken separately, the appreciative value of the two exchanged objects is equal for both parties; but it must not be forgotten that this appreciative value is none other than the averaging of the two esteem values given to the objects of exchange by the contracting parties. Now, it is quite possible that this average result is radically different in the two exchanges settled separately, because the esteem values depend on the way in which each considers the objects of his needs, on the degree of usefulness which he assigns to them among his other needs; they are different for each individual. Consequently, if one only considers the two individuals on the one side and the two individuals on the other, the average result may be very different. It is quite possible that the contracting parties of one of the exchanges are less sensitive to cold than the contracting parties of the other; this circumstance is sufficient to cause them to attach less esteem value to wood and more to corn. Thus while in one of the exchanges four bags of corn and five armfuls of wood will only be equivalent to two bags of corn, which will not prevent that, in each contract, the value of the two objects is exactly equal for the two contracting parties, since one is given for the other.

Let us now bring our four men together, let us enable them to communicate with one another to learn of the conditions offered by each of the owners, either of wood or of corn. It follows that the person who would consent to give four bags of corn for five armfuls of wood, will no longer be willing to do so when he finds out that one of the owners of wood consents to give five armfuls of wood for only two bags of corn. But the latter, learning in his turn that four bags of corn may be had for the same quantity of five armfuls of wood, will change his mind too, and will no longer content himself with two. He would be quite prepared to take four, but the owners of corn would no more consent to give them to him than the owners of wood would be willing to content themselves with two. The conditions of the projected exchange will thus be changed and a new *evaluation* will take place, a appreciation of the value of wood and corn. It is immediately clear that this appreciation will be the same in the two exchanges and for the four dealers, that is, that for the same quantity of wood the owners of corn will give neither more nor less corn, and that for the same quantity of corn the owners of wood will give neither more nor less wood. At first glance it can be seen that if one of the owners of corn were to demand less wood than the other for the same quantity of corn, the two owners of wood would address themselves to him in order to profit from this reduction in price. This competition would urge this owner to demand more wood than he first demanded for the same quantity of corn; in his turn, the other owner of corn would lower his demand for wood, or raise his offer of corn, in order to win back the owners of the wood he needs, and this effect would take place until the two owners of corn offered the same quantity of corn for the same quantity of wood.[5]

---

[5] This paper was never finished. (Note by du Pont.)

Plan for a Paper on Taxation in General, on Land Taxes in Particular, and on the Project of a Land Register

Turgot presents a detailed plan for taxation of France. He argues that a plan cannot be confined to immediate measures but must be based on a full theoretical analysis. It is only on this basis that one can ask, what can be done? Following the Physiocrat Quesnay, Turgot holds that taxation should fall only on the proprietors of land. He strongly criticizes all other taxes, which he terms "indirect." In doing so, he anticipates a great deal of later work on the effects of taxation. Taxes on particular goods will discourage production of those goods and can sometimes have a debilitating effect on an entire town. Turgot also anticipates the "supply-side" argument that high taxes can end up reducing revenue because of their deleterious effects on production. Attempts to put the burden for taxes on foreigners through taxes on trade will not work. In addition, indirect taxes encourage corruption and evasion.

CHAPTER 9

Plan for a Paper on Taxation in General, on Land Taxes in Particular, and on the Project of a Land Register

The subject on which M. le Contrôleur-Général[1] has consulted the Intendants is one of the most interesting which can be examined. It contains the foundations of the whole political administration of a nation.

The question is no less than the determination of the most advantageous manner, for the sovereign and for the people, of securing the revenues of the State, and of distributing the contribution which the society as a whole owes itself for the supply of all public expenditures.

M. le Contrôleur-général has contented himself with asking some questions; but I think that since each of these questions is closely related to the first principles of the matter, they cannot be resolved in a satisfactory and practical manner unless this matter is treated fully and its principles are developed in their natural order. It seems to me that this is the only way of realizing what is the best thing to do; for it is always the best with which theory should be concerned. Neglecting this procedure, on the pretext that what is best is not practical in actual circumstances, is

---

Written 1763.

[1] The Contrôleur-général to whom this paper was directed was presumably Bertin (1719–1792), who held this post from 1759 to 1763. He was keenly interested in agricultural reform, and took charge of a new secretariat d'Etat which included agriculture, in 1763.

like wishing to resolve two questions at the same time. It is like surrendering the advantage of putting questions in the simplicity which alone can render them susceptible to proof. It is like rushing into an inextricable labyrinth without any clues and like wishing to unravel all the paths at the same time, or rather, like voluntarily closing your eyes to the light by making it impossible for you to find it.

I will therefore treat the subject with all the rigor of theory by a separate study and discussion of the following two very different questions: What should be done? And what can be done?

I will not conform to the order in which the succinct questions have been put forward. The answer to each of these questions will be discovered as a matter of course through the development of the principles, and I will take care to recall them and to recapitulate them separately.

To the questions on the land register, M. le Contrôleur-général has added some questions on the establishment of corporations. This subject is so important in itself that I believe I must treat it in a separate paper in which I also intend to approach it from the two points of view of the best possible, and the most feasible.

Plan of the Various Chapters

Of the necessity of taxation, or of the contribution to public expenditure.

Examination of Rousseau's idea that the *corvées* are preferable; show how much more costly this is, how much less equitably distributed, and impractical in a large society.

General principles of the distribution of taxation.

Of distributive justice.

Of the necessity of never injuring the sources of wealth.

False ideas of some people on distributive justice.

On Land Taxes and a Land Register

Who is liable to taxation? Proof that only the proprietor of the soil is liable [to taxation], (because he alone earns a net revenue which is ascertainable), for the maintenance of all other types of property of which the conservation and free use necessarily turn to his profit.

Refutation of the arguments used in attempts to prove that people with *purely personal property* have the same interest.

Different types of taxation.

There are only three possible types.

Direct taxation of landed property.

Direct personal taxation, which becomes a tax on the use of labor.

Indirect taxation or that on consumption.

Indirect taxation is divided into general taxation on consumption, like sales tax (*aides*) and excise duties; and into local taxation.[2]

The latter is subdivided into duties or impositions on consumption by virtue of their admission into the place where they are to be consumed;

Taxes on trade or on commodities passing through certain places, like tolls;

Taxes on certain transactions in the society, sales, etc., which are direct in some respects, and indirect in others;

And monopolies, like those of salt or tobacco.

All these different types of taxation ultimately fall entirely on the proprietors of the soil.

In order to demonstrate this, it is necessary:

---

[2] The *aide* and *accise* were taxes on consumption goods.

To develop accurately the concept of the revenue, and to prove that only the proprietor has a revenue;[3]

Proof that industry has no revenue at all; distinction between profit and revenue.

Enumeration of different taxes. Their incidence.

Only the tax on consumption admits of difficulty. Now, it is obvious that the proprietor pays it by buying services more dearly, and selling his products at a lower price, or by the decrease either of the price or of the quantity of consumption: the decline in quantity leads also to the decline in price.

Examination of the question whether the proprietor pays the indirect tax twice.

The loss may be greater or smaller, but whatever the proportion and the manner in which the question is decided, there is no doubt that preference must be given to direct taxation.

Firstly, because, as I have said already, only the proprietor is liable [to taxation];

Secondly, because direct taxation is less expensive to levy, and thus the proprietor gains the whole amount of the costs and the gain of the chief collectors, tax farmers or agents;

Thirdly, because the indirect taxation imposes a multitude of constraints on commerce; because it entails lawsuits, frauds, penalties, the loss of a large number of people, a war between the government and its subjects, a lack of proportion between crime and punishment, and a continual and almost irresistible temptation to fraud, which is yet subject to cruel punishment;

---

[3] I have heard a man calculating the revenue of a province by saying: There are so many men; each man, in order to live, spends so many *sous* per day, therefore the province has so much revenue. Tax a similar revenue proportionately, and these people must die of hunger, or at least from misery. I believe that it all comes back to the great question of the soup of the Franciscans; it is in them when they have eaten it. It is the same with the so-called revenue from industry. When a man has eaten the reward proportioned to his talent or to the usefulness of his service, he has nothing left, and taxation cannot be levied on nothing. (Note by Turgot.)

Fourthly, because indirect taxation attacks liberty in a thousand ways;

Fifthly, because it is greatly prejudicial to consumption, and by this destroys itself;

Sixthly, because the expenses of the State are increased by it, since the State pays it on its own expenditure and on that of all its agents;

Seventhly, because it gives a competitive advantage in trade to foreign merchants;

Eighthly and finally, because its results cannot be calculated precisely, while a proprietor is always able to determine what proportion of his revenue he pays.

In the case of direct taxation, the State knows what it is inflicting; it also clearly knows what it is able to inflict. Everything desirable in administration is present in it, that is, simplicity, surety, and rapidity.

Direct Taxation

On persons or on the land.

That on persons, by its very nature offends reason; only laziness, and undue haste can have suggested it.

It cannot possibly be uniform.

Firstly, because there are people who own nothing;

Secondly, because, if the whole idea is to tax the individual, who is but a mass of wants, it would at any rate be necessary to tax at the rate appropriate to the lowest class of society; and at such a low rate, taxation would not yield a great deal.

It is therefore necessary to come back to classifying people more or less according to their means. Then this is no more than taxation of wealth, imposed arbitrarily and without rules.

If all so-called means are included in this, such as industry, commerce, their wages, the profits necessary for the exercise (of their business), etc., this poll-tax is in this respect an indirect tax.

The part proportioned to the means originating from landed property is direct taxation; but it has all the disadvantages of arbitrariness.

It is still possible to distinguish between personal and real taxation, even in the case where the personal taxation would be proportioned to landed property only, for the taxation resting on landed property may be payable by the person, as in the *taille personnelle*, or by the capital, as in the *taille réelle*. This is the difference from real taxation with regard to the assessment and with regard to the collection.

If all direct taxation were left in existence in amended form, a great deal of the taxation would still remain and fall directly on the soil, and it would still have to be imposed in the most equitable way possible, and even then the indirect taxes would still hit landed property on the rebound.

It is therefore of some use to discuss the question in general terms, and to run through the particular disadvantages of the various types of indirect taxation.

Indirect Taxation

Impositions on general consumption; their disadvantages. They cause the payment of the same tax on products of the same type, some of which are costly, and others not. Poor consumers are taxed excessively. And similarly, the same tax is paid on output of which a part, originating from fertile soil, has cost little, while the rest, from barren ground, has cost a great deal which it barely repays. These taxes therefore bear no relation to the revenue, and cause the abandonment of cultivation of mediocre soil, the output of which would only cover costs.

The import duties of towns. They have the same disadvantages and, moreover, this difficulty, that their rates could not be made to follow the relative value of commodities; because, for commodities with a high value, smuggling would increase in line with the duties.

The less necessary commodities are, the more duties will diminish their consumption.

A sure yield can therefore be counted on only to the extent that the taxes are imposed on commodities which the people use, which they cannot do without, and which are at the same time sufficiently bulky to prohibit fraud; but then the poor pay, or, at least advance, the whole of the tax, which causes them great hardship. The wealthy, who repay this advance, at first pay almost nothing, and even in the end pay only tardily.

It is a common belief that through these duties the towns are made to pay; but in reality, it is a charge on the country side which produces the taxed commodities. For the inhabitants of towns have limited revenues, and can pay the tax only by offering a lower price to the producers and the initial sellers of the commodity, or by curtailing their consumption. And we have already seen that these two transactions which naturally occur together, have the same results.

The ridiculous tariffs which the inhabitants of the towns have been allowed to establish, have almost completely the objective of placing the whole burden of the tax on what they call *foreigners*.

Foreign merchandise must therefore be sold at a higher price than local goods. This gives the local merchants a monopoly which is prejudicial to the ordinary inhabitants of the towns.

In the case of most of these duties, it is felt that everything must be taxed. Because of this, an inextricable labyrinth of valuations, disputes, etc. has been created.

Moreover, taxation of commerce tends to reduce its volume.

The natural result of all these urban taxes would be to change the location of towns, or to extend them beyond the genuine convenience of the inhabitants by building in the suburbs in order to evade the duties. The only reason which prevents this effect is another evil, which is even worse: It is the sad condition of the inhabitants of the countryside and the manifold vexations which pursue them, while the city dwellers, by reason of their wealth and their proximity to the government, their better education and greater prestige, and because, through closeness, they form a much more imposing body than those living in the country, even though the latter are twice as numerous, have been able to avoid much of the wrongs and the bad treatment which the cultivators have had, and still have, to endure.

If the countryside were subjected to territorial taxation only, the majority of the town dwellers would soon settle there, and this would not be a bad thing, for then consumption would come closer to the place of production; there would be fewer wasteful expenses of transportation and the cultivator, enjoying the whole of the consumer's expenditure, would be able to extend his activities profitably to less fertile lands of which the additional produce would enable citizens to live whose existence is at present impossible, because if they were born, they would have no sustenance.

Taxation by way of monopoly is much worse still. By the extreme disproportion in price, it becomes a cruel lure to smuggling. The king is made to play the same role as those people who scatter corn for the birds in order to trap them.

With all indirect taxation, the maladministration of the customs officers is impossible to avoid. In order to ascertain frauds, it is necessary to give customs officers the privilege of being believed on the basis of their reports, and this may become a source of vexations which cannot be curbed.

The intricacy of the tariffs and the laws which regulate their collection and which seek to prevent their violation, make it a physical impossibility for the people to hold out against these vexations, for in the midst of so many obscurities, what individual would dare to hazard the expenses of a lawsuit against the agents of the authorities?

The taxation on transfers of property and commercial deeds, is a type of taxation no less odious.

It seems that Public Finance, like a greedy monster, has been lying in wait for the entire wealth of the people, and all this through a gross misunderstanding. For why so many tricks when all real wealth is *out in the open*, as the saying goes?

The hundredth penny (*centième*) takes a portion from property itself. However, when people agreed to pay taxes to preserve the society of which they are members, they did this only to preserve their property, and not to lose it.

There are undoubtedly cases in which people would consent to sacrifice part of their property in order to save the remainder, but this would not be the normal case. They want an assured and constant tenure of property, and they also want their sacrifice to be constant. Taxation must therefore be levied on the revenue and not on the capitals.

Moreover, the State has the greatest possible interest in preserving the stock of capitals. It is this stock which provides the advances of all agricultural and commercial enterprises, as well as the acquisition of real property. These capitals are formed by the slow process of thrift. To cause payment, as revenue of the State, of part of these capitals, which are accumulated for the advances necessary for work, is to destroy in part the source of these same revenues.

Having decided that direct taxation of landed property is the only form of taxation conforming to our principles, it is necessary to establish: firstly, on what part of the product of landed property it should be levied, and then how it can be distributed and collected.

I have already said that only the owner of real property is liable to contribute to taxation; a first ground for this is that he alone has a stake in the preservation of an abiding social order. What does it matter to a working man what becomes of the government? He would always own the same resources in the form of his arms; he is perfectly indifferent as to whether it is Jack or Peter who furnishes the work. A second ground, and the more peremptory, is that only the owner of landed property has a true revenue.

Discussion of the Revenue

M. Quesnay was the first to establish the correct notion of the revenue, when he learnt to distinguish the *gross product* from the *net product*, and not to include the profits of the cultivator in the *net product*. These products are the bait, the sufficient and necessary motive for cultivation; why would the cultivator work if he could not count on his legitimate profit? And will he not work with all the more eagerness and success as he is assured that he will not labor in vain?

An estate may produce commodities in quite large quantities and not yield any net product; for this result it is sufficient to assume that it costs more to till than the sale of its fruits can yield.

It is well known that soil, manured and ploughed to the point where it is as light as that of an ants nest, yields a prodigious harvest; but if in order to work the soil in this manner, spades and many days' labor are required, this output may become expensive. If the quantity of output is such that it is not matched by consumption, and has no exchange value, the revenue will be zero in spite of the abundance of the harvest. When the philosophers' stone is discovered, its inventor would not be any richer from it if he could only make gold to the value of a hundred *louis* by spending the value of a hundred *louis* on charcoal, and if it were to cost him a hundred and one *louis* he would certainly leave the trade.

This truth is well known; but what has not been so well realized is that it is just as necessary to subtract similarly from the gross product the recovery of the expenses of the cultivator in order to ascertain the *net product*.

M. Quesnay has developed the mechanism of agriculture which is based entirely on very large original advances and requires in addition annual advances which are equally necessary. It is therefore necessary to deduct from the sale of the produce: firstly, all the expenses or *annual advances*; secondly, the interest on the *original advances*; thirdly, their maintenance and the replacement of their inevitable decay, at least equal to the interest; fourthly, the subsistence and reasonable profit of the entrepreneur farmer and his agents, the wages of their labor and of their industry.

The cultivator has made these calculations when he leases a piece of land. It is the surplus which he gives to the proprietor that makes up the revenue, and it is only on this revenue that taxes can be levied. When the proprietor cultivates the land himself, he has no greater disposable revenue, but he combines in one person his revenue as a proprietor and his profits as a cultivator, a profit which is not disposable at all.

M. Quesnay has, moreover, demonstrated that, if the exchange value is diminished, the revenue would diminish gradually to the point where finally the soil would produce nothing beyond the reproduction of advances and the profit of the cultivator; that from then on, there would be no more letting out of land; that the proprietor, it is true, would still be able to farm it for his own subsistence, by making the advances himself, but that this slender revenue would no longer be disposable. And it would be possible that, in a nation where the estates would be reduced to this sort of cultivation, there would be absolutely no revenue, no means of sustaining the State, other than by gradually consuming the capitals; this situation would be self-destructive and of necessity transitory.

To appreciate this, it is sufficient to consider that the proprietors must have their livelihood. Let a family need a hundred *écus* in order to subsist, and let the land be so distributed that each proprietor, by farming it himself, earns only one hundred *écus*, and he will not be able to pay the tax without taking from his subsistence.

This so-called revenue would only be the wages of his labor. The true revenue is the portion of the proprietor over and above that of the cultivator, that which the cultivator gives to the proprietor in order to acquire the right to work his field. All other notions of the revenue are illusions. When landed property is purchased, it is this revenue alone which is purchased.

Now it is obvious that it is this revenue alone in which the tax can share, since it could not encroach upon the share of the cultivator without removing his interest in cultivation, without forcing him to consume his advances and consequently to reduce his activities and his productive expenditure. As the output of successive years becomes less, the encroachment of the tax would become more and more destructive, and the output and the sources of the

State's revenues would be exhausted together with the revenue of the proprietors.

There is no further need to return to indirect taxation, which would destroy the capitals even more quickly, for the very reason that its blows would at first be less perceptible and would give less warning of the danger.

In this context the question is solely one of territorial taxation; and since it has already been shown that taxation should respect the portion of the cultivator, it follows directly that it must be paid by the proprietor. For if it were demanded from the farmer, the latter would be intelligent enough to withhold it from the proprietor in the price of his lease. Thus, the taxing of the cultivator as such would never have been considered, but for the impediments placed in the way of true principles by the privileges of the Nobility and the Church which the lawmaker desires to dodge. The disadvantages of this method will be discussed below. For the time being, we will deal with the question considered by itself, and, in a nation where no obstacle is placed in the way of pursuing correct principles, there is no doubt but the proprietors would be approached directly.

However, this proposition is contrary to the opinion held by those who originally conceived of the device of the royal tithe (*dîme royale*),[4] or those who have praised it. This method may in fact dazzle one by its simplicity, by the ease with which it is collected, by the appearance of distributive justice, and at least, because each knows what he must pay. The ecclesiastical tithe is a fascinating example among the poor and non-trading people. This form of taxation may be established more easily than any other. It is certain that the taxpayer always has the wherewithal to pay; he pays immediately and

---

[4] The system of the *dîme royale*, or royal tithe, had been suggested by Sébastien Le Prestre de Vauban in the book *Dîme Royale*, which appeared in 1707. The *dîme royale* consisted of a tax levied proportionately on everything bearing a revenue, and was to be modeled on the *dîme ecclésiastique* which was then in existence in France. Vauban's scheme was severely criticised at the time by Boisguilbert, in a mémoire to Chamillart, then Contrôleur-Général. (Note by Turgot.)

without expense. This mode of taxation is established in China. Yet, it has a number of disadvantages.

First disadvantage of the tithe: its lack of proportion. No regard whatsoever to the expenses of cultivation. It is possible that the gross tithe is greater than the net product. If by expending the value of nine *setiers* of corn, one managed to produce ten *setiers* per *arpent*, the net product would be only one *setier*. This would yet be a very sufficient revenue for engaging in agriculture: well, the tithe would take it all; it would therefore destroy the whole revenue; and if the cultivation had been more expensive, the tithe would destroy itself; it would destroy the motive for cultivation, and put an end to it.

Second and more direct reason, but which is partly contained in the first. The tithe, being a portion of the crop, may encroach upon the share of the cultivator, and may therefore take more than it should. The whole crop belongs at first to the cultivator; it is up to him to make his calculations in order to know what he ought to give up to the proprietor, and it is only on this portion, surrendered to the proprietor, that taxation may and should be levied.

Proposing to set up a cadaster for the tithe in order to remedy these shortcomings, and to ask less from land that produces less relative to the expenses, would mean rushing into a difficulty greater than that of evaluating the revenues in terms of money, because, for the latter operation, the leases and contracts of sale can be used at least, while there is nothing like this for evaluating the expenses of cultivation, which can only be ascertained through an analysis of cultivation. This is impossible for anyone but the cultivator, who knows how to calculate them accurately. The farmers calculate them approximately, and come closer by trial and error.

The tithe would be an excessive tax in some provinces; but it would be far from adequate for the public needs, unless it was extremely outrageous, which would make it more unequal, and even more destructive of cultivation, and consequently of itself, on land of inferior quality.

If it is assumed that the clergy have no other revenue than the tithe (setting off its other wealth against the enfeoffed tithes, and other tithes it does not own), the whole of the tithe, levied, it is true, at a multitude of different rates, would not go much beyond sixty million, and I do not believe the clergy to be a great deal more wealthy.

Let us thus turn back to approaching the proprietor directly, and asking from him in coin that part of his revenue which the State needs.

What would be asked of him? How would it be asked from him?

Two different systems.

Ask from each a part of the revenue, a constant proportion. This is the method of the *dixième*, of the *vingtième*, this is what has been put forward in the *Théorie de l'impôt*, in the *Philosophie Rurale*, it is the method used in the English land tax.

On the other hand, a fixed sum may be exacted from the nation, from each province, from each municipality; this sum being distributed among all the proprietors in proportion to their prosperity.

This second system, embodied in the arbitrary *taille*, has also been adopted in the provinces with land surveys or with *taille réelle* (property tax). In fact, it is only to this system that the land survey is truly appropriate. For what purpose would an unchangeable land survey serve in the case where a proportional part of a variable revenue is demanded? However, when a tax distribution is made, a fixed table is required. In all, there are only four possible methods of distributing the land tax.

Firstly, that of a portion proportional to the crop. This is the method of the tithe, of which I have already spoken and whose advantages and disadvantages I have sufficiently discussed.

Secondly, that of a portion proportional to the revenue. This is the method of the *vingtième*.

Thirdly, that of a fixed sum distributed each year among the taxpayers according to their mutual knowledge of the produce. This is more or less the method of the arbitrary *taille*, confined to landed property.

Fourthly, that of a fixed sum, distributed according to an invariable valuation of the property. This is the method of the land survey or the *taille réelle*.

The method based on the tax proportional to the revenue would have considerable advantages.

An unchangeable law could forever put an end to all the disputes between the government and the people, especially if it fixed one proportion for war and one for peace. People would compound at this rate in purchases and sales, and the part of the net product belonging to taxation would not be bought any more than that belonging to the priest is bought. After some time, in truth, no one would be paying taxes. But the king would be proprietor of a proportional part of the revenue of all the estates.

This revenue would increase with the wealth of the nation, and if the increase in wealth should augment the needs, it would be equally sufficient in that case. The wealth of the king would be the measure of the wealth of the people, and the administration, always affected by the repercussions of its mistakes, would learn once and for all, that is, by the simple calculation of the yield of the tax.

These advantages are considerable, especially in a monarchy; for in a republic or a limited monarchy like England, the people might not be so pleased if the prince would never have to reckon with them. With a law like this, the English Parliament would lose its greatest influence, and the king would soon be as absolute a monarch as in France, since it would no longer be to any one's advantage to oppose him.

If, therefore, it were possible to succeed in establishing a tax like this, proportional to the revenue, there could be no hesitation in preferring this manner of levying the public revenue to any other.

But I confess that this seems completely impossible to me: under this system, the king or the government stands alone against all, and every one is interested in hiding the value of his wealth. In the provinces where the *grande culture* exists, the value of the leases serves as a valuation; but firstly, not all land is leased; and secondly, I think it impossible to guard against the disadvantage of defeasances. I know it is said that an administration which inspires confidence, as that of the States could be, would persuade people to declare accurately; but I believe this to be a lack of understanding of human nature. Fraud would be very common, and straightaway would no longer be deemed dishonorable. Even in the case of the distribution method, where all frauds are regarded as odious in that they affect all the taxpayers, people scarcely scruple to commit fraud. The principles of honesty and patriotism have far from taken root in the provinces; only in the course of time and by the slow means of education could they be established.

It is proposed to make defeasances null and void, but this would encourage false testimony. The proper remedy for fraud is to take away all advantage in it.

Moreover, there still remains the objection relating to the provinces where lease holding is not practiced, that is, more than two thirds of the kingdom. Would declarations be demanded from the proprietors? What has been their use for the *vingtième*? But, it is said in the *Théorie de l'impôt*, the old forms of taxation can be left in existence in the provinces where there is no lease holding, until cultivation has made sufficient progress there for this to be introduced. This is all right in the case of an entire province, but in connection with parishes for the distribution among the proprietors of each estate, it would entail returning to estimates.

And then, it would be rather a long wait until lease holding is established everywhere. I will show below, when I will be concerned with developing the progress of *la grande culture*, that this will not be as speedy as M. de Mirabeau images it will be.

The restoration of agriculture must start with the proprietors. The stock of capitals required for the establishment of rural enterprises will take a long time to eventuate.

It is therefore necessary to rest content with the distribution of a fixed sum, except that its increase could be regulated according to a certain proportion with the revenues of the nation; I will show below that this is possible, and how it may be done.

This distribution cannot be made arbitrarily without incorporating many of the disadvantages with which the *taille* has been reproached. I say a part, not all, for it must be understood that part of the disadvantages of the current taxation arises from the fact that it is not levied directly on the proprietor but on the cultivators, and on the unfortunate inhabitants of the countryside. Yet many of the disadvantages would remain.

One can be sure that in this annual distribution the poor proprietors would always be overburdened, and that the large proprietors, whose voice would always be preponderant....[5]

---

[5] This paper was not finished, and the manuscript has not been found.

Extracts from "Paper on Lending at Interest"

The next selection shows Turgot's strong opposition to laws that limit or prohibit interest on loans. Anti-usury laws show no awareness of the importance of risk. In order to have economic progress, enterprises requiring large amounts of capital are necessary. Many of these enterprises are risky; if lenders are not allowed to derive a profit, they have no incentive to lend. The very fact that usury laws are always evaded shows their necessity. An activity that invariably takes place cannot reasonably be said to be wrong. Further, since lenders own the money they lend, they have the right to come to whatever terms they are able to secure. In the course of arguing against usury, Turgot defends an unusual interpretation of the then-common view that an exchange involves an equality of value. He takes this "equality" to be the fact that each person in an exchange values what he gains more than what he gives up. Although he retains the term "equality," he in fact abandons its usual interpretation.

CHAPTER 10

Extracts from "Paper on Lending at Interest"

Sections I–III. *Reasons for the paper and background.* Some months ago a complaint was made to the magistrate at Angoulême against an individual who allegedly had exacted usurious interest rates in credit transactions. This complaint has caused a great deal of consternation as well as further complaints against lenders, and has thrown the whole credit structure of the area into confusion. Because credit has been so widely interrupted, bankruptcies are rapidly increasing. This financial crisis is of such importance, that the Royal Council should be informed. This paper has been written to provide the Council with a resume of events, and a solution to the problem.

In order to appreciate the facts of the case, some background material about the district is provided. Angoulême ought to be a flourishing town, because of its geographical location, but unfortunately scarcity of capital has prevented this. At present, its major commerce is connected with the manufacture of paper, the brandy trade, and some iron works.

The paper trade, in general has steady prices; the opposite applies to that in brandy: this commodity is subject to huge variations in price. These variations lead to very hazardous speculations, which may

---

This paper was written in connection with a lawsuit in Angoulême in 1769 between two debtors and their creditor. Because part of the paper deals with particulars of the lawsuit and with moral arguments against canon law on the subject of usury, only those parts of economic interest have been translated in full. The other sections have been condensed; the condensed parts are placed in square brackets.

either procure immense profits, or entail ruinous losses. The enterprises of the iron masters, which supply the navy, require very large and lengthy advances from them, which return to them with profits which are all the more considerable as they return later. To avoid losing the opportunity of a large order, they are forced to obtain money at any price, and they find the greater advantages as, by paying in cash for the ore and the wood, they obtain a very considerable reduction in the price of these raw materials for their enterprises.

IV. *Cause of the high interest rate in Angoulême*. It is easy to understand that the combination of a trade which is equally susceptible to large risks and large profits, and an area where capitals are in short supply, as found in the town of Angoulême, must have resulted in a fairly high current rate of interest, and generally higher than it is in other places of commerce. Indeed, it is notorious that for a period of about forty years, most of the financial transactions have been made at the rate of 8 or 9 per cent per annum, and sometimes at a rate of 10 per cent, depending on the size of the demand, and the risk involved.

Sections V–X. *The details of the legal dispute, and some of its consequences*. In this type of commercial situation, bankruptcies are frequent. Two of these bankrupts, in collusion with some friends, fraudulently obtained money by issuing bills on each other, which were endorsed by their friends and discounted with the defendant at a fairly high interest rate. When the bills fell due, the two bankrupts, instead of paying, denounced their creditor to the magistrate for charging usurious interest rates. This action has intimidated other lenders, who are now refusing to discount bills until they are sure of the legal position. This has disrupted the whole credit system of Angoulême.

XI. *Disastrous effects of this unrest on the credit and commerce of Angoulême*. As expected, the effect of the lawsuits has been the total loss of credit for the whole trade of Angoulême. The license given to the dishonesty of the borrowers has closed the purses of all the lenders, whose wealth, moreover, has been severely shaken by this blow. No expired obligations are renewed, all enterprises come to a halt, the manufacturers are exposed to failure through the impossibility of finding credit in expectation of the return of their funds. At the beginning of this paper I already referred to the large number of bills of exchange which have been protested since these disturbances started.

I have been informed that the merchants who deal in cloth for the consumption of the town, having addressed themselves to Lyon, according to their custom, in order to place their orders, have received the reply that no transactions will be made with people from Angoulême except on cash terms. This disrepute has even affected the subsistence of the people: since the harvest has failed in the province, they need the resources of trade to fill the gap. It would be expected that the town of Angoulême, being situated on a navigable river, would always be abundantly provided, and that her merchants would be eager to set up stores, not only for local provisions, but even for those of part of the province; but the inability of undertaking any form of speculation, which the general disrepute has brought about, makes this expedient worthless.

Sections XII–XIII. It is necessary to put an end to these difficulties, but it is not easy to remedy their causes, because of the prejudices contained in the law concerning interest.

XIV. *Defects of our laws on the subject of interest; impossibility of observing them rigorously; disadvantages of the arbitrary limits which have been imposed in practice*. I will not mince words. The laws recognized in the courts on the subject of the interest of money are poor; our legislation conforms to the extreme prejudice about usury introduced during the era of ignorance by theologians who understood the meaning of Scripture no better than the principles of natural right. The rigorous observation of these laws would mean the destruction of all commerce; consequently, they are not observed rigorously: they forbid all stipulation of interest without the alienation of capital; they prohibit, as illegal, all interest stipulated at a rate higher than that fixed by the ordinances of the Prince. And it is a well-known fact that there is no commercial centre on earth where the majority of transactions do not depend on the borrowing of money without the alienation of capital, and where interest rates would not be fixed by convention, according to the relative abundance of money on the spot, and the relative certainty of the solvency of the borrower. The rigidity of the law has yielded to the force of circumstances: jurisprudence has had to moderate in practice its theoretical principles, and has openly come to allow borrowing by bill, by discount, and other types of financial transactions between merchants. This will always happen when the law prohibits what the nature of things requires. However, this situation—where laws are not observed, but continue to exist without being repealed, and are even still partly enforced—entails very great disadvantages. On the one hand, the known disregard of the law reduces the respect which citizens should have for everything which carries its authority; on the other hand, the existence of this law maintains a troublesome prejudice, stigmatizes something which is legal in itself, with which society cannot dispense, and which consequently, a large group of citizens should be permitted to do. This class of citizens is degraded by this, and the onset of this degradation in the opinion of the public weakens the restraints imposed by its honor, that valuable support of integrity. The author of *Esprit des Lois* has aptly stated that: "When the laws prohibit a necessary thing, they only succeed in making dishonest men of those who do it."

The virtual non-observance of this law has meant that it has become most arbitrary, because there is no certainty as to when it will be invoked. The penalties for transgressions of this law are also most severe and include: compensation to the borrower, banishment; and for the second offence, condemnation to the galleys for life, or banishment for life. In the law, no distinction has been made between usury proper or exorbitant interest rates, and acceptable rates of interest. This makes the law even more arbitrary.

XV. What has happened in Angoulême proves the disadvantages arising from the arbitrariness of the law on interest.

XVI. This makes it imperative that the Government must settle the matter: either by repealing the law altogether, or by making it more specific.

XVII. The reform of the law is a difficult matter. It is therefore necessary to have knowledge of the true facts surrounding interest, in order to combat the prejudice of vested interest in this matter.

XVIII. In order to examine the question in the light of natural right, an extensive discussion is required which will weigh up the evidence for, and against, the taking of interest on loans. I must apologize for setting out this argument at length, since the prejudice surrounding this topic is sufficiently great to warrant such treatment.

XIX. *Proof of the legitimacy of lending at interest, based on its absolute necessity for commerce; development of this necessity.* First of all, the absolute necessity of lending for the prosperity and the maintenance of commerce is a very strong proof against the principles adopted by dogmatic theologians on the subject of lending at interest, for what man who is reasonable and religious at the same time can presume that Providence has forbidden a thing which is absolutely essential for the prosperity of society? Now, the necessity of lending at interest for commerce, and consequently, for civilized society, is proven from the first by the tolerance which the absolute need of commerce has forced to be given to this type of transaction, in spite of rigid prejudices of both theologians and legal experts. Moreover, this necessity is a self-evident thing. There is no commercial centre on earth where enterprises do not depend on borrowed money; there is not a single merchant perhaps who has not frequently been obliged to have recourse to the purse of others; even the richest in capitals could not be sure of never needing this expedient except by keeping part of their funds idle, and consequently, by diminishing the extent of their enterprises. It is no less obvious that those outside capitals necessary to all merchants can only be confided to them by their owners to the extent that the latter discover an advantage in it capable of compensating them for the deprivation of money which they could have used, and for the risks attached to all commercial enterprises. If the money lent for uncertain enterprises did not yield an interest higher than that on sound mortgages, people would never lend to merchants. If it was prohibited to draw interest from money which had to be returned on a fixed date, all money for which the owners could foresee a need in a certain time, while not needing it currently, would be lost to commerce during this interval. It would be utterly lost to those who have an urgent need for it. The rigorous enforcement of such a prohibition would remove immense sums from the circulation, which are now made available through the certainty of recovering them in case of need, to the mutual advantage of lenders and borrowers; and the lack of them would necessarily make itself felt by the rise in the rate of interest, and by the cessation of a large part of commercial enterprises.

XX. *Necessity of leaving the determination of interest in commerce to the agreements of the merchants, and to the operation of the different factors which cause it to vary: indication of these factors.* It is thus from absolute necessity, and to maintain confidence and the circulation of money, without which there is no commerce at all, that the lending of money at interest without the alienation of capital, and at a rate higher than the interest (le denier) fixed for Government stock, is sanctioned in commerce. It is essential that money is considered in commerce as a genuine commodity whose price depends on agreement and varies, like that of all other commodities, according to the ratio between offer and demand. Interest being the price of loanable funds, it rises when there are more borrowers than lenders; it falls, on the contrary, when there is more money offered than is demanded for borrowing. It is in this way that the normal rate of interest is established, but this normal rate is not the only rule which is followed, nor should it be followed to fix the rate of interest for individual transactions. The risks which the capital may run in the hands of the borrower, the needs of the latter, and the profit which he hopes to draw from the money which he borrows, are the circumstances which, when combined in different ways, and with the normal rate of interest, will often carry the rate to a higher level than it is in the ordinary course of trade. It is quite obvious that the lender would decide to lend his capital only through the lure of a high profit, and it is no less obvious that the borrower would decide to pay an interest which is all the higher as his needs are more urgent, or as he hopes to draw a greater profit from this money.

XXI. *Inequalities in the rate of interest because of the inequality of risks are no more than just.* What injustice can there be in this? Can it be expected that an owner of money risk his funds without any compensation?

He can refuse to lend, it is said; undoubtedly, and this is just what proves that, when lending, he can expect the profit to be proportionate to his risks. For, why deprive persons who, when they borrow cannot give security of an assistance they most urgently need? Why deprive them of the means to attempt enterprises from which they hope to get rich?

No law, civil or canon, forces anybody to render them gratuitous assistance; why should civil or canon law prohibit them to procure it at a price which they consent to pay for their own benefit?

XXII. *The legitimacy of lending at interest is independent of profit.* Scholars have tried to disprove the legitimacy of interest by arguing that the borrower does not always profit from the loan, while the lender always profits from the interest. This argument is invalid.

XXIII. *The legitimacy of interest is a direct consequence of the ownership which the lender has in the object he lends.* The legitimacy of lending at interest arises from the inviolable right of private property. The owner of an object can do with it what he likes: he can sell it or let it. The buyer or the lessee voluntarily buys or leases it, and the price he pays will be just, as long as neither of the parties is fraudulent.] Property in money is no less absolute than that in furniture, in a piece of cloth, or in a diamond; the owner is no more bound to dispose of it gratuitously; giving it, lending it gratuitously is a laudable action inspired by generosity, sometimes demanded by charity and humanity, but which is never in the nature of strict law. A person may similarly give or lend all sorts of commodities, and he ought to do so in certain cases. Apart from these circumstances, in which charity demands sacrifices to help the unfortunate, money may be sold, and is sold, in fact, when it is placed in an annuity; it is sold for money when money in one place is given in exchange for the receipt of money in another, the type of transaction known as *foreign exchange*, in which less money is given at one place to receive more of it in another, just as, in a transaction of lending at interest, less money is given at one time in order to receive more at another, because the difference in time, like that in space, causes a real difference in the value of money.

XXIV. *The ownership of money entails the right to sell it and the right to draw a rent from it.* Since money is sold like any other possession, why should it not be let like any other possession? And since interest is only the rent of money lent for a period of time, why would it not be permissible to receive it? By what strange whim does morality or law forbid a free contract between two parties who both derive advantage therefrom? And can it be doubted that they derive such advantage since they have no other motive to decide them on it? Why would the borrower offer a rent for this money for a period of time, if during this time, the use of this money were not advantageous to him? And, if it is replied that necessity forces him to submit to these terms, is not the gratification of real need a benefit? Is this not the greatest benefit of all? It is similarly necessity which forces man to fetch bread at the baker's; does the baker have any less right to receive the price of the bread he sells?

XXV. *False ideas of the scholastics on the alleged sterility of money; false consequences they have drawn from it.* The scholastic theologians, following Aristotle, have argued that money is sterile because money does not yield money. But since only the soil and cattle yield natural fruit, have they not forgotten to include other types of personal property such as jewels, furniture, etc.? Have they not forgotten that for individuals money is equivalent to real objects, and that money in this sense is indispensable to all productive enterprises? Have they also not forgotten that those who use money in their enterprises generally draw a profit from it?

XXVI. Another reason against the legitimacy of interest: the property in money passes to the borrower at the moment of the loan, so that no charge can be made for it. This argument is derived from St. Thomas Aquinas.

XXVII. *Refutation of this reasoning.* This reasoning is only a web spun of errors and misunderstandings which are easily cleared up.

The first proposition, that, in every contract, none of the parties can, without injustice, exact more than he has given, has a true foundation; but the manner in which it is put forward entails a false meaning, which may lead to misunderstanding. In every exchange of

Lending at Interest

value against value (and every agreement, properly so called, or subject to payment, can be regarded as an exchange of this type), there is an interpretation of the word *value*, in which the value is always equal on both sides; but this is not at all through a principle of justice, it is because things cannot be otherwise. The exchange, being free on both sides, can only be motivated by the preference of each of the contracting parties for the thing he receives over the thing he gives. This preference presumes that each attributes a greater value to the thing he acquires than to the thing he gives up, relative to his individual use and to the satisfaction of his needs and desires. But this difference in value is equal on both sides; it is this equality which causes the preference to be exactly mutual, and the parties to be in agreement. It follows from this that in the eyes of a third party, the two values exchanged are exactly equal, and that, consequently, in every transaction between men, equal value is always given for equal value. But this value depends solely on the opinion of the two dealers as regards the degree of usefulness of the things exchanged for the satisfaction of their desires or their needs: it does not, in itself, have any reality which may be used as a basis for arguing that one of the parties has wronged the other.

If there are only two *dealers*, the terms of their contract are entirely arbitrary, and unless one of the two has used duress or fraud, the conditions of the exchange do not concern morality in any way. When there are several *traders*, as each is interested in not paying more to one for what another agrees to give him at a lower price, a normal value is established, by the comparison of all the offers and demands, which differs from that established in the exchange between two men only in that it is the mean of the different values which would have resulted from the chaffering of the parties in each exchange considered separately. But, this mean or normal value does not acquire any reality apart from the opinion and comparison of mutual needs; it is continually susceptible to variation, and no obligation can be derived from it to give such and such a good for such and such a price. The owner is always free to keep it, and consequently, to determine the price at which he agrees to part with it.

It is quite true that in a brisk trade, carried on by a multitude of hands, each individual buyer and seller has so little influence on the formation of this general opinion and on the current evaluation which results therefrom, that this evaluation may be regarded as an independent phenomenon. In this sense, common practice permits this normal value to be called the true value of the thing; but since this expression, convenient rather than precise, cannot impair in any way the absolute right which ownership confers to the seller over his merchandise and to the buyer over his money, it cannot be concluded that this value may serve as a basis for any moral rule; and it remains strictly true that the conditions of any exchange cannot be unjust except to the extent that duress and fraud have influenced them.

If a young stranger is overcharged in a purchase, the injustice arises from the fact that the trader has taken advantage of his ignorance of the normal value. This transaction is not unjust because the trader has charged more than an "intrinsic value," since the normal value is not intrinsic in any way. The transaction is unjust because it involved a form of fraud.

The conclusion to be drawn from this explanation is that, in every exchange, in every agreement which is based on two reciprocal terms, injustice can only be based on duress, fraud, dishonesty, the abuse of confidence, and never on an alleged metaphysical inequality between the thing sold and its price.

The second proposition in the reasoning which I am attacking is based once more on the gross misunderstanding and on an assumption which is precisely the one in question. "What the lender demands," it is said, "over and above the principal, is something he receives in excess of what he has given, since by receiving the principal alone he receives the exact equivalent of what he has given." It is true that in repaying the principal, the borrower returns exactly the same weight of metal which the lender had given him. But where have our logicians observed that in a loan it is only necessary to consider the weight of the metal lent and repaid, and not the value and the usefulness it has for the lender and the borrower? Where have they observed that to determine this value, it is only necessary to consider the weights of the metal handed over at two different dates, without comparing the difference in usefulness which exists at the date of borrowing between a sum currently owned and an equal sum which is to be received at a distant date? Is not the difference well known, and is not the trivial proverb, *a bird in the hand is better than two in the bush*, a naive expression of this well-known fact? Now if a sum actually owned is worth more, is more useful, is preferable to the assurance of receiving a similar sum in one or several years' time, it is not true that the lender receives as much as he gives when he does not stipulate interest, for he gives the money and receives only an assurance. Now, if he receives less, why should this difference not be compensated by the assurance of an increase in the sum proportioned to the delay? This compensation is precisely the rate of interest.

The distinction often made in discussions about the legitimacy of interest between an object hired and consumed during use, and an object which is not consumed during hire, is also invalid. In hiring an object which is not consumed, such as a diamond, usefulness is obtained which must be paid for.

But, it is replied, this usefulness does not have to be paid for, since it is transferred together with the ownership during the period of hire.

Again, an unfortunate misunderstanding. It is true that the borrower becomes the owner of the money considered physically, as a certain quantity of metal. But is he really the owner of the value of the money? Certainly not, since this value is only confided to him for a time, to be repaid on the expiration of the contract. But, without entering into this discussion which amounts to a real quibble about words, what can be concluded from my alleged ownership of the money? Do I not obtain this ownership from the person who has lent me the money? Is it not by his consent that I have obtained it, and have the conditions of this consent not been settled between him and myself? That is so, the use which I make of this money will be the use of my property, the usefulness which it yields me is an accessory to my ownership. All this will be true, but when? When the money is mine, when this ownership has been transferred to me; and when will this be so? When I have bought it, and paid for it. Now, at what price do I buy this ownership? What do I give in exchange? Is it not clear that it is my commitment to return on a certain date a certain sum, whatever it may be? Is it not also quite clear that in order to determine this equivalent in such a way that our gain will be equal on both sides, we must take account of the usefulness which this ownership I will acquire, but which I do not yet have, will yield me, and the usefulness which this ownership could yield to the lender during the time he is deprived of it? If you like, the reasoning of the legal experts will prove that I do not have to pay for the use of a thing when I already have acquired ownership of it; but it does not prove that I could not, when deciding to acquire this ownership, fix the price in consideration of this use which is attached to the ownership. In short, the object still assumes that which is in question, that is, that the money received today and the money which must be repaid in a year's time are exactly equal. In reasoning in this manner, it is forgotten that it is not the value of the money when it has been repaid that has to be compared with the value of the money when it is lent, but that it is the value of the promise of a sum of money which has to be compared with the value of a sum of money available now. The assumption is that it is the money paid back which is, in a loan contract, the equivalent of the money lent, and this assumption is absurd, for it is at the time of the contract that the respective conditions must be considered, and it is at this time that equality has to be established between them. Now, at the time of lending there certainly only exist a sum of money on the one hand, and a promise on the other. If it is assumed that a thousand francs and a promise of a thousand francs are exactly of the same value, an even more absurd assumption is made; if these two things are equivalent, why do people borrow?

It is very curious that the principle of the equality of values which must be present in agreements is the starting point for the establishment of a theory according to which the whole of the gain is for one of the parties, and none of it for the other. Surely, nothing is more tangible; for, when at the end of a few years, a sum of money is returned to me which I had lent without interest, it is very clear that I have gained nothing and that, after having been deprived of its use and having risked its loss, I have precisely only what I would have had if I had kept it in my coffers during that time. It is just as clear that the borrower has benefited from this money, since he had no other motive for borrowing than this; I would therefore have given something for nothing, I would have been generous; but if, in my generosity, I gave something real, I accordingly could have sold it without being unjust.

It is doing unwarranted honor to sophistries like those attacked, to discuss them at such length, but then, they are backed with the authority of education and of the church.

XXVIII. *Examination and refutation of arguments drawn from Scripture against the legitimacy of interest.* The mistaken arguments discussed above partly derive from misinterpretations of passages from the Scriptures: namely, the saying of Jesus in Luke, chapter VI, verse 35, and some passages of the Mosaic Law from the *Old Testament*. These passages are irrelevant to the problem.

XXIX. *True origin of the opinions condemning interest.* The condemnation of interest arose from the fact that in non-commercial societies, the major class of borrowers was that which borrowed for consumption purposes. In some of these cases, it would have been a charitable act to lend without charging interest. In these societies, the risks of the lender were also greater, which drove interest to exorbitant heights. (In ancient Rome, 12 per cent was considered to be a moderate rate.) Because of high interest rates and the predominance of consumption loans at that time, the Church fathers took such a rigid view of this subject; but this is now completely outdated.

XXX. *Lessening of the causes which made lending at interest odious to the nations.* The causes, which formerly made lending at interest odious, have ceased to operate with as much force. Since slavery has been abolished among us, insolvency has less cruel consequences; it no longer entails capital punishment or the loss of freedom. Imprisonment (for debt), which we have retained, is in truth a hard and cruel law for the poor; but its harshness has at least been mitigated by many restrictions and limited to a certain type of debt. The suppression of slavery has given an activity to the arts unknown to ancient peoples, among whom each well-to-do individual used to let his slaves manufacture at home nearly everything he needed. Today, the practice of the mechanical arts is an expedient open to every working man. This multitude of works, and the advances they necessarily require, offer profitable employment to money on all sides; the infinitely increasing enterprises of commerce use immense capitals. The poor, who are reduced to absolute misery by their inability to work, find aid in the superfluity of the wealthy and the various charities, which does not appear to have existed among the people of antiquity, and which, indeed, was less necessary there, since in the constitution of societies, the poor, when reduced to the final degree of destitution would naturally fall into slavery. On the other hand, the vastness of the capitals accumulated from century to century by that spirit of thrift which is inseparable from commerce, swollen especially by the abundance of treasure brought from America, has, throughout Europe; caused the rate of interest to fall. All these circumstances together have caused that the borrowing for subsistence by the poor is no more than a fraction of the total of loans; that the majority of loans are made to the rich, or at least to industrious men who hope to obtain large profits from the use of the money they borrow. Consequently, lending at interest inevitably became less odious, since, through commercial activity, it has, on the contrary become a source of profit to the borrower. It has become common in all commercial towns to the extent that the magistrates, and even theologians, have come to tolerate it. The condemnation of lending in itself, or of interest exacted without the alienation of capital, has become a form of speculation left to dogmatic theologians, and in practice, all commercial and financial ventures depend on lending at interest without the alienation of capital.

XXXI. *The stigma attached to the name of usurer is now limited to a few types of usury*. The name of usurer is now reserved for the small money lender who lends to the poor and unfortunate on a weekly basis, and who charges exorbitant rates of interest.

XXXII. *The usurers whose occupation is to lend to the poor are really harmful to society*. The usurers who lend to the poor are harmful to society, not because they charge interest, but because they take advantage of the pressing needs of others by charging excessive rates. It is because of this that they should be punished.

XXXIII. *The prohibition of usury is not at all the solution to this particular problem.*

XXXIV. *Consequences of what has been said on the true causes for the disrepute of lending at interest, and on the changes which have occurred in public opinion in this regard.* The changes in society discussed above have made the general prohibition of interest archaic practice. Only usury proper must be forbidden.

XXXV. *General consequence: no ground for the prohibition of lending at interest.*

XXXVI. *Interest is the price of money in commerce, and this price must be left to the course of events, to the competition of commerce.* If the natural order is adhered to, money must be regarded as a commodity which the owner has the right to sell or let; consequently, the law should not demand the alienation of capital in order to allow the stipulation of interest. There is no more reason for the law to fix the rate of this interest. This rate must be determined, like the price of all things in trade, by the chaffering between the dealers and by the relationship between offer and demand. There is no commodity for which the most enlightened, the most meticulously careful, and the most accurate administration can take the responsibility of balancing all the circumstances which must influence the determination of the price, and of setting one which is disadvantageous to neither the seller nor the buyer. Now, the rate of interest is even more difficult to determine than the price of any other kind of commodity, because this rate depends on even more critical and variable circumstances and considerations; that of the time at which the loan is made, that of the date stipulated for its repayment, and above all, that of the risk or the judgment of the risk which the capital is bound to run. This judgment varies continually: a momentary alarm, the occurrence of some bankruptcies, rumors of war, may spread a general concern, which suddenly makes all monetary transaction dearer. The judgment and the reality of the risk vary even more from one man to another, and increase or diminish in every possible degree; therefore, there ought to be as many variations in the rate of interest. A commodity has the same price for everybody, because everybody pays for it with the same money, and commodities in general use, whose production and consumption naturally adjust to each other, have more or less the same price for a long time. But money on loan does not have the same price, either for all men or at all times, because in lending, money is paid for with a *promise* only, and because, if the money of all buyers looks the same, the promises of all the borrowers are not the same. To fix the rate of interest by law, is to deprive someone who cannot offer security proportioned to the lowness of the legal rate of the expedient of borrowing; it is, consequently, to make a multitude of commercial enterprises, which cannot be carried out without risking capital, impossible.

XXXVII. The only justification for setting a legal rate is to give judges a rule by which to determine whether a loan is usurious or not. Due to the various circumstances which influence particular loan contracts, and the price charged for them, this is impossible.

XXXVIII. *Advantages which will arise for commerce and for society in general from a law which conforms completely to the principles which have been developed here.* The trade in money should be free, as all trade ought to be. The result of this freedom would be competition, and the effect of this competition would be a low rate of interest: not only because the shame and risks attached to lending at interest are a surcharge which the borrower always pays, just as the buyer of prohibited commodities always pays for the risks of the smuggler, but even more, because a very large quantity of money which lies idle in chests, would enter the circulation when prejudice, no longer consolidated by the authority of law, would slowly give way to reason. Thrift would become all the stronger in accumulating capitals, when the money trade is an outlet which is always open to money. Today, loans can only be placed in large quantities. An artisan is inconvenienced by his small savings; they are sterile for him until they become large enough to be placed on loan. He must keep them, always exposed to the temptation of dissipating them in taverns. If the trade in money were to acquire the degree of activity which would result from complete freedom and the destruction of prejudice, money merchants would start business, and gather small sums; in the towns and in the country they would collect the savings of the working people, to turn them into capitals and to supply them to commercial centers, just as, from village to village, right up to the heart of Normandy, merchants are seen gathering butter and eggs which are produced there, in order to sell them in Paris. This facility of allowing their savings to bear fruit, open to the people, would be for them a most powerful encouragement to thrift and sobriety, and would offer them the only possible means of preventing the misery into which they are thrown by the smallest mishap, by sickness, or, in any case, by old age.

Sections XXXIX–LIII. Concluding remarks. If this proposed change in the law appears to be too sudden, the change could be more gradually introduced. Some proceedings against usurers, for instance, could still be started. A change in the law however, would prevent occurrences like those described at Angoulême happening in the whole of France, and it would therefore safeguard the needs of trade.

The magistrates, moreover, would not have to admit the charges made at Angoulême. In the new legislation, the type of money lender ought to be immaterial, while a rate of interest greater than 6 per cent should not be taken as an excuse to start criminal proceedings. Unfortunately, the officers of justice at Angoulême do not hold these principles, so that the Intendant and the Contrôleur-général will have to interfere. The Royal Council would probably be the best tribunal to settle the matter. It could appoint a special commission to investigate. However, the following ought in any case to be done. The originators of the trouble at Angoulême should be punished for the disruption to commerce which they caused; and a proposal made by the judges in the case should also be examined. They suggested the appointment of a special officer who would investigate this type of case, and who would be able to fix the proper rate of interest. This type of proposal, as has been fully discussed above, has many disadvantages. Final conclusion: In the opinion of the author, the matter should be taken from the hands of the local judges and placed in the hands of a special commission appointed by the Royal Council.]

Written in Limoges, 27 January, 1770.

Extracts from "Letters to the Contrôleur-général on the Grain Trade"

In several letters, Turgot opposes restrictions on the grain trade. He replies to the argument that free trade in grain will help only the proprietors of land, not cultivators of land or consumers. In response, Turgot notes that gains to the proprietors will help cultivators and consumers, since the proprietors will have more money to make purchases, It is not true that free trade will lead to an increase in the price of grain: to the contrary, increased production is likely to lower prices. If it is argued that any gains to cultivators will be passed on to the proprietors, Turgot answers that this will not immediately be the case. In the time that it takes for rents to be readjusted, the cultivators will gain. Turgot reiterates his view that all taxes are ultimately paid by owners of land.

CHAPTER 11

Extracts from "Letters to the Contrôleur-général on the Grain Trade"

FIRST LETTER

Limoges, 30 October

[The first letter is more or less a preamble to what is to follow. Turgot's argument in it can be summarized as follows: I have promised to write you on the advantages of the free trade in grain, and propose to deal with this subject in a considerable amount of detail. You have not given me enough time to reply to your request for advice on this subject, since it deserves to be treated at book length and time is too pressing. However, you owe it to the public, to the King, and to yourself as minister, to treat this matter carefully, since it has repercussions on the whole country and not just on agriculture. The problem is also controversial; on the one hand, *the economists* have supported freedom of the grain trade; while on the other, many reputable writers have opposed this policy.]

Turgot's letters to Abbé Terray, who was then Contrôleur-Général, on the subject of the grain trade, which were written at the end of 1770, have been considered to be one of his more important pieces of economic work. Of the seven letters originally written, only four have survived, since Turgot was unable to have copies made of the second, third and fourth letters. They were all written while Turgot was on a tour of inspection of his district, and therefore show signs of haste. Since the letters are long, only selections with theoretical interest have been translated. To give some continuity to the text, part of Turgot's argument has been summarized. These summaries have been placed in square brackets in the text.

SECOND, THIRD, AND FOURTH LETTERS

Tulle, 8 November; Egletons, 10 November; Bort, 13 November

[These letters have unfortunately been lost, and only du Pont's summaries have been preserved. These are reproduced by Daire and Schelle, but will not be summarized here. The second letter deals with the "interests of the cultivator," the third with the possibility of establishing grain stores, and the fourth with a statistical analysis of the average price of grain, and some further conclusions on grain stores.]

FIFTH LETTER

Saint-Angel, 14 November

Sir, at the end of the letter which I had the honor of writing you from Bort yesterday on the freedom of the grain trade, I promised you a fifth letter, intended to discuss the arguments with which you presented me at Compiègne, and with which you then appeared to be greatly taken.

"Three types of people," you said, "are interested in the selection of a plan for the policy of grain: the proprietors of landed estates, the cultivators, and the consumers.

I agree that the system of freedom is immensely favorable to the proprietors.

In connection with the cultivators, the advantage of such a system for them is purely a temporary one, since on the expiration of the leases, the proprietors are well versed in appropriating the whole of this advantage for themselves by increasing their rents.

Finally, the consumers obviously suffer the greatest harm from the freedom, which raises the prices to a level which no longer has any relation to their means of subsistence, and which increases all their expenses."

You even added on that occasion "that, in the last few years, it had cost the King several million for the excess value of bread which it was necessary to grant the troops."

You concluded from this that "the policy of freedom was favourable only to a very small number of subjects; that it is immaterial to the cultivators, and that it is most harmful by far to the greatest number of the King's subjects."

I do not think I am mistaken in the exposition of your arguments; allow me now, sir, to take up its three aspects in succession.

You agree, first of all, that *the policy of freedom is very advantageous to the proprietors, whose revenues it increases*. We are certainly very much in agreement on this conclusion; but I doubt whether we are as much in agreement on the principles from which we derive it, and, as these principles are very important, I will stop to discuss them.

First of all, however, I want to point out all the advantages you granted me by admitting that the policy of freedom increases the revenue of the proprietors.

This revenue, sir, is the security for all the mortgaged income from landed property.

It is the source of the greater part of the wages, which enable the people to live, for the people, the day-laborer, the artisan, have nothing by themselves; they live on the produce of the soil; they obtain this produce only by buying it with their labor, and can buy it only from those who gather it and who pay them for their work with that produce or with the money which represents it. It is therefore the sum of subsistence goods or rather, the mass of values produced annually by the soil which forms the fund of the wages for distribution to all classes of society. The cultivator immediately consumes what is necessary for his subsistence; the rest is divided between him and the proprietor; and both, by their expenses, whether these have as objective the continuation or the improvement of cultivation, or whether they are limited to the satisfaction of their needs, distribute this remainder in wages to all the other members of society as the price of their labor. The values which the latter have received return to the hands of the cultivators through the purchases of commodities they consume, to leave them again by a circulation the continuity of which is essential to the life of the body politic, just as the circulation of the blood is essential to the life of the animal body. Anything that increases the sum of values produced by the soil increases, therefore, the sum of wages to be distributed among the other classes of society.

Finally sir, the revenues of the proprietors are the only source from which the State can draw its revenue. No matter in what manner the taxes are levied, and in what form they are collected, in the final analysis they are always paid by the proprietors of landed estates, either through the increase of their expenses, or through the decrease of their receipts.

The self-evidence of this truth is very easily shown, for it is quite clear that every tax imposed on consumption will be paid forthwith, in part by the proprietors, in part by the cultivators, in part by the stipendiary class, since these three classes consume and since every consumer is included in one of these three classes.

There is no problem with respect to the portion which the proprietor pays on his own consumption.

The part paid by the cultivator is evidently an increase in the costs of cultivation, since these costs consist of the whole of the cultivator's expenditure, they must return to him every year, with a profit, in order that he may be able to continue his cultivation, and he must necessarily deduct the whole of these costs from the products before determining the portion of the proprietor, or *the rent*, which is reduced accordingly. The proprietor therefore still pays this portion of the tax through the reduction of the revenue.

The part which the wage earners pay on their consumption thus remains; but it is very clear that if the competition of workmen on the one hand, and those who spend, on the other, had fixed the daily wage at 10 *sous*, and the wage earner lived on those 10 *sous* (it is well known that the wage of a man who has only his arms is ordinarily reduced to what is necessary for the subsistence of himself and his family); if, I say, it is then assumed that a new tax on his consumption increases his expenses by 2 *sous*, it is necessary that his day's work be paid more dearly, or that he reduce his consumption. It is obvious that if he is paid more for his day's work, this is at the expense of the proprietor or the cultivator, since they alone have the wherewithal to pay, and when it is the cultivator who pays, it is still at the expense of the proprietor, as I have shown above; but the less well off the laborer, the less domineering he can be, and the proprietor will at first not give in easily to the increase in wages. It will be necessary for the wage earner to reduce his consumption and to suffer. Now, this decrease in consumption will diminish the demand for commodities in proportion, and in the final analysis, always that for subsistence goods. These goods, consequently, will decrease in value; now, this decrease in value, on whom does it fall? On the seller of the commodity, on the cultivator, who, deriving less from his cultivation, will give proportionately less to his proprietor in rent. The latter therefore pays all in every case.

In reality, this forced reduction in the consumption of the day laborer could not be permanent, because it puts him in a state of penury. Before the tax, wages were on a level with the customary price of commodities, and this level, which is the result of a multitude of causes combined and balanced with each other, must tend to re-establish itself. It is certain that competition, by causing wages to be at a lower level, reduce those of the simple unskilled workers to what is necessary to their subsistence. It should not be thought, however, that this necessity is thus reduced to the essentials for avoiding starvation to such an extent, that nothing remains outside it, which these men may have at their command either to obtain some little luxuries, or, if they are thrifty, to create a little movable fund which becomes their resort in unforeseen cases of sickness, or times of high prices, or unemployment. When the objects of their expenditure increase in price, they first begin to cut down on this little superfluity and the enjoyments it can procure for them. But it is of this type of *luxury* especially, that it can be said that it is *a most necessary thing*; it is essential that there is a little of it, just as it is necessary that there is *some play* in every machine. A watch of which all the wheels would work into each other with mathematical precision and without the smallest gap, would soon cease to go. If by an unexpected decrease in wages or increase in expenses, the worker can put up with being reduced to strict essentials, the same causes which had forced wages to rise a little above the necessary of yesterday, continue to operate and cause them to rise once more until they attain a higher level, in the same proportion with the necessary of today. If an absence of the ability to pay stands in the way of this return to the natural proportion, if the decrease of the revenue of the proprietors persuaded them to resist this increase in wages, the worker would go elsewhere to look for the competency without which he cannot exist; population would diminish up to the point where the decrease in the number of workers, by curtailing their competition, enables them to lay down the law and to force the proprietors to raise wages. I admit, if the lowness of the price of produce caused by the decrease in consumption continued, the increase in wages would be less considerable; but this lowness of the price of commodities having diminished the profits of the cultivator, would force him to diminish his productive expenditure, and consequently, production: now, from the smaller production an increase in price must result. If each of these effects occurred to the fullest extent, the loss resulting from the new tax would fall on the proprietors in several different ways, since he would have less revenue and would not be able to obtain the same objects of enjoyment with the same revenue, which would cause a double loss. But there is reason to believe that the one compensates the other, without it being possible to determine just how they compensate, and if they balance completely. In whatever way this compensation occurs, and even supposing it to be complete, it follows at least that the proprietor always bears the whole of the new tax, either in the increase of his expenses, or in the decrease in his revenue.

The question of who pays import duties must also be considered. In a large State, foreign trade is small as compared with domestic trade, because objects of foreign trade are usually luxuries. There are some exceptions to this, like the trade with the American colonies, which is a trade in necessities. The only enduring type of trade is that trade where imports and exports balance in the long run, and where the balance of trade is therefore small compared with the volume of trade. In such trade, import duties will reduce the volume of trade and raise the price of imported commodities, which increase is ultimately borne by the revenue of the proprietors.

Be that as it may, the principle that the whole of the tax is paid by the proprietors and from the revenue of the soil, must be regarded as unchangeable. And it is very essential that the revenue of the soil, that is, the part of the produce which remains after the deduction of the expenses of cultivation, the wages and profit of the cultivator, pays the whole of the tax; for everything else, whether produce from the soil, or profit of any type whatsoever, is destined for the reproduction and the continuation of work of every kind, on which the whole edifice of society depends. In the world, there is only land and human labor: it is by labor that the land produces; it is the produce of the soil which pays the wages of labor, and, generally, all the labor which is required in the service of society, and which occupies the different classes of men.

From the produce of the soil, the cultivator must first deduct his subsistence, and that of his family, since this is the indispensable wage of his labor, and the motive which induces him to cultivate; next, the interest on his advances, and this interest must be sufficiently high for him to discover an appreciable advantage in placing his capitals in agricultural enterprises, rather than in any other form. Without these two conditions, agriculture would lack advances, and advances are no less necessary there than human labor. The cultivator must also appropriate the wherewithal to meet all the expenses which the continuation of his cultivation requires, for without these expenses, the reproduction of the following year would cease.

This then is the share of the cultivator; it is inviolable, and tyranny could encroach upon it only at the risk of stopping the reproduction, and of damaging the source of taxation. In vain the cultivator is taxed personally; he must either be able to pass on the tax to the proprietor, or reduce his cultivation.

The surplus produce, that which remains after the portion of the cultivator has been deducted, is the *net product* or the revenue of the soil. It is this net product which the cultivator is able to hand over, and which indeed he does hand over to the proprietor in order to obtain permission from him to cultivate. It is also from this net product, at the expense of the revenue of the proprietor, that all the charges on the land are taken: the tithe of the Clergy, the rent of the lord, and the tax levied on behalf of the King. And it is very essential that all this is taken from the net product, for only this net product is disposable; only this portion of the fruits of the earth is not absolutely necessary for the reproduction of the following year. The remainder is the share of the cultivator, an inviolable share as has been said, which cannot be encroached upon without stopping all activity in the political system.

All the *wages* of the workmen, all the *profits* of the entrepreneurs in every type of manufacture and trade, are paid, partly by the cultivator, namely, for the expenditure required by the satisfaction of their needs, or by the work of their cultivation; partly by the proprietors and the other partakers of the net product, such as the clergy, the fund holder, the sovereign, for the expenses they pay from this net product to obtain all the objects of pleasure, or usefulness, whether individual or public. All these wages, all these profits, are no more disposable than the share of the cultivators in the fruits of the earth; competition necessarily limits them to what is essential for the subsistence of the simple working man, to that interest on the advances of all manufacturing and commercial enterprises, and to that indispensable profit of the entrepreneurs, without which they would prefer other uses of their money, which would entail neither the same risk nor the same effort. I have demonstrated above how the whole part of the tax which, it might be imagined, they could be made to pay, would, in the final analysis, always fall on the proprietor alone.

This digression is longer than I had intended, but the importance of the revenue to the kingdom had to be demonstrated to you. I will now return to the major objective of this letter, that is, the discussion of the three points put forward by you.

Your arguments rest on your erroneous assumption that the effect of the policy of freedom will be *dearer* grain. This is not necessarily true, as the statistics of average grain prices show. The assumption, so often put forward, that a large part of the harvest will be exported when the policy of free trade is adopted, similarly does not necessarily follow. The English, in spite of their encouragement of exports, do not export a great deal of grain.

There are, on the contrary, some very strong reasons to believe that the average price will fall. I have pointed out above that the price is determined by a comparison between demand and total production. It must therefore fall when total production increases at a faster rate than total requirements. Now, this increase in production is more than likely. If the extension of cultivation is a consequence of the increase in the profits of the cultivator, as soon as the earth produces more, it must follow, at least until the number of consumers is increased, that the commodity falls in price. This fall is assured as long as it does not conflict with the profit of the cultivator.

Recall, sir, what I had the honor to explain at length in my letter written Thursday last from Tulle, on the difference between the average price to the producer and the average price to the consumer. I think I showed there that the mere equalization of the prices, true aim and unfailing effect of the policy of freedom, without raising the price for the consumer to any extent, and simply by bringing this price together with that of the producer-seller, assures the latter of a tremendous profit. This profit is sufficiently large for much of it still to remain even when it decreases a little by the lowering of the price to the advantage of the consumer. Now, if there is still some profit for the cultivators when the price falls, the competition among the cultivators will cause it to fall. Perhaps, subsequently, the increase in the revenues, by increasing the sum total of wages, will cause an increase in demand; those who used to eat only buck wheat porridge will then eat bread; those who used to be limited to rye bread will add some wheat. The increase in public affluence will increase the population and by this increase in wants a slender increase in price will be generated; fresh encouragement to cultivation which, through the increase in production, will again cause its value to fall. It is by these alternating, small fluctuations in price that the whole nation will slowly progress to the highest state of cultivation, affluence and population which it is able to enjoy relative to the size of its territory. The revenues and the public wealth will increase without involving an increase in the average price for the consumer; this price may even fall a little.

All this can be shown from the experience of free trade at various points of time both in France and England, and by a comparison between England and France at the present time. These statistics prove that freedom of the grain trade will not necessarily increase the average price of grain.

SIXTH LETTER

Angoulême, 27 November

In my last letter I stated that I would answer your three points on the benefits for the three classes which are affected by a policy of free trade in grain. I have already discussed the interest of the proprietors and now turn to that of the cultivators who, contrary to your assumption, would not be indifferent to it. The reason you gave for this assumption is that their gains are short lived, and that they will lose them on the renewal of their leases. Even if we assume that this is the case, there is still a great deal of advantage in the temporary increase in the wealth of the farmers.

Now, this increase in wealth for the class of farmer-cultivators represents a tremendous benefit for them and for the State. If it is assumed that the real increase in the produce of the land is one sixth of the rents, which is not far from the truth, and probably an underestimate, this sixth, accumulated over six years to the profit of the cultivators, forms for them a capital equal to the revenue of the rented lands. I say a capital, for the profits of the cultivators are not squandered on luxuries. If it is assumed that they place it in the national debt, in order to draw interest from it, this would certainly be a net profit for them, and it cannot be denied that they will be the richer for it: but they are not so stupid, and they have a much more lucrative use for their funds. This use is to pour them back into their agricultural enterprises, to increase the sum total of their advances with them, to buy cattle and agricultural implements, to increase all kinds of manures and fertilizers, and to plant and marl the estates, if they can obtain a second lease on these terms from their proprietors.

Letters on the Grain Trade

All these advances have as their immediate objective to increase the amount of produce, to the benefit of the entire State, and to give the cultivators an annual profit. It is essential that this profit is greater than the ordinary interest of loan money, for otherwise, the owner of the capital would prefer to lend it. It is also necessary that this profit is kept completely for the farmer-cultivator, without him yielding the least part to the proprietor: for if this profit was not entirely for the farmer, he would prefer to invest his money in another manner, so as not to share the interest with anyone else. Here then a permanent increase in wealth, to the advantage of the cultivators, equal at least to the interest of the annual revenue of all the leases, converted into capital. This is surely a great deal.

This item is altogether unrelated to the increase in the leases which causes the gain for the proprietor; it only makes the revenue more secure by further assuring the solvency of the farmer.

But this is not all; this capital and this interest, firmly assured to the farmer-cultivator, and steadfastly used by him to swell the advances of cultivation, must, following the present course of events, increase the produce in a much greater proportion than the interest of these new advances. Undoubtedly, the cultivator will in time agree to yield the proprietor his share in this increase in profit; but this will always happen only after he has wholly benefited from it himself up to the time of expiry of the lease: the argument I have put forward as regards the initial profit resulting directly from the policy of freedom is applicable to the second profit, and also to that resulting from this second increase in wealth. Hence, there results a progressive increase in the wealth of the cultivators, in the advances in agriculture, in the total produce and the values gathered annually from the soil. This progression may be fast or slow: but if the outlets continually raise sales, either by regular exportation, or by an increase in population, it will have no other limit than the physical one of the fertility of the soil.

This happy picture must be contrasted with the unhappy results of the curtailing of the freedom of the grain trade. In this case, the value of the produce of the soil will decline, and the cultivators will be impoverished.]

You have also argued that on the expiration of the leases, the proprietors appropriate all the profit of the farmers. This assumption is a lot further from the truth than you suppose. It is, of course, essential that the proprietors can appropriate the whole of the net product over and above the necessary advances of cultivation, but the tenant has the interest of these advances for the further accumulation of new capitals. The proprietors cannot risk appropriating either the advances or the interest on these advances, for that would cause the decline of cultivation and produce. It is true, however, that at the end of the lease, competition will ensure that the new rent is equal to the net product of cultivation, after all costs have been met.]

No sir, it is not at all in this sense that it must be, or has been, said, that the freedom of the grain trade is of tremendous benefit to the cultivators. The situation of the cultivators taken individually must be improved by it; but this result is but a trifle compared to the immense advantage which must result from it for cultivation in general, through the growth of the capitals used for drawing the produce from the soil, and from the increase in the number of cultivators.

I must insist on this observation, because it attacks directly the major flaw in the arguments which you have permitted me to criticize. As soon as the raising of rents has as its sole cause the competition among a great number of agricultural entrepreneurs, when each of them, individually, would not gain any more, would not draw a better share than previously from his capital and labor, it would still remain true that the number of laborers and agricultural entrepreneurs would be greater, that the sum of capitals employed in agriculture, and consequently the produce, would be greatly increased. Now, that is what really interests the State as a whole.

The benefits of large advances in agriculture are seen in the provinces of Flanders, Picardy, Normandy, etc., where the land is exploited by wealthy tenant farmers who can afford to pay large rents. If these farmers were deprived of a market, or if their market were diminished, their enterprises would decline, and the prosperity would disappear from these districts.

In the poorer provinces, land has a much smaller value. This is not caused by the different fertility of the soil; it is caused by the less capital intensive cultivation. It is to be hoped that all provinces will follow the more capital intensive methods in the future, to the ultimate benefit of the whole of the State. On the calculation of M. Dupré de Saint-Maur, these poor provinces are more than four sevenths of the whole nation. Freedom of the grain trade should greatly diminish this proportion.

Do not believe, sir, that this will be harmful to the consumers. In my next letter, I will deal with the interest of this class of people in the policy of a free trade in grain.

SEVENTH LETTER

Limoges, 2 December

Sir, in my last letters, written from Saint-Angel and from Angoulême, I dealt with the interest of the *proprietors* and that of the cultivators in the freedom of the grain trade. To complete the reply to your objections against this freedom, I have to discuss the interest of the *consumers*, whom you believe to be injured by the suppression of the constraints of the old regulations.

As for me, sir, I together with many others, am thoroughly convinced that the policy of freedom is no less advantageous, and that it is even more necessary, for the consumers than it is for the cultivators and the proprietors. I even dare to feel sure I can convince you of this, if you will be so good as to consider my arguments carefully.

Two things are necessary for the livelihood of the consumer: firstly, the existence of the produce; secondly, that it is within his reach, and that he has sufficient means to obtain it. How then could his interest be opposed to that of the cultivator and the proprietor of the land, since it is from them that he receives both the produce and the wage with which to purchase the produce?

Consumption first of all implies production: thus, the livelihood of men is no less based on cultivation than is the revenue of the soil. Now cultivation only takes place because it is profitable to cultivate, and if the cessation of that profit destroys the revenue, it also destroys cultivation and the livelihood of men.

The profits of the cultivator, divided between him and the proprietor, form, through the expenses they pay from them to procure the different objects of their wants, the unique wages-fund of all the other classes of society. These wages are the price of labor and of industry, but labor and industry have only as much value as there is the wherewithal to pay for them, that is, as much as agriculture has generated in consumable produce suitable for the enjoyment of man, over and above what is necessary for the subsistence of the cultivator; the consumer there is doubly dependent on agriculture; he has a double interest in its prosperity, both in order that his livelihood exists, and in order that he, as a consumer, has the means to buy it by selling his labor. He has an interest in selling his labor at a price high enough to enable him to pay for the commodities he needs with the price he receives for it, and he must pay for these commodities at a price high enough for those who sell them to draw from this price the means to generate an equal quantity of produce in the following year, as well as the means to continue to buy his labor. Without this exact proportion, either the cultivator would cease to make the earth produce commodities and revenue, or the wage earner would cease to labor, or rather, these two things would occur at the same time, because cultivator and wage-earner, wages and labor, being necessarily correlated, and equally dependent on one another, must either exist, or be destroyed, together. Consequently, if this proportion did not exist, population would diminish and society would destroy itself. Let us not forget to observe that this reduction in the number of men would begin with the class of consuming wage-earners. If less subsistence is produced, someone must starve, and that will not be the cultivator, for before sharing his harvest with anyone else, he begins by taking what he needs himself. If there is only enough grain for himself, he will not give any of it to his shoemaker to pay for a pair of shoes: he will go barefoot and survive. If the production decreases to the point where it yields only just the necessary subsistence for the cultivator, the last grain of corn will be for him, and the proprietor will be forced to cultivate for himself to avoid starvation.

It can, therefore, be said that in a sense the consumer is more interested in the extension of cultivation than the cultivator and the proprietor. For the latter two, the question is only that of being more or less wealthy, of living more or less comfortably; but for the wage-earning consumer, existence is at stake; it is a matter of life or death.

If every man consumes three *setiers* of corn or other equivalent subsistence, as many men must be deducted as the number of times three *setiers* of corn are taken from the annual production. And these men who are deducted will be taken from the class of the wage-earning consumers, or, as they are called, the *laboring poor*.

For the existence of society it is essential that the necessary proportion between the price of commodities and the price of labor exists normally. But this proportion does not consist of a point so precise and indivisible that it cannot vary and gradually move away from the equilibrium which is most just and advantageous for the two classes. In that case, either one or the other suffers more or less, and both of them a little. Between health and death there is the middle state of sickness; there are even a thousand degrees of weakness between sickness and health. The proportion can be disturbed for shorter or longer intervals in such a way that a great number of men experience all the excess of misery, and that societies are in a state either of crisis and convulsion or weariness and decline. What ought to be desired? Two things: firstly, that this proportion between the price of wages and the price of commodities is the fairest, the closest to equilibrium, the most advantageous possible for the cultivators and the proprietor on the one hand, and the wage-earner on the other; the most suitable, in short, to procure for the whole of society the greatest amount of production, of enjoyment, of wealth and of strength; secondly, that the disturbances occasioned by natural causes are as rare, as short-lived, and as light as possible.

There, sir, is the true end of legislation on the matter of subsistence. All that is required now is to examine what means lead to this end in the best way, whether freedom, or prohibitions and regulations. I venture to say that this way of stating the nature of the question decides it, for the right price and the constant price both result necessarily from free trade, and can only result from free trade. I will not develop this idea any further here as it would lead me too far afield, and would cause me to digress from the particular aim of this letter. It is sufficient to have indicated at the outset the source of the wages of the consumer, and the manner in which his interest is linked with that of agriculture. I will now turn to an enumeration of the advantages which the consumers must derive from the free trade in subsistence goods.

The consumers certainly gain from the increase and improvement in cultivation which is caused by the policy of free trade. They also gain from the increase in produce brought to market as a result of free trade, because this raises the value of grain by extending the market, and makes the long term storage of grain more profitable, thereby preventing the use of grain for alternative employments.]

There are two methods of restoring prices to their level, despite the un-evenness of harvests. The one consists in transporting grain from provinces where the harvest is good to those where it is bad; the other is to store it up in abundant years for use in famine years. These two methods entail costs, and free trade will always choose that which, all told, entails the least cost. Barring special circumstances, this is usually transportation, since, on the one hand, the return of the funds is speedier, and, on the other, the waste product is less considerable, the grain being consumed the sooner. But if the government, by placing obstacles in the way of transportation, leaves no other alternative than storage, it is evident that it increases the share of the rats and weevils to no purpose; it increases it even more by prohibiting storage by the merchants, who, having no other occupation nor any other interest than to preserve their grain, are a great deal more attentive and skilled in this than the farmers, whose true occupation is to grow it, and who need all their attention for this.

There are several ways of overcoming these difficulties in the storing of grain; they have been described and practiced on previous occasions by people concerned with this matter. But to continue with the question at hand, production is proportioned to consumption, and as consumption increases, so will production. The problem of famine can therefore best be solved by encouraging consumption, including foreign consumption by exportation. The stimulus to production and capital formation given by the policy of free trade will increase the sum of produce in the nation, and therefore the fund from which everyone can consume. The increase and improvement of cultivation will also increase the possibilities for employment, thereby making it easier for the people to earn their living.]

But these advantages are not confined to finding work more easily; for, from the very fact that labor is more sought after, wages must rise by degrees, because laborers will become scarce relative to the wages offered. It is a well-known fact that in the last few years, while the building trade has been brisk in Paris, masons have been given higher wages. This increase is inevitable as long as the number of laborers does not increase in proportion to the new values put into the wages fund for distribution. The greater quantity of wages offered, and the affluence of the people, increase the population: but this increase, following the natural order, is much less speedy than that of production. The year after a field has been cleared, manured, and sown, it returns the wherewithal to feed a man; but, before a man is brought up, twenty years are necessary, and before these twenty years have passed, production would have had time to increase more and more if its progress were not hampered and restrained by the limits of consumption. Workmen coming from abroad can also prevent the increase of wages: however, men are too strongly attached to their native country for this immigration ever to be too large. But whether the increase in population comes from the influx of foreigners, or from the multiplication of the species, it will always be the result of the affluence of the people, and will always presuppose it. Here then, in the increase in values brought about by the policy of free trade, is an obvious advantage for the class of wage-earning consumers, since it causes a greater wages fund to be available for distribution, which produces: firstly, a greater certainty of finding work, and, for each laborer, a greater number of useful working days; secondly, an actual increase in the price of wages, through the competition of cultivators and proprietors, who will raise it in emulation of one another to attract workmen; thirdly, an increase in population, consequence of the greater affluence of the people.

The equalization of prices is another advantage of the policy of freedom. This results from the process of distributing grain evenly between provinces in times of harvest failure by allowing free transportation. It can also result from a policy of public granaries which distributes the grain more evenly over good and bad years. This has been done in various small states, and also in France on several occasions. It will of course require capital formation, but this should not be a difficulty. The people will also have to be convinced of the wisdom of the procedure. The profit made by these public granaries will, however, be an offsetting advantage to the treasury. This policy of purchasing in abundant years and selling in lean years will have the desirable result of greatly stabilizing grain prices.]

One of the great disadvantages of the inequality of the price for the consumer is based on the fact that the proportion which is established between the price of subsistence goods and the price of a day's work, does not follow the average price exactly, but constantly remains below it, to the detriment of the day laborer; so that, if the prices of dear, average and cheap years were distributed in such a way that they were more or less equal every year, wages would be higher, to the advantage of the consumer, than they are when wages vary a lot. This is easy to demonstrate. The daily wage, like the price of every thing else, is determined by the relationship between offer and demand, that is, by the reciprocal need of those who give work and those who have to live by working. Wage-earning people, in good and bad years alike, have no other means to live than by working; they will, therefore, offer their labor, and competition will force them to settle for the wage necessary for their subsistence. They will not foresee and forecast the possibility of a dearth in order to force those who pay them to raise their wages; for, whatever this distant future may be, they must live at the present time, and if they make themselves too hard to please, their neighbor would take the work at a lower price. It is, therefore, on the customary rate that the price of wages will settle itself; it will even fall below this proportion in years of low prices, because, if on the one hand, this low price makes the people lazy and reduces the competition among the laborers, on the other hand, it deprives the cultivators, and, by repercussion, the proprietors, of the means of giving work. Then again, the increase in prices in dear years does not only fail to be considered in the determination of wages, but tends, rather to decrease them. Indeed, the misery of the people banishes idleness, and makes work so necessary for them, that they give it at a lower price. All those among the proprietors who have a fixed revenue, and even, in the case of excessive dearth, all those who are in a situation of giving employment, themselves suffer by the increase of their expenses, and are not compensated for this by the increase in their revenue (for it cannot be repeated too often that only the equality of prices causes the increase of the revenue of the cultivators, and that they are not compensated by a high price in the years of dearth, for the low prices of the years of abundance, because the quantity which they sell is proportionately far less than the rise in the price). They are themselves, therefore, in no situation to give employment; most often, they decide to do so only from motives of charity, and by profiting from the readiness of the workers to lower their wages. Thus, not only do the wage-earners fail to share in any way in the jolt which the transitory dearth gives to the price, but they do not even participate to the extent that the transitory dearth increases average prices. Yet it is mainly the years of dearth which raise average prices, even in the countries where the absence of free trade maintains a customary, rather low price, which is far below the mean price. It follows from this that, without the mean price of subsistence goods rising to the loss of the consumer, the price of wages will rise to his benefit by the simple equalization of the mean price between abundant and unfruitful years, because then the mean price will coincide with the customary price, and it is always to the customary price that the price of wages is related.

I cannot deny myself a reflection here. In my letter written from Tulle, and in even more detail in that from Bort, I showed you that the policy of free trade and the equalization of prices alone—the mean price remaining the same for the consumers—must assure the cultivators, the proprietors and the State of an immense increase in profits and revenues. I believe I showed you in this letter that, with the mean price still remaining the same for the consumers, by the mere effect of the equalization of prices and the policy of freedom, the consumers will gain by being remunerated in a proportion which is more advantageous for them, since their current wage is determined by its proportion with a price lower than the mean price, and since it will then be proportioned to the mean price, that is, to their real expenses. It appears to me that the combination of these two truths ought to inspire a great deal of confidence in the results of the policy of freedom.

I add that the advantage to the consumers will still be very great even when the mean price of consumption goods would rise, and that the welfare which would be procured for wage-earners by the re-establishment of the proportion between their wage and their expenses will always be equally real, even if the mean price were to rise, provided that it was always constant, or almost invariable.

I further add that the observation which has been developed here, completely refutes the objection which the adversaries of the freedom of the grain trade are so often heard to repeat. Experience shows, they say, that the price of wages does not rise with the price of grain, and, as they always assume that freedom increases the price of grain, they conclude from this that freedom is fatal to the consumers.

I believe to have shown, on the contrary, that even when the momentary dearth failed to increase the price of wages, and even when it lowered it below its natural proportion, it must be concluded that the evil lies in the momentary dearth, and, in order to remedy this, it is necessary to establish a price as constant and equal as possible, that is, to give trade complete freedom.

This can be shown by statistical data from England and France. Examples can be given which show the difference in the behavior of the average price over periods when there was free trade and when there was not. Forbidding the trade in grain between districts makes the people liable to the harmful effects of harvest failure and high prices. From free trade, as I have shown, only good results can follow.

I would also like to mention some specific dues which ought to be abolished: that of the *droits de ménage et de péage*, of the *maîtrise des boulangers*, and of the *banalité des moulins*.[1] These three raise the price of bread unnecessarily.]

I cannot help making some reflections on the danger of some remarks in the preface to your plan, which perhaps I have already made, but to whose repetition there can be no objection.

To announce to the people that the dearth which they experience is the *result of scheming* and not of the disturbance of the seasons, to tell them that they suffer *dearth amidst plenty*, this is to sanction all the *past, present, and future* slanders to which they themselves resort but too readily, and to which many people are eager to rouse them, against the administration and administrators of every rank. This is, at the same time, to become accountable for the dearths which may continue, or occur in the future, it is to undertake personally to provide them with *abundance*, whatever may happen: now, it is essential to be very sure about your facts before making such a promise. I admit that no plan for regulation would inspire me with such confidence. I would prefer to base my security on physical necessity and on justice. The people are well aware of the fact that the Government cannot command the seasons, and they must understand that it has no right to violate the property of the husbandmen and the grain merchants. It is a sign of strength, even in the eyes of the people, when they can be told: *What you ask of me is an injustice.* Those who are not satisfied with this reasoning, will never be satisfied with any, and will always slander the government, no matter what measures it takes to please

---

[1] *Droits de ménage et de péage*: These were seigneurial toll rights dating back to feudal times. Many were abolished during the reign of Louis XIV, but there were plenty of them left in the eighteenth century. *La Maîtrise des boulangers*: master craftsmanship in the bakers guild which was difficult and costly to obtain, and therefore raised the price of bread. *La banalité des moulins*: the feudal right of the seigneur to force peasants to hire his mill for the grinding of their grain.

them; for it will not gratify them seeing that it is impossible for the government to procure cheap grain for the people when the harvests have failed, and that there is no possible means of obtaining it at a lower price than that which would result from complete freedom, that is, from the observance of rigorous justice.

Letter to l'Abbé Terray on the "Marque des Fers"

Readers will not be surprised to learn that Turgot strongly opposes duties on iron. (The "marque des fers" mentioned in the letter is a duty on iron.) The only way to attain prosperity is to have unlimited freedom of trade. Opponents of free trade claim that restrictions will benefit home products at the expense of foreigners. These contentions are just an excuse by those who are attempting to secure a monopoly position at the expense of consumers. Those who claim to gain by restrictions ignore the fact that they lose as consumers when other people use restrictive measures to their own advantage. Even if one disregards the general argument for free trade, there is still excellent reason to avoid a duty on iron. If restrictions have to be imposed, they should be on consumption goods rather than on a commodity such as iron, which is essential for the production of numerous goods. A duty on iron would have a bad effect on the entire economy.

CHAPTER 12

Letter to l'Abbé Terray on the "Marque des Fers"

Limoges, 24 December, 1773

I am honored to report to you on the state of the ironworks and mills in the Generality of Limoges which are engaged in the manufacture of iron articles.

You have requested this account of me several times; I would have liked to have been able to send it to you more promptly, and, above all, in a more finished state; but in spite of the trouble to which I went to obtain as detailed an account on each of the ironworks as you seem to require, you will observe that there still remains a great deal of uncertainty about the output of iron from these different works. You will also notice that this uncertainty derives largely from the purely physical circumstances which cause variations in the output, such as the shortage or abundance of water in the different factories. The variations in the market and in the wealth of the entrepreneurs also have an influence on the fluctuations in output, almost as great as the physical causes.

As for the observations you seem to require on the means of instilling more life into this branch of industry, or of restoring to it that which it is said to have lost, I have few to offer. I know of no

---

Written 1773. Turgot's letter on the "marque des fers" was written in response to a request by l'Abbé Terray in connection with a project to raise a new duty on iron, which he had apparently foreshadowed in 1771. The "marque des fers" or "le droit de marque des fers" was a duty on iron and iron commodities first established in the seventeenth century during the reign of Henry IV.

means whatever of stimulating any trade or industry other than that of giving it the greatest freedom, and freeing it from all those burdens which the mistaken interest of the treasury has inordinately increased upon all kinds of commodities, and particularly upon the manufactures of iron.

I cannot conceal from you that one of the chief causes of my delay in responding to your inquiries, has been the rumor which is circulating to the effect that their object was the imposition of new duties, or the extension of old ones. The opinion, founded on too many precedents, that the investigations of the government have for their sole object the discovery of ways of extracting more money from the people, has given rise to a general distrust, and the majority of those to whom inquiries are directed do not reply, or seek to mislead by replies sometimes false and sometimes incomplete. I cannot believe, sir, that you would intend to impose new burdens on a trade which, to the contrary, you say you want to encourage. If I had thought this, I confess I would congratulate myself on the involuntary delay in my furnishing you with the information you have requested, and I would regret not being able to prolong the delay even more.

If, after complete liberty has been obtained by the relief from all taxes on the manufacturing, transportation, sale and consumption of commodities, anything remains to be done by the government to encourage a branch of trade, it can only be by means of education, that is, by encouraging the research of men of science and craftsmen who tend to perfect the craft, and, above all, by extending the knowledge of the practical processes which greed seeks to keep as so many secrets. It would be useful for the government to incur some expenses in sending young men to foreign countries in order to learn processes of manufacture unknown in France, and to publish the results of these researches. These means are good; but freedom of commerce and deliverance from taxes are much more efficient and much more necessary.

You appear, in the letters with which you have honored me on this subject, to believe that certain obstacles which might be placed on the importation of foreign iron would act as an encouragement

Letter to l'Abbé Terray

to our national trade. You intimate even that you have received repeated representations from different provinces as regards the favor which these iron articles from abroad obtain, to the prejudice of the commerce and manufacture of native iron commodities. I believe, indeed, that iron masters, who know only about their own iron, imagine that they would earn more if they had fewer competitors. There is no merchant who would not like to be the sole seller of his commodity. There is no branch of trade in which those who are engaged in it do not seek to ward off competition, and do not find some sophisms to make people believe that it is in the State's interest to prevent at least the competition from abroad, which they most easily represent as the enemy of the national commerce. If we listen to them, and we have listened to them but too often, all branches of commerce will be infected by this kind of monopoly. These fools do not see that this same monopoly which they practice, not, as they would have the government believe, against foreigners, but against their own fellow-citizens, consumers of the commodity, is returned to them by these fellow citizens, who are sellers in their turn, in all the other branches of commerce where the first in their turn become buyers. They do not see that all these associations of men engaged in a particular trade will not fail to arm themselves with the same pretexts in order to obtain from the misled government the same exclusion of foreigners; they do not see that in this balance of annoyance and injustice between all kinds of industry, in which the artisans and the merchants of each kind oppress each other as sellers, and are oppressed as buyers, there is no advantage to any party; but there is a real loss to the whole of national commerce, or rather, a loss to the State, which buying less from abroad, similarly will sell less to them. This forced increase in price for all buyers necessarily diminishes the sum total of enjoyment, the amount of disposable revenues, the wealth of the proprietors and of the sovereign, and the amount of wages to be distributed to the people. This loss is doubled again, because in this war of reciprocal oppression, in which the government lends its authority to all against all, the only sector of industry excepted, is that of the tilling of the soil, which is oppressed by everybody in concert through these national monopolies, and which, far from being able to oppress anyone, cannot even take advantage of the natural right to sell its commodity either to foreigners or to those of its fellow-citizens who would buy it, so that from all the classes of working citizens, only the small farmer suffers from monopoly as buyer, and at the same time as seller. He alone cannot freely buy from abroad any of the things he requires; he alone cannot freely sell abroad the commodity he produces, while the cloth merchant or any other, buys as much wheat as he wants from the foreigner and sells him as much as he can of his cloth. Whatever sophisms are collected by the self-interest of a few merchants, the truth is that all branches of commerce ought to be free, equally free, and entirely free; that the system of some modern politicians who fancy that they encourage national commerce by prohibiting the importation of foreign merchandise is plain delusion; that this system results only in setting all branches of commerce as enemies against one another, in nourishing among nations a germ of hatred and of war, of which even the lightest effects are a thousand times more costly to the people, more destructive of wealth, population and happiness, than all those paltry mercantile profits which people fancy they will ensure benefit the nations which allow themselves to be misled. The truth is that in wishing to hurt others, we only hurt ourselves, not only because the retaliation to these prohibitions is so easy to devise that other nations do not fail to think of it in their turn, but also because we deprive our own nation of the incalculable advantages of a free commerce; advantages so great that, if a great State like France were willing to experience them, the rapid advancement of her commerce and industry would soon compel the other nations to imitate her in order not to be impoverished by the total loss of their own commerce.

But supposing these principles not to be, as I am quite convinced they will be, clearly proven, supposing even that we admit the expediency of prohibition in some branches of commerce, then I would be so bold as to say that iron should be excepted for an incontrovertible reason, which is also peculiar to it.

This reason is that iron is not merely a consumption good useful for the different purposes of life: the iron used in household goods, in ornaments, in weapons, is not the largest part of the metal produced and sold. Above all, it is as an implement necessary in the execution of all crafts, without exception, that this metal is so important and so valuable in commerce. It is, in this respect, the raw material of all the crafts, manufactures, of agriculture even, to which it furnishes the greater part of its implements. For this reason it is a commodity of the first necessity. For this reason, even if we were to adopt the idea of encouraging manufactures by prohibitions, iron ought never to be subject to them, because these prohibitions, in the opinion even of those who support them, ought to be placed only on goods manufactured for consumption, and not on commodities used in manufacture, such as the raw materials and the implements required in production; since, according to this system, the buyer of iron implements used in his manufacture or in the cultivation of his land ought to enjoy all the advantages which the principles of this system give to the seller over the ordinary consumer.

To prohibit the importation of foreign iron, therefore, is to favor the iron master not only at the expense of the domestic consumers, as in the ordinary cases of prohibition, it is to favor them at the expense of all manufacturers, of all branches of industry, and at the expense of agriculture, and the production of all foodstuffs, in a special and even more direct manner than the effect of all other prohibitions by which, it must be admitted, it is still constrained.

I am persuaded that this thought, which no doubt has occurred to you, will prevent you from complying with the inconsiderate entreaties of the iron masters and of all those who can only consider this branch of commerce by itself and as isolated from all other branches with whom it has relations of the first necessity.

I will add here two further considerations which, in my opinion, deserve your full attention.

Firstly, many crafts not only need iron, but iron of various qualities, and adapted to the nature of each work. For some, relatively soft iron is needed, for others, more brittle iron. The most important manufactures employ steel, and steel again varies in quality; that of Germany is suited for certain purposes, that of England, which is more valuable, for others. Now there are certain kinds of iron which our Kingdom does not supply, and which must be obtained abroad. With regard to steel, it is well known that very little of it is produced in France, that this kind of production is only just in the experimental stage, and that, however successful the trials may have been, it may take half a century perhaps before enough steel can be produced in France to supply a reasonable part of the use made of it by manufactures, during which time it will be necessary to obtain from abroad ready made tools, because they cannot be made in France with the necessary precision, and because the products would lose too much of their value and price if they were made with imperfect instruments. Thus, to prohibit the importation of foreign types of iron would be to ruin our own manufacture; it would mean destroying those in which steel is employed, and all those which need special quality iron. To charge these types of iron with excessive duties would be to lead these manufactures to an inevitable decay, in time; it would mean sacrificing a large part of our national commerce to the very mistaken self-interest of the iron masters.

It seems to me that the first consideration proves that in the current state of trade in manufactures and the domestic iron industry, it would be imprudent to restrain the importation of foreign iron. What remains to be discussed will prove that this importation will never cease to be necessary, and that, on the contrary, the need for it will probably never cease to grow with the passing of time.

Indeed, it is sufficient to consider the tremendous quantity of charcoal which is consumed by the smelting of the ore and by its reduction into metal, and the equally large quantity which is consumed by the ironworks where the metal is refined, in order to be convinced that, however abundant the ore may be, it can only be developed to the extent that it is situated in the neighborhood of a very large quantity of cheap wood. However plentiful a forest situated near a river flowing to Paris may be, the establishment of an ironworks would certainly never be found expedient there, because the wood has a value there which could never be recovered from the sale of the iron which is manufactured with it. Moreover, the principal benefit expected from the establishment of an ironworks is that of giving a value and a market to forests which did not have any before. It follows from this that as the woods become scarce, as they acquire value through new markets, through the opening of roads and navigable canals, through the increase in agriculture and population, the smelting and production of iron articles must become less profitable and gradually decline. It follows from this that the longer nations have been developed, relative to the progress they have made toward wealth and prosperity, they must manufacture less iron, and obtain more from abroad. It is for this reason that England, which, of all nations in Europe, is the most advanced in this regard, obtains only a small amount of crude iron domestically, and buys a great deal of it in Germany and in the Baltic, which she increases in value by converting it into steel and hardware. The trade in iron is assigned by nature to new peoples, to people who possess vast virgin forests, far removed from all markets, where there is still profit in burning very large quantities of wood just for the sake of the value of the salts which are extracted by washing the ashes. This trade, declining in England, still quite flourishing in France, much more so in Germany, and in the Baltic countries, must, in the natural order of things, proceed to Russia, to Siberia, and to the American colonies, until these countries become populated in turn, and, all nations being more or less in balance in this regard, the increase in the price of iron will become sufficiently great for the advantage in manufacturing it to be restored even in the country where its production had been abandoned, for want of the ability to maintain a competitive position with the poor nations. If this decline of ironworks resulting from the increase in wealth, population and the multiplication of markets for trade generally was a misfortune, it would be an inevitable misfortune, which it would be useless to attempt to prevent. But it is not a misfortune at all if this trade declines only to be replaced by more profitable ones. It is necessary to reason about France relative to other nations, just as it is necessary to reason about the provinces supplying Paris with consumption goods relative to the provinces of the interior; the proprietors in the neighborhood of the Seine certainly do not regret that their woods have too high a value to enable the establishment of ironworks in that area, and they resign themselves quite happily to purchasing, with the revenue from their wood, the iron which other provinces sell to them.

To persist in opposing this necessary result, from a narrow-minded political viewpoint which thinks it is possible to grow everything at home, would be to act just like the proprietors of Brie who thought themselves thrifty by drinking the bad wine from their own vineyards, which really cost them more in the sacrifice of land suitable for good wheat, than they could have bought from the proceeds of their wheat. It would be to sacrifice a large profit in order to retain a smaller one.

Thus our policy should surrender itself to the course of nature, and the course of commerce, which is no less necessary and no less irresistible than the course of nature, without seeking to direct this course. For, in order to guide it without disturbing it, and without injuring ourselves, it would be necessary for us to be able to follow all the changes in the needs, the interests, and the industry of mankind. It would be necessary to know these in such detail as would be physically impossible to obtain, and in which even the most skilful, the most active and the most painstaking government will risk always to be wrong in half the cases, as is observed or acknowledged by Abbé Galiani in a work[1] in which he nevertheless vindicates with the greatest zeal the system of prohibitions just on the type of trade where they are most disastrous, to wit, the grain trade. I add that, even if we had for all these particulars the mass of knowledge which is impossible to gather, the result would only be to let things go precisely as they would have gone by themselves, by the simple action of the self-interest of man, enlivened and held in check by a free competition.

But, if we ought not to drive away the foreign iron which we need, it does not follow that we should burden our own iron with duties, or rather, taxes, on their manufacture, or on their transport. Quite the contrary, the manufacture and transport of French iron should be left perfectly free, in order that they may draw the greatest advantage from our mines and forests, as long as the entrepreneurs

---

[1] I.e., Ferdinando Galiani, *Dialogues sur le commerce des blés*, (Paris: 1770).

find it profitable, and that, by their competition, they may help to supply our agriculture and our crafts with the implements that they require at the lowest possible price.

For my own conscience's sake, sir, I felt it my duty to communicate to you all the thoughts which were prompted by a fear that you might yield to proposals which I consider dangerous, and which would injure the trade which you desire to encourage. I know that you do not disapprove of the boldness with which I have openly expressed what I believe to be the truth.

I am, etc.

Six Projects of Edicts

Turgot suggests six edicts to be enacted to the king that would result in comprehensive economic freedom for France. The arguments he gives for abolishing the corvée, compulsory labor to construct roads, are characteristic. Forced labor is inefficient, since workers who are not paid have no incentive to do good work. In addition, the compulsory laborers are taxed twice: not only do they receive no pay for their work, but they are prevented from doing productive work for pay during the term of their forced labor. Claims that forced labor allows more roads to be built at the same time than relying on the market fail because the roads are useless unless supplemented by other facilities provided by the market. Likewise, the guild system is inefficient and ought to be curtailed. It is a harmful restriction on free labor. Turgot's other edicts propose eliminating other restrictions on the free market, such as taxes on grain and suet.

CHAPTER 13

Six Projects of Edicts
Together with Explanatory Preambles Enacting Sundry Reforms

EDICT OF THE KING
Which Suppresses the Corvée and Decrees the Construction of Highways for a Money Price

Louis, etc., The utility of roads designed to facilitate the transport of commodities has been recognized during all time. Our predecessors have regarded their construction and repair as one of the most worthy objects of their vigilance.

Never have these important works been prosecuted with greater ardor than under the reign of the late king, our venerated lord and grandfather. Many provinces are reaping the fruits of these activities in the rapid increase in the value of their lands.

The protection we owe to agriculture, the true foundation of plenty and public prosperity, and the favor we will to accord to commerce as a further encouragement to agriculture, cause us to seek to bind more and more by facile communications all parts of our realm, both among themselves and with outside districts.

Desiring to secure these advantages to our people by the means least burdensome to them, we have investigated carefully the means

---

Published in February, 1776, and registered at a Lit-de-Justice on the 12th day of March of the same year.

which have been employed heretofore for making and repairing public roads.

We have noted with pain that, with the exception of a small number of provinces, works of this kind have been executed, for the most part, by means of corvées required of our subjects, and even from the poorest part, while they have been paid no wages for the time they were so employed. We have been unable to escape being struck by the discomforts inherent in the nature of that contribution.

To draft the cultivator forcibly to these labors is always to do him a real wrong, even when he is paid for his day's work. One would seek in vain to select, for demanding forced labor, a time when the peasants were unoccupied; the work of cultivation is so diversified and so incessant that no time is without its employment. Such times, when they do exist, differ in contiguous places, and frequently in the same place, owing to the varying nature of the soil, or different kinds of cultivation. The most attentive administrators cannot know all these variations. Besides, the necessity of assembling under foremen a sufficient number of laborers demands that the summary writs be general in the same district. Error on the part of the administrator may cause to the cultivators a loss of days for which no salary could repay them.

To take the time of the laborer, even for pay, is equivalent to a tax. To take this time without paying for it is a double tax; and that tax is out of all proportion when it falls on a simple day laborer who has nothing for his subsistence but the labor of his hands.

The man who works under compulsion and without recompense works idly and without interest; he does, at the same time, less work, and his work is poorly done. The peasants (*corvoyeurs*), obliged to travel frequently ten miles or more to report to the foreman, and as much more to return to their homes, lose a great part of the time demanded from them, without any labor return for it. The multiplied complaints, the embarrassment of tracing out the work, of distributing it, of executing it with a lot of men gathered haphazard, most of them as devoid of intelligence as they are of initiative, consume a further part of the remaining time. In this way the work which is done costs the people and the state, in day's labor of men and vehicles, twice and often three times what it would cost if done for a money consideration.

The little work wrought so dearly is always poorly done. The art of making stone ballasts, although simple, has, nevertheless, principles and rules which determine the manner of laying out the embankments, of choosing and laying out curbs, of placing the stones according to their bulk and durability, and in accordance with the nature of their composition by which they are rendered more or less susceptible of resisting the weight of vehicles and atmospheric influences. On the attentive observation of these rules depend the solidity and durability of the roads; and that sort of attention cannot be looked for, nor can it be demanded, from the men who are drafted to the corvée, who have, all of them, a different business, and who work on the roads only a few days in each year. In work paid for in money, all the details which pertain to the perfection of the work are specified to entrepreneurs. The laborers whom they choose, instruct and oversee, make the construction of roads their regular business, and they know it; the work is well done, because if it is done poorly the contractor knows he will be obliged to reconstruct it at his own expense. The work done by the corvée remains poorly done, because it would be too harsh to demand from the wretched peasant a double task, to repair the imperfections committed through ignorance. As a result, the roads are less solid and more difficult to repair.

There is a further cause which makes the work of repair done by the corvée very much more costly.

In places where these labors are based on a money consideration, the entrepreneur charged with keeping a part of the road in repair, watches closely for the slightest disintegrations; he repairs them at small cost at the moment they are forming and before they are greatly increased; consequently the road is always in good condition and never requires costly repairs. The roads, on the contrary, which are kept in repair by the corvées, are never repaired until their grievous condition is forced upon the attention of the persons charged with keeping the roads in repair.

As a result of this, it happens that on these roads, made in the first place, as is usual, of embankments of large stones, and very crude from the beginning, the vehicles always follow the same track and wear ruts which frequently cut entirely through the ballast.

The impossibility of issuing writs of corvée at all times brings it about in most of the provinces that the repairs needed for maintenance are made twice a year, before and after the winter season, and that between these times the roads come to be in wretched disorder. It is necessary to secure new stone entirely for the work of repair; hence, aside from the inconvenience of making each time a ballast as unsatisfactory as a new one must ever be, there is involved an annual expense in days' labor of men and of carts, approaching very near the first cost of construction.

Any industry which requires such intelligence is impossible of being carried on by means of the corvée. It is on this account that in making roads by that method we are obliged to confine ourselves to embankments constructed of ill-assorted stones, without being able to substitute a ballast of paving stones when the nature of the stones demands it or when their scarcity and the distance from which they must be brought render the construction by paving incomparably cheaper than that of general stone ballasts, which consume a very great quantity of stone. That difference in price, frequently greatly to the disadvantage of stone ballasts, is an increase in the actual expense and in the burden resting upon the people which results from the custom of the corvée.

There must be added a multitude of accidents: the loss of animals which, arriving at the place of work already exhausted by long travel, succumb to the labor demanded of them; the loss even of men, heads of unfortunate families, maimed, consumed by the maladies which the intemperance of the season occasions, or by the work itself; a loss most sad when those who perish succumb to a hazardous demand, and who have been compensated by no salary whatever.

There must be added further the expenses, the law costs, the fines and penalties of all kinds which are made necessary by resistance to a law too harsh to be executed without complaint; perhaps the secret vexations which the greatest vigilance of those who are charged with the execution of our orders cannot entirely avoid in an administration so extensive and so complex as that of the corvée, and where distributive justice goes astray in a multitude of details; where authority subdivided, so to speak, to infinity is shared among so great a number of hands, and entrusted in its final analysis to subalterns whom it is almost impossible to choose with careful discretion and very difficult to oversee.

We believe it impossible to appreciate all the corvée costs the people.

By substituting for this system, so burdensome in its effects and so disastrous in the means employed, the custom of constructing highways for a sum of money, we will have the advantage of knowing precisely what will result to our people; the advantage of drying up at once so prolific a source of vexations and rebellion; the advantage of having no longer to punish nor to command to that end, and of economizing the exercise of authority, which it is so disastrous to squander. These different motives are sufficient to move us to prefer to the use of the corvée the more pleasant and less costly means of making roads at a definite money cost. But a still more powerful and decisive motive fixes our determination: it is the injustice which is inseparable from the use of the corvée.

The weight of that charge does not fall, nor can it ever fall, anywhere else than upon the poorest part of our subjects, upon those who have no property other than their hands and their industry, upon the peasants and on the farmers. The landowners, almost all of whom are *privilégiés*, being exempt, contribute but very little.

Nevertheless it is to the landowners that the public roads are useful, by the value which increased channels of communication give to the products of their lands. It is not the actual farmers nor the day laborers who work for them that are profited. The successors of the present farmers will pay to the proprietors that increase of value in increase of rents. The class of day laborers will gain, perhaps, some day an increase of wages proportionate to the increased price of commodities; they will profit by participating in the general increase of public welfare; but the class of landowners alone will receive a prompt and immediate increase of wealth, and that new wealth will not be scattered among the people except in so far as the people will purchase it through increased labor.

It is then the class of proprietors of land which receives the fruit of the construction of roads; it is that class which ought alone to make the necessary advances, since they finally secure the benefits.

How can it be just to compel those to pay it who have nothing? to force them to give their time without wages? to take from them their only resource against misery and starvation in order to set them to work for the profit of those citizens who are richer than they are?

A wholly opposite error has often led the administration to sacrifice the rights of proprietors, in the misdirected desire to relieve the poorer part of the subjects, in compelling them by prohibitive laws to give up the commodities in their possession for less than their actual value. Thus injustice was worked, on the one hand, against the landowners in order to procure bread at a low price for the wage-workers; and on the other, in favor of the landowners, these unfortunates were robbed of the legitimate fruit of their toil and sweat. It was feared that the cost of subsistence would be too high for them to obtain it by their wages; and the government, demanding from them for nothing a labor, which would have been paid for if those who profited by it had borne the expense, took away from them the medium of competition best calculated to make their wages reach their proper level.

It has injured equally the property and liberty of different classes of our subjects; it has impoverished now one and now the other in order unjustly to favor each in turn. It is thus that one is misled when he forgets that justice only can maintain the equilibrium between all rights and all interests. This will be throughout the basis of our administration; and it is in order to render justice to the most numerous part of our subjects, whose especial need for protection will always command our most particular attention, that we have made haste to bring to an end the corvées in all parts of our realm.

We have not, however, wished to yield to the promptings of our heart without first having examined and appreciated the motives of our predecessors, by which they have been led to introduce and to suffer to subsist a custom, the embarrassments of which are so evident.

It may have been thought that, since the method of the corvée made it possible to work at once on all routes in all parts of the kingdom, communication would be more quickly opened, and that the state would enjoy more promptly the wealth due to the activity of trade and to the increase in the value of the articles produced.

Experience has not been slow to dispel that illusion. It was quickly seen that some of the sparsely populated provinces were precisely those where the construction of highways, owing to the nature of the country and of the soil, required immense labors which one could not flatter himself he might accomplish with a small number of hands without keeping them at it for more than a century, perhaps.

It was seen that, even in the more populous provinces, it was impossible, without crushing the people and ruining the fields, to draft peasants a sufficient number of days to complete within a short time any considerable part of the road.

It was proved that the peasants could not give their time advantageously without being directed by intelligent employees, whom it was necessary to pay; that to furnish the necessary utensils, to keep them in repair, to meet the cost of shops and store-houses, involved expenses proportionate to the number of men annually employed.

It was discovered that, on a fixed length of roadway built by corvée, many indispensable pieces of work had to be done, such as bridges, rock escarpments and walls of earth, which could be accomplished only by skilled workmen and for a price in money; that consequently it was fruitless to hasten the construction of works of corvée, if the impossibility of accelerating in like proportion the skilled work left the roads broken and useless to the public.

We are convinced, in short, that the quantity of the work accomplished annually by corvée has a necessary relation to the quantity of skilled work which the disposition of the fund for bridges and culverts permits to be done each year, and that it is impossible and useless to pass beyond this proportion; that one flatters himself in vain that all the roads may be made at once, and that the pretended advantage of the corvée is reduced to the possibility of beginning a large number of roads at the same time, without actually accomplishing any more work than could be done by the method of constructing them by contract, by which one part is not undertaken until another is finished and thrown open to the enjoyment of the public.

The present condition of the roads in most of our provinces, and what remains to be built after all these years during which the corvées have been vigorously enforced, prove how false it is that that system can hasten the construction of highways.

Some, also, are dismayed at the expense involved in the construction of roads by contract. It is not believed that the treasury of the State, drained by many wars and the extravagance of former reigns, and charged with an enormous debt, will be able to provide for that expense. Some fear to impose further taxes on the people, already too heavily burdened; and it is deemed preferable to demand from them gratuitous labor, imagining that it is better to demand from the country people, during certain days, the hands they have rather than the money they have not.

Those who reason thus forget that they must not demand from those who have nothing but their hands either what they have not or the hands which are their sole means of support for themselves and their families.

They forget that the charge for building roads, doubled and tripled by the sluggishness, the loss of time and the imperfection inherent in corvée labor, is incomparably more heavy upon the unfortunates who have nothing but their hands, than would be a charge, incomparably less, imposed in money upon the proprietors who are able to pay; who, by the increase of their revenue, would immediately reap the fruits of that outlay, and whose contribution, becoming to them a source of wealth, would at the same time relieve those men who, having nothing but their hands, can live only as those hands are employed and paid. They forget that the corvée is itself a tax, a tax most heavy, most unequally apportioned, far more disastrous than that which they dread to have established.

The facility with which roads have been made by contract in some of the states-districts, and the relief experienced by the people in certain *généralités* of assembly districts, where the administrators substituted for the corvée a contribution in money, have demonstrated clearly enough how preferable that contribution is to the inconvenience which accompanies the use of the corvée.

Another very obvious reason has doubtless greatly influenced the decision which has been made to adopt the method of the corvée for the construction of highways, and that is the fear that the recurring needs of the Royal treasury would impel the administrators to divert from their destination the amounts imposed for the making of roads to some more urgent item of expense, especially in time of war; that the sums, once diverted, would remain so, and that the people might one day be forced, at the same time, both to pay the tax designed originally for the roads and to provide in some other manner, perhaps even by the corvée, for their construction.

The administrators themselves have feared this; they have wished to be so placed that it would be impossible to commit an infidelity of whose danger all too many examples have made them sensible.

We commend the motives of their fear, and we appreciate the force of that consideration; but it in no way changes the nature of things; it does not make it just to demand a tax from the poor to enrich the wealthy, and to compel those to sustain the construction of highways who have no interest in them.

All concede that in the time of war the first of all needs is the defense of the state; it is necessary then, it is just, to suspend all expenses which are not of absolute necessity; the outlay for the roads should be reduced to repair merely. The tax designed to provide for that expense should be reduced in proportion to relieve the people charged with extraordinary taxes occasioned by the war.

In time of peace, the interest the sovereign has in causing commerce and tillage to flourish, and the necessity of roads to secure that end, ought to allay the fear that the works will be abandoned or that new sums proportionate to the needs will not be provided by the re-establishment of the tax suspended on the occasion of the war. Nor need there be any fear that so simple a method would be abandoned in favor of a re-establishment of the corvées, if the latter had once been abolished because they were recognized to be unjust.

On our part, the exposition we have made of the motives which have led us to suppress the corvée guarantees to our subjects that they will not be re-established during our reign; and perhaps the memory which our people will cherish of this testimony of our love will give to our example, in the eyes of our successors, an importance which will prevent them from reimposing on their subjects a burden which we have abolished.

Further, we will take all measures in our power that the sums arising from the tax levied for the construction of highways cannot be diverted to other uses.

In this mind, we have wished that that tax should never be regarded as an ordinary tax and of fixed amount, and that it can never be turned into our royal treasury. We will that it be regulated each year in our Council, for each *généralité*, and that it shall never exceed the sum which it will be necessary to employ in that year for the construction and repair of causeways or other works which have hitherto been made by corvée, while we reserve the right to construct bridges and other works of skill by the same funds which have been so used until the present, and which are imposed in our kingdom for that end. Our intention is that the whole sum arising from the contribution in each *généralité* may be used there, and that no sum may be imposed the following year except in consequence of a new edict decreed in our Council.

In order that our subjects may be informed of the objects for which the said contribution will be employed, we have deemed it proper to ordain that a writ shall be prepared in our Council, in the ordinary form, showing all the contracts for works which it will be necessary to undertake in the year; that that writ shall be deposited, both in the office of our Bureaux of Finance which are charged with the execution of the edicts of the king, and in those of our Courts of parlement, Chambers of Accounts and Courts of Aides, and that each of our subjects may have free access.

We have willed that in case the sums be not used in the year, the sums remaining for use be deducted from the levy of the following year, without being confused, under any pretext whatever, with the mass of our finances and turned into the royal treasury. We have believed it necessary also to order, by the present edict, the accounting of the sums arising from that contribution, both by our Chambers of Accounts and by our Bureaux of Finance, and of engaging the fidelity those tribunals owe us to permit at no time any use of those sums foreign to the object for which we have destined them.

By the reckoning we have made of the roads to be built and repaired in our different provinces, we believe we are able to assure our subjects that the expense of that object will in no year exceed the sum of *ten millions* or all the assembly districts.

That tax, having for its object an expense useful to all proprietors, we will that all proprietors, privileged and non-privileged, concur in it as is customary in all local charges; and for that reason, we intend that even the lands of our domain may not be exempt, either in our hands or in the hands of others, by whatsoever title they may be held.

The same spirit of justice which moves us to suppress the corvée and to charge the expense of making roads to the proprietors who have an interest in it, determines us to provide for the legitimate indemnity of proprietors of heritages, who are deprived of some part of their property, whether by the laying out of roads or by the extraction of material which must be used. If the necessity of public service obliges them to surrender some part of their goods, it is just that they should suffer no damage, and that they should receive the price of that part of their property which they are obliged to surrender.

For these reasons, etc., by advice of our Council, etc., we have, by the present edict, perpetual and irrevocable, decreed, enacted and ordained, etc., as follows:

Article I. There will no longer be demanded from our subjects any labor, either gratuitous or forced, under the name of *corvée*, or under any other name whatever, for the construction of roads or for any other public work, except in case that the defense of the country in time of war demands extraordinary labors; in such case it will be provided by virtue of our orders addressed to governors, commandants, or other administrators of our provinces. We forbid, in every other circumstance, all those who are charged with the execution of our orders, to command or require it, reserving to ourselves the right to pay those who are compelled by circumstances, in such cases, to be taken away from their ordinary work.

Article II. Works hitherto accomplished by corvées, such as the building and repair of roads, and other works necessary to communication between the provinces and cities, will be carried out in the future by means of a contribution from all proprietors of landed property or real estate subject to twentieths, and the apportionment will be made in proportion to their payments according to the regular tax lists.

Article III. With regard to the construction of bridges and other works of skill, provision will be made from the same funds which have been used for this purpose heretofore.

Article IV. We will that the proprietors of land and of structures which it will be necessary to cross or demolish in the building of roads, as well as those who may be injured by the extraction of material from their property, may receive the value of the said lands, heritages or injuries; and they will be paid by the funds arising from the tax decreed by article II herein.

Article V. The amount of tax in each *généralité* shall be regulated each year by the cost of construction, repair and damages which we will ordain in the said *généralité* in that year; to this end there shall be each year a separate writ decreed by our Council which shall include all the said expenses.

Article VI. Estimates and specifications shall be prepared, contracts for the said work and bills for their repair shall be drawn up in the form which will be prescribed; and the writ ordained by us in our Council, mentioned in the preceding article, shall include the amount of the said contracts and bills; reserving to ourselves and to our Council, as in the past, the control of routes, estimates, contracts, and all the clauses, appurtenances and provisions which they may include.

Article VII. A report shall be made to us in our Council each year, of the employment of the sums arising from the tax ordained; and in case the sum shall not be entirely consumed, mention shall be made of this fact in the writ of the following year, and the sum which has not been employed shall be deducted from the tax of the said following year. On the contrary, in case some unforeseen cause requires an expense which had not been included in any of the contracts, an account shall be made of it, and if that expense is approved by us, it will be included in the writ ordained for the following year.

Article VIII. As soon as the said edict shall be promulgated by us, four copies of it for each *généralité* will be deposited, one in the office of our Court of parlement, the second in that of our Chamber of Accounts, the third in our Court of Aids, and the fourth in our Bureaux of Finance of the *généralité*, with the intent that all persons of whatever quality or condition they may be, may have access to it without cost or inconvenience; and the said writs will serve as a basis for the reports made to the Chamber of Accounts by our Treasurers, as will be explained in Articles X and XI.

Article IX. The recovery of the sums arising from the said tax, ordained by article II of the present edict, will be made in the same manner as that of the twentieths.

Article X. The sums collected shall be remitted to the ordinary receivers of taxes, who shall withhold from the receipts, month by month, a deduction of four deniers per livre of these taxes, which shall be turned into the hands of the commission of treasurers established by us for the control of bridges and culverts in each *généralité*, and that commission shall deliver the said amounts to the contractors of these works, in the form which will be prescribed by us. The said sums may not under any pretext whatever be diverted to any other use or even turned into our royal treasury.

Article XI. The said treasurers will not be discharged finally of the said sums except on the delivery of the receipts of the contractors. We make express inhibition and prohibition to the commission of the said treasurers against paying out the said sums for any other purpose whatever, on penalty of being compelled to recover the entire sum which they would have paid according to the dispositions of the present article. We enjoin upon our Chamber of Accounts and our Bureaux of Finance, each according to its duty, to hold exactly to these instructions.

Thus we give by commandment, etc.

EDICT OF THE KING

Decreeing the Suppression of Craft-Guilds

Louis, etc. We owe it to our subjects to assure them the full and complete enjoyment of their rights; we owe that protection especially to that class of men who, possessing nothing but their labor and industry, above all others have the need and right of employing to the limit of their capacity their sole resources for subsistence.

We have viewed with pain the multiplied blows which have been struck at this natural and common right of ancient institutions, blows which neither time, nor opinion, nor even the acts emanating from the authority, which seems to have sanctioned them, have been able to make legitimate.

In nearly all the cities of our realm, the exercise of various arts and trades is concentrated in the hands of a small number of *maîtres* incorporated in a guild, who may, to the exclusion of all other citizens, make or sell the particular objects of commerce of which they enjoy the exclusive privilege; consequently, those of our subjects who, by inclination or by necessity, desire to exercise the arts and trades, may do so only by acquiring the mastership (*maîtrise*), to which they are ineligible until they have passed an apprenticeship as long and arduous as it is superfluous, and after they have satisfied claims and multiplied exactions by which a part of the money they so greatly need to establish their trade or to open their shop, or even for their subsistence, they find consumed in sheer waste.

Those who are so unfortunate as to be unable to meet these expenses are reduced to a precarious existence under the domination of *maîtres*, condemned to waste their lives in indigence, or to carry on outside their country an industry they might have made useful to the State.

Citizens of all classes are deprived of the right to choose what laborers they would employ, and of advantages competition would give them in the low price and excellence of labor. Often one cannot execute the simplest work without having recourse to many workmen of different guilds, without enduring the delays, the infidelities, the exactions which necessitate or favor the pretensions of the various guilds, and the caprices of their arbitrary and injurious regime.

Thus the effect of these institutions, on the part of the state, is an appreciable diminution of trade and of industrial labor; with respect to a numerous part of our subjects, a loss of wages and means of subsistence; on the part of the inhabitants of the cities in general, complete subjection to exclusive privileges, the effect of which is exactly analogous to that of an effective monopoly, a monopoly of which those who control it against the public are themselves the victims whenever they in their turn have need of the commodities or trade controlled by another guild.

These abuses crept in by degrees. They were originally brought about by the interests of private individuals who established them against public interests. It was only after a long interval of time that authority, possibly deceived, possibly seduced by the appearance of utility, gave to them a sort of sanction.

The source of evil is in the privilege accorded to artisans of the same trade of assembling and combining into a single body.

It appears that when the cities began to be freed from feudal servitude and to be formed into communities, the facility of classifying the citizens according to their profession introduced that custom which was unknown until that time. The different professions thus came to be regarded as the private societies of which the general community was composed. The religious fraternities, by drawing more closely the bonds which united them with persons of the same professions, gave them more frequent occasion of assembling and of occupying themselves in the associations, with the interests common to that particular guild; an interest which they pursued with continuous activity, to the prejudice of those of society in general.

The corporations once formed promulgated their rules, and, under different pretexts, came to be authorized by the police.

The foundation of these rules is from the first to exclude from the exercise of a trade any one who is not a member of the guild; their general purpose is to restrict as far as possible the number of masters, and to render the acquisition of a mastership a difficulty almost insurmountable to any except the children of the existing masters. It is to this end that they have contrived the multiplicity of expenses and formalities of admittance, the difficulties connected with the arbitrary judgment of trial-pieces, especially the costly and needlessly protracted apprenticeships, and the prolonged servitude of the journeyman: institutions which have the further object of giving the masters gratuitously, during many years, the enjoyment of the fruits of the labors of the aspirants.

The guilds devote themselves especially to excluding from their territory foreign commodities and labor; they lay great stress on the pretended advantage of excluding from commerce such commodities as are supposed to be poorly made. The pretext led them to demand for themselves regulations of a new kind, tending to prescribe the quality of raw materials, their use and their manufacture; these regulations, whose execution was entrusted to officers of the guilds, gave to them an authority which became a means, not only of more effectually excluding aliens when suspected of infraction, but in addition of subjecting the masters of the guilds to the domination of leaders, and of compelling them, under fear of being prosecuted as suspected offenders, never to separate their interests from those of the association, and thus making them accomplices in all the maneuvers inspired by the spirit of monopoly animating the leading members of the guilds.

Among these arrangements, unreasonable and carried out to an infinite number of minute rules, but always dictated by the greatest interests of the masters of each guild, is the one which excludes entirely all others than the sons of masters or those who marry the daughters of the masters. They reject, besides, those whom they call *foreigners*, that is to say, those who are born in another city. In a large number of the guilds, to be married is sufficient to exclude one from apprenticeship, and consequently, from a mastership.

The spirit of monopoly which has prompted the contrivance of these regulations, has been able even to exclude women from trades most appropriate to their sex, such as that of embroidery which they may not exercise even for their own account.

We will not pursue further the enumeration of the bizarre arrangements, tyrannical and contrary to humanity and good manners, which fill these obscure codes, conceived by greed, adopted without examination in times of ignorance, and which only need to be known to become the object of public indignation.

These guilds, however, came to be authorized in all the cities, together with all their statutes and privileges, sometimes by the letters of our predecessors, obtained under different pretexts or by means of money which they paid for their confirmation from reign to reign, frequently by the writs of our courts, sometimes by the simple decisions of police or even by custom alone.

At length the custom prevailed of regarding the restrictions put upon industry as common law. The government was accustomed to make a financial resource of the taxes imposed on the guilds and of the multiplication of their privileges.

Henry III. gave, by his edict of December 3d, 1581, to that institution the scope and form of a general law. He established the arts and trades in corporations and guilds in all the cities and villages of the kingdom; he subjected all artisans to the *maîtrise* and to the trade corporations. The edict of April 5th, 1587, enlarged yet more these arrangements by subjecting all merchants to the same laws as the artisans. The edict of March, 1673, purely fiscal, by ordaining the execution of the two preceding edicts, added to the guilds already existing, other corporations unknown before that time.

The Department of Finance sought more and more to extend the resources which it found in the existence of the societies. Independently of the taxes and establishment of the guilds and of new *maîtrises*, there was created in the guilds a class of offices under different names, and those holding the offices were obliged to purchase them by means of loans which they were compelled to contract, and on which they paid the interest with the product of the profits on the duties which were alienated to them.

It was doubtless the allurement of this means of finance which prolonged the delusion concerning the immense injury which the existence of guilds causes to industry, and concerning the blows which it struck to natural right. That delusion has been carried among some persons to the point of contending that the right of labor is a royal right, one that the Prince could sell and that the subjects ought to purchase. We hasten to place beside this another maxim:

God, by giving to men needs and making them dependent upon the resource of labor, has made the right of labor the property of all men, and that property is primary, the most sacred and most imprescriptible of all.

We regard it as one of the first obligations of our justice, and as an act in every way worthy of our beneficence, to emancipate our subjects from all the restraints which have been laid upon that inalienable right of humanity. Wherefore, we will to abolish the arbitrary institutions which do not permit the indigent to live by their labor; which exclude the sex whose weakness implies greatest needs and fewest resources, and which seem, by condemning it to inevitable misery, to encourage seduction and debauch; which stifle emulation and industry and make useless the talents of those whom circumstances exclude from admission into the guild; which deprive the state and art of all the advantages which foreigners might furnish; which retard the progress of the arts by the difficulties which inventors find multiplied by the guilds, who thus dispute the right to exploit discoveries which they themselves have not made; which, by means of the inordinate expenses artisans are compelled to incur in order to acquire the liberty of labor, by the exactions of all kinds they must endure, by the multiplied penalties for so-called offenses, by expense and extravagance of every sort, by the endless litigations which arise between the different associations because of their respective claims concerning the scope of their exclusive privileges, surcharge industry with an enormous tax, grievous to the subjects and with no corresponding advantage to the state; which, in short, by the facility they afford to members of the guilds to combine among themselves and to compel the poorer members to submit to the rule of the wealthy, become an instrument of monopoly and give rise to schemes whose effect is to increase beyond all natural proportion the price of commodities which are most necessary for the subsistence of the people.

We shall not be deterred in this act of justice by the fear that a multitude of artisans will take advantage of the liberty bestowed upon all and embark in trades of which they are ignorant, and that the public will be inundated with poorly wrought articles. Liberty has not produced such evil effects in places where it has been established for a long time. Laborers in the suburbs and in other privileged places do not work less effectively than those in the interior of Paris. The whole world knows, besides, how illusory is the police of the craft-guilds, so far as concerns the perfection of work done, and that, all the members of the guilds being moved by the *esprit de corps* to stand by one another, any individual who complains finds himself nearly always condemned, and is harried by prosecution in court after court until he finds the course of justice more intolerable than the object of his complaint.

Those who understand the development of trade know that all important enterprises, whether of traffic or of industry, require the concurrence of two industrial classes, entrepreneurs who advance the raw material and the necessary implements of trade, and simple laborers who work for the account of the first for wages agreed upon. Herein lies the real distinction between entrepreneurs or masters and laborers or journeymen; it is based in the nature of things and does not depend on the arbitrary institution of corporations.

Surely, those who embark their capital in a business have the greatest interest to entrust their material only to good workmen; and there is no ground for fear that they will take the risk of employing poor workmen who can only mutilate their merchandise and drive away their purchasers. And it must be presumed, as well, that entrepreneurs will not put their fortunes into a business about which they do not know enough to be able to choose good workmen and to oversee their labor. We have no fear then, that the suppression of apprenticeships, of journeymen and master pieces, will expose the public to unacceptable service.

Nor do we fear that the sudden influx of a multitude of new workmen will ruin the older ones, and give a disastrous shock to business.

In places where business is freest, the number of merchants and laborers of all kinds is limited always, and necessarily in proportion to the need, that is to say, to consumption. It will not pass that proportion in places where liberty is restored. No new entrepreneur will risk his fortune by sacrificing his capital in a venture where success is doubtful, and where he has reason to fear the competition of all the masters at present established in the enjoyment of the advantage of a settled business and patronage.

The masters who today compose the guilds, by losing the exclusive privilege they have as sellers, will profit as buyers by the suppression of the exclusive privilege of all other guilds. The artisans will profit by the advantage of not being dependent, in the fabrication of their articles, upon the masters of many other corporations, each of which claims the privilege of furnishing some indispensable part. The merchants will gain the privilege of selling all the assortments accessory to their chief trade. All will profit especially by being independent of the leaders and officials of their guild, and in having no longer to pay the fees of frequent visits, in having release from a multitude of contributions for wasteful or prejudicial expenses, costs of ceremonies, banquets, conventions, law suits, all as frivolous in their object as they are ruinous by their multiplicity.

In suppressing the guilds for the general advantage of our subjects, we owe it to their legitimate creditors who have entered into contracts with them in the period of their authorized existence to provide for the security of their credits.

The debts of the guilds are of two classes; the one arise from loans made by the guilds, the amounts of which have been turned into our royal treasury for the acquisition of the offices created and now abolished; the other arise from loans they were authorized to make in order to meet their own expenses of all kinds.

The taxes alienated to these offices, and the fees the guilds have been authorized to collect, have been devoted hitherto to the payment of the interest on the debts of the first class, and even in part to the repayment of the capital. The amount of the same profits will continue to accumulate in our accounts, and the same fees will be collected in our name, to be devoted to the payment of interest and capital of these debts until they are wholly discharged. The part of their revenue which has been used by the guilds for their private expenses, being now released, will serve to augment the sinking fund which we design for the repayment of the capitals concerned.

With regard to the debts of the second class, by the reckoning we have secured of the condition of the guilds in our good city of Paris, we are assured that the amounts they have in bank, or which are due to them, and the chattels they hold and which their suppression will make subject to sale, will be sufficient to discharge what remains to be paid of those debts; and if they are not sufficient, we will provide the balance.

We believe we thus render all justice due the guilds; for we think we ought not repay to their members the taxes required of them from reign to reign, for the right of confirmation or enjoyment. The object of those taxes, which frequently did not come into the treasury of our predecessors, has been attained by the enjoyment the guilds had of their privileges during the reign under which the taxes were paid.

The privilege had to be renewed in each reign. We have restored to our people the sums our predecessors were accustomed to collect for their enjoyment; but we have not renounced the right, inalienable from our sovereignty, of summoning for examination the privileges too readily granted by our predecessors, and of refusing them confirmation if we judge them prejudicial to the welfare of the state and contrary to the rights of our other subjects.

It is for this reason that we have determined not to confirm them, and to revoke expressly the privileges accorded by our predecessors to guilds of merchants and artisans, and to pronounce that revocation general throughout our kingdom, because we owe the same justice to all our subjects.

But that same justice requires that at the moment when the suppression shall be effected provision be made for the payment of their debts, and since the explanations we have requested of the condition of those in the different cities of our provinces have not yet been furnished, we have decided to suspend, by a separate article, the application of our present edict to the guilds of the provincial cities until we shall have taken the necessary measures to provide for the discharge of their debts.

We regret that we are forced to except, for the present, from the liberty we are giving to all kinds of business and industry, the guilds of barbers, wig-makers, and bath-keepers, which institutions differ from other bodies of the same kind, in that the masterships of these callings were created by virtue of offices, the revenue from which has been received in our casual revenue, with the privilege extended to the officials of retaining their ownership by the payment of 1 per cent. We are compelled to defer the emancipation of this kind of industry until we may make arrangements for the extinction of those offices, and we will do this as soon as the condition of our finances will permit.

Certain vocations are susceptible of abuse and affect the confidence of the public, or the general police of the state, or even the safety and life of men: these trades require a surveillance and special precaution on the part of the public authority. These vocations are pharmacy, gold-smithing, and printing. The rules to which these have been subject are parts of the general system of craft-guilds, and without doubt, in that respect, they ought to be revised; but the special features of that reform, the arrangements which it will be best to preserve or to change are objects so important as to demand careful examination and reflection. And while we reserve the right to make known later our intentions in the matter of the rules to be fixed for the practice of these trades, we believe that, for the present, they should not be changed from their existing state.

In assuring to business and industry entire liberty and the full competition it should enjoy, we will take such measures as the preservation of public order may require, in order that those who follow the different crafts, arts and trades may be known and established, at the same time, under the protection and the discipline of the police.

To this end, the merchants and artisans, their names, residence and employment will be exactly recorded. They will be grouped, not on the basis of their vocations, but according to the quarter where they have their domicile. And the officials of the guilds abolished will be replaced advantageously by syndics established in each quarter or *arrondissement*, to guard public order, to report to the magistrates charged with the police, and to transmit their orders.

All the guilds have numerous law suits: all litigation which the corporations have among themselves will be quashed because of the reform of the exclusive rights they claimed. If, on the dissolution of corporations and guilds, it is found that some cases have been begun and prosecuted in their name which present objects of permanent interest, we will provide that these be carried to a final judgment, for the preservation of whatever rights pertain thereunto.

We will provide further that that class of suits at law, which are frequently raised between artisans and those who employ them, concerning the perfection or the price of labor, may be ended by whatever means are most simple and least costly.

For these causes, etc., etc.,

Article I. It shall be free to all persons, of whatever quality and condition they may be, even all foreigners who may not yet have obtained letters of naturalization from us, to embrace and to exercise in all our kingdom, and especially in our good city of Paris, such kind of business and such profession of arts and trades as may seem good to them, even combining many: to this end we have abolished and suppressed, we will to abolish and suppress all corporations and guilds of merchants and artisans, as well as masterships and craft-guilds. We abrogate all privileges, statutes and regulations given to the said corporations and guilds, by reason of which none of our subjects may be annoyed in the prosecution of his business and his trade, for any cause or under any pretext whatsoever.

Article II. And it will be required, nevertheless, that all those who desire to pursue the said profession or business shall make preliminary declaration before the Lieutenant-General of Police, which will be inscribed in a record provided for that purpose, and will contain their names, surnames and domiciles, the kind of trade or business they purpose to undertake, and in case of change of residence or of business, or of retiring from business or labor, the said merchants or artisans will be required in like manner to make their declaration to the said recorder, free from all expense, on penalty against those who pursue their callings without having made the said declaration, of seizure and confiscation of their articles and merchandises, and a fine of 50 livres.

We exempt, however, from that obligation the present masters of corporations and guilds, who will not be required to make the said declarations except in case of change of domicile, of business, of new combination of trades, or retirement from business and labor.

We exempt further those who are now, or who may wish to become, wholesale merchants, our intention being not to subject such to any rules or formalities to which wholesale dealers have not been subject hitherto.

Article III. The declaration and inscription in the police records, ordained in the preceding article, concerns only those merchants and artisans who labor for their own account and sell to the public. With regard to the common laborers, who are not answerable directly to the public, but to entrepreneurs or masters, for whose account they work, the said entrepreneurs or masters will be required, on every requisition, to submit to the Lieutenant-General of Police a statement containing the name, domicile and kind of work of each of them.

Article IV. We do not intend, further, to include in the dispositions effected by articles I. and II. the vocations of pharmacy, goldsmithing, printing and book-selling, with regard to which there will be no innovation until we may enact for their control whatever pertains thereunto.

Article V. We exempt in like manner from the provisions of the said articles I. and II. of the present edict the guilds of master *barbiers-perruquiers-étuvistes* in the places where their business is exercised until otherwise ordained by us.

Article VI. We will that the present masters of the guilds of butchers, bakers and others whose trade has to do with the daily subsistence of our subjects may not abandon their business within one year after the declaration which they will be required to make before the Lieutenant-General of Police that they intend to withdraw from their business and trade, on penalty of 500 livres fine, and heavier punishment if it befall.

Article VII. Merchants and artisans who are obliged to keep a record of the names of those persons from whom they buy certain commodities, such as silver-smiths, haberdashers, second-hand dealers and others, will be required to abide faithfully by those records, and to submit them to the officials of police on the first requisition.

Article VIII. Any drugs, the use of which may be dangerous, shall not be sold except by apothecaries or by merchants who shall obtain special written permission from the Lieutenant-General of Police, and besides, shall be required to inscribe in a record, signed by the Lieutenant-General of Police, the names, rank and residence of the persons to whom they may wish to sell them, under penalty of 1000 livres fine, even of extraordinary prosecution, according to the requirements of the case.

Article IX. Such arts and trades as may occasion in their operation dangers or exceptional inconvenience, either to the public or to private individuals, will continue to be subject to police regulations, made or to be made, in order to preclude those dangers and inconveniences.

Article X. *Arrondissements* will be formed in the different quarters of the cities of our kingdom, and especially in our good city of Paris, in each of which a syndic and two assistants will be appointed by the Lieutenant-General of Police, for the first year only, and after the registration and then upon the execution of the present edict; afterward, the said syndics and assistants shall be chosen annually by ballot by the merchants and artisans of the said *arrondissement*, in an assembly held for that purpose in the house of and in the presence of a commissioner appointed by the Lieutenant-General of Police; which commissioner shall draw up an official report free of expense; then the said syndics and assistants shall take oath before the Lieutenant-General of Police, to exercise supervision over the traders and artisans of their *arrondissement* without distinction of condition or business, to report to the said Lieutenant-General of Police, to receive and to transmit his orders, and those who are appointed syndics and assistants may not refuse to discharge the functions appointed them, nor by reason of the same may they demand or receive from the said merchants or artisans any sum, either as a present, by virtue of their honors, or as an exaction: we expressly forbid this on penalty of the law on malversation of public moneys.

Article XI. Law suits which arise because of bad workmanship or defects in finished goods will be brought before the Lord Lieutenant-General of Police, to whom we delegate exclusive jurisdiction, in order that, on the agreement of experts commissioned for that purpose by him, immediate judgment may be had, without cost, and in final resort, except in case the demand for indemnity exceeds the sum of 100 livres; in which case the matter will be tried in the ordinary form.

Article XII. In like manner there will be brought before the Lord Lieutenant-General of Police, for immediate judgment, without cost and in last resort, up to the amount of 100 livres, the law suits which may arise over the execution of engagements of time, apprentice contracts and agreements made by the masters and the laborers working for them, relative to that labor; and in case the sum at issue exceeds the value of 100 livres, they will be tried in the ordinary form.

Article XIII. We expressly forbid wardens or officials in charge of corporations or guilds to make hereafter any visits, inspections, seizures; to institute any action in the name of the said guilds; to convoke, or to assist to convoke any assembly under any pretext whatever, even under the pretext of acts of fraternities, which custom we abolish; and in general, to discharge any function in the capacity of wardens, and especially to demand or to receive any sum from members of their guilds, under any pretext whatever, on penalty of the law respecting malversation of public moneys, excepting, however, such sums as may be due to us for the taxes of the members of the said corporations and guilds, and the collection of these sums, both for the current year and what remains to be collected for preceding years, shall be made and continued in the usual form until payment is complete.

Article XIV. We forbid in like manner all masters, journeymen, laborers and apprentices of the said corporations and guilds to form any association or assembly among themselves under any pretext whatever. Wherefore, we have abolished and suppressed, do abolish and suppress, all fraternities which may have been established either by the masters of corporations and guilds or by journeymen and laborers in the arts and trades, even though set up by the statutes of the said corporations and guilds or by all other private claims, or even by letters-patent from us or our predecessors.

Article XV. With regard to the chapels erected on account of the said fraternities, endowments of the same and property included in the endowments; we will that provision for their employment be made by the bishops of the dioceses, in whatever manner they may deem most useful as well as to acquit the endowments; and letters patent will be drawn up, addressed to our court of parlement, in accordance with the decrees of the bishops.

Article XVI. The edict of the month of November, 1563, establishing consular jurisdiction in our good city of Paris, and the declaration of March 18, 1728, will be executed, as to the election of Consular Magistrates, in all that is not contrary to the present edict. Wherefore, we will that the presiding Consular Magistrates of the said city may be required to summon and assemble, three days before the expiration of their year, merchants to the number of sixty, citizens of the said city, provided that not more than five from each of the three guilds not suppressed may be summoned, apothecaries, gold-smiths and printer-booksellers, and not more than twenty-five appointed from among those who follow the vocations and business of dry goods, groceries, haberdashery, furs, hosiery, and wine selling, whether they conduct these trades singly or combine with them other branches of trade or of arts and commerce, amongst whom will be admitted by preference the wardens, syndics and assistants of the three guilds not suppressed and also those who are exercising, or who may exercise the functions of syndics or assistants of merchants or artisans in the various *arrondissements* of the said city; and with regard to those whom it may be necessary to add in order to fill out the number of sixty, they may be summoned up to the number of twenty by the said magistrates and consuls, from merchants and business men or other prominent *bourgeois* who are versed in business affairs; these sixty, together with the five Consular Magistrates presiding, and no others, thirty-two of them choosing, shall proceed, in the form and according to the provisions decreed by the said edict and the said declaration, to elect new magistrates and consuls; these shall take the oath of office in the great hall of our parlement in the accustomed manner.

Article XVII. All law suits now pending, in whatever court, between the said corporations and guilds, arising out of their claims or privileges or any other pretense whatever, shall be terminated by virtue of the present edict.

We forbid all *gardes-jurés* who have power of attorney, and all other agents whatever of the said corporations and guilds, to take any action by reason of the said suits, on pain of nullity and of answering in their person and private name for all costs which may be incurred. And with regard to suits resulting from seizures of chattels and merchandises, or whatever may have been given in place of them, we will that they in like manner be and remain terminated, and that the said chattels and merchandises be returned to those from whom they were seized, by virtue of a plain receipt which they shall give to the persons who happen to be in charge of the goods or acting as depositaries; reserving the provision for costs incurred until the day appointed for payment shall be set by the Lieutenant-General of Police, whom we appoint to this end, at which time the restitutions, damages, interests and costs which may be due to private individuals shall be taken from the sums belonging to the said guilds, if they are sufficient to cover the said amounts; if they are not, other provision will be made by us.

Article XVIII. With regard to the law suits of the said corporations and guilds which involve landed property, sites, payments on arrears of profits and other objects of like nature, we reserve to ourselves the right to provide the means of securing prompt investigation and trial by the courts where they are now on the docket.

Article XIX. We will that, within the space of three months, all wardens, syndics, and magistrates, both those who are now presiding and those who are about to relinquish their offices, as well as those who have not yet made their reports of their administration, be required to submit them, namely, in our good city of Paris, to the Lieutenant-General of Police, and in the provinces to commissioners whom we shall appoint for that purpose, in order that writs and revisions may be executed in the ordinary form, and constraints issued for the payment of the balance as shall be enacted by us, in order that all sums arising may be used to discharge the debts of the said guilds.

Article XX. To the end of providing for the payment of the debts of the said guilds of the city of Paris and for securing the claims of their creditors, there will be placed, without delay, in the hands of the Lieutenant-General of Police, schedules of the said debts, of payments made, of what remains to be paid, of means on hand for their payment, both fixed real estate and property and chattels and accounts which may happen to belong to them. All those who claim to be creditors of the said guilds will be required in like manner, within three months from the day of publication of the present edict, to submit to the Lieutenant-General of Police the titles of their credits, or certified copies of the same, in order that provision for their payment may be assured in whatever sums may belong to them.

Article XXI. The product of duties imposed by the kings, our predecessors, on different materials and merchandises, the collection and control of which have been granted to some of the corporations and guilds of the city of Paris, as well as the profits which have been assigned to them through the purchase of offices created at various times, and which have been included in the list of charges upon our finances, will continue to be exclusively devoted to the payment of arrears and to the payment of the capital of the loans made by the said guilds. We will that any sum in excess, arising from these products, above what will be necessary to discharge the arrears, as well as the entire saving resulting either from the diminution in the cost of collection or from the extinction of the expenses of the guilds which were taken out of these products, or from the diminution of interest charges because of successive reimbursements, be used as a sinking fund for the entire extinction of the capital of the said loans; and to this end a particular bank will be designated by us, under the inspection of the Lieutenant-General of Police, into which will be turned annually the amount of the said profits as the product of the said administrations, to be used only for the payment of arrearages and the repayment of capital.

Article XXII. Proceedings will be brought before the Lieutenant-General of Police for the sale of the land and other real estate as well as of the chattels of the said corporations and guilds, the product of which shall be used in the discharge of their debts, as has been enacted by article XX. herein. And in case the product of the said sale exceeds, for any corporation or guild, the amount of its debts, both to us and to private individuals, the said excess shall be divided in equal portions among the present masters of the said corporation or guild.

Article XXIII. With regard to the debts of corporations or guilds established in our provincial cities, we enact that, in the said space of three months, those who claim to be creditors of the said corporations or guilds be required to put into the hands of our Lieutenant-General of Police the titles of their said credits, or summarized schedules of the same, in order that the amount of the said debts may be determined by us and provision be made for their payment; and until we have taken the necessary measures to accomplish that end, we suspend in our provincial cities the suppression ordained by the present edict.

Article XXIV. We have made void and do make void by the present edict, all edicts, declarations, letters-patent, writs, statutes and regulations contrary to this present edict.

So given and commanded, etc., etc.

DECLARATION OF THE KING

Which Repeals Certain Rules Concerning Which the Letters-Patent of November 2, 1774, had Treated, Suppressing All Taxes Established in Paris on Wheat, Méteils, Rye, Flour, Peas, Beans, Lentils and Rice, and Moderating Those on Other Grain Products

Louis, etc., One of the first duties we felt we owed to the felicity of our peoples was to assure their daily subsistence by recalling, by the decree of our Council of September 13, 1774, and the letters-patent expediting the same of November 2 following, to its true principles legislation concerning the trade in grain. We desire that these principles be exposed clearly and in detail, in order to make known to our people that the surest means of procuring abundance is to maintain free circulation, so that the commodities may pass from places of abundance and supply to those of want and demand; to protect and to encourage the trade so that the doors will more surely be open to the places where there is the greatest consumption and a more certain market.

We have had the satisfaction of seeing the measures we have taken justified by experience, even in the midst of popular prejudice, of the inquietudes and annoyances arising from these prejudices, and of devastations committed by an ignorant or deluded populace. After an unusually poor harvest, the inadequacy of which was attested by the amount of new grain which provisioned the markets, even before the following harvest was garnered, and despite the disarrangement and cessation of trade which the renewal of old rules that are contrary to liberty wrought in the speculations of dealers, and the interruption of the trade in grain which resulted from these regulations during many years, the commodity, nevertheless, was not lacking; the afflicted provinces were relieved by the resources of those which were better supplied; a considerable quantity of grain was imported into the realm; and the price, though higher than we could have desired, was not so excessive, however, as we have often seen it under the prohibitive regime, even in years when the harvest was generally much better than that of the year 1774.

At least, a better harvest restored abundance. We may not hasten too quickly to turn to advantage these days of tranquility and complete the removal of all obstacles which may yet retard the activity and progress of commerce, in order that, if crop failure afflicts our provinces anew, our people may find resources prepared in advance against famine, and that they may not be exposed longer to the excessive variations in the value of grains which destroy all semblance of proportion between the level of wages and the cost of subsistence.

Great cities, and especially capitals, naturally attract abundance by the wealth and number of consumers. Our good city of Paris seems in particular to be destined to become the *entrepôt* of a most extensive trade.

The rivers Seine, Yonne, Marne, Oise and Loire, by the canals of Briare and Orleans, establish ready communication between this city and the most fertile provinces of our kingdom; they offer a natural passage by means of which the wealth of all the provinces should circulate freely and be distributed among them; the vast extent of the consumption of Paris includes necessarily a great part of commodities of all kinds, if nothing arrests them in their course; it would even have at its disposal all the commodities which a free commerce would be impelled to secure for it and turn into it from all contiguous provinces.

Nevertheless, we admit with regret that the provisionment with grain of our said city, far from being abundant and ready as it would be in a state of free circulation, has been for many centuries an object of sore care for the government and of solicitude for the police, and that these attentions have tended only to repress the commerce entirely.

In giving our letters-patent of November 2, 1774, we proposed to ourselves to seek out, by the most rigid examination of the separate police regulations of our said city of Paris, the causes which set themselves in opposition to the facility of its provisionment, as we announced by article 5 of the said letters-patent our intention to ordain concerning those rules by a new law.

We have had before us accordingly the ordinances, decrees and regulations of police pertaining to the trade in grain and the provisionment of Paris.

We discover that in calamitous times of trouble and civil war, in the centuries when commerce had no existence, and its principles could not be known, the kings, our predecessors, Charles VI, Charles IX, and Henry III, promulgated some ordinances covering that matter; that, without the concurrence of royal authority, many police rules have been added to form a body of legislation equivalent to a prohibition of bringing grain into Paris; that custom and precedent have maintained it, and sometimes confirmed it; that, even when government began to bring to bear on that object a more enlightened attention, vigorous claims were made for the conservation of that police; that it has been preserved as if it had been the safeguard of the facility of subsistence.

That officials, created at different times in connection with the market and port, were charged with the oversight of its execution, and were nevertheless authorized to collect taxes which further injured the sale of grain.

That, finally, for some few years, a tax has been laid on that trade for the construction of a market and warehouse.

Thus, in combining the different effects of the police designed to assure the necessities of life in Paris, it results that not only do the taxes of various nature increase the price of grain and flour, but that these regulations prevent their abundance, and that all parts of this legislation are so mutually contradictory and so opposed to their object, that the one indispensable thing required to reform them is to expose, by the simplest statement, these regulations and their effects.

An ordinance of February, 1415, renewed by a decree of August 19, 1661, forbids any one to store or to remove the sacks of grain or flour arriving by land, to unload, to store in granaries or *magasins*, or even under awnings, the same commodities arriving by water; as a result, according to these regulations, they have to remain exposed to the atmosphere, to the rain and the damp, which destroys them. The same decree of 1661 forbids accumulating any store of grain, and allowing it to be stopped in the places where purchased, or at the ports of lading, or on the roads by which it should arrive.

These combined restrictions prevent Paris from having any means of keeping a supply of grain and flour within its borders or of having any supply in its environs.

The same ordinance of 1415 imposes on the merchants who bring grain to Paris the obligation to sell before the third market day, on penalty of being compelled to sell at the lower price of the preceding markets; and the decree of August 19, 1661, and the Ordinance of Police of March 31, 1635, after having taken away from all merchants the privilege of making any purchase in Paris, forbid in like manner all bakers from purchasing more than two hogsheads of wheat at a single bargain.

Thus the same police, by its contradictory dispositions, forces the sale and forbids the purchase.

By conforming strictly to that police, the capital could never have provision for more than eleven days' consumption; for the interval between three markets is only eleven days, and, on one hand, the merchants, assured of not having free disposition of their commodity after that interval, and of being forced, perhaps, to sell at a loss, would bring into Paris only the grain necessary for eleven days' subsistence; while on the other hand, the city could have no provisions in its private *dépôts*, since they are prohibited there; nor even in the bake-shops, since they are forbidden to buy more than two hogsheads of grain.

If that police be observed, every time that high or low water, or ice and snow interrupted navigation or land travel for more than eleven days, the inhabitants of Paris would wholly lack subsistence in the most fruitful years, and in the midst of the abundance which the rest of the kingdom enjoys.

A decree of Parlement on August 23, 1565, forbade grain merchants, on penalty of corporal punishment, to export from the city, either by land or by water, going either up or down the river, the grain they had brought into it; two ordinances of police, of 1622 and 1632, added to the rigor of that decree by forbidding the purchase and the removal of any grain for a greater distance than ten leagues from Paris, on penalty of confiscation and arbitrary fine.

These dispositions tend to banish trade in grain from the city of Paris, where the *négociant* is deprived of liberty and almost of the property right in his commodity, and especially of the allurement, so essential to trade, of being able to take it where there is hope of receiving profit; that police informs him that he can neither enter the city nor pass within the *arrondissement* of ten leagues, and that space becomes an insurmountable point of separation between all the provinces which might have profited by the advantages of navigation, for their mutual succor; in this way Bourgogne and Champagne, having an over-supply of grain, cannot relieve Normandy afflicted by famine, for the sole reason that the Seine traverses Paris and its *arrondissement*: in the same way scarcely any relief could be brought from Normandy to Paris and beyond, by ascending the Seine, until, by our edict of June, 1775, suppressing the offices of privileged merchants and carriers of grain, and abolishing the right of *banalité* of the city of Rouen, we removed the obstacles which intercepted the grain trade in that city.

The police ordinance of 1635, cited above, and confirmed by an edict of 1772, forbade merchants who had begun the sale of a cargo of wheat to increase the price; and by an obvious injustice, the merchant subject to hasards which might have diminished the price at the commencement of his sale could not profit by those which, before the end of that sale, might have made the price more advantageous.

The same rules enjoin further, that all traders who bring grain to Paris shall conduct the sale there in person or by some member of the family, and not by brokers (*facteurs*); it ignored the fact that the laborer can not then abandon the tasks of cultivation, or the trader the care of his business, to follow a part of his merchandise; that neither of them can leave without expense; and that these expenses, having to be defrayed out of their trade, would uselessly augment the price of grains.

The prohibition laid on wagoners (*voituriers*), by the edict of 1661, from selling grain along the road, and even from untying the sacks, on penalty of confiscation, is without object in regard to the trade, which should not be throttled by being bound up with such details; it is inhuman toward those of our subjects who may happen to have immediate and pressing needs; it is still more inconvenient and repulsive to the dealer whom it exposes to anxiety and to unjust punishment, perhaps, if some accident obliges him to touch the sacks of grain which he is conveying.

Finally, the obligation imposed by the same decree of 1661 on those who carry on the grain trade for Paris, to submit their invoices to notaries, to present them to the officials of grain, and to register them in a public record, is a formality contrary to all the customs and interests of commerce, which demands above all else good faith, secrecy and celerity of transaction; and that law has no other object than to occasion expenses which increase the cost of sales.

It is by such rules that it was deemed most fit in other times, and almost to our day, to provide the subsistence of our good city of Paris. The *négociants*, whose function is that of necessary agents of circulation and who carry abundance unfailingly wherever they find liberty, security and markets, have been treated as enemies who must be harassed on the way and loaded with chains when they arrive; the grain they bring to the city cannot be taken out: but they can neither keep it nor protect it from the ravages of climate and corruption; they are forced to hasty sales; they are stopped from making purchases; the merchant must sell his grain by the third market day or lose control of it; the purchaser can provide for his wants only slowly and in small quantities. Diminution in prices brings a loss to the trader; their increase can profit him nothing; the grain merchants, dismayed by the rigors of the police, are moreover exposed to public hatred; the trade is oppressed, slandered on all sides, and driven from the city; a district twenty leagues in diameter divides the provinces of greatest abundance from each other and from our city; and yet all precautions were forbidden in the interior of the city and the outskirts; they seem even to have conspired against future harvests, by requiring that the laborer quit his work to follow his grain and sell it himself.

That disastrous police produced in former times the effects which might be expected; periods of excessive and protracted scarcity rapidly succeeded years of abundance; these were prolonged without actual famine; they led to violent and dangerous remedies, which only prolonged them because commerce, destroyed by these rules, could offer no help.

Such at least are the effects which our city of Paris experienced in 1660, 1661, 1662, 1663; in the years 1692, 1693, 1694; in the years 1698 and 1699; then in the year 1709, and later in the years 1740 and 1741, sad times when the price of grain, though moderate in the provinces, was nevertheless excessive in Paris; when the excess of price was determined, not by the effective quantities of goods, but by the greed of a small number of merchants to whom the sale of grain was granted, under a regime which permitted neither trade, nor circulation, nor competition. Only the disregard of these exasperating restrictions, based on the laws of necessity, has been able to make less uncertain the provisionment of our good city of Paris; they were a ceaseless menace of famine and high prices; it was necessary to tolerate resources against frost and floods; to have *magasins* in the district of ten leagues, and even in the interior; to permit the merchants to preserve their grain against climatic conditions, to allow them time to make their sales, and the privilege of employing agents: it is only by the non-execution of the laws that Paris has been able to provide its subsistence.

But the non-execution of such laws is not sufficient to reassure the trade, which their existence continually menaces; it has not recovered its functions; the government, being unable to rely on it, believes it necessary to proceed by itself to secure the provisionment of the capital. It has found that that precaution, reputed necessary, involves the greatest possible inconvenience; that the commerce conducted under its orders admits neither the extent and celerity, nor the economy of the ordinary commerce; that its authorized agents, in all the markets where they appear, bring alarm and sudden rise in prices; that they by reason of their very functions commit many abuses; that operations of that kind completing the discouragement and absolute ruin of ordinary trade, enormously increase the expenses, and by consequence the burdens of our subjects who supply the funds; and finally, that they do not accomplish their object.

It is especially in recent times that the multiplied inconveniences of the laws have been conspicuously apparent. The declaration of May 25, 1763, seemed to open the way to agricultural prosperity and facility of subsistence, by ordaining that the circulation of grain should be entirely free in all parts of the kingdom; but a multitude of particular and local obstacles thwarted the general intent of the law and embarrassed all communication; they were not yet recalled or removed.

The edict of July, 1764, was in force for only a very short time, when its provisions were changed: that legislation, yet incomplete, needed careful attention; and yet the poor harvests caused every proposed innovation to be regarded with timidity, until the decree of the Council of December 23, 1770, and the letters-patent of September 16, 1771, recalling the prohibitive régime of past centuries, refastened the shackles from which the grain trade was barely disentangled, and surcharged it with numerous and complex formalities which made it impossible.

At that time the inequality of harvests ceased to be the measure of the value of grains; their true price existed nowhere; they were given an excessive value in some places, and moderate and even low valuation in places immediately contiguous. Wheat and rye were lacking in our most frequented ports, and they could be brought from other ports where abundance reigned, only when directed by the Admiralty office. The appearance of some local famine, always at hand, burdens the government with solicitude, with excessive expenses and with compulsory operations which give the people much disquiet and too little real relief; and in the spaces of time when many successive harvests have been sufficiently good, the general price of grain has been higher than in 1775, after the poor harvest of 1774.

The examination of these facts, which are well known to the public, convinces us that only a commerce emancipated from all annoyance and all fear will suffice for all needs, prevent the inequalities in price and the sudden and startling variations which so often come without any actual cause; that it alone, in case of misfortune, will be able to remedy the actual famines in a way that all government expenditures can never succeed in doing.

Determined to give, on all occasions, proofs to our people of our love for them, and to make what sacrifices their welfare and the facility of their subsistence may demand of us, we will to choose in preference and to make known to them those things of which the utility is most certain and most direct; we purpose to establish abundance within their walls, by repealing the rules which banish it, by freeing grain from the taxes which increase the price and which vex the trade; finally, by delivering it from the troublesome functions of certain offices created to oversee the execution of these rules, and which it is in our mind to suppress, along with other offices of the same kind, by our edict of this month.

We are determined to exempt from all taxes and to grant the enjoyment of absolute immunity to wheat, *méteils*,[1] rye, flour, peas, beans, lentils and rice, destined for consumption by the people of our said city; but, while exercising our beneficence in the present extinction of taxes, we would not forget that it is in our justice to provide for indemnities due by reason of the suppressions which we purpose to ordain.

One part of the duties which are collected on grain has been conceded to the *prévôt* of merchants and aldermen of our good city

---

[1] Mixed grains.

of Paris, by the declaration of November 25, 1762, for the establishment of a new market and warehouse. The revenue is assigned to the payment of present charges, the acquittal of which will be provided for by us until January 1, 1783, at which time the payment of the claim for market and warehouse should cease, by the terms of the same declaration.

Another part of the same taxes was devoted to the offices of measurers and carriers of grain, established in connection with the market and ports by the edict of the month of June, 1730, and which are included in the general suppression ordained by our edict of this month.

The order effectually to establish the indemnities assured to these offices by our edict requires that we reserve, to be collected to our profit, a part of the taxes, attributed to the same offices, on oats, grain and grain products other than wheat, *méteils*, rye, flour, peas, beans, lentils and rice, and less useful to the subsistence of our people than the kinds we specifically emancipate.

We will, however, to distinguish and to abolish only that portion of the taxes which represents the wages of porters actually employed in the service of the markets; we will continue to collect that part reserved to the officials, as an interest in their finance.

We have no doubt that commerce delivered from all encumbrances and encouraged by our laws will provide for all the needs of our good city of Paris. Therefore a constant abundance and just prices for the necessities of life ought to be the consequence and effect of the reform of a vexatious police, of the protection we accord to trade, of the freedom of communication, and finally, of the absolute immunity from all taxes which increase the price; and the good we shall accomplish for our subjects will be the most grateful recompense for the pains we take in their behalf. For these causes, etc.

Article I. We will that it may be free to all persons, of whatever quality and condition they may be, to bring in and to hold in storage or *magasin*, both in our good city of Paris and in the circumscribing district of ten leagues and elsewhere, grain and flour, and to sell them in such places as shall seem good to them, even away from boats and markets.

Article II. It shall be likewise free to all persons, even to bakers of our good city of Paris, to buy grain and flour at all hours, in such quantities and in such places, both within the said city and elsewhere, as they judge fit.

Article III. Those who have grain and flour, whether in the markets and ports, or in granaries or *magasins* in the said city of Paris, shall not be constrained to sell them at the third market day, or at any other fixed time.

Article IV. Those who have grain to sell in our said city may also increase as well as lower the price, in conformity with the course of trade, without being compelled, under the pretext of uncovering a pile or cargo of grain, and commencing the sale from one or both, to continue the sale at the same price.

Article V. It shall be equally free to all those who have grain or flour in the said city of Paris to sell them in person or by brokers or agents.

Article VI. Those who carry on trade in grain in our city of Paris, or for it, may not be in any case constrained to submit any declarations, bills of lading or invoices before notaries, or to record them in any public record.

Article VII. It shall be free to all persons to remove, both from the city of Paris and from its circumscribing district of ten leagues, the grain and flour they may have brought in, or which they may have purchased therein, without needing, for that end, any permission.

Article VIII. We have abolished and suppressed, do abolish and suppress the taxes on wheat, *méteils*, rye, flour, peas, beans, lentils and rice, which we have included in the suppression ordained, by our edict of the present month, of different offices created in connection with the ports and markets; all of which taxes on the commodities most necessary to life, we do give and restore to the inhabitants of our good city of Paris. We forbid, under severe penalty, all persons, under pretext of the same, to make any such collection, beginning from the day of publication of our present declaration.

Article IX. We have in like manner abolished and suppressed, do abolish and suppress the tax for market and warehouse levied on wheat, *méteils*, rye, flour, peas, beans, lentils and rice, together with the 8 sous per livre assessed on account of the same tax; and, in consequence of the provisions enacted by the present article and by the preceding article, the said grain and flour are exempt from all taxes whatsoever in our good city of Paris. We will, furthermore, that the collection of the said tax for market and warehouse, on all other commodities and merchandises which are subject to it, and which are not specifically freed by our present declaration, shall continue to be made for the benefit of the *prévôt* of merchants and aldermen of our good city of Paris, until January 1, 1783, when the said collection should cease, in accordance with the letters-patent of November 25, 1762, by which it was established.

Article X. We have reserved and do reserve (as is herein set forth), to be collected to our profit, the taxes attributed to the offices of measurers and carriers of grain, levied on oats, malt, grains and grain products other than wheat, *méteils*, rye, peas, beans, lentils and rice. We will that the said collection be made at the barriers by the agents and clerks of the Farmer General of our taxes, who shall be held to strict account, in conformity with the provisions of article III of the edict of the present month, enacting the suppression of guilds of officials to whom the taxes have been assigned.

Article XI. We ordain that, under the taxes reserved and designated by the preceding article, a separation be made of that part answering to the wages of labor, which the said officials may have received in connection with the grain in the markets and ports; and that from the day of publication of our present declaration, the said portion shall cease to be collected; and the other part of the same taxes, which we have intended to reserve, shall be collected on the basis of, and in conformity with, the tariff attached under the counter-seal of our present declaration.

Article XII. Provision will be made by us for the indemnity due the said *prévôt* of merchants and aldermen of our good city of

Paris, by reason of the extinction ordained, by article IX herein, of the market and warehouse tax on grain and flour announced in the said article, and from funds which shall be designated by us for that purpose.

Article XIII. Furthermore, our letters-patent, given concerning the commerce in grain on November 2, 1744, shall be executed for our good city of Paris, and for the circumscribing *arrondissement* of ten leagues. We annul all ordinances, edicts, declarations, letters-patent, decrees and regulations contrary to the same.

So given by commandment, etc.

EDICT OF THE KING

Enacting the Suppression of the Exchange of Poissy, and the Conversion and Modification of Duties

Louis, etc. It not infrequently happens, in the necessities of the State, that it is sought to adorn the taxes, which must needs be imposed, by some pretext of public utility. That subterfuge, to which the kings our predecessors sometimes believed it necessary to descend, has rendered the taxes, the birth of which it marked, more onerous. One of its results was that the taxes endured long after the need which had been their real cause, by reason of the apparent utility by which they were disguised, or that they were renewed under the same pretext, which favored various private interests.

Thus in January, 1690, to sustain the war begun in the preceding year, sixty offices of *jurés-vendeurs* of cattle were created, to which was granted 1 sou per livre of the value of the cattle consumed in Paris, on condition that they pay foreign merchants the cash for the animals they brought in: this appeared likely to encourage the trade and to procure abundance by preventing the delays to which the drovers were exposed so long as they dealt directly with the butchers.

The first trial gave rise to innumerable complaints on the part of both foreign merchants and the butchers, who represented that the creation of *jurés-vendeurs* of cattle was a grievous burden on their trade instead of an advantage to it; that there was no need of any intermediary between the men who supplied the animals and those who retailed to the public; that Paris had been provisioned before without any one appointed to advance payments to the vendors of animals; and that the tax of 1 sou per livre necessarily raised the price of meat and lessened the demand. These representations were regarded; and, by a declaration of March 11th of the same year, the king, Louis XIV, "wishing," said he, "to treat with consideration the said foreign merchants and the butchers of the said city of Paris, and to procure an abundance of cattle for it," suppressed the sixty offices of *jurés-vendeurs*. However, at the end of seventeen years, in 1707, in the course of an unfortunate war, after having exhausted all other resources, recourse was again had to the arguments which produced the edict of 1690: it was alleged that certain individuals were exacting from the butchers usurious charges, and one hundred offices of Treasury-Counsellors of the Bourse of the markets of Sceaux and of Poissy were created, with the view of having a bureau in daily oversight of the market, to advance to foreign merchants the price of the animals sold by them to butchers and other solvent merchants; and these officials were authorized to collect 1 sou per livre of the value of all animals sold, even of those for which they had not advanced the price. This institution, so strongly suggestive of the times of calamity, was suppressed again when peace was assured.

The trade in cattle, freed from fees and kindred shackles, recovered its natural course and continued for thirty years without interruption. During that period Paris was abundantly provisioned, and the raising of cattle flourished in many of our provinces.

But the expenses of a new war urged the government, at the end of 1743, to make use of the same financial resource which was supported by the same pretext. It was supposed to be necessary to lower the price of animals by putting the foreign merchants in position to supply the greatest possible number. It was held that the most plausible means of accomplishing this was to pay them in cash, and that this advantage would not be too dear at a deduction of 1 sou per livre. But although that deduction was established for all sales of animals, the bank was exempted, as in 1707, from advancing the price to those who sold to butchers not of recognized solvency; the period of credit to others was limited to two weeks. These rules restricted the usefulness of the bank, practically, to collecting a fee of 1 sou per livre.

That fee was farmed: it has continued from that time to be a part of the revenue of the State. One-fourth sou per livre was added by the edict of 1747, and continued in force by lettres-patent of March 16, 1755, and of March 3, 1767.

In bringing these edicts and letters-patent to our attention, we have been unable to escape the conviction that their provisions were directly opposed to the effects it was hoped and promised would be accomplished by them.

The duty of 6 per cent, which raised the price of each animal more than *fifteen livres*, did not fail to raise the price of meat instead of lowering it, and to cut down the profits of the breeders who raised and fattened the stock; it discouraged that industry and annihilated the abundance, not only of meat in the shops, but still more of the herds which the pastures might have supported, had there been adequate profit in raising the greatest possible number.

On the other hand, if it seems advantageous that the majority of the foreign merchants should receive in cash the price of the cattle brought in by them, it is no less contrary to every principle of justice that the wealthy butchers who are able to pay their bills in cash for themselves, should, notwithstanding that, be compelled to pay interest on an advance they do not need; and that the butchers who happen to be in less easy circumstances and to whom credit is refused on the ground that they are not regarded as unquestionably solvent, be also compelled to pay the interest on an advance which is not made for them at all.

The edict which created the exchange fixed fifteen days as the limit of time for the butchers to acquit themselves of their obligations to the bank of Poissy, and gave to the farmers of that exchange the right of corporal constraint in the third week; the result is that the effective advance of amounts loaned is never equal to one-twelfth of the amount of the sales; it should be much less than that, inasmuch as the bankers, having the right to refuse credit to butchers of questionable solvency, are far from making advances for all the sales.

Nevertheless, the interest has to be paid just as if the whole amount of the sale had been advanced, and in like manner if the sale is made on the first day of the year, interest must be paid as if it was for the full year. The tax that is paid ought, then, to be regarded less as the price of advances made to butchers as a genuine tax on cattle and on butcher's meat.

We would desire that the condition of our finances permitted us to sacrifice entirely that branch of revenue; but since that is impossible, and we cannot tolerate it in its present form, we have preferred to replace it by an increase of duty collected on entry into Paris, both on live animals and on meat destined for consumption. The simplicity of that method of collection, which involves no new expense, places us in position to relieve our subjects, at the present time, from about two-thirds of the burden laid on them to provide the fees of the Exchange of Poissy.

Besides, we are convinced that the greatest advantage our subjects will derive from the change will result from the greater freedom which the suppression of the Exchange of Poissy will bring to the trade in cattle. It is from that liberty, from the competition it will beget, and the encouragement it will give to production, that there may be attained the reestablishment of abundance of herds and moderation in the price of so large a part of the subsistence of our subjects.

For these causes, etc., we have, by the present edict, enacted and ordained as follows:

Article I. We will that, beginning from the first day of Lent of the present year, the fee of 1 sou per livre of the value of animals designed for the provisionment of Paris, established by edict of 1744, and the additional one-fourth sou per livre of the said fee, established by the edict of September, 1747, both continued by letters-patent of March 16, 1755, and March 3, 1767, and collected by virtue of the same at the markets of Sceaux and Poissy, be and remain suppressed.

Article II. In order to make good in part the diminution which will be effected in our revenues by the suppression of fees enacted by the preceding article, in the future, there will be collected, beginning from the first day of Lent next following, at the gates and entries of our good city of Paris, in addition to, and in increase of, the duties which are now established, the extra fees herein announced:

	Livres	Sous	Deniers
For each bullock	5	1	1
cow	3	10	
calf	11	10	45
sheep	6		
pound of dressed beef, veal and mutton	5	12	75

Article III. The supplemental duties established by the preceding article being entirely destined to replace that part of our revenue, which came from the duty of 1 sou per livre and the one-fourth sou per livre of the same, established on the sale of animals in the markets of Sceaux and Poissy, and which we have suppressed by the preceding article; the said supplemental duties cannot be subject to, nor give place to, any duty of first or second twentieths, old or new sous per livre, fees of officials, gratuitous gift, fee of service, and sous per livre of the same in favor of the General Hospital of the city of Paris, of any *titulaires* of offices, of any administration, or of the highest bidder of our *fermes*.

Article IV. The duty on each pound of veal will be lowered to a total of six and sixteen twenty-fifths deniers, and reduced to the same basis as that per pound of beef, veal or mutton, reserving the right of indemnity to whatever amount may pertain thereto.

Article V. We have suppressed, and in like manner do suppress, beginning from the same day, the Caisse or Bourse of the markets of Sceaux and Poissy, established and prorogued by the edicts and declarations of 1743, 1755, and 1767; we cancel the former lease to Bouchinet and his sureties; and we release him from the engagements under it, reserving to ourselves to provide whatever indemnity the highest bidder of our *fermes-générales* may claim because of the one-fourth sou per livre included in his lease.

Article VI. We authorize the said Bouchinet and his sureties to recover, within the accustomed period, the sums they may happen to have advanced before the said first day of Lent: we will that they cease to make new advances, and we confirm them in the right of prosecution and privilege which they have enjoyed heretofore for the recovery of their funds.

Article VII. We permit butchers and foreign merchants who bring in animals to them, to make among themselves such agreements as they judge fit, and to stipulate such credit as shall seem good to them.

Article VIII. We permit, also, among those who have managed for us the said Caisse or Bourse of Poissy, and to all others of our subjects, to loan, on conditions which shall be mutually and voluntarily accepted, their money to butchers who believe they have need of it in the conduct of their business.

Thus do we give and command, etc.

LETTERS-PATENT

Of February 6, 1776, Enacting a Change and Modification of Taxes on Suet

Louis, etc. Having rendered an account in our Council of the different police regulations, decisions and writs interfering in the matter of trade in suet in our good city of Paris, and also of the taxes of different nature which are collected on that commodity, and of the form of their collection, we have discovered that the imaginary precautions, taken during a period of two centuries, to procure the abundance and cheapness of a substance so essential to meet the needs of our people, have had necessarily effects directly opposite to what was intended; that, by the old rules of 1567 and 1577, maintained by later decisions, and particularly by a writ of August 19, 1758, no permission was granted either to the butchers who collect and render the suet to handle it themselves and to sell it freely, or to the chandlers who made use of it, to supply themselves with whatever quantity they deemed necessary for their work; that the suet had to be set out for sale on fixed days, and divided among the master chandlers, who could pay only a uniform price on penalty of fine; that what it became necessary to import in order to supply what was lacking in our kingdom, was subject to the same rules and a like division, and that as a result, no private individual could be permitted to speculate in this useful branch of trade; that the whole guild of chandlers could not do so, even if they were free, because of the heavy duties laid upon the importation of that material, until they had persuaded the late king, our very honored lord and grandfather, to moderate them by the writ of his Council of November 28, 1768. We have been unable to discover in that police, so contrary to all the principles of trade, anything other than a consequent abuse resulting from the vicious constitution of corporations and guilds which we are determined to suppress. Our purpose being that for the future the business of butcher and chandler, as well as all others, shall be freely followed, the method of exposing for public sale and division among the master chandlers can no longer continue; and, the taxes to which it has been subject being no longer suffered to be collected in the manner hitherto followed, it is necessary to substitute a method simpler and more advantageous to the people. Wherefore, we have provided this by a writ issued this day in our Council, in our presence, and we have ordained that for its execution all necessary letters shall be drawn up. For these causes, etc., We have decreed as follows:

Article I. Trade in suet shall be free for the future in our good city of Paris, and the obligation of exposing it for sale for division among the chandlers, shall remain abrogated, beginning from the publication of the writ of this date and these presents, notwithstanding all decisions of police and writs in confirmation of the same, which we will to be regarded as null and void; wherefore, all butchers shall be free to sell, as well as all chandlers to purchase the said commodity, in such times or places, and in such quantity as shall seem good to them.

Article II. The tax of a sou per pound levied on the sale of suet in the interior of Paris, shall be suppressed and shall cease to be collected beginning from the same day.

Article III. In order to supply the amount of the said tax, it will be replaced by a tax on the animals which produce the suet, in proportion to the average quantity taken from them; which tax, moderate in itself, will be collected only at the entries and barriers of Paris, at the rate of 2 livres 12 sous 2 25deniers per bullock, 1 livre 5 sous 5 15deniers per cow, and 5 sous 2 deniers per head of mutton.

Article IV. The said tax of entrance established by the preceding Article shall not be subject to any additional fees in favor of the city of Paris, of the General Hospital, or of our Farmers-General, since the tax is only by way of replacement and the tax which it replaces was not subject to any additional fees.

Article V. The main tax of 100 sous per quintal, on the entrance of foreign suet into Paris, will be reduced to 1 livre 10 sous 9 35deniers, so that, with the fees of domain, *barrage*, *poids-le-roi*, and sou per livre of the same, which amounts to 11 sous 2 25deniers, it will make the sum of 2 livres 10 sous per quintal, or 6 deniers per pound of suet or of tallow.

Article VI. All additional taxes of first and second twentieths, 4 sous per livre of the first twentieth, *gare*, gratuity, twentieth of gratuity, and 8 sous per livre of the same, established on the entry of foreign suet, shall be and remain suppressed, we reserving, if it so happen, the right to make whatever indemnity may pertain thereto.

Article VII. The taxes established by articles III. and V. herein shall be administered and collected by the contractor (*adjudicataire*) of our *fermes-générales*, for our account; therefore, the managers for us who are in charge, under the name of *ouache*, of the recovery of the combined taxes will be absolved from making any account, as well of the product of taxes on the sale of suet in the interior of Paris, as of that which is secured from the suburbs, and also of the principal tax *d'entrée* on foreign suet; and this is in effect from the day the *adjudicataire* of our taxes shall begin to administer the taxes established by way of replacement.

Article VIII. We abrogate all ordinances, writs, and regulations contrary to the provisions of the preceding articles.

EDICT OF THE KING

Enacting the Suppression of Offices Connected with the Ports, Quays, Stalls and Markets of Paris

Louis, etc. The resolution we have made to direct our attention to everything which may procure the welfare of our subjects, has caused us to examine the different edicts by which the kings, our predecessors, successively created, suppressed and restored different offices, of which the greater part remain in existence, in connection with the port, quays, stalls and markets of our good city of Paris, and the concessions of various sorts which were alienated to these offices.

We have discovered, by the conditions of the period in which they were created, that they owe their origin to the extraordinary needs of the state in times of calamity, and we are assured that in times more fortunate it has always been proposed to suppress them as burdensome to the people and useless to the police regulations, which had served as the pretext for their creation.

It was in accordance with these motives that the suppression of all offices of that kind which were created since 1688 was decreed by the edicts of May, 1715, and September, 1719, and all these offices remained abolished and suppressed without making any change in public order and police, after the said years 1715 and 1719, until the years 1727 and 1730, when the late king, our honored lord and grandfather, decided to restore them, and did so by the edicts of January and June of the said years.

By article II of the edict of 1730, it was specifically ordained that the former incumbents of the offices which had been suppressed might acquire the offices newly created upon the payment of sums fixed by the roles decreed by the Council: namely, one-seventh in money and six-sevenths in liquidation of the former offices, in arrears of the same liquidations, and in supplemental contracts with the city; and with regard to those who had not been incumbents formerly, they were permitted to acquire the offices in like manner upon payment of one-sixth in money and five-sixths in contracts.

The taxes alienated to these offices having been compared, in 1759, with other taxes of the same kind re-established by the edict of December, 1743, and farmed out, it was discovered that there was a great disproportion between the products of these taxes and the finances of the offices. The late king, by his edict of September, 1759, ordained that the offices should be suppressed; that the taxes should be collected to his profit and that the product should be destined to the repayment of so much of the finances of the holders of the offices as was comprised in the sums loaned by them.

That edict announced to the people freedom from many branches of burdensome restrictions, and to the state the recovery of part of its revenue.

New requirements prevented its execution: the edict of March, 1760, permitted the holders of the offices suppressed to continue for a time the exercise of their functions and to enjoy their privileges; it ratified their suppression, however, by postponing the collection which would effect their reimbursement, the time of which was fixed at January 1, 1771, and to be completed in 1782. Circumstances continuing to be contrary to these provisions, it became necessary to provide by the declaration of December 5, 1768, that the beginning of repayment should be deferred until January 1, 1777, and be finished in 1788.

The edict of 1760 and the declaration of 1768, although permitting a temporary enjoyment of their privileges by the incumbents, did not revoke the suppression decreed by the edict of September, 1759. That disposition remains in full force and ought to be put into execution at the moment when the holders of the offices may receive the indemnity which they have a right to claim by virtue of their warrants (*titres*).

That indemnity, fixed for them by article II of the edict of June, 1730, consists for part of them of one-seventh of their finances in money and six-sevenths in mortgage-contracts on the product of the same taxes; for the other part of them, it consists of one-sixth in money and five-sixths in contracts. Therefore, since the holders of the offices are assured of that indemnity the suppression ordained by the edict of 1760 ought to be in force.

The creditors of the guilds of officials should receive their payment in preference to the officials themselves, because the offices are encumbered and their profits mortgaged.

It is in accordance with our justice to preserve their rights and to assure the capital and interest of the credits which are due to them according to the profits of the taxes alienated to the said offices, until the execution of the arrangements ordained by the declaration of September 5, 1768.

Such an operation is equally advantageous to the officials, to their creditors, and to the people.

Most of the guilds complain that the products they enjoy at present are diminished to the point of being insufficient to acquit them of the charges with which they are burdened. Thus the incumbents of offices lose their value, and their creditors see the security of their credits diminishing and becoming inadequate.

On the part of our subjects, to whom we desire to give, on every occasion, tokens of our affection, their interest requires that the taxes heretofore alienated to these guilds be henceforth reunited in our hand and administered under our order, in order that, during the time that the state of our finances will not permit us to cease collecting them altogether, we may have, at least, the best opportunity to make them less annoying by effecting in them such modifications and reductions as would be impossible if the existence of offices, continued in actual exercise, furnished pretexts to the incumbents to disarrange by demanding indemnities, the plans we purpose to adopt for the greatest advantage of our people.

For these causes, etc., we have, by our present edict, enacted and ordained as follows:

Article I. Article I of the edict of the month of September, 1759, will be executed; accordingly, all offices created by the edicts of January, 1727, and June, 1730, connected with the ports, quays, stalls and markets of our good city of Paris, will continue suppressed, beginning from the day of publication of the present edict. We prohibit those who may be found holders of them, their clerks and officers, from continuing to exercise their functions in the future.

Article II. We except, however, the offices of supervisors, gaugers and measurers, *jurés-vendeurs* and comptrollers of wines and liquors, commission brokers of wines, and others such as have been combined in the domain and patrimony of our good city of Paris, by the declaration of August 16, 1733, and by the edicts of June, 1741, and August, 1744, of which offices the taxes will continue to be collected to the profit of the said city.

Article III. The taxes heretofore attributed to the guilds of officials, the suppression of which we specifically ordain, as well as the taxes combined in our *fermes*, will continue to be collected to our profit by the highest bidder for our taxes (*fermes*) beginning from the day of publication of the present edict and continuing until otherwise ordered by us, with the exception at all times of the taxes united in the domain and patrimony of our city of Paris, mentioned in the preceding article, which it will continue to enjoy as in the past.

Article IV. The proprietors of offices suppressed by the present edict will be reimbursed regularly from funds set apart for the purpose by us, pursuant to the liquidation provided by the edict of March, 1760, and in the same manner as the finances of the said offices were paid into our casual revenue. Wherefore, those of the said proprietors who acquired the offices by paying one-sixth of the sums in money, will be repaid the said sixth in money, and those who acquired the offices by paying one-seventh only in money, will receive similarly only the said seventh. And with regard to the balance of the finance of the said offices furnished in collaterals, mortgages at 4 per cent, will be delivered to each of the said proprietors, the arrears of which, special effects under the product of the taxes heretofore attributed to them, will commence to run from the day they cease to exercise the functions of the said offices and to collect the taxes, and shall continue until they are wholly repaid.

Article V. Arrears of profits, due by the guilds of officials suppressed by the present edict, will be paid on the same basis as the said profits would be liquidated by the edict of March, 1760, and as the proprietors of the said privileged profits and mortgages on the product of taxes restored to our hand in consequence of the said suppression, will be paid.

Article VI. The balance of the product of these taxes, as well as the funds we shall designate from our finances, shall be used to reimburse the capital sums; namely, by preference, to reimburse the profits now due by the said guild of officials, and subsequently the capital sums of the mortgages we shall give them to complete the finance of offices. We will that the interest on the sums repaid be employed progressively to augment the sinking funds until the profits of the offices are wholly reimbursed, and that the product of the said taxes or the said interests be not diverted to any other use.

Article VII. We reserve the right to suppress, to simplify or to modify the said taxes reunited in our hand which may seem to us too burdensome to our people, either by reason of their nature or because of the formalities required for their collection. And if it happens that the product be diminished, the balance will be provided for by us by assigning some other branch of our revenues to the payment of arrears and the reimbursement of the capital due to the said officials and their creditors.

Article VIII. We annul all edicts, ordinances, declarations, decrees and regulations in all that may be contrary to the provisions of the present edict.

So given by commandment, etc.

PART II
Philosophy

A Philosophical Review of the Successive Advances of the Human Mind

Turgot presents a brief outline of human progress. The fact that human beings have similar experiences does not imply that all nations ar alike. People have different abilities, and the results of individual genius may bring some cultures to the fore. The growth of knowledge is traced, with developments in Athens an early highlight. Turgot argues that we learn through the senses; like Hume, he holds that deductive knowledge is limited to showing the connections between ideas. Language is essential to knowledge, and Turgot warns that languages that develop first can become fixed and overly elaborate and impede knowledge. The contemporary age is one in which knowledge has developed more than ever before. Descartes was a pioneer in this recent growth, but Newton and Leibniz are the greatest modern thinkers.

CHAPTER 14

A Philosophical Review of the Successive Advances of the Human Mind

The phenomena of nature, governed as they are by constant laws, are confined within a circle of revolutions which are always the same. All things perish, and all things spring up again; and in these successive acts of generation through which plants and animals reproduce themselves time does no more than restore continually the counterpart of what it has caused to disappear.

The succession of mankind, on the other hand, affords from age to age an ever-changing spectacle. Reason, the passions, and liberty ceaselessly give rise to new events: all the ages are bound up with one another by a succession of causes and effects which link the present state of the world with all those that have preceded it. The arbitrary signs of speech and writing, by providing men with the means of securing the possession of their ideas and communicating them to others, have made of all the individual stores of knowledge a common treasure-house which one generation transmits to another, an inheritance which is always being enlarged by the discoveries of each age. Thus the human race, considered over the period since its origin, appears to the eye of a philosopher as one vast whole, which itself, like each individual, has its infancy and its advancement.

We see the establishment of societies, and the formation of nations which in turn dominate other nations or become subject to them. Empires rise and fall; laws and forms of government succeed one another; the arts and the sciences are in turn discovered and perfected, in turn retarded and accelerated in their progress; and they are passed on from country to country. Self-interest, ambition, and vainglory continually change the world scene and inundate the earth with blood; yet in the midst of their ravages manners are softened, the human mind becomes more enlightened, and separate nations are brought closer to one another. Finally commercial and political ties unite all parts of the globe, and the whole human race, through alternate periods of rest and unrest, of weal and woe, goes on advancing, although at a slow pace, toward greater perfection.

In the time placed at my disposal I could not hope to portray for you the whole of so vast a panorama. I shall try merely to indicate the main lines of the progress of the human mind; and this discourse will be wholly taken up with some reflections on the origin and growth of the arts and sciences and the revolutions which have taken place in them, considered in their relation to the succession of historical events.

Holy Writ, after having enlightened us about the creation of the universe, the origin of man, and the birth of the first arts, before long puts before us a picture of the human race concentrated again in a single family as the result of a universal flood. Scarcely had it begun to make good its losses when the miraculous confusion of tongues forced men to separate from one another. The urgent need to procure subsistence for themselves in barren deserts, which provided nothing but wild beasts, obliged them to move apart from one another in all directions and hastened their diffusion through the whole world. Soon the original traditions were forgotten; and the nations, separated as they were by vast distances and still more by the diversity of languages, strangers to one another, were almost all plunged into the same barbarism in which we still see the Americans.

But natural resources and the fertile seeds of the sciences are to be found wherever there are men. The most exalted mental attainments are only and can only be a development or combination of the original ideas based on sensation, just as the building at whose great height we gaze in wonder necessarily has its foundation in the earth upon which we tread. The same senses, the same organs, and the spectacle of the same universe, have everywhere given men the same ideas, just as the same needs and inclinations have everywhere taught them the same arts.

Now a faint light begins occasionally to penetrate the darkness which has covered all the nations, and step by step it spreads. The inhabitants of Chaldea, closest to the source of the original traditions, the Egyptians, and the Chinese apparently lead the rest of the peoples. Others follow them at a distance, and progress leads to further progress. The inequality of nations increases; in one place the arts begin to emerge, while in another they advance at a rapid rate toward perfection. In some nations they are brought to a standstill in the midst of their mediocrity, while in others the original darkness is not yet dissipated at all. Thus the present state of the world, marked as it is by these infinite variations in inequality, spreads out before us at one and the same time all the gradations from barbarism to refinement, thereby revealing to us at a single glance, as it were, the records and remains of all the steps taken by the human mind, a reflection of all the stages through which it has passed, and the history of all the ages.

But is not nature everywhere the same?—and if she leads all men to the same truths, if even their errors are alike, how is it that they do not all move forward at the same rate along the road which is marked out for them? It is true that the human mind everywhere contains the potential for the same progress, but nature, distributing her gifts unequally, has given to certain minds an abundance of talents which she has refused to others. Circumstances either develop these talents or allow them to become buried in obscurity; and it is from the infinite variety of these circumstances that there springs the inequality in the progress of nations.

Barbarism makes all men equal; and in early times all those who are born with genius are faced with virtually the same obstacles and the same resources. Societies are established and expanded, however; national hatreds and ambition—or rather greed, the only ambition of barbarous peoples—cause war and devastation to increase; and conquests and revolutions mix up peoples, languages, and customs in a thousand different ways. Chains of mountains, great rivers and seas confine the dealings of peoples with one another, and consequently their intermingling, within fixed boundaries. This results in the formation of common languages which become a tie binding several nations together, so that all the nations of the world become divided as it were into a number of different classes. Tillage increases the permanence of settlements. It is able to feed more men than are employed in it, and thus imposes upon those whom it leaves idle the necessity of making themselves either useful or formidable to the cultivators. Hence towns, trade, the useful arts and accomplishments, the division of occupations, the differences in education, and the increased inequality in the conditions of life. Hence that leisure, by means of which genius, relieved of the burden of providing for primary necessities, emerges from the narrow sphere within which these necessities confine it and bends all its strength to the cultivation of the arts. Hence that more rapid and vigorous rate of advance of the human mind which carries along with it all parts of society and which in turn derives additional momentum from their perfection. The passions develop alongside genius; ambition gathers strength; politics lends it ever-widening perspectives; victories have more lasting results and create empires whose laws, customs, and government, influencing men's genius in different ways, become a kind of common education for the nations, producing between one nation and another the same sort of difference which education produces between one man and another.

United, divided, the one raised up on the other's ruins, empires rapidly succeed one another. The revolutions which they undergo cause them to run the whole gamut of possible states, and unite and disunite all the elements of the body politic. Like the ebb and flow of the tide, power passes from one nation to another, and, within the same nation, from the princes to the multitude and from the multitude to the princes. As the balance shifts, everything gradually gets nearer and nearer to an equilibrium, and in the course of time takes on a more settled and peaceful aspect. Ambition, when it forms great states from the remains of a host of small ones, itself sets limits to its own ravages. Wars no longer devastate anything but the frontiers of empires; the towns and the countryside begin to breathe

the air of peace; the bonds of society unite a greater number of men; ideas come to be transmitted more promptly and more widely; and the advancement of arts, sciences, and manners progresses more rapidly. Like a storm which has agitated the waves of the sea, the evil which is inseparable from revolutions disappears: the good remains, and humanity perfects itself. Amidst this complex of different events, sometimes favorable, sometimes adverse, which because they act in opposite ways must in the long run nullify one another, genius ceaselessly asserts its influence. Nature, while distributing genius to only a few individuals, has nevertheless spread it out almost equally over the whole mass, and with time its effects become appreciable.

Genius, whose course is at first slow, unmarked, and buried in the general oblivion into which time precipitates human affairs, emerges from obscurity with them by means of the invention of *writing*. Priceless invention!—which seemed to give wings to those peoples who first possessed it, enabling them to outdistance other nations. Incomparable invention!—which rescues from the power of death the memory of great men and models of virtue, unites places and times, arrests fugitive thoughts and guarantees them a lasting existence, by means of which the creations, opinions, experiences, and discoveries of all ages are accumulated, to serve as a foundation and foothold for posterity in raising itself ever higher!

But what a spectacle the succession of men's opinions presents! I seek there for the progress of the human mind, and I find virtually nothing but the history of its errors. Why is its course, which is so sure from the very first steps in the field of mathematical studies, so unsteady in everything else, and so apt to go astray? Let us try to discover the reasons. In mathematics, the mind deduces one from another a chain of propositions, the truth of which consists only in their mutual dependence. It is not the same with the other sciences, where it is no longer from the intercomparison of ideas that truth is born, but from their conformity with a sequence of real facts. To discover and verify truth, it is no longer a question of establishing a small number of simple principles and then merely allowing the mind to be borne along by the current of their consequences. One must start from nature as it is, and from that infinite variety of effects which so many causes, counterbalanced one by the other, have combined to produce. Notions are no longer assemblages of ideas which the mind forms of its own accord and of whose range it has exact knowledge. Ideas emerge and are assembled in our minds almost without our knowing it; we are beset by the images of objects right from the cradle. Little by little we learn to distinguish between them, less by reference to what they are in themselves than by reference to their relation to our habits and needs. The signs of language impress themselves on the mind while it is still undeveloped. At first, through habit and imitation, they become attached to particular objects, but later they succeed in calling up more general notions. This chaotic blend of ideas and expressions grows and becomes more complex all the time; and when man starts to seek for truth he find himself in the midst of a labyrinth which he has entered blindfold. Should we be surprised at his errors?

Spectator of the universe, his senses show him the effects but leave him ignorant of the causes. And to examine effects in an endeavor to find their unknown cause is like trying to guess an enigma: we think of one or more possible key words and try them in turn until one is found which fulfils all the conditions.

The natural philosopher erects hypotheses, follows them through to their consequences, and brings them to bear upon the enigma of nature. He tries them out, so to speak, on the facts, just as one verifies a seal by applying it to its impression. Suppositions which are arrived at on the basis of a small number of poorly understood facts yield to suppositions which are less absurd, although no more true. Time, research, and chance result in the accumulation of observations, and unveil the hidden connections which link a number of phenomena together.

Ever restless, incapable of finding tranquility elsewhere than in the truth, ever stimulated by the image of that truth which it believes to be within its grasp but which flies before it, the curiosity of man leads to a multiplication of the number of questions and debates, and obliges him to analyze ideas and facts in a manner which grows ever more exact and more profound. Mathematical truths, becoming from day to day more numerous and hence more fruitful, point the way to the development of hypotheses which are more far-reaching and more precise, and indicate new experiments which, in their turn, present new problems for mathematics to resolve. Thus the need perfects the tool; thus mathematics is sustained by natural philosophy, upon which it sheds its light; thus everything is bound together; thus, in spite of the diversity in their development, all the sciences render mutual aid to one another; thus, by feeling his way, by multiplying systems and draining them, as it were, of their errors, man at last attains to the understanding of a great number of truths.

What ridiculous opinions marked our first steps! How absurd were the causes which our fathers thought up to make sense of what they saw! What sad monuments they are to the weakness of the human mind! The senses constitute the unique source of our ideas: the whole power of our mental faculties is restricted to combining the ideas which they have received from the senses: hardly even can they form combinations of ideas of which the senses do not provide them with a model. Hence that almost irresistible tendency to judge of what one does not know by what one knows; hence those delusive analogies to which the first men in their immaturity abandoned themselves with so little thought; hence the monstrous aberrations of idolatry. Men, oblivious of the original traditions, when affected by sensible phenomena, imagined that all effects which were independent of their own action were produced by beings similar to them, but invisible and more powerful, whom they substituted for the Divinity. When they were contemplating nature, it was as if they fixed their gaze on the surface of a deep sea instead of on the sea-bed hidden by the waters, and saw there only their own reflection. All objects of nature had their gods, which, being created after the model of man, shared his attributes and vices. Throughout the world, superstition sanctified the caprices of the imagination; and the only true God, the only God worthy of adoration, was known only in one corner of the earth, by the people whom he had expressly chosen.

In this slow progression of opinions and errors, pursuing one another, I fancy that I see those first leaves, those sheaths which nature has given to the newly-growing stems of plants, issuing before them from the earth, and withering one by one as other sheaths come into existence, until at last the stem itself makes its appearance and is crowned with flowers and fruit—a symbol of late-emerging truth!

Woe be to those nations, then, in which the sciences, as the result of a blind zeal for them, are confined within the limits of existing knowledge in an attempt to stabilize them. It is for this reason that the regions which were the first to become enlightened are not those where the sciences have made the greatest progress. The respect for the new-born philosophy which the glamour of its novelty inspires in men tends to perpetuate the first opinions: the sectarian spirit comes to be attached to it. Such a spirit is natural for the first philosophers, because arrogance feeds on ignorance, because the less one knows the less one doubts, and because the less one has discovered the less one sees what remains to be discovered. In Egypt, and long after in the Indes, superstition, which made the dogmas of the ancient philosophy the patrimony of the priestly families, who by consecrating them enchained them and incorporated them in the dogmas of a false religion; in great Asia, political despotism, the result of the establishment of great empires during the centuries of barbarism; the civic despotism born of slavery and of the plurality of wives which is a consequence of it; the want of vigor on the part of princes; the prostration of their subjects; in China, the very care which the Emperors took to regulate research and to tie up the sciences with the political constitution of the state, held them back forever in mediocrity: these trunks which since their origin had been too productive of branches soon ceased to grow higher.

With the passing of time new peoples came into being. In the course of the unequal progress of nations, the civilized peoples, surrounded by barbarians, now conquering, now conquered, intermingled with them. Whether the latter received from the former their arts and their laws together with servitude, or whether as conquerors they yielded to the natural empire of reason and culture over brute force, the bounds of barbarism steadily retreated.

The Phoenicians, inhabitants of a barren coast, had made themselves the agents of exchanges between peoples. Their ships, spread out over the whole Mediterranean, began to reveal nation to nation.

Astronomy, navigation, and geography were perfected, one by means of the other. The coasts of Greece and Asia Minor came to be filled with Phoenician colonies. Colonies are like fruits which cling to the tree only until they have reached their maturity: once they had become self-sufficient they did what Carthage was to do later, and what America will one day do.

Out of the intermingling of these colonies, each independent of the others, with the ancient peoples of Greece and with the remnants of all the swarms of barbarians who had successively ravaged her, there arose the Greek nation, or rather that family of nations comprised of a large number of small peoples who were prevented from aggrandizing themselves at one another's expense by the fact that they were all equally weak and by the nature of the terrain, which was broken up by mountains and sea, and who were intermingled, divided, and reunited in a thousand different ways by their associations, their public and private interests, their civil and national wars, their migrations, the reciprocal duties of colonies and metropolises, one language, customs, a common religion, trade, public games, and the Amphictyonic league. In the course of these revolutions, and by means of these manifold interminglings, there was formed that rich, expressive, and sonorous language, the language of all the arts.

Poetry, which is no more than the art of painting with words, and the perfection of which depends so greatly on the genius of the languages which it employs, assumed in Greece a grandeur which it had never previously known. It was no longer, as it had been with the first men, a succession of barbarous words chained to the beat of a rustic song and to the steps of a dance as uncouth as the riotous joy which it expressed. It had decked itself out in a harmony which was all its own. The ear, ever more difficult to please, had laid down stricter rules; and if the burden of these had become heavier, the new expressions, turns of phrase, and felicitous boldnesses of style, which had increased in proportion, lent greater strength to bear it.

Good taste had finally succeeded in outlawing those involved figures and elephantine metaphors which we object to in Oriental poetry.

In those countries of Asia where societies arrived earlier at a stable state, and where writers appeared earlier, languages became stabilized at a point nearer to their first origin, and as a result were marked by that high-flown style which is characteristic of a language in its first imperfect stage. Languages are the measure of men's ideas: thus in early times there were names only for the objects which were most familiar to the senses; and to express these imperfect ideas it was necessary to have recourse to metaphors. A word which is coined signifies nothing, so that one must try, by putting together the signs of the ideas which are nearest akin, to set the mind on the track of what one wishes to communicate to it. The imagination attempts to grasp the thread of a certain analogy which binds together our senses with their different objects. An imperfect or farfetched analogy gives birth to those clumsy and abundant metaphors which necessity, more ingenious than fastidious, employs, which good taste disavows, of which the first languages are full, and of which even now etymologists find vestiges in the most cultivated.

Languages, which are necessarily used by all men, and thus often by men of genius, are always perfected over time, when they are not immobilized by written works which become a permanent standard by which to judge of their purity. The habitual use of the spoken word leads continually to new combinations of ideas, calls attention to new relationships between them and to new shades of meaning, and makes felt the need for new expressions. Moreover, through the migrations of peoples, languages blend with one another like rivers and are enriched by the coming together of several languages.

Thus the Greek language, formed by the intermingling of a greater number of languages, and stabilized later than those of Asia, unites together harmony, richness, and variety. Homer consummated its triumph, poured into it the treasures of his genius, and lifted it to the greatest heights by the harmonious character of his poetry, the charm of his expression, and the splendor of his images.

Following on this, liberty, which as the result of a revolution natural to small states came to be established in all cities on the ruins of the government of a single man, gave a new stimulus to the genius of the Greeks. The different forms of government into which the opposing passions of the powerful and the people turn by turn precipitated them, taught the legislators to compare and to weigh up all the different elements in society, and to find the proper equilibrium between their forces; while at the same time the combined quarrels and interests of so many ambitious, weak, and jealous neighboring republics taught the states to fear one another, to keep constant watch on one another, and to counterbalance successes with leagues, and led at the same time to the perfecting of politics and the art of war.

It was only after several centuries that philosophers appeared in Greece—or rather it was only then that the study of philosophy became the business of particular thinkers and appeared sufficiently extensive in its scope to occupy them fully. Until then, the poets had been at the same time the only philosophers and the only historians. When men are ignorant it is easy to know everything. But ideas were not yet by any means clear enough. A sufficiently large number of facts was not available; the time of truth had not by any means arrived, and the systems of the Greek philosophers could not yet be anything but adroit. Their metaphysics, shaky on the most important truths and often superstitious or blasphemous, was scarcely more than a collection of poetic fables or a tissue of unintelligible words; and their natural philosophy itself was nothing but shallow metaphysics.

Morality, although still imperfect, was less affected by the infancy of reason. The recurring needs which constantly call men into society and force them to bow to its laws; that instinct, that feeling for the good and the honorable which Providence has graven on all our hearts, which comes before reason, and which often seduces it in spite of itself, leads the philosophers of all ages to the same fundamental principles of the science of behavior. Socrates guided his fellow-citizens along the path of virtue; Plato sowed this path with flowers; the charm of his eloquence beautified even his errors. Aristotle, the most wide-ranging, profound, and truly philosophical mind of all antiquity, was the first to carry the torch of exact analysis into the sphere of philosophy and the arts. Unveiling the principles of certitude and the springs of feeling, he subjected the development of reason and even the fire of genius to constant rules.

Happy centuries, in which all the fine arts spread their light on every side, and in which the passion of a noble emulation was swiftly transmitted from one city to another! Painting, sculpture, architecture, poetry, and history grew up everywhere at the same time, as we see in the expanse of a forest a thousand different trees springing up, growing, and being crowned together.

Athens, governed by the decrees of a multitude whose tumultuous waves the orators calmed or agitated at their pleasure; Athens, where Pericles had taught the leaders how to buy the state at the expense of the state itself, and how to dissipate its treasures in order to exempt themselves from giving an account of them; Athens, where the art of governing the people was the art of amusing them, the art of feasting their ears, their eyes, and their curiosity always greedy for novelties, with festivities, pleasures, and constant spectacles, Athens owed to the very vices of its government which made it succumb to Lacedaemon that eloquence, that taste, that magnificence, and that splendor in all the arts which have made it the model of nations.

While the Athenians, the Spartans, and the Thebans are in turn arrogating to themselves superiority over the other cities, the Macedonian power, unnoticed, like a river which overflows its banks, slowly extends into Greece under Philip, and violently inundates Asia under Alexander. This host of regions and states, from which the conquests of the Assyrians, the Medes, and the Persians, in successively swallowing one another up, had formed this great body, the product of so many conquerors and so many centuries, breaks up with a crash on the death of the conqueror of Darius. Wars between his generals establish new kingdoms; Syria and Egypt become a part of Greece, and receive the language, the customs, and the sciences of their conquerors.

Commerce and the arts render Alexandria the rival of Athens. Astronomy and the mathematical sciences are carried there to an even higher level than they have ever been before. Above all we see flourishing there that erudition with which until then the Greeks had been little acquainted—that kind of study which is concerned less with things than with books, which consists less in producing and discovering than in assembling together, comparing, and evaluating what has been produced and what has been discovered; which does not move forward at all, but which turns its gaze backwards in order to survey the road which has been taken. The studies which demand the most genius are not always those which imply the greatest progress in the mass of mankind. There are minds to whom nature has given a memory which is capable of assembling together a large number of pieces of knowledge, a power of exact reasoning which is capable of comparing them and arranging them in a manner which puts them in their full light, but to whom at the same time she has denied that fire of genius which invents and which opens up new roads for itself. Created to unite past discoveries under one point of view, to clarify and even to perfect them, if they are not torches which shine with their own light, they are diamonds which brilliantly reflect a borrowed light, but which total darkness would confound with the meanest stones.

The known world, if I may put it like that, the commercial world, the political world, had expanded as a result of the conquests of Alexander. The dissensions of his successors began to present a vaster spectacle, and, amid these clashes and these oscillations of the great powers, the little cities of Greece, situated in the midst of them, often the arena of their struggles and a prey to the ravages of all the parties, were no longer conscious of anything but their weakness. Eloquence was no longer the mainspring of politics: henceforth, degraded in the obscurity of the schools by childish declamations, it lost its brilliance along with its power.

But for several centuries already, Rome, in Italy as if in a world apart, had been advancing by a continual succession of triumphs toward the conquest of the world. Victorious over Carthage, she appeared suddenly in the midst of the nations. Peoples trembled and were brought into subjection: the Romans, conquerors of Greece, became aware of a new empire, that of intellect and learning. Their austere uncouthness was tamed. Athens found disciples, and soon rivals, among her conquerors. Cicero displayed, at the Capitol and on the rostrum, an eloquence derived from the lessons of the Greeks, of which its enslaved masters no longer knew anything but the rules. The Latin language, softened and enriched, brought Africa, Spain, and Gaul under orderly government. The boundaries of the civilized world were identical with those of the Roman power, and two rival languages, Greek and Latin, shared it between them.

The laws of Rome, created to govern one city, sank under the burden of the whole world: Roman liberty was extinguished in waves of blood. Octavius alone finally gathered in the fruit of the civil strife. Cruel usurper, temperate prince, he gave tranquility to the earth. His enlightened protection stimulated all the arts. Italy had a Homer, less productive than the first, but wiser, more equable, just as harmonious, and perhaps more perfect. Sublimity, reason, and the graces united to create Horace. Taste was perfected in every sphere.

Knowledge of nature and of truth is as infinite as they are: the arts, whose aim is to please us, are as limited as we are. Time constantly brings to light new discoveries in the sciences; but poetry, painting, and music have a fixed limit which the genius of languages, the imitation of nature, and the limited sensibility of our organs determine, which they attain by slow steps and which they cannot surpass. The great men of the Augustan age reached it, and are still our models.

From this time until the fall of the Empire, we see nothing but a general decadence in which everything is plunged. Do men raise themselves up, then, only to fall? A thousand causes combine to deprave taste more and more: tyranny, which degrades minds below all things which are great; blind luxury, which, born of vanity, and judging works of art less as objects of taste than as symbols of opulence, is as opposed to their perfection as a civilized love of magnificence is favorable to it; enthusiasm for new things among those who, not having enough genius to invent them, only too often have enough wit to spoil the old; the imitation of the vices of great men and even the misplaced imitation of their beauties. Writers proliferate in the provinces and corrupt the language: I know not what remnants of the old Greek philosophy, mixed up with oriental superstitions, confounded with a host of empty allegories and magical spells, take possession of men's minds and smother the healthy natural philosophy which was beginning to spring up in the writings of Seneca and Pliny the Elder.

Soon the Empire, abandoned to the caprices of an insolent militia, becomes the prey of a host of tyrants, who, in the process of seizing it from one another, bring desolation and havoc to the provinces. Military discipline is destroyed, the northern barbarians penetrate on every side, peoples fall upon peoples, the cities become deserted, the fields are left uncultivated, and the western Empire, weakened by the transference of all its power to Constantinople, ruined everywhere by so many repeated ravages, at last suddenly collapses, and the Burgundians, Goths, and Franks are left to quarrel over its far-flung ruins and to found kingdoms in the different countries of Europe.

Could it be, in this sanctuary, that I should pass over in silence that new light which, while the Empire was proceeding toward its ruin, had spread out over the world—a light a thousand times more precious than those of letters and philosophy? Holy religion, could it be that I should forget you? Could I forget the perfecting of manners, the dissipation at last of the darkness of idolatry, and the enlightenment of men on the subject of the Divinity! Amid the almost total ruin of letters, you alone still created writers who were animated by the desire to instruct the faithful or to repel the attacks of the enemies of the faith; and when Europe fell prey to the barbarians, you alone tamed their ferocity; you alone have perpetuated the knowledge of the discarded Latin tongue; you alone have transmitted to us across so many centuries the minds, so to speak, of so many great men which had been entrusted to that language; and the conservation of the treasure of human knowledge, which was about to be dissipated, is one of your benefactions.

But the wounds of the human race were too deep; centuries were necessary to heal them. If Rome had been conquered by one people alone, their leader would have become a Roman, and his nation would have been absorbed in the Empire together with its language. We would have seen what the history of the world presents to us more than once: the spectacle of a civilized people invaded by barbarians, communicating to them its manners, its language, and its knowledge, and forcing them to make one people with it. Cicero and Virgil would have sustained the Latin language, just as Homer, Plato, and Demosthenes had defended theirs against the Roman power. But too many peoples, and too many ravages, succeeded one another; too many layers of barbarism were added one after the other before the first had time to disappear and yield to the force of the Roman sciences. Too many conquerors, too single-mindedly devoted to war, were for several centuries too much occupied with their quarrels. The genius of the Romans was extinguished and their language was lost, confounded with the Germanic languages.

It is a consequence of the intermingling of two languages that a new one is formed from them which is different from each; but a long time passes before they can be combined in a really intimate manner. Memory, wavering between the two, decides at random between the expressions of one and the other. Analogy, that is, the art of forming conjugations and declensions, of expressing the relationships between objects, and of arranging the expressions in discourse, has no longer any fixed rules. Ideas are associated in a confused manner; there is no longer any harmony or clarity in the language. Pour two liquids into the same vessel: you will see them become turbid and cloudy, and not recover the transparency they had when they were separate until time has rendered their mixture more intimate and more homogeneous. Thus, until a long succession of centuries has succeeded in giving the new language a uniform quality of its own, poetry, eloquence, and taste disappear almost completely. Thus new languages grew up in Europe, and in the chaos of their first formation ignorance and vulgarity ruled everywhere.

Unhappy empire of the Caesars, must new misfortunes be visited even upon those remnants which have escaped from thy wreck! Must it be that barbarism destroys at once all the refuges of the arts! And thou too, Greece, thine honors are then eclipsed! Finally the north seems to become exhausted, and new storms gather in the south against the only provinces which are not yet groaning under a foreign yoke!

The standard of a false prophet unites the wandering shepherds in the Arabian deserts; in less than a century Syria, Persia, Egypt, and Africa are covered by a raging torrent which ravages the whole territory from the Indian frontiers to the Atlantic Ocean and the Pyrenees. The Greek empire, confined within narrow boundaries, devastated in the south by the Saracens and then by the Turks, and in the north by the Bulgarians, laid waste internally by factions and by the instability of its throne, falls into a state of weakness and lethargy, and the cultivation of letters and arts ceases to occupy a debased, slack, and indolent populace.

In vain does Charlemagne in the west try to revive a few sparks of a fire which is buried under the ashes; their glow is as evanescent as it is feeble. Soon the quarrels of his grandsons disturb his empire; the north once again raises and sends forth new destroyers; the Normans and the Hungarians once again cover Europe with new ruins and a new darkness. Amid the general weakness, a new form of government puts the finishing touch to the ruin: the annihilated royal power gives way to that host of small sovereignties, subordinate one to another, among which the feudal laws maintain I know not what false semblance of order in the midst of the very anarchy which they perpetuate.

The kings without any authority, the nobles without any constraint, the peoples enslaved, the countryside covered with fortresses and ceaselessly ravaged, wars kindled between city and city, village and village, penetrating, so to speak, the whole mass of the kingdoms; all commerce and all communications cut off; the towns inhabited by poor artisans enjoying no leisure; the only wealth and the only leisure which some men still enjoy lost in the idleness of a nobility scattered here and there in their castles who do nothing but engage in battles which are useless to the fatherland; the grossest ignorance extending over all nations and all occupations! An unhappy picture—but one which was only too true of Europe for several centuries!

But nevertheless, from the midst of this barbarism, perfected arts and sciences will one day rise again. Amid all the ignorance, progress is imperceptibly taking place and preparing for the brilliant achievements of later centuries; beneath this soil the feeble roots of a far-off harvest are already developing. The towns among all civilized peoples constitute by their very nature the centers of trade and the backbone of society. They continued to exist; and if the spirit of feudal government, born of the ancient customs of Germany, combined with a number of accidental circumstances, had abased them, this was a contradiction in the constitution of states which was bound to disappear in the long run. Soon we see the towns revive again under the protection of the princes; and the latter, in holding out their hands to the oppressed peoples, reduce the power of their vassals and little by little re-establish their own.

Latin and theology were already being studied in the universities, together with the Aristotelian dialectic. For a long time the Mussulman Arabs had been teaching themselves Greek philosophy, and their learning was spreading to the west. Mathematics had been extended as a result of their work. More independent than the other sciences of the perfection of taste and perhaps even of precision of intellect, one cannot study mathematics without being led to the truth. Always certain, always pure, its truths were emerging, encompassed about by the errors of judicial astrology. The chimerical search for the philosophers' stone, by encouraging the Arab philosophers to separate and to recombine all the elements of bodies, had led to the blossoming under their hands of the vast science of chemistry, and had spread it to all places where men were capable of being imposed upon by their greedy desires. Finally, on all sides, the mechanical arts were coming to be perfected by virtue of the simple fact that time was passing, because even in the decline of the sciences and taste the needs of life preserve them, and because, consequently, among that host of artisans who successively cultivate them it is impossible not to meet every now and then with one of those men of genius who are blended with the rest of mankind as gold is blended with the clay in a mine.

As a result, what a host of inventions unknown to the ancients and standing to the credit of these barbarous ages! Our art of musical notation, our bills of exchange, our paper, window glass, plate glass, windmills, clocks, spectacles, gunpowder, the magnetic needle, and the perfection of navigation and commerce. The arts are nothing but the utilization of nature, and the practice of the arts is a succession of physical experiments which progressively unveil nature. Facts were accumulating in the darkness of the times of ignorance, and the sciences, whose progress although hidden was no less real, were bound to reappear one day augmented by this new wealth, like those rivers which after disappearing from our view for some time in a subterranean passage, reappear further on swollen by all the waters which have seeped through the earth.

Different series of events take place in different countries of the world, and all of them, as if by so many separate paths, at length come together to contribute to the same end, to raise up once again the ruins of the human spirit. Thus, in the night, we see the stars rise one after the other; they move forward, each in its own orbit; they seem in their common revolution to bear along with them the whole celestial sphere, and to bring in for us the day which follows them. Germany, Denmark, Sweden, and Poland through the efforts of Charlemagne and the Othos, and Russia through trade with the Greek empire, cease to be uncultivated forests. Christianity, in bringing together these scattered savages, in settling them in towns, is going to dry up forever the source of those inundations which have so often been fatal to the sciences. Europe is still barbarous; but the knowledge brought by her to even more barbarous peoples represents for them immense progress. Little by little the customs introduced by Germany into the south of Europe disappear. The nations, amid the quarrels of the nobles and the princes, begin to fashion for themselves the principles of a more stable government, and to acquire, in accordance with the different circumstances in which they find themselves, the particular character which distinguishes them. The wars against the Mussulmans in Palestine, by giving a common interest to all Christian states, teach them to know one another and to unite with one another, and sow the seeds of that modern political state of affairs in which so many nations seem to comprise nothing but one vast republic. Already we see the royal authority reviving again in France; the power of the people establishing itself in England; the Italian towns constituting themselves into republics and presenting the likeness of ancient Greece; the little monarchies of Spain driving the Moors before them and little by little joining up again into one whole. Soon the seas, which have hitherto separated the nations, come to be the link between them through the invention of the compass. The Portuguese in the east and the Spaniards in the west discover new worlds: at last the world as a whole is known.

Already the intermingling of the barbarous languages with Latin has during the course of the centuries produced new languages, of which the Italian, less removed from their common source and less mixed with foreign languages, takes precedence in the elegance of its style and the beauties of its poetry. The Ottomans, spreading through Asia and Europe with the swiftness of a violent wind, end by overthrowing the empire of Constantinople, and disseminate in the west the feeble sparks of those sciences which Greece still preserved.

What new art is suddenly born, as if to wing to every corner of the earth the writings and glory of the great men who are to come? How slow in every sphere is even the least progress! For two thousand years medals have presented to all eyes characters impressed upon bronze—and then, after so many centuries, some obscure individual realizes that they can be impressed upon paper. At once the treasures of antiquity, rescued from the dust, pass into all hands, penetrate to every part of the world, bear light to the talents which were being wasted in ignorance, and summon genius from the depths of its retreats.

The time has come. Issue forth, Europe, from the darkness which covered thee! Immortal names of the Medici, of Leo X, of Francis I, be consecrated for ever! May the patrons of the arts share the glory of those who cultivate them! I salute thee, O Italy!—happy land, for the second time the homeland of letters and of taste, the spring from which their waters have spread to fertilize our territories. Our own France still only beholds thy progress from afar. Her language, still tainted by remnants of barbarism, cannot follow it. Soon fatal discords will rend the whole of Europe; audacious men have shaken the foundations of the faith and those of the empires; do the flowered stems of the fine arts grow when they are watered with blood? A day will come, and it is not far off, when they will beautify all the countries of Europe.

Time, spread your swift wings! Century of Louis, century of great men, century of reason, hasten! Already, even amidst the turmoil of heresy, the long-disturbed fortunes of states have ended by settling down, as if as the result of a final shock. Already the unremitting study of antiquity has brought men's minds back again to the point where its progress was arrested; already that host of facts, experiments, instruments, and ingenious exercises which the practice of the arts has accumulated over so many centuries, has been rescued from obscurity through printing; already the productions of the two worlds, brought together before our eyes as the result of a far-flung commerce, have become the foundation of a natural philosophy hitherto unknown, and freed at last from alien speculations; already on every hand attentive eyes are fixed upon nature: the remotest chances, turned to profit, give birth to discoveries. The son of an artisan in Zealand brings together for amusement two convex glasses in a tube; the boundaries of our senses are made to recede, and in Italy the eyes of Galileo have discovered a new firmament. Already Kepler, seeking in the stars for the numbers of Pythagoras, has discovered those two famous laws of the movements of the planets which one day in the hands of Newton will become the key to the universe. Already Bacon has traced out for posterity the road which it must follow.

Who is the mortal who dares to reject the learning of all the ages, and even those notions which he has believed to be the most certain? He seems to wish to extinguish the torch of the sciences in order to relight it all on his own at the pure fire of reason. Does he wish to imitate those peoples of antiquity among whom it was a crime to light at other fires that which was made to burn on the altars of the Gods? Great Descartes, if it was not always given to you to find the truth, at least you have destroyed the tyranny of error.

France, whom Spain and England have already outstripped in the glory of poetry; France, whose genius finishes forming itself only when the philosophical spirit begins to spread, will owe perhaps to this very backwardness the exactitude, the method, and the austere taste of her writers. Rarefied and affected thoughts, and the ponderous display of an ostentatious erudition, still corrupt our literature: a strange difference between our progress in taste and that of the ancients! The real advancement of the human mind reveals itself even in its aberrations; the caprices of Gothic architecture are never found among those who possess nothing but wooden huts. The acquisition of knowledge among the first men and the formation of taste kept pace, as it were, with one another. Hence a crude severity and an exaggerated simplicity were their prerogative. Guided by instinct and imagination, they seized little by little upon those relations between men and the objects of nature which are the sole foundations of the beautiful. In later times, when, in spite of the imperfection of taste, the number of ideas and perceptions was increased, when the study of models and rules had caused nature and feeling to become lost from men's view, it was necessary for them through reflection to take themselves back to where the first men had been led by blind instinct. And who is not aware that it is here that the supreme effort of reason lies?

At last all the shadows are dispelled: and what a light shines out on all sides! What a host of great men in every sphere! What a perfection of human reason! One man, Newton, has subjected the infinite to the calculus, has revealed the properties of light which in illuminating everything seemed to conceal itself, and has put into his balance the stars, the earth, and all the forces of nature. And this man has found a rival. Leibnitz encompasses within his vast intellect all the objects of the human mind. The different sciences, confined at first to a small number of simple notions common to all, can no longer, when as a result of their progress they have become more extensive and more difficult, be envisaged otherwise than separately; but greater progress once again unites them, because there is discovered that mutual dependence of all truths which in linking them together illuminates each through the other; because, if each day adds to the vast extent of the sciences, each day also makes them easier, because methods are multiplied with discoveries, because the scaffolding rises with the building.

O Louis, what majesty surrounds thee! What splendor thy beneficent hand has spread over all the arts! Thine happy people have become the centre of refinement! Rivals of Sophocles, of Menander, and of Horace, gather around his throne! Arise, learned academies, and unite your efforts for the glory of his reign! What a multitude of public monuments, of works of genius, of arts newly invented, and of old arts perfected! Who could possibly picture them? Open your eyes and see! Century of Louis the Great, may your light beautify the precious reign of his successor! May it last for ever, may it extend over the whole world! May men continually make new steps along the road of truth! Rather still, may they continually become better and happier!

In the midst of these vicissitudes of opinions, of sciences, of arts, and of everything which is human, rejoice, gentlemen, in the pleasure of seeing that religion to which you have consecrated your hearts and your talents, always true to herself, always pure, always complete, standing perpetuated in the Church, and preserving all the features of the seal which the Divinity has stamped upon it. You will be her ministers, and you will be worthy of her. The Faculty expects from you her glory, the Church of France her illumination, Religion her defenders. Genius, learning, and piety are united to give ground for their hopes.

On Universal History

Turgot gives a much more extensive account of human civilization and the growth of knowledge than in the previous selection. He describes the growth of states, in particular drawing a contrast between despotism and cities. The Ottoman Empire is analyzed at length. Turgot then turns to an account of intellectual progress. Ideas arise from the senses, and more general concepts arise by abstraction from sensory information. People at first ascribe natural occurrences to minds; they know how they themselves can produce effects in the external world and assume that nature is the effect of other minds. Later, they assume that the abstractions they derive from the senses are really existing essences with causal powers. It is only later that true scientific investigation begins, based on empirical investigation. Turgot's account of these stages of intellectual growth prefigures the three-stage theory of Auguste Comte.

CHAPTER 15

On Universal History

Prefatory Note by du Pont

Turgot rendered to Bossuet the homage which the loftiness of his thought and the energy of his expression deserve. He admired the noble and rapid flow of his style, its wealth of expression, its grandeur, and its harmonious dignity. But after having paid this tribute to his excellence as a writer, he regretted that his *Discourse on Universal History* was not more rich in insights, in reason, and in true perceptions. It was with sorrow that he saw it as not living up to the high-minded design of the author, to the interesting position in which he found himself as the tutor of a king, and to the majestic talent which no other French orator has yet equaled.

Nevertheless it was not in M. Turgot's nature to disparage a celebrated work and to slight a great man.

He preferred to rewrite the book, to give it the far-reaching scope which he would have wished it to have, and to embody in it principles which the illustrious Bishop of Meaux had passed over in silence, had not perhaps conceived, and would not perhaps have accepted.

Such a work could not be executed at one stroke. M. Turgot therefore judged it proper, before undertaking it, to sketch out a plan of it, not limiting himself to a bald and simple list of the subjects which he wanted to write about and develop, but delineating them with strokes of a brush as great artists do in their skilful outlines of a portrait.

This plan was not completed, but we have found the first sketch of it, which we are reproducing here.

The work is unfinished, but not one of its pages could have been written by a man who had not conceived it in its entirety, and who had not considered with deep attention and in all their aspects the multitude of subjects which it was to encompass.

PLAN OF THE DISCOURSES ON UNIVERSAL HISTORY
Idea of the Introduction

Set by his Creator in the midst of eternity and immensity, and occupying in them but one point, man necessarily enters into relations with a multitude of things and beings, while at the same time his ideas are concentrated in the indivisibility of his mind and of the present moment. He knows himself only through his sensations, which all have reference to external objects, and the present moment is a centre at which a host of interlinked ideas converge.

It is from this interlinking, and from the order of the laws which all these ideas follow in their continual variations, that man acquires the consciousness of reality. Through the relation of all his different sensations he becomes aware of the existence of external objects. A similar relation in the succession of his ideas reveals the past to him. The relations of beings with one another are by no means passive relations. All may act on one another according to their different laws, and also according to their distances from one another. This real world, of whose limits we are ignorant, has for us very narrow ones, which depend more or less on the perfection of our senses. We have knowledge of a small number of links in the chain, but the extremities in the great and the small equally escape us.

The laws governing bodies constitute physics: always constant, they are described, not recounted. The history of animals, and above all that of men, presents quite a different spectacle. Men, like animals, succeed to other men to whom they owe their existence, and they see, as animals do, their fellows spread out over the surface of the globe which they inhabit. But, being endowed with a more developed reason and more liberty of action, man's relations with his fellows are much more numerous and varied. Possessor of the treasure-house of signs, which he has had the ability to multiply almost to infinity, he can assure himself of the possession of all his acquired ideas, communicate them to other men, and transmit them to his successors as a heritage which is always being augmented. A continual combination of this progress with the passions, and with the events they have caused, constitutes the history of the human race, in which each man is no more than one part of an immense whole which has, like him, its infancy and its advancement.

Thus Universal History encompasses a consideration of the successive advances of the human race, and the elaboration of the causes which have contributed to it; the early beginnings of mankind; the formation and intermingling of nations; the origin of governments and their revolutions; the progress of languages, of natural philosophy, of morals, of manners, of the arts and sciences; the revolutions which have brought about the succession of empire to empire, of nation to nation, and of religion to religion; the human race always remaining the same during these upheavals, like the water of the sea during storms, and always proceeding toward its perfection. To unveil the influence of general and necessary causes, that of particular causes and the free actions of great men, and the relation of all this to the very constitution of man; to reveal the springs and mechanisms of moral causes through their effects—that is what History is in the eyes of a philosopher. It is based upon geography and chronology, which measure the distances between times and places.

In presenting, according to this plan, a picture of the human race, following roughly the historical order of its progress and laying stress on the main epochs, I do not want to go into things deeply but only to give an outline, a mere sketch of a great study, and to afford a glimpse of a vast arena without traversing it; just as we see through a narrow window all the immensity of the heavens.

PLAN OF THE FIRST DISCOURSE

On the Formation of Governments and the Intermingling of Nations

The whole universe proclaims to us a supreme Being. Everywhere we see the print of the hand of a god.

If we want to arrive at a knowledge of something more precise, we are surrounded by mists.

Every day we see arts invented; in some parts of the world we see peoples who are civilized and enlightened, and in other parts nomadic peoples in the depths of the forests. In an eternity of time this inequality of progress would have been bound to disappear. Thus the world is not eternal; but we are bound at the same time to conclude that it is very old. Just how old? We do not know.

Historical times cannot be traced further back than the invention of writing; and, when it was invented, men could at first make use of it only to record vague traditions, or a few leading events to which no dates were ascribed, and which were mixed up with myths to such an extent as to render discrimination impossible.

The pride of nations has led them to shift their origins far back into the depths of antiquity. But in relation to time, men, before the invention of numbers, could scarcely have extended their ideas beyond the few generations with which they were acquainted, that is, three or four. It is only within a century or a century and a half that tradition, unaided by history, can indicate the period of a known event. Thus no history can be traced much further back than the invention of writing, unless it be by means of a mythical chronology, which men took the trouble to create only when nations, revealed to one another through their commerce, had converted their pride into jealousy.

In this silence of reason and history, a book has been given to us as a repository of revelation. It tells us that this world has existed for six thousand or eight thousand years (according to the different copies); that we all owe our origin to a single man and a single woman; that it was through the punishment of their disobedience that man, born for a happier state, was reduced to a degree of ignorance and poverty which he was able partly to dispel only by means of time and labor. It deftly sketches out for us the invention of the first arts, the fruit of men's first needs, and the succession of generations, up to the point at which the human race, almost completely engulfed by a universal flood, was once again reduced to a single family, and thus obliged to start afresh.

This book, then, does not by any means stand between us and what we are looking for—the way in which men have come to be spread out over the earth, and political societies to be organized. It offers a new point of departure for these significant events, similar to that which would have been adopted even if the facts which it relates to us had not become an article of our faith.

Without provisions, and in the depths of forests, men could devote themselves to nothing but obtaining their subsistence. The fruits which the earth produces in the absence of cultivation are not enough: men had to resort to the hunting of animals, which, being limited in number and incapable in a given region of providing many men with food, have for this very reason accelerated the dispersion of peoples and their rapid diffusion.

Families or small nations widely separated from one another, because each required a very large area to obtain its food: that was the state of hunters. They have no fixed dwelling-place at all, and move extremely easily from one spot to another. Difficulty in getting a living, a quarrel, or the fear of an enemy are enough to separate families of hunters from the rest of their nation.

So they move aimlessly wherever the hunt leads them. And if another hunt leads them further in the same direction, their separation from one another increases. Thus peoples who speak the same language sometimes find themselves at distances of more than 600 leagues from one another, and surrounded by peoples who do not understand them. This is common among the savages of America, where we see, for the same reason, nations of fifteen or twenty men.

It is nevertheless not rare to find that wars and quarrels, motives for which barbarous peoples are only too clever at thinking up, have brought about interminglings which out of a large number of nations have sometimes formed one single nation through a general similarity of customs, and of languages which are distinguished from one another only by a large number of dialects.

The custom among the savages of America of adopting their prisoners of war in place of the men whom they lose in their expeditions must have made these interminglings very frequent. We see languages holding sway over vast stretches of country, such as that of the Hurons in the vicinity of the St. Lawrence river, that of the Algonkins extending down to the Mississippi, that of the Mexicans, that of the Incas, that of the Topinambours in Brazil, and that of the Guaranis in Paraguay. The boundaries between them are commonly great mountain ranges.

There are animals which allow themselves to be brought into subjection by men, such as oxen, sheep, and horses, and men find it more advantageous to gather them together into herds than to chase after wandering animals.

It did not take long for the pastoral way of life to be introduced in all places where these animals were met with: oxen and sheep in Europe, camels and goats in the east, horses in Tartary, and reindeer in the north.

The way of life of hunting peoples is maintained in the parts of America where these species are lacking. In Peru, where nature has placed a species of sheep called *llamas*, the people are shepherds, and this is obviously the reason why that part of America has been more easily civilized.

Pastoral peoples, whose subsistence is more abundant and more assured, were the most numerous. They began to grow richer, and to understand better the idea of property. Ambition, or rather greed, which is the ambition of barbarians, was able to inspire them with the inclination to plunder, and at the same time with the will and the courage to hold their own. Tending herds involved trouble from which hunters were free, and herds sustained more men than were required to look after them. Thus a disproportion was bound to arise between the quickness of movement of the disposable population and that of the nation. Thus a nation could not shun the fight against a horde of determined men, whether hunters or even members of other pastoral nations, who would remain masters of the herds if they became conquerors, but who were also sometimes repelled by the cavalry of the shepherds, if the herds of the latter consisted of horses or camels. And as the conquered could not flee without dying of hunger, they shared the fate of the beasts and became the slaves of the conquerors, whom they sustained by tending their herds. The masters, relieved of all these cares, for their part went on subjecting others in the same manner. Thus small nations were formed which in their turn formed large ones. So these peoples spread out over a whole continent, until they were stopped by what appeared to be impenetrable barriers.

The incursions of pastoral peoples leave more traces than those of hunters. Susceptible to a greater number of desires, as a result of the idleness which they enjoyed, they went rushing to wherever they hoped to find booty and seized hold of it. They remained wherever they found pasturage, and intermingled with the inhabitants of the country.

The example of the first encouraged others. The course of these torrents widened, with peoples and languages constantly intermingling.

But these conquerors soon disappeared. When there was nothing left to pillage, the various hordes had no further interest in remaining together, and, besides, the multiplication of herds forced them to separate. Each horde had its chief. But some principal chief, or one who was more warlike, would retain a certain superiority over the others throughout his nation, and would exact from them various gifts as tokens of homage.

At last false ideas of glory entered the picture. What had formerly been done for the purpose of pillage was now done in order to exercise domination, to raise their own nation above others; and, when trade between peoples had made them acquainted with the attributes of different foreign countries, to exchange a barren country for a fertile one.

Every prince who was in any way ambitious made raids on the lands of his neighbors, and extended his power until he encountered someone capable of resisting him; then there was a battle; and the conqueror added the power of the conquered to his own and made use of it for new conquests.

Hence all those inundations of barbarians which have so often ravaged the earth—those ebbs and flows which constitute their whole history.

Hence those different names which peoples of the same country have successively borne, the variety of which confounds the researches of scholars. The name of the dominant nation became the general name for all the others, which nevertheless kept their particular names. Such were the Medes, the Persians, the Celts, the Teutons, the Cimbri, the Suevians, the Germans, the Allemands, the Scythians, the Getae, the Huns, the Turks, the Tartars, the Mogols, the Manchurians, the Kalmucks, the Arabs, the Bedouins, the Berbers, etc.

All conquests were not equally extensive; barriers which would not have stopped a hundred thousand men would stop ten thousand; thus a much greater number of small conquests took place within countries which were cut off. Revolutions were bound to be much more frequent there, and more intermingling of nations was bound to occur. Rivers, and to an even greater extent mountain ranges and the sea, formed impenetrable barriers for a great number of these would-be Attilas. Thus, in between the mountain ranges, the rivers, and the seas, small scattered peoples were reunited, fused together by the multiplicity of revolutions. Their languages and their customs were intimately blended together to assume, as it were, a uniform color.

Beyond these first natural barriers, conquests were more extensive and interminglings less frequent.

Particular customs and dialects form different nations. All obstacles that diminish communication, and consequently distance, which is one of these obstacles, heighten the distinctions which separate nations; but in general the peoples of one continent are mingled together, at any rate indirectly: the Gauls with the Germans, the latter with the Sarmatians, and so on as far as it is possible to go so long as great seas do not separate them. Hence those customs and those words which are common to peoples very distant and very different from one another. Languages, customs, and even human forms seem to me like colored bands running across all the nations of a continent in all directions and forming a succession of perceptible gradations, each nation being tinged with a shade intermediate between those of the nations which neighbor it. Sometimes all the nations are blended together; sometimes one transmits to another what it has itself received. But almost all these revolutions are unknown to history; they leave no more traces than storms do on the sea. It is only when their course has encompassed civilized peoples that the memory of them is preserved.

Pastoral peoples in fertile countries were no doubt the first to move on to the state of agriculture. Hunting peoples, who are deprived of the assistance of animals to manure the soil and to facilitate labor, were unable to arrive so soon at agriculture. If they cultivate any land at all, it is only a small quantity; when it is exhausted they move their habitation elsewhere; and if they are able to abandon their nomadic life it is only by infinitely slow steps.

Husbandmen are not by nature conquerors; the cultivation of the land keeps them too busy. But, being more wealthy than the other peoples, they were obliged to defend themselves against violence. Besides, with them the land can sustain many more men than are necessary in order to cultivate it. Hence people who are unoccupied; hence towns, trade, and all the useful arts and accomplishments; hence more rapid progress in every sphere, for everything follows the general advancement of the mind; hence greater skill in war than in the case of barbarians; hence the division of occupations and the inequality of men; hence slavery in domestic form, and the subjection of the weaker sex (always bound up with barbarism), the hardship of which increases in proportion to the increase in wealth. But at the same time a more searching enquiry into government begins.

The inhabitants of the cities, who were cleverer than those of the countryside, brought the latter into subjection; or, rather, a village which by means of its situation had become a convenient centre where the neighboring population gathered for purposes of trade, and which had a larger number of people, became the dominant one, and, leaving in the other villages only those who were necessary for the cultivation of the land, drew to itself, either by means of slavery or through the attraction of government and commerce, the largest number of inhabitants. The blending together and union of the different departments of government became more intimate and more stable. And in the leisure of the cities, the passions were developed alongside genius.

Ambition gathered strength, politics lent it perspectives, and the progress of the mind enlarged them: hence a thousand different forms of government. The first were necessarily the product of war, and thus implied government by one man alone. We need not believe that men ever voluntarily gave themselves *one master*; but they have often agreed in recognizing *one chief*. And the ambitious themselves, in forming great nations, have contributed to the designs of Providence, to the progress of enlightenment, and thus to the increase in the happiness of the human race, with which they were not concerned at all. Their passions, even their fits of rage, have led them on their way without their being aware of where they were going. I seem to see a huge army, every movement of which is directed by some mighty genius. When the military signals are given, when the trumpets sound tumultuously and the drums beat, whole squadrons of cavalry move off, the very horses are filled with a passion which has no aim, and each part of the army makes its way through the obstacles without knowing what may result from it: the leader alone sees the combined effect of all these different movements. Thus the passions have led to the multiplication of ideas, the extension of knowledge, and the perfection of the mind, in the absence of that reason whose day had not yet come and which would have been less powerful if its reign had arrived earlier.

Reason, which is justice itself, would not have taken away from anyone what belonged to him, would have banished wars and usurpations for ever, and would have left men divided up into a host of nations separated from one another and speaking different languages. As a result the human race, limited in its ideas, incapable of that progress in all kinds of understanding, and in the sciences, arts, and government, which takes its rise from the collective genius of different regions, would have remained for ever in a state of mediocrity. Reason and justice, if they had been more attended to, would have immobilized everything, as has virtually happened in China. But what is never perfect ought never to be entirely immobilized. The passions, tumultuous and dangerous as they are, became a mainspring of action and consequently of progress; everything which draws men away from their present condition, and everything which puts varied scenes before their eyes, extends the scope of their ideas, enlightens them, stimulates them, and in the long run leads them to the good and the true, toward which they are drawn by their natural bent. It is like the wheat which is shaken over and over again in a winnowing-basket, and which under its own weight always falls more and more purified of the light chaff which was debasing it.

There are the gentle passions which are always necessary, and which are developed all the more as humanity is perfected; and there are the others, violent and terrible, such as hatred and vengeance, which are developed more in times of barbarism; they are also natural, and thus also necessary. Their explosion brings back the gentle passions to ameliorate them. In the same way, violent fermentation is indispensable in the making of good wine.

Men who are taught by experience become more and more humane; and it would appear that in recent times generosity, the virtues, and the tender affections, which are continually spreading, at any rate in Europe, are diminishing the dominion of vengeance and national hatreds. But before laws had formed manners, these odious passions were still necessary for the defense of individuals and peoples. They were, so to speak, the leading-strings with which nature and its Author guided the human race in its infancy.

Man is still barbarous in America; and in early times in the rest of the world he was almost always cruel to foreigners. This blind partiality toward his own country, which lasted until Christianity and afterward philosophy taught him to love all men, resembles the state of those animals which during the winter are covered with thick and hideous coats of fur which they will shed in the spring; or, if you like, his early passions resemble the first leaves which sheathe and hide the new stem of a plant, later withering with the emergence of other sheaths until as a result of these successive growths the stem is revealed and becomes crowned with flowers and fruits. This theory is not at all derogatory of Providence. The crimes which were committed were the crimes of men. Those who indulged in them were not happy; for no happiness can lie in the guilty passions. Those who drew on courage and virtue to resist them had their first reward in the consciousness of this courageous virtue. The struggle of one against the other increased the knowledge and the talents of all, and gave to the perception of the good a character of certainty which from day to day appeals more strongly to man's conscience, and a charm which will end by governing the hearts of all. If we look at the world from a broad point of view, then, and see it in the context of the whole concatenation of events which has characterized its progress, it becomes the most glorious witness to the wisdom which presides over it.

It is only through upheavals and ravages that nations have been extended, and that order and government have in the long run been perfected; just as in those forests of America, as old as the world, where from century to century oaks have succeeded to oaks, where from century to century, falling into the dust, they have enriched the soil with all the fruitful juices which the air and the rain have helped to provide, where their remains, furnishing a new source of fecundity to the earth which had given them birth, have served to produce new shoots, still hardier and more vigorous. Thus, over the whole surface of the earth governments have succeeded to governments, empires have been raised up on the ruins of empires, and their scattered remains have been gathered together again; the progress of reason under the early governments, freed from the constraint of the imperfect laws imposed by absolute power, has played a greater part in the constitution of later governments. Repeated conquests extended states; the impotence of barbarian laws and the limitations of civil authority forced them to divide. In some places, peoples weary of anarchy threw themselves into the arms of despotism; in others, tyranny carried to excess gave rise to liberty. No change took place without bringing about some gain; for none took place without adding to experience, and without extending or improving, or paving the way for, man's education. It was only after centuries, and by means of bloody revolutions, that despotism at last learned to moderate itself, and liberty to regulate itself; that the situation of states at last became less fluctuating and more stable. In this way, then, through alternate periods of rest and unrest, of weal and woe, the human race as a whole has advanced ceaselessly toward its perfection.

When quarrels first took place in nations, a man who was superior in strength, in valor, or in prudence persuaded and then forced the very people whom he was defending to obey him.

This superiority alone suffices to give a chief to men who have gathered together. It is not exactly true that ambition is the sole source of authority. People are induced to choose a chief; but they have always wished him to be reasonable and just, not foolish and arbitrary.

In nations of a small size it is impossible for despotic authority to become consolidated; the dominion of a chief can in such a nation rest on nothing but the consent of the people, or on a veneration either for a person or for a family. Veneration for a person disappears when power is abused; and when the veneration is for a family, this abuse provides a motive for palace revolutions for the benefit of another member of the family who seeks to gratify public opinion to a greater extent.

In small nations, the whole state is under the eyes of each individual. Each shares directly in the advantages of the society, and could not find any greater benefit in oppressing it on account of another. There is not enough wealth which could be used arbitrarily to bribe dishonest people. There is no populace: a kind of equality prevails. The kings could not live in isolation from their subjects; their people necessarily constitute their only guards and their only court. They love them better, and, when they are wise, they are better loved by them. If they are not wise, protests are soon made to them, and these could be followed by resistance. It is easy to assemble together. The means and the art of forcing the greater number, in spite of their size, to obey the smaller number cannot exist.

Five hundred thousand men can keep in subjection fifty million, but two hundred men can never keep in subjection twenty thousand, although this is the same proportion. This explains why despotism has never held sway among peoples who are separated into small nations, Savages, Tartars, Celts, Arabs, etc., at any rate when some superstitious belief has not blinded men's eyes, as in the case of the subjects of the Old Man of the Mountain. This also explains why monarchy itself, which was everywhere the first form of government—since it is easier to control men than to get them to agree, and because military authority, always concentrated as it is in one hand, must have rendered a similar concentration of civil power natural and often necessary—was after a certain period replaced by republics in almost all those cities which were reduced to their adjoining territories or to distant colonies. Here the spirit of equality cannot be banished, because the spirit of commerce rules: the collective industry of men never fails to make it dominate in cities, when their ways of life are not corrupted and swallowed up by the general impulsive force of a huge state which encompasses them all: whether by the spirit of despotism, as in the case of the Asiatics; or whether, as in the case of the ancient Franks, by the military spirit of a nobility which resided in the countryside, and which had derived its original modes of behavior in nomadic nations which could have no commerce. Also the spirit of commerce presupposes a property in goods which is independent of every power other than that of the laws: it cannot become inured to oriental *avania*.

In states which were confined to a single city, it was impossible that the monarchy could be long maintained. There its least transgressions are and are seen to be more tyrannical; there tyranny has less power and faces more energetic resistance. There, too, monarchy more easily degenerates. The passions of the man are more confounded with those of the prince. He or those in his circle may be tempted by some individual's fortune, or by his wife. Less elevated above his subjects, he is more sensitive to their affronts, and more susceptible to anger. In the infancy of human reason, it is easy for a prince to grow angry at the obstacles which the laws put in the way of his passions, and for him not to appreciate that these barriers between him and his people do not defend him less against his subjects than they do his subjects against him. But since in a small state he is never the strongest, the abuse of power, which is bound to be more frequent there, is also less easily defended against the revolt which is its consequence. Thus republics arise, at first aristocratic and more tyrannical than monarchy, because nothing is so horrible as obedience to a multitude which always knows how to exalt its passions into virtues; but at the same time more lasting, because the people are more debased. The powerful and the weak unite against a tyrant; but an aristocratic senate, above all if it is hereditary, has only the populace to combat. In spite of this, republics confined to one city tend naturally toward democracy, which also has its serious drawbacks.

The domain of a city could be extended only by colonies and conquests. Colonies could be established in the vicinity of a city only in the earliest times. Soon the territory which surrounded the city became occupied; colonies were then removed to a distance, and consequently remained linked to the metropolis only in so far as they were not firmly enough established to be able to do without it, like those layers which remain attached to the trunk until they have grown strong enough, and which are then detached from it by the slightest accident; or like the fruit which clings to the tree until its maturity causes it to fall to the ground, germinate, and produce new trees. Nevertheless, by the use of a metaphor which was natural enough, the relations between the metropolis and the colonies were expressed by the words *mother* and *daughter*; men, who at all times have been bound by their own language, inferred analogous duties from these expressions, and the exercise of these duties was for a long time maintained solely by the force of custom, which always finds defenders among the men whom it subjugates, just as laws do among the authorities who maintain them.

It is rare for cities to make conquests. They go in for them only when, so to speak, they have nothing better to do. Moreover, there is commonly found among them a kind of equilibrium and a degree of jealousy sufficient to result in the formation of leagues against any city which exalts itself too much.

Love of country, above all in republics, makes it almost impossible for the sovereignty of a city to be destroyed by forces which are the equal of its own.

Thus a city is rarely a conqueror, barring some unusual combination of internal constitution and external circumstances which was never found, I believe, except in the case of the Roman people.

But when cities were still under the sway of kings, it was easier to make conquests. A warlike king gave a considerable superiority to his city; he could make a number of conquests and bring several cities under his domination; and the more his city was extended the stronger became his authority, and the more possible it became for him to crush one party through the instrumentality of the others. The authority of the prince became the sole centre of power, and whatever interest individuals might have or appear to have in throwing off the yoke, it was impossible for them to be brought together except through a long series of secret intrigues; but the king was usually powerful enough for fear or hope of reward to induce some accomplice to betray such a secret.

Unreasoning ambition often drove the first conquerors to spread out far and wide, and when it proved impossible, either for want of troops or because the distances were too great, to maintain their conquests, they contented themselves with exacting tribute, which was only paid so long as the people concerned were weaker.

Hence a perpetual succession of wars, and a continual alternation of victories and defeats, of nations in turn dominating one another, according as chance gave them kings who were conquerors.

In the case of those princes ruling over agricultural peoples who were up to a point civilized, their states were bound, because of the inequality in the progress of their neighbors, to find themselves surrounded by barbarous peoples. When they were in their vigorous stage, they extended their power by making conquests, by turning the neighboring territories into colonies and gradually civilizing them. But when such states relapsed into weakness, the barbarians attacked them in their turn and had the best of it; the desire to dominate a rich country pricked the ambition of the chiefs and the greed of a fierce people.

These inundations, these migrations of peoples which among barbarians succeed one another without leaving any trace, sometimes encompassed in their course peoples who were already civilized, and it is only in this way that the memory of them has been able to come down to us today. In such cases the barbarian people adopted the civilization of the conquered, as a result of the influence which knowledge and reason are always certain to exercise over force when conquest does not involve extermination. The barbarians, having become civilized, themselves civilized their first place of abode. The two peoples were formed into a single people; it became a more extensive empire under one chief.

Civilized peoples, who are more wealthy, more peaceful, and more accustomed to a soft or at any rate sedentary life, above all in the fertile regions which were the first to be cultivated, soon lose that vigor which made them into conquerors when a learned discipline puts no obstacle at all in the way of softness. The conquerors then give way to new barbarians; empires are extended, going through their ages of vigor and decline; but their very downfall helps to perfect the arts and improve the laws. Thus the Chaldeans, the Assyrians, the Medes, and the Persians succeeded one another, the domination of the latter being the most far-reaching.

It was in this way that the kingdom of Lydia, when it had acquired a degree of superiority, swallowed up all the little kingdoms of Asia Minor, which had been softened by the Greek way of life. Later, like those rivers which, swollen by the contributions of a thousand others, eventually lose themselves in the sea, Lydia was in its turn invaded by Cyrus, who appeared with a new nation. This nation, at first barbarous, retained under the conqueror's successors nothing but pride and ambition. The softness of the vanquished was soon transmitted to the victors. That discipline which alone can offset force, and by means of which the reason of enlightened peoples makes up for the violence of barbarians, was known only by the Greeks. The whole of the great Persian power broke down against Greece, which had taken shape and developed in the midst of civil wars.

The territory of Greece, broken up by islands and mountains, could not be subject to the same vicissitudes. It was difficult in early times for great empires to be formed there. A host of small states, almost always at war, kept up the military spirit, and made advances in tactical skills, the perfection of arms, and boldness in battle. Civilization was also extended by means of commerce. In general it is peoples from the mountains and from cold or infertile countries who have conquered the plains, and who have either formed empires or held out against them. They are poorer, more hardy, and more inaccessible; they can choose their time when they are attacking and their positions when they are defending themselves. And when they are desirous of becoming conquerors, they have more to gain from it, and a greater aptitude for it.

The great empires, formed as we have just said by barbarians, were despotic. Despotism is easy. To do what you want to do, is a rule which a king learns very quickly; art is necessary to persuade people, but none is necessary to give them orders. If despotism did not revolt those who are its victims, it would never be banished from the earth. A father wishes to be a despot over his children, and a master over his servants. Honesty does not safeguard a prince against this poison; he wishes for the good, and makes a virtue of wishing everyone to obey him. The larger the state the easier despotism is, and the greater would be the difficulty involved in establishing a moderate government. For that, it would be necessary for there to be an established order in all parts of the state; one would have to determine the position of each province and of each city, and to allow its municipal administration all the liberty which it would not be possible for it to abuse. How many different departments would have to be combined and equilibrated, and what difficulties would face him who had no idea that this was necessary! A conquest carried out by barbarians, which is the product of force and accompanied by devastation, puts a state into such disorder that to mend matters would require the greatest genius, the most dexterous hand, the most moderate and active virtue, and the purest and noblest heart.

Since it was impossible to answer for everything, one could devise nothing better than to install governors who were as despotic to the people as they were servile to the prince. It was easier to look to them to levy taxes and keep the people down than to arrange the details of this oneself.

The prince forgot the people. The best governor was the one who gave him the most money and who knew best how to obtain the menials and flatterers who frequented the palace. The governors had underlings who acted in the same way. Despotic authority made the governors dangerous; the court treated them with the utmost severity, and their position depended upon its slightest caprice. Pretexts were sought to deprive them of the treasure they had plundered; and the people gained no relief at all, for greed is a natural characteristic of barbarian kings.

Originally taxes were never conceived as subventions to meet the needs of the state; but the prince demanded money, and people were forced to give it to him. Throughout the east presents are made to them; the kings there are simply individuals who are powerful and greedy.

All power was thus concentrated in a single person, who was not even shrewd enough to divide up that part of it which he was unable to exercise. Princes, governors, and underlings were alike subordinate tyrants who exerted pressure on one another only in order to crush the people with all their united strength.

Despotic princes, never having come across laws, scarcely dreamed of making any. They were their own judges: in general, when the power which makes the laws and that which applies them are one and the same, the laws are useless. Punishments remain arbitrary; they are usually cruel when they are imposed by the prince, and pecuniary in character when they are imposed by underlings who draw profit from them. So far as the civil disposition of inheritances is concerned, custom or the will of the father decides it.

It can also be seen from this that a despotic government which comes on the scene after laws and customs have been established does not involve the same disadvantages as these early conquests made by barbarians did.

The Neros and the Caligulas, if I may venture to say so, had in them more wickedness than the evil they actually committed. As a result of the rules of conduct accepted in the state under the first Caesars, the people were not at all oppressed; the provinces enjoyed a high degree of tranquility; and distributive justice was equitably enough carried out. The governors did not dare to give way to their greed: they would have been punished by the emperors. The court held, between the people and the great, that balance which it ought to hold in a well-directed government.

In general, the most moderate of the great states are those which are formed by the union of several small ones, above all when this union is brought about slowly.

At bottom, the monarch has no interest at all in involving himself with the details of municipal government in places where he is never present: he is led to leave it as it is. Princes can be partial to despotism only when it is around them, because their passions (or those at least which are most subject to caprice) are relative only to what is in their neighborhood: like the rest, they are not more than human. That is why the despotism of the Roman emperors did less harm than that of the Turks.

With the Turks, despotism enters into the constitution of their government. It infects all parts of the state; it fetters all its departments. Each pasha exercises over the people who are subject to him the same authority which the Grand Seigneur has over him. He is alone entrusted with and responsible for all the tribute. He has no other revenue than that which he extracts from the people over and above what he is obliged to furnish to the sultan; and he is forced to redouble his harassments in order to provide for the countless presents which are necessary to keep him in his office. There is no law in the empire to regulate the raising of money, and no formal procedure in the administration of justice. Everything is done in military fashion. The people have no one at all at court to protect them against the abuse of power by the great, in the fruits of which the court itself shares.

When it is the conqueror who has himself installed governors in the provinces, his ignorance is bound to lead him to take his own government as a model, and thus to establish an administrative despotism, which then becomes as it were a great tree whose branches spread out far and wide over the whole empire, and which smother all the produce of the land which they cover with their shadow.

When a military government is the only thing which keeps the state together, forming a nation only by making it the slave of a prince, this government is despotic in principle, and if manners do not moderate it, it will also be so in practice. Military discipline necessarily presupposes despotism and rigor. But we must not confuse nations ruled by a military government with nations wholly composed of warriors, such as the barbarians, Germans and others. Far from it: their government gives birth to liberty. There war is by no means an exclusive occupation which has to be specially studied, and which gives those who carry it on a superiority of force over the rest of society. Such a nation maintains its rights. A prince can enslave his people by means of soldiers, because the people are weaker. But how can he enslave a people of soldiers? It is not courage, nor the military spirit, which extinguish liberty, but the very reverse.

The kingdoms of Europe conquered by the northern barbarians, therefore, were saved from despotism, because these barbarians were free before the conquest, which was carried out in the name of the people and not in that of the king. The Roman way of life which was established, and the religion which the barbarians embraced, also contributed to protect them from despotism.

Private individuals were spread throughout the country; they shared territorial power and the gains of victory with the prince.

It was not the same in Asia, where the conquered peoples were already accustomed to despotism, because the first conquests, which had taken place before the period when manners could have been formed, had been very extensive and rapid.

Despotism gives birth to revolutions; but all that these bring about is the exchange of one tyrant for another, because in great despotic states the power of the kings is established only by means of their troops, and their security by means of their guards. The people are never strong or united enough to check such a military power, which substitutes one king for another, assured of being the instrument of the tyranny of the successor as it had been of that of his predecessor.

One suspects that the total effects of these causes must have been infinitely various, depending upon the way in which they were intermixed with the ideas of the received religion, and, as we have already noted, with veneration for a particular family, because in the absence of any other power men are ruled by habit. It would have been just as easy for the janissaries, if they had wanted to, to choose a sultan from among the populace as from the Ottoman family; but such was the respect for that family which was instilled into them from infancy that they would not have wanted this.

This power of education is one of the main sources of the capacity of governments to endure, to the point of maintaining them when the whole driving force of the empire is weakened, and of concealing its decline: in such a way that at the slightest disturbance one is astonished to see the state fall to the ground, like those trees which look healthy, because their bark is undamaged, whereas all the wood inside it is reduced to powder, and no longer offers any resistance to the wind. In despotic states, education is wholly employed to break down people's courage. Fear and deference seize hold of the imagination. The sovereign, wrapped in formidable obscurity, seems to govern from the depths of a storm cloud, from which come thunder and lightning to inspire terror and dazzle.

It may be added that in these vast despotic states there is also introduced a despotism which extends over social manners, which dulls men's minds even more; which deprives society of the greater part of its resources, its delights, and the co-operation of women in the running of the family; which by forbidding the social intercourse of the two sexes reduces everything to uniformity, and induces in members of the state a tired lethargy which is opposed to all change and therefore to all progress.

When everything is conducted by force (as it necessarily has to be in a society where a host of slaves and women—in each wealthy house as in the state itself—are sacrificed to a single master), the fire of the intellect is extinguished; it is locked in the shackles of barbarian laws. Despotism perpetuates ignorance, and ignorance perpetuates despotism. What is more, this despotic authority becomes common practice, and common practice confirms the abuses.

Despotism is like an enormous weight which, pressing down on wooden pillars, weakens their resistance and causes them from day to day to sink and subside.

I shall therefore say something about slavery, polygamy, and the softness which is their consequence; and under this head I shall deal with the causes of differences in manners among men.

The enslavement of women to men is based over the whole world on the inequality of their physical powers. But as rather more men are born than women, wherever equality has reigned monogamy has been natural. It is so, therefore, among all small peoples, shepherds, hunters, and husbandmen; it is so among peoples divided up into small societies where the states are confined within the walls of cities as in Greece, and above all in the democratic republics; it is so among poor peoples, and among all the less wealthy individuals in the very countries where polygamy is most in vogue; it is the same in the empires whose customs date from the time when the people were still under republican governments, like the Roman empire and that of Alexander's successors, which although despotic never knew polygamy.

Nevertheless the barbarians, who show little refinement in matters of love, were all inclined toward plurality of wives. Tacitus reports that the chiefs of the Germans sometimes had three or four wives; but among a people which was nomadic and poor the evil could not have been contagious. Thus it was with the growth in the wealth and the size of empires that polygamy was established; and with slavery its extent was increased.

The first men were cruel in their wars; it was only after a long time that they learned moderation. Hunting peoples massacre their prisoners; or, when they do not kill them, they incorporate them in their own nation. A mother who has lost her son chooses a prisoner to serve as a son to her; she loves him because he is useful to her. The ancients, among whom children were a form of wealth, and who received services from them, were inclined toward the adoption of children. Thus there were few slaves, or none at all, among hunting or primitive peoples.

Pastoral peoples began to be familiar with slavery. Those who captured herds were obliged, in order to be able to devote themselves to new expeditions, to maintain those who tended them.

Agricultural peoples carried slavery further. They had more varied services and more tiring work for slaves to perform, and in proportion to the extent to which the manners of the masters became more civilized, slavery became harsher and more degrading, because the inequality was greater. The wealthy ceased to work; slaves became a luxury and a commodity; parents even sold their children. But the slaves who were captured in war, or who were born of parents who were themselves slaves, always made up the greatest number.

In the house, they were used for all the lowest duties. They had neither goods nor honor of their own; they were stripped of the elementary rights of humanity. The laws gave limitless authority over them, and this was quite easy, because it was their masters who made the laws; and these masters thought to assure oppression by means of oppression. In despotic states the princes had a host of slaves, as did the governors and even wealthy individuals. The vast size of the states brought the inequality of fortunes to the highest pitch. The capitals became like chasms, where the wealthy from all parts of the empire gathered together, along with their hosts of slaves.

The female slaves formed part of the master's pleasures. This can be seen in the manners of the ancient patriarchs, for the crime of adultery (and this was still the case in the statute law of antiquity) was never a reciprocal one as it is with us. It was only the husband who was regarded as being injured by it. This was a consequence of the great inequality between the two sexes which barbarism brought about. Among the ancient peoples women never had any rights in the marriage relation. It was only poverty which prevented polygamy from being established everywhere.

When in later times the manners and laws of a nation became settled, the intermingling of families restored to women those rights which they had not enjoyed since the earliest times, because, above all in republics, they used the power of their brothers against the tyranny of their husbands.

In these republics, where everyone was equal, the parents of a girl would never have agreed to let her go out of their sight for ever. Polygamy and the cloistering of women could never become established there. But in the first empires of which we are speaking, peopled as they were by a host of slaves, where women had no rights, and men had rights over their slaves, the plurality of wives became a practice which was as common as the limits of individual fortunes allowed. Jealousy is a necessary consequence of love: it inspires husband and wife with a wise sense of mutual propriety which assures the future of their children. This sensible attitude, and still more the presumption of dishonor which was associated with a wife's infidelity, increased along with polygamy.

The impossibility of subjecting women to this law of fidelity, when neither their hearts nor their senses could be satisfied, led to the practice of shutting them up. Princes, and later those individuals who were wealthy enough, established seraglios for themselves.

Jealousy brought it about that men were mutilated in order to guard the women. Thence a softness entered into manners which did not mollify them but on the contrary rendered them more cruel.

The princes shut themselves up with their wives and their slaves; and their subjects, whom they never saw, were scarcely regarded by them as human beings. Their political government was always that of barbarians. It was crude, because they were ignorant and lazy; it was cruel, because less time is required to cut down a tree than to gather in its fruits, and because the art of making men happy is of all arts the most difficult, the one in which the most elements have to be combined.

The same softness spread through the whole state. Thence that sudden weakening of the monarchies of the east. Those of the Chaldeans, the Assyrians, the Medes, and the Persians scarcely survived the first conquerors who had founded them. It was as if they had remained in being for some time only while waiting for an enemy to come and destroy them. If these monarchies, by the weight of their armies, sometimes overwhelmed weak nations, they broke down in the face of any courageous resistance; and as soon as Greece had been united, it overthrew this immense colossus with hardly any effort.

There is only one means available to counter this general degeneracy of a nation, and that is a militia which is kept under martial discipline, like the Turkish janissaries or the Egyptian mamelukes; but such a militia often becomes an object of terror to its masters.

One thing that should be pointed out is that these harmful effects of despotism and the plurality of wives have never been extended so far as under Mohammedanism. This religion, which does not allow any laws other than those of the religion itself, opposes the wall of superstition to the natural march of improvement. It has consolidated barbarism by *consecrating* that which existed when it appeared, and which it adopted through national prejudice. Neither in the history of the ancient monarchies, nor in the manners of China and Japan, can one find such an excess of abasement as that of the Mohammedan peoples.

Despotism, and the uniformity and thus the imperfection of manners, laws, and government, were maintained in Asia and wherever great empires were formed at an early stage; and I have no doubt that the existence of the vast plains of Mesopotamia contributed to this. When despotism was later extended along with Mohammedanism, this was to some extent only as a result of the transmission of manners from one country to another.

The peoples who were preserved from despotism were those who remained shepherds or hunters; those who formed small societies; and the republics. It was among such peoples that revolutions were useful; that nations participated in them and thus drew gain from them; that tyranny was unable to consolidate itself sufficiently to enslave men's minds; that the profusion of particular bodies of law and of revolutions which pointed out the errors of the founders of the state, and the fall of an old and rise of a new sovereign authority which brought about a re-examination of the laws, in the long run perfected the laws and government. It was among such peoples that equality was maintained, that intellect and courage showed great activity, and that the human mind made rapid progress. It was among them that manners and laws in the course of time learned how to direct themselves toward the greatest happiness of the people.

After this glance at the progress of governments and their morality, it will be useful to trace the progress of the human mind in all its revolutions.

SKETCH OF THE SECOND DISCOURSE
Of Which the Subject will be the Progress of the Human Mind

Let us start from that state of confusion in which the mind knows nothing but sensations, in which sounds, more or less loud and more or less shrill, the temperature and resistance of surrounding objects, and pictures of bizarre, differently colored forms, come to assail the mind on every hand, and throw it into a kind of intoxication which is nevertheless the germ of reason.

The manner in which ideas begin to become a little distinct in our minds, and to exercise an influence on our will, depends on a kind of spiritual mechanism common to all men. It may be the work of a few moments; at any rate this would seem to be proved by the example of animals which know how to find their food, and, what would appear more difficult, which know how to go and look for it shortly after their birth.

Although pertaining to the history of nature rather than to that of facts, this period must be studied with care, since in every sphere the first steps determine the direction of the journey.

It was movement which cleared up this state of confusion, and which gave men the ideas of distinction and unity. Without it, they would never have thought of reflecting on the difference between colors; they would have been content merely to experience it. But the arrangement of the parts of this picture which is presented to the mind often changes the picture itself. The mind learns to observe the course of these variations. During the first experience of these changes, no distinction at all was yet made between the parts which maintained the same position relative to one another, whether the whole appeared to be in motion, as in the case of animals, or whether it appeared to be fixed in one spot, as in that of a tree. Thus, however much the images presented to our senses were only the result of all the individual colored or resistant points of which they were composed, the mind conceived them, so to speak, only in bulk.

The first individual ideas were thus necessarily collective in relation to the parts of which they are composed; at no time was it possible, nor will it ever be possible, for the analysis of the works of men to be carried to the highest degree. Properly speaking, there are no such things as simple ideas; they all resolve themselves into the results of sensations, the elements and different causes of which can be analyzed up to a point whose limit is unknown to us.

But the analysis of the first men was not carried very far. The stock of ideas was divided up only to the extent of the experience afforded by the diversity of phenomena and above all of needs. Men's needs are relative only to this stock; it is unnecessary to anatomize fruits in order to feed on them, and even less necessary to analyze the ideas which inform us of their presence. Ideas are a language and true indicators by means of which we recognize the existence of external objects. It is never by means of reasoning that we perceive their relations with ourselves. Providence, by inspiring us with desires, has wisely spared us so long a journey. As a result of this, men have necessarily related their sensations to the external objects which they assume to exist. Where would we be if, before going in search of their food, men had been obliged, from their own sensations regarded solely as affections of their minds, to infer the existence of objects outside themselves?

Thus men began by giving names which were relative to the existing stock of ideas. Ideas, being the indicators of the existence of external objects, do not represent them at all exactly; from a distance an oak looks like an elm, and thus arises the idea of *a tree*—not because I have the idea of a tree which is neither an oak nor an elm, but because I have an idea which informs me of the existence of a tree without telling me whether it is the one or the other. This is the origin of abstraction. The idea is simple, no doubt, if one considers it in itself, independent of its relations—i.e., if we take it as always representing a certain form and a certain color; but experience teaches us that this form and this color are equally an indicator of the existence of an oak or of an elm.

It is the same with the signs of language. The first time they were used they designated only some definite object; but as they were applied to several objects they became general. Little by little different circumstances were distinguished, and in order to import more clarity into language, names were given to *modes* or *manners of being*, which in relation to our ideas are only relations of distance, or rather relations to the different sensations which are excited in us by the different languages which the objects speak to us, if I may put it that way.

Thus the ideas of *modes* were given names after those of *substances*, which were regarded as the principal ideas, although the senses acquire them for us at one and the same time. Thus it was by extracting the signs of language from their undue generality that the mind familiarized itself little by little with more abstract ideas. One suspects that ideas were multiplied in proportion as languages were perfected. The words which expressed affirmation, negation, the act of judging, existence, and possession became the bond of all our reasoning. Habit caused these same ideas to be applied in similar cases to all the roots of languages.

Little by little, by giving names in this way to the different relations which objects have with one another or with ourselves, the possession of all these ideas was assured, and as a result the operations of the mind acquired a considerable facility. But at the same time the labyrinth of ideas became more and more encumbered; it was natural to believe that to each word there corresponded one idea, and yet the same words are rarely synonymous with one another; they have different meanings according to the way in which they are applied. In conversation we guess more than we actually hear.

The mind, by an almost mechanical operation which owes its origin to the linking together of ideas, seizes quite quickly the meaning of words determined by the circumstances. Having believed that words corresponded exactly to ideas, men were quite astonished to see that their precise determination could not be agreed upon; it was a long time before they began to suspect that this arose from the fact that ideas were different according as one wanted to extract the general idea from different particular cases; people lost their way among misleading definitions which took in only one part of the object, and everyone gave a different definition of the same idea.

The complex notions of substance, which, because they relate to real objects, necessarily include a greater or lesser number of parts, according as the object is more or less understood, were regarded as pictures of the objects themselves. Instead of asking by what stages a certain number of different kinds of things had been gathered together under a general name, an effect of which the cause would have been found in their general resemblance, men sought for that common essence which the names expressed; they invented genera, species, individuals, and those *metaphysical degrees* whose nature has caused so many disputes, as cruel sometimes in their effects as they were frivolous in their object.

Instead of regarding these names as signs which are relative to the manner in which we perceive the range of existing things which we extend according to the resemblances we discover, and which we cannot extend too far without running the risk of confusing one with another, men invented *abstract and incommunicable essences*. Latterly they have gone so far as to apply this also to concepts relating to products of the human mind, such as comedy and tragedy. People have seriously argued about whether a poem belongs to this or that genus, and only rarely has it been realized that the argument is merely about words.

The error was still greater with regard to the signs which were used to express the relations between things. Such are all the moral ideas which have been reasoned about as if they were objects existing independently of the things which have these relations with one another.

Man receives his various ideas in his infancy, or, rather, the words are engraved on his mind. They are linked up at first with particular ideas; and little by little there is formed that confused assemblage of ideas and expressions whose use is learned through imitation. Time, by means of the progress of languages, has multiplied ideas to infinity; and when man seeks to retire within himself, he finds himself in a labyrinth which he has entered with blindfolded eyes. He can no longer find the marks of his footsteps; nevertheless his eyes open, and he sees on all sides paths of whose interconnection he is unaware. He clings to a few truths which he is unable to doubt; but whence does this certainty come to him? He knows nothing except through his ideas, and he is thus bound to believe that his ideas bring certainty with them; for whence could he derive it before having analyzed the manner in which these ideas are formed in his mind? This is an immense task, which requires several generations.

Without understanding very well what it is to have an idea of a thing, he lays down as a principle that everything which his ideas tell him about an object is true. This is a delusive principle, because in reality it is an art to draw from notions once they have been determined, even arbitrarily, inferences which are incapable of taking one in. Success, in this case, becomes another source of error. People have more confidence in the principle, and misuse of it does not arouse any aversion to it at all. For the same reason that everyone is convinced that he has the true idea of an object, one is never tempted to challenge a court, to which no one has recourse without believing that he will hear it pronounce in his favor. From this in all ages there has arisen the obscurity of logic and metaphysics; from this have arisen arbitrary definitions and divisions.

This darkness could only be dissipated little by little; the dawn of reason could only rise by imperceptible degrees, to the extent that men analyzed their ideas more and more; not that they at first recognized the necessity of distinguishing between all the parts of their ideas: but their very disputes led them toward this, because truth seems to fly away and escape from our investigations until we have arrived at the primary elements of ideas; because while advancing little by little we are always aware of a gap; and finally because curiosity always makes us act until it has exhausted the subject of its investigations, and because no question can be exhausted except by means of the truth.

Progress was more or less rapid, depending on circumstances and aptitudes.

A fortunate arrangement of the fibers of the brain, a greater or lesser degree of power or refinement in the organs of sense and memory, a certain degree of quickness in the blood—these are probably the only differences which nature herself creates as between one man and another. Their minds, or the power and character of their minds, have a real inequality, the causes of which will always remain unknown to us and which could never be the subject of our reasoning. All the rest is the effect of education; and this education is the result of all the sensations we have experienced, and of all the ideas which we have been able to acquire from infancy. All the objects with which we are surrounded contribute to this; and the instruction of our parents and our masters makes up only the smallest part of it.

The original aptitudes are distributed equally among barbarous peoples and among civilized peoples; they are probably the same in all places and at all times. Genius is spread through the human race very much as gold is in a mine. The more ore you take, the more metal you will get. The more men there are, the more great men you will have, or the more men capable of becoming great. The chances of education and of events either develop them, or leave them buried in obscurity, or sacrifice them before their time, like fruits blown down by the wind. One is compelled to admit that if Corneille, brought up in a village, had followed the plough all his life, that if Racine had been born in Canada among the Hurons, or in Europe in the eleventh century, they would never have unfolded their genius. If Columbus and Newton had died at sixteen, America would perhaps not have been discovered until two centuries later, and we would still perhaps be ignorant of the true system of the world. And if Virgil had perished in infancy we would have had no Virgil, for there have not been two of them.

Progress, although inevitable, is intermingled with frequent periods of decline as a result of the occurrences and revolutions which come to interrupt it. Thus progress has been very different among different peoples.

Men who are separated from one another and who have no commerce have moved forward at much the same rate. We have found small nations which live by hunting at the same point of development, with the same arts, the same arms, and the same manners. Genius was of little benefit with respect to unrefined needs; but as soon as the human race succeeded in escaping from the narrow sphere of these elementary needs, the circumstances which put this genius in a position to develop, combined with those which presented it with facts and experiences which a thousand others would have seen without taking advantage of them, soon introduced one or another kind of inequality.

Among barbarous peoples, where education is more or less the same for everyone, this inequality could not be very great. When labor was divided according to men's aptitudes, which is in itself very advantageous since everything is then done better and more quickly, the unequal distribution of goods and social responsibilities meant that the majority of men who were employed in rough and lowly work were unable to make the same progress as the other men, to whom this distribution gave leisure and the means of advancing themselves.

Education brought about an even greater difference between the various parts of one and the same nation than did wealth, and as between different nations it was the same.

The people which were the first to acquire a little more knowledge quickly became superior to its neighbors; and each step in its progress made the next one easier. Thus the development of one nation accelerated from day to day, while others stayed in their state of mediocrity, immobilized by particular circumstances, and others remained in a state of barbarism. A glance over the earth puts before our eyes, even today, the whole history of the human race, showing us traces of all the steps and monuments of all the stages through which it has passed from the barbarism, still in existence, of the American peoples to the civilization of the most enlightened nations of Europe. Alas! our ancestors and the Pelasgians who preceded the Greeks were like the savages of America!

A reason for these differences which are found between nations has been sought in differences of climate. This view, modified a little and rightly restricted only to those climatic influences which are always the same, has recently been adopted by one of the greatest geniuses of our century. But the conclusions which are drawn from it are hasty, to say the least, and are extremely exaggerated. They are belied by experience, since under the same climates peoples are different; since under climates which resemble one another very little we very often find peoples with the same character and the same turn of mind; since the fervor and despotism of the Orientals can arise from barbarism alone when it is combined with certain circumstances; and since that metaphorical language which is presented to us as an effect of the greater proximity of the sun was that of the ancient Gauls and Germans, according to the accounts given by Tacitus and Diodorus Siculus, and is still that of the Iroquois in the icy regions of Canada. It is in fact that of all peoples whose language is very limited, and who, lacking the appropriate words, multiply comparisons, metaphors, and allusions in order to make themselves understood, and who manage this sometimes forcefully but always with little exactitude and clarity.

Since physical causes act only upon the hidden principles which contribute to the formation of our mind and our character, and not upon the results, which are all that we see, we are right to evaluate their influence only after having exhaustively examined that of the moral causes and assured ourselves that the facts are absolutely inexplicable by the latter, of whose principle we are conscious, and whose operation we can follow in the depths of our hearts.

The ideas of the first men were limited to objects perceptible by the senses, and thus their languages were confined to designating them. The formation of a host of abstract and general ideas, still unknown to a large number of peoples, was the work of time, and consequently it was only after a long period that men arrived at an understanding of the art of reasoning.

The class of objects which were the first to be designated in languages was the same everywhere, just as were the first metaphors and the first abstract ideas which govern conjugations, declensions, and analogy in the most barbarous languages (none of which we know in its original state); for whatever the way in which barbarism arrests the progress of a body of men, it is only by depriving them of opportunities to perfect themselves. In the course of time genius never fails to appear. Thus in the constant use of languages it is impossible that the variety of combinations of ideas which present themselves for expression should not indicate the need for new signs, in order to denote new connections or new shades of meaning between the ideas. And this need, which is a consciousness of our poverty, in revealing the latter to us teaches us how to remedy it, and becomes the source of our wealth.

Thus the languages of the most barbarous peoples are today very far removed from their first attempts. It is the same with all progress, which is always real but sometimes very slow; there are few arts and sciences whose origin cannot be traced back to these first epochs; all the arts are based on homely ideas, on experiences which are common to and within the reach of all men.

We see the immense progress which the sciences have made, and we have lost sight of the imperceptible chain by which they are linked to the first ideas. In the beginning, men observed the heavenly bodies with the naked eye; the horizon was the first instrument, and the 360 days of the lunisolar year are the model for the division of the circle into 360 degrees. The stars, from the first to the fourth magnitude, are visible to all men. The alternation of days and nights, and the changes in the phases of the moon, were natural measures of time; the alternation of heat and cold, and the needs of tillage, led to a comparison of the path of the sun with that of the moon. Thence the year, the months, and the names of the principal constellations.

Then navigation made it necessary to perfect astronomy, and showed how to relate it to geography.

Music, dance, and poetry, again, have their source in the nature of man. Created to live in society, his joy manifests itself externally: he leaps and shouts. A common joy expressed itself in swaying movements, in leaps, and in simultaneous and confused shouts. Little by little people became accustomed to leap in a similar manner; the steps were marked by sounds; and the latter were separated by regular intervals. The ear, with very little experience, and by following nature alone, learned to appreciate the primary relations between sounds. When it was desired to communicate the reason for one's joy in words, these were arranged according to the beat of the sounds. This was the origin of dance, of music, and of poetry, which was at first written in order to be sung. It was only with time that people began to get satisfaction simply from the harmony which was characteristic of it, and which they became familiar with only after it had been sufficiently perfected to give pleasure by itself alone. To the extent that the arts are perfected, they are separated from one another because they need particular talents. Pauses were indicated by similar sounds, and the ear thus learned to take account of the number of syllables. The necessity of conforming in this way to the beat must have contributed to the progress and softening of languages; versification daily became less free; the ear, by dint of experience, subjected itself to stricter rules; and if the burden of these became heavier, this was fortunately compensated for by the fact that the perfection of languages and the proliferation of new turns of phrase and felicitous boldnesses of style also lent greater strength to bear it.

Among uncultivated peoples, the capacity to remember verses, together with national vanity, induced them to set down in songs their most memorable actions. Such are the songs of the savages of our own day, those of the ancient bards, the runic rhymes of the inhabitants of Scandinavia, some ancient canticles included in the historical books of the Hebrews; the chou-king of the Chinese, and the ballads of the modern peoples of Europe. These were the only histories which existed before the invention of writing—histories without chronology, and, as we might expect, often full of untrue circumstances.

The poverty of languages, and the necessity for metaphors which resulted from this poverty, led to the employment of allegories and fables to explain physical phenomena. They are the first steps of philosophy, as can still be seen in India.

The fables of all peoples resemble one another, because the effects to be explained, and the patterns of the causes which have been invented in order to explain them, resemble one another. There are some differences, because although there is only one truth, and although imagination takes only one course which is very much the same everywhere, the individual steps do not all correspond with one another. Moreover, the mythological beings who were supposed to exist were brought into histories of the facts, which thus came to vary greatly. The sex of the gods, often depending as it did on the gender of a word in a language, was also bound to bring about variations in the fables of different peoples. Very many circumstances in these fables were peculiar to them, without destroying their general interrelationship. The intermingling of nations, and trade between them, gave birth to new fables through ambiguities of expression; and poorly understood words increased the number of the old fables.

Regarding imaginary beings as real, men sometimes multiplied the number of gods by including those which different nations had invented to explain the same effects, and at other times they took those which had similar attributes to be the same. Thence the confusion in the history of these gods. Thence too the multiplicity of their actions, above all when two peoples with the same mythologies were mixed together, as in the case of the Indians. Natural philosophy changed, but people did not stop believing in fables, because of their twofold love of antiquity and the marvelous, and also because the fables were transmitted from century to century by education.

The first histories were also fables, invented in the same way to make up for ignorance of the origin of empires, arts, and customs; it is very easy indeed to recognize their falsity. Everything which men invent is linked only to what seems to be the truth, that is, to the opinions of the century in which the fact concerned is invented. But what men recount is linked to the truth itself, and can never be contradicted by subsequent observations. Moreover, before the invention of writing, men had no records other than songs and a few stones beside which the songs were repeated. It is clear that men were more concerned to seek amusement and glory in these songs than they were to avoid exaggeration in them. Even Herodotus was still a poet. It was only after him that it was felt necessary that history should tell the truth.

Herodotus wrote four centuries after Homer, and yet what does Herodotus amount to? What then did those four centuries amount to? What were the times of Homer like? Why had poetry risen so high while history remained so low? Herodotus is vastly inferior in his field to Homer in his; and one of the great defects of Herodotus is that he is too like Homer, seeking all the time to decorate his account with the ornaments of fable. To know that men are greedy for the marvelous, to have enough genius to use it with vigor and grace, and to give general pleasure—that was Homer. More reflection was necessary, and a slower rate of progress, before it was understood that there were occasions when these marvels could not give as much pleasure as the unvarnished truth; that men's curiosity could find in the certainty of things a pleasure and a tranquility which more than compensated for the number, variety, and singularity of the adventures; and finally that a means of giving pleasure which had been tried a thousand times could not be assured of success for ever.

This reflection and this progress were reserved for times after Homer's, and more than four centuries after. When Herodotus wrote, these times had not yet arrived. Often a thing which demands less genius than another requires more progress among mankind as a whole.

The arts of design, sculpture, and painting have many connections with poetry in the feelings which the artist experiences, and in those which he strives to communicate. They had a natural origin in the desire to preserve historical or mythological records; and genius in this sphere was heightened by that patriotic or religious zeal which sought to express with feeling, depth, and force the ideas and memories which these records were bound to recall.

All these arts depend a great deal on the different states of mankind—whether they are hunters, shepherds, or husbandmen. The latter, being the only ones who could have a large population, and needing as they did a greater amount of positive knowledge in order to direct their labor, would necessarily make much greater progress.

Men's knowledge, all of which is contained within actual sensation, is of different kinds. One kind consists in pure combinations of ideas, such as abstract mathematics. Another is concerned with external objects, but takes in, so to speak, only their surface and the effects they have on us: such are poetry and the arts of taste. Another, finally, has for its object the very existence of things. It goes back from effects to causes, from the senses to the body, from the present to the past, from visible bodies to invisible ones, from the world to the Divinity. The belief in the existence of bodies, and that of past objects which are recalled by the memory, came before reasoning. No one ever had any doubts about the immediate cause of our sensations: the causes of the movements of bodies constituted physics; and at first the action of bodies upon one another was often confused with that of the Divinity.

Aristotle, in a work which, although scoffed at today, is none the less one of the finest endeavors of the human spirit, was able to carry analysis to its perfection by examining the manner in which our minds pass from a known truth to an unknown one; he was able to derive from this the rules of the art of reasoning, and by demonstrating the effects of a certain combination of ideas he showed how we could make certain that one proposition was legitimately deduced from another. It must be admitted that in the rest of his philosophy he was unable to make any analysis as perfect as this, because the enumeration of the ideas was not nearly as easy. But however useful one takes his work to be so far as consequences are concerned, it could not serve to ascertain causes. Although Aristotle had put forward the notion that all ideas came from the senses, it was a very long time before anyone began looking for causes other than the so-called abstract ideas and going back to their origin. *Bacon* was the first to feel the necessity for submitting all these notions to examination again. It was a great deal at that time to encourage scholars to do this. We must forgive him for having himself proceeded only in a timid fashion. He was like a man who walks trembling along a road filled with ruins, doubting and feeling his way. After him, *Galileo* and *Kepler*, as a result of their observations, laid the true foundations of philosophy. But it was Descartes who, bolder than they, meditated and made a revolution. The system of occasional causes, the idea of reducing everything to matter and movement, constituted the essence of this lively philosopher, and presuppose an analysis of ideas of which the Ancients had provided no example at all.

In shaking off the yoke of their authority, he still did not challenge sufficiently the knowledge which he had first received from them. It is astonishing that a man who ventured to question everything he had learned did not seek to follow the progress of his new knowledge from his first sensations. One might say that he was frightened by the solitude in which he had put himself, and that he was unable to endure it. All at once he throws himself back into the very ideas of which he had been able to divest himself. He conjures up, as did the Ancients, pure abstractions; he regards his ideas as realities. He invents for them causes which are proportionate to their scope. He is seduced by these ancient preconceptions even while he is combating them. If I were not held back by the respect and gratitude due to such a great man, I would compare him to Samson, who, in pulling down the temple of Dagon, was crushed beneath the ruins.

The members of his sect attributed our errors to illusions of the senses, and the exaggerated zeal with which they attacked the senses had a good effect. In trying to work out the way in which our senses deceive us, men learned to analyze the way in which they give us an account of external objects. *Locke* succeeded in carrying this analysis much further, and *Berkeley* and *Condillac* followed him. They are all the children of Descartes.

When *Descartes* looked at nature, it was as if he cast a piercing glance at it, encompassed it completely, and took as it were a bird's-eye view of it.

Newton examined it in more detail. He described the country which the other had discovered.

Some people have made it their business to sacrifice the reputation of Descartes to that of Newton. They have imitated those Romans who, when one emperor succeeded another, simply knocked off the head of the first and substituted for it that of the second. But in the Temple of Glory there is room for all great geniuses. A statue can be erected for everyone who is worthy of it.

In between these two mighty geniuses, there happened what always happens in every field. A great man opens up new paths for the human mind. For a certain period all men are still only his pupils. Little by little, however, they level the paths which he has mapped out; they unite all the parts of his discoveries; they bring together and catalogue their valuable and authoritative features, until a new great man rises up, who soars as high above the point to which his predecessor had led the human race as that predecessor did above the point from which he set out.

Newton, without the experiments of *Richer*, would perhaps not have dreamed that his principles would lead him to give the world the shape of a spheroid. The greatest genius is never tempted to go deeply into theory unless he is stimulated by the facts. It is rare for men to give themselves up to reasoning. There are people who have the need to feel, but a more pressing need is required before they venture to make a leap forward.

It is said that M. *Frenicle* suspected that gravity, which made bodies fall to the ground, also kept the planets in their orbits. But from such a vague and uncertain idea to that piercing perspective, that vision of genius of *Newton*, which penetrated the immensity of the combinations and relationships of all the heavenly bodies, to that unyielding boldness which feared neither the profundity of calculation nor the beauty and difficulty of the problems, and which rose so far as to put into its balance the sun, the stars, and all the forces of nature—that is the distance from Frenicle to Newton.

Descartes discovered the art of putting curves into equations. *Huigens*, and above all Newton, suddenly carried the torch of reason into the abyss of the infinite.

Leibnitz, mighty genius and conciliator, wanted his works to become a kind of centre where all human knowledge would be united. He wanted to gather together into one bundle all sciences and all opinions. He wanted to resuscitate the systems of all the ancient philosophers, like a man trying to build a proper palace from the ruins of all the buildings of ancient Rome. He wanted to make of his Theodicy what Peter made of St. Petersburg.

We owe to these great men the pattern and the laws of analysis, the lack of which had for such a long time retarded the progress of metaphysics, and even that of physics.

It could be said that there is one general respect in which these two sciences both differ from those which are called mathematical. All sciences, no doubt, have their origin in the senses. But mathematics has this advantage, that it is an application of the senses which is not susceptible to error.

The necessity of measuring fields, aided by the property which space has of being itself measured in relation to the room it occupies, gave rise to the first elements of mathematics. Ideas of numbers are neither less simple, nor less familiar; it was from these few simple ideas, which are easily combined together, that the mathematical sciences were formed. Everything which is capable of being considered as a quantity may be their subject. They are only the consequences of abstract definitions which include such a small number of ideas that it is easy to encompass all of them. A chain of truths, all depending upon one another, is formed: a chain in which men have only to recognize all the steps they have taken in order to accumulate truth upon truth. These truths become more and more fruitful; the more we advance in speculation, the more we discover of those general formulae of calculation from which we can descend to particular truths by particularizing the hypotheses. The truths, when they are combined, are increased in number and combined again; and from this springs a new increase, because each becomes the source of a host of truths which are no less fruitful than the first.

To the extent that the number of these known truths increased, to the extent that the properties of a greater number of shapes were investigated, their common properties were expressed in formulae and general principles which contained everything that was known. Thus even in mathematics men began by investigating a few familiar figures, a small number of properties of lines; the general principles were the work of time.

Thus, since it was believed that the best order was that in which a multiplicity of consequences was derived from one principle alone, men were obliged, in order to incorporate it in mathematical works, to recast from century to century the whole method of instruction. It was not realized that this allegedly natural order was in fact arbitrary; that in geometry, where the general relationships of figures are set out, these relationships are reciprocal; that one may equally infer the principle from the consequence, or the consequence from the principle; the equation of the ellipse can be deduced from its construction, as its construction can be deduced from its equation.

Thus, if any method is to be preferred, it is that of tracing the steps of the human mind in its discoveries, of bringing home the general axioms which spring from all the particular truths, and at the same time making known the manner in which all the preceding truths are bound up in them. Thus the picture of the progress of mathematics is like the Olympus of the poets, which was pointed toward the earth, and which, to the extent that it moved away from the earth, expanded until it touched the sky. Thus geometry has expanded up to the infinite. Particular truths lead to more and more general formulae; and even in mathematics it is from the particular to the general that one must advance.

But when the general principles are found, what rapid progress they bring about in these sciences! Algebra, the reduction of curves to equations, the analysis of the infinite! Here there is a sequence of hypothetical truths, certain for that very reason, and at the same time verified by nature, because the first hypotheses were by no means arbitrary, but based on the ideas of extent which our senses present to us, and which they present to us only because things possessing extent really exist in nature.

Mathematics sets out from a small number of ideas, and combines their relationships *ad infinitum*. It is quite the contrary in the physical sciences, where it is a question not of a sequence of ideas and relationships, but of facts and ideas which concern an object actually existing either in the past or the present (the future can only be mathematical), and the truth of which consists in the conformity of our opinions with this object.

Under the heading of physical sciences I include logic, which is the body of knowledge concerning the operations of our minds and the generation of our ideas; metaphysics, which deals with the nature and origin of things which exist; and finally physics properly so-called, which examines the mutual action of bodies upon one another, and the causes and interconnections of sensible phenomena. One could also add history, the certainty of which can never be as great, because the concatenation of events can never be as close, and because events which took place a long time ago can only with difficulty be submitted to a new examination. Nature being always consistent with itself, we may, by means of experiments, bring before our eyes once again the same phenomena, or produce new phenomena; but if the first witnesses of an event are not very trustworthy, the event must always remain surrounded by uncertainty, and its precise effects can never be known to us.

I am not speaking here of sciences like morals and politics which depend on self-love regulated by justice, which is itself only a very enlightened form of self-love. What I have said in a general way about the differences between sciences of combination and sciences of observation may be applied to them. In the latter, man cannot confine his attention to a small number of principles. He is assailed simultaneously by a whole mass of ideas, and is forced to gather them together in large numbers, because all things which exist are bound up with one another by their mutual interaction; and he is obliged at the same time to analyze these ideas carefully until he arrives at their most simple elements.

Logic is based on the analysis of language and the reduction of the images of objects to the simple sensations of which they are composed. Metaphysics was bound to feel the effects of the small amount of progress made in this analysis. Before we had analyzed our sensations and understood their causes, the real uniformity of material substances was not apparent to us. A body which is blue and a body which is red are bound to appear different, and we would scarcely have been able to contemplate the conformity which they possess if the senses had not revealed bodies considered in themselves as existing outside ourselves, capable of assuming various colors and manifesting themselves with different sensible qualities. Thence the distinction between *substance* and *mode*; but this did not at first prevent men from conceiving the *modes* as so many things existing outside ourselves, even though they could not in fact exist without a subject. Thence the errors of the majority of philosophers.

There is nothing so confused among the Ancients as all these ideas of substance, essence, and matter, which were due to the absence of proper knowledge about the way in which they originated from the first sensible ideas. They were nevertheless employed in all their ambiguity. In order to explain them, how much progress had to be made in physics itself, whose errors were holding back development!—for metaphysics and physics have a mutual need of one another. How much time was necessary to discover that all sensible phenomena could be explained by shape and movement! Descartes was the first to see this truth clearly. Before him, for want of this degree of analysis, physics remained more or less confounded with metaphysics.

The errors of metaphysics relate to the manner in which we receive, through our sensations, the idea of things existing outside ourselves. It is only by relating colored points that we create for ourselves the idea of visible extent; it is by the gathering together of a number of sensations, which produce in us the resistance of external bodies to our own, that we create for ourselves the idea of tangible extent. It is only by reasoning that we assure ourselves of the existence of the bodies which constitute the bond and common cause of the sensations associated with them; but instinct, or, if you like, the combining together of ideas derived from experience, came before reasoning, and men confused the bodies themselves with their sensible qualities. This idea was bound to lead to that obscurity in the whole of metaphysics of which I am speaking, and which is easy to understand if we consider that the judgment we pass on the existence of external objects is only the result of their relations with us, of their effects on us, of our fears, of our desires, and of the use which we make of them. Our senses being given to us only for the preservation of our lives and our welfare, sensations are simply the true signs of our ideas about these external things, which are sufficient to make us seek or avoid them without understanding their nature. Our judgments are simply the abbreviated expression of all the movements which these bodies excite in us, an expression which guarantees for us the reality of these bodies by the reality of their effect itself. Thus our judgment on external objects does not in any way presuppose the analysis of such ideas; we judge in bulk.

On the other hand it must be observed that language, in relation to metaphysics, resembles the application which is made of geometry to physics. But apart from the fact that in language, the use of which is habitual and easy, we do not always bother not to allow ourselves any contradiction, we would be able to succeed in this only by first defining all our ideas, as a result of which we would tire ourselves out in the formulation of a series of truths which had little applicability to the usage of society, which is after all the chief aim of language.

Complete meticulousness would lead to there being no contradictions in terms, and to the formulation of a chain of hypothetical truths; but that is not enough in sciences which have to be compared with real objects. Often the problems of physics (because all the elements which concur in producing the effect have not been clearly seen) lead to a result which is absolutely contrary to experience, even though there are no mathematical errors involved. Words recall rather than express ideas. Given correct logic, we can deduce consequences very effectively; but who will vouch for the causes? And if they happen to be false, how far would the very truth of the consequences become removed from reality, if men, driven by their needs to their senses and to society, were not often forced to be inconsistent? Two contradictory ideas do not look like the object; but why do they not look like it? Usually it is because they are abstract ideas whose objects have no existence at all.

In general, the principles of the sciences in which we do not wish to stray from reality can be nothing other than facts. In metaphysics, facts can be known only through the analysis of our sensations, which in relation to external causes are only the effects which indicate them. In physics, they can be known only through a profound examination of all the circumstances, which, when it is found to be impossible, comes to constitute the necessary limit of our researches. He who is familiar with only one of the coasts of a country is uncertain whether it is an island or the mainland. That is the position we are in so far as all the objects of our ideas are concerned when we begin to reflect, and it is still the position so far as a great number of them are concerned after a great deal of reflection.

This twofold confusion of language and ideas has undoubtedly had a considerable influence on physics. Men, when they began to reason about the phenomena which confronted them, at first sought for the cause itself before they had properly understood the phenomena; and since the true causes could be discovered only in the course of time, they invented false ones. Whenever it is a question of finding the cause of an effect, it is only by way of hypothesis that we can succeed, when the effect is all that is known.

We go back, as best we can, from the effect to the cause, in our endeavors to decide what is outside ourselves. Now in order to divine the cause of an effect when our ideas do not present it to us, it is necessary to invent one: we must verify a number of hypotheses and try them out. But how can we verify them? By working out the consequences of each hypothesis and comparing them with the facts. If all the facts which are predicted on the basis of the hypothesis are found in nature precisely as the hypothesis would lead us to expect, this conformity, which cannot be the effect of chance, becomes its verification, in the same way that one identifies the seal which has made an impression when one sees that all the characteristics of the latter are included in those of the seal.

Such was the course of the progress of physics. Facts which were poorly understood, poorly analyzed, and few in number were bound to lead to the invention of totally false hypotheses; the necessity of making a host of suppositions, before finding the true one, was bound to produce many. Further, the difficulty of deducing the consequences of these hypotheses and comparing them with the facts was in the beginning very great. It was only by the application of mathematics to physics that men were able from those hypotheses, which are only combinations of what necessarily happens when certain bodies are moved according to certain laws, to infer the effects which necessarily followed from them; and thereafter research was bound to increase with time. The art of making experiments, too, was perfected only in the course of time; fortunate accidents, which nevertheless happen only to those who often have these objects before their eyes and who understand them; and, much more commonly, a multiplicity of refined theories and little systems relating to details, often aided once again by mathematics—apprised men of the facts, or indicated to them the experiments which ought to be carried out together with the way to make them successful. Thus we see how the progress of mathematics supported that of physics, how everything is bound up together, and at the same time how the need to examine all the hypotheses necessitated a host of mathematical investigations which, by multiplying truths, increased the generality of the principles, thereby leading to the development of a considerable facility in calculation and the perfection of this art.

From all this it may be concluded that men were bound to pass through a thousand errors before arriving at the truth. Hence that host of systems, each one less sound than the other, which nevertheless represent real progress, real gropings toward the truth; systems, moreover, which give rise to research and are for this reason useful in their effects. Hypotheses are not harmful: all those which are false destroy themselves. The so-called systematic classifications which are really only arbitrary dictionaries would seem on the whole to check the advance of natural history, by treating it as if it were complete, whereas it can never in fact be so; and nevertheless these systems themselves represent progress. Pliny is no more scholarly a naturalist than Linnaeus; on the contrary, he falls far short of him. But Pliny was familiar with fewer objects, and fewer relations between these objects. Linnaeus is more aware of the extent to which his account is overburdened with detailed lists of objects, and of the fact that in order to identify them one must understand their relationships. He often looks for arbitrary ones—well, they will give way to the knowledge of the imperceptible gradations which unite the species. The first step is to find a system; the second is to become disgusted with it.

Let us go back to our physical hypotheses, whose diversity, as we see, is necessary, and whose uncertainty does not prevent us from being able in the end to find the true ones, at any rate when the details of the facts can be sufficiently ascertained. But besides the difficulty of analyzing the facts and developing the hypotheses, there is in the manner in which they have been formed another source of error which is still more considerable. This is the only too tempting taste for analogy; ignorance sees resemblances everywhere, and unfortunately it is ignorance which passes judgment.

Before men were conversant with the mutual interconnection of physical effects, nothing was more natural than to suppose that these were produced by intelligent beings, invisible and resembling ourselves; for what else would they have resembled? Everything that happened, without men having a hand in it, had its god, in respect of whom fear or expectation soon led to the establishment of a cult; and this cult was once again devised on the model of the respect which people might have for powerful men. For the gods were only more powerful men, more or less perfect according to whether they were the product of a century which was more or less enlightened about the true perfection of humanity.

When the philosophers had recognized the absurdity of these fables, without yet having acquired any real understanding of natural history, the idea struck them to explain the causes of phenomena by way of abstract expressions like *essences* and *faculties*: expressions which in fact explained nothing, and about which men reasoned as if they were *beings*, new gods substituted for the old ones. Following these analogies, *faculties* were proliferated in order to provide a cause for each effect.

It was only much later, through observation of the mechanical action which bodies have upon one another, that men derived from this mechanics other hypotheses which mathematics was able to develop and experiment to verify. That is why physics did not cease degenerating into bad metaphysics until a long period of progress in the arts and in chemistry had multiplied the combinations of bodies, and until, with the development of closer communications between societies, geographical knowledge had become more extensive, the facts had become more certain, and the practice of the arts had itself been brought to the attention of the philosophers. Printing, literary and scientific journals, and the transactions of Academies increased the degree of certainty until today it is only the details which remain in doubt.

There is another kind of progress of the human mind, less recognized and acknowledged, but nevertheless real—that which is relative to the arts of taste, to painting, poetry, and music. Whatever the admirers of antiquity say about this, we have become more knowledgeable about these arts, without having surpassed or even attained in the arts of design that sublime beauty of which Greece (over a very short period) provided the models.

Since it is nevertheless very difficult to apprehend true taste without being arbitrary, and since its nature can be easily dulled by all kinds of habits, it has been subject to a large number of revolutions. Painting depends upon imitation; architecture was at first subject only to the method of building which convenience dictated. The techniques of these two arts were perfected, but eccentric fashions brought about variations in taste. That delicacy of feeling upon which the perfection of taste depends is not associated with either barbarism or laxity. It depends upon an elegance of manners, upon a temperate luxury which does not hinder the spread of enlightenment, but which is sufficient to ensure a market for pleasing objects and the employment of second-rate artists, among whom the great artists who shine out from them are formed. No art can continue to exist unless it succeeds in employing a number of men sufficient to carry it on as a simple craft.[1] Extravagant luxury, where vanity causes ornaments to be accumulated because it regards them less as

---

[1] The English for many years have spared nothing to acquire beautiful pictures; and their nation has still not been able to produce a single great painter.

The Italians, the French, and the Flemish, and a very small number of Germans and Spaniards, have been the only ones to be successful in this art. The reason for this is that the English pay only for good pictures. By banning images from the churches, they deprived themselves of the means of supporting bad painters, and even second-rate ones. And in all crafts where bad workers cannot gain a livelihood, and second-rate workers are not comfortably off, great men are not created. Our painters of Notre-Dame bridge, who supply all the little village churches with pictures, constitute an indispensable nursery for the rearing of a few great painters. When starting in an art one is hardly assured of success in it. Thus if one had to be certain of rising to the highest rank in a craft in order to get one's bread, fathers would never set their children to it.

That is why among the English there is only a very small number of painters. Nearly all the Dutch painters have painted only landscapes, seascapes, or rustic scenes; and I do not believe that one can name a single painter of history who is at all well-known who was not a Catholic. (Note by Turgot.)

ornaments than as symbols of affluence, smothers taste. Men no longer seek for the pleasure which things afford to the senses and the mind; they no longer search their own hearts. They no longer listen to anything but fashion. The sure way to judge badly in any sphere is not to judge with one's eyes. When each individual judges, the multitude judges well, because its judgment is that of a large number of people; but when no one does anything but listen, the multitude judges badly. Another cause of bad taste was often the progress of technique in the arts. Men are always liable to mistake the difficult for the beautiful. Arts, virtues—everything is infected by this error; hence the false virtues of many philosophers.

Only after a very long time did it become known that virtue among men, as well as beauty in the arts, depended on certain relationships between objects and our organs. The intellect naturally delights in apprehending these relationships, and the arts are perfected when they have reached this point. Artistic techniques, when they are perfected, appear as merits in the worker who thinks of demonstrating his dexterity, and who does not think at all about the manner in which objects ought to please, which is difficult to elucidate when one does not apprehend it with a kind of instinct. Hence Gothic architecture, which is abandoned only when antiquity is taken as a model, that is, the period when men had felt this inspiration.

Greece, too, had lost good taste, which shows that it is not barbarism alone that smothers it; but it was less conscious that it had lost it, because it had not had to endure that period of palpable barbarism which warned Europe to look for models in happier times.

With regard to painting and sculpture, since these two arts are very difficult, they were bound to fall into a decline as soon as the protection of enlightened princes came to be lacking. Not even sales in the churches, nor individual luxury, could keep them going, for individuals were impoverished: and because of the paucity of trade in all parts of Europe there was little choice. The taste which is formed through the repeated comparison of beautiful things is lost when trade between nations does not put them before one's eyes. The dauber on the corner is enough for those who enjoy only an unrefined luxury. Moreover, painting is an art which is undertaken for money and which requires genius, and the forms of government in Europe, degrading as they did everyone who was not a gentleman, reduced it to pure technique. As for Greece, it was too broken and too ravaged, both by the instability of its monarchy and by the invasions of the Saracens and the Bulgarians, to be able to cultivate the agreeable arts with success. However, it contributed to the revival of Rome in the fourteenth century through the enthusiasm which it inspired for antiquity.

There were parts of the arts of taste which could be perfected with time, for example perspective, which depends on optics. But local color, the imitation of nature, and the expression of the passions itself are of all times. Thus those great men who at all times have pushed art forward to a certain point, acquire, in relation to the following centuries, a certain equality, and as a result they are in a way more fortunate than philosophers, who necessarily became out of date and useless through the progress of their successors.

Great men in the fields of eloquence and poetry have the same immortality, and in a way a still more lasting one, because their works are perpetuated and multiplied by means of copies. Their progress depends on languages, on circumstances, on manners, and on the chance which causes several great geniuses to arise in a nation.

One point about eloquence should be noted—that when we speak of its progress and its decline, we are thinking only of studied eloquence, of set speeches; for at all times and among all peoples, the passions and public affairs have produced men who were truly eloquent.

The histories are full of examples of powerful and persuasive eloquence in the depths of barbarism. Cardinal de Retz was more eloquent in Parliament than in the pulpit. See also Segesta, Arminius, and Vibulinus in Tacitus.

I am not at all surprised at the fall of eloquence in Greece and Rome. After the division of Alexander's empire, the kingdoms which were established on its ruins eclipsed all the small republics in which eloquence had shone with such brilliance. Alexandria and

Antioch became the centers of commerce and the arts. Athens was no longer anything but a town in Greece without any authority, where young men were still sent to study, but where talent did not lead to a large fortune. Ambitious people were found at the Court of Kings, where what was necessary was not eloquence but intrigue. What took place in the public square in Athens no longer gave an impetus to the whole of Greece.

When one reads the speeches of Demosthenes, one finds that there were scarcely any which he was able to deliver in that debased and degenerate Athens. Clever teachers, whatever talents and whatever taste one may suppose them to have possessed, were thus unable to preserve true eloquence there.

They brought it about that young people, as still happens in our colleges, were presented with *amplifications* on all kinds of subjects. Nothing is more liable to distort the mind and even to destroy sincerity of character; an honest heart is not warmed by cold. Eloquence is a serious art, which persons of real worth will never play at. A man of genius will never make a parade of eloquence and waste his time in inveighing against Tarquin or Sylla, or in trying to persuade Alexander to live in peace. Thus we see that after the fall of the republics there were declaimers but no longer orators. In Rome, where the same causes had led to the same effects, several emperors, who were in love with eloquence and who condescended to engage in the composition of a number of discourses, failed to produce any Ciceros because they failed to reproduce the circumstances which had given birth to them. Men are never eloquent when they have nothing to say. They must have someone who is to be moved or convinced.

Our bar does not lend itself, or seldom lends itself, to bursts of eloquence. Cicero, accusing or defending a citizen before a popular assembly or a Roman senate invested with legislative power, could give himself up to his genius. But when it is a question of examining in a tribunal whether, according to the law, a certain inheritance should belong to Peter or to James, all that is required is a quite simple didactic tone. All that is required is to establish the truth; and any discourse which does nothing but establish the truth is not capable of giving pleasure when one has no personal concern with the subject.

As soon as political matters no longer came within the province of orators, the ancients did not know where to find a place for eloquence. They did not have the resource which we find in a great number of philosophical and moral problems which with us have given birth to a kind of eloquence which we call academic, and which, in order to achieve the success of which it is capable, still requires that those who engage in it should never indulge in *amplifications*.

The pulpit, which has carried eloquence to the highest point, has been known only to the moderns. The grandeur of God, the majestic obscurity of the mysteries, the pomp of religion, and the powerful interest of the life to come, have opened up a huge field for the sublime and moving genius of the Bossuets and the Saurins. The grandeur of the subject has even in a way given shape to another kind of florid eloquence employed by Fléchier and Massillon, who are certainly much more eloquent than Lysias and Isocrates, without attaining to the great bursts of eloquence of Bossuet.

It is perhaps surprising that the ancient fathers did not in the same way seize this opportunity to bring about a revival of eloquence among the Greeks and the Romans. It is true that we find in some of them, and above all in the Greeks, some admirable traits. *Salvianus*, speaking to the inhabitants of Treves who after their city's revolution were demanding gladiatorial games, is not far below the level of Demosthenes who similarly reproached the Athenians for their love of entertainments. But in general these traits of the fathers were rooted out by the power of their subject. Their discourses, which they put in the form of homilies, always had something didactic about them which was more fitted to instruct than to move. Often a love of simplicity led them to pay no heed to nobility of imagery and the other ornaments of discourse. It would appear that *St. Augustine* often sought to be eloquent. Sometimes he succeeded in this: but his beauties of style were swamped beneath a deluge of witticisms and frivolous conceits into which he was drawn by the bad taste of his century, and which he had picked up in his profession as a teacher of rhetoric.

What is called bombast is, so to speak, nothing but a counterfeit of the sublime. True eloquence employs the boldest and most lively figures; but these must be produced as the result of real enthusiasm. One never moves without being moved; and the language of enthusiasm has this in common with that of all the passions, that it is ridiculous when it is only imitated, because it is always only imperfectly imitated.

An arrow which is correctly shot ascends to the target and sticks to it; if it is aimed higher it falls to the ground—an illustration of a natural figure and an extravagant one.

The intermingling of languages puts them into a state of continuous movement until their analogy is determined; and during the very time when they are changing they are softened, until great writers become the models to judge of their purity. Before this coming together, languages are never in a settled state. It is obvious that when two languages whose constructions are different come to intermingle, time will be necessary before a uniform whole results. Further, bookmen wish to retain the old language, and speak it badly because they speak it only from books; the people without books speak an unrefined language, devoid of rules and harmony; there is no more poetry in either the one language or the other; or, if a few verses are made, since it is unrefined men who make them, the verses are barbarous. It should be noted that among peoples who through time have advanced in the arts and made a certain amount of progress in ideas, the common people are more ignorant than the leading citizens even of a still-barbarous nation. Further, the mechanical arts and the subjection of the people cause minds to deteriorate. Men's first ideas have a certain analogy with the imagination and the senses, which abstract ideas, together with the progress of philosophy, cause them to lose. No doubt these new ideas are capable of being reconciled with the imagination, but new progress is required to bring this about.

Good poets do not emerge, and taste and elegance do not begin to be formed, until languages have acquired a certain richness, and above all until their analogy becomes stable. Nearly all languages are a mixture of several languages. In so far as they are intermingled, the result will consist partly of one and partly of the other. During this time of fermentation, conjugations, declensions, and the ways in which words are formed have nothing settled about them. Constructions are encumbered, and thought is obscured as a result of this encumbrance. Further, the half-formed technical languages frequently change. Poetic terms cease to be in use shortly after their invention, so that poetic language cannot grow richer. Once the language has been formed, there begin to be poets who use it. But it becomes stabilized only when it has been used in the writings of a number of great geniuses, because only then is there a point of comparison from which to judge of its purity. It is perhaps a misfortune for languages to be stabilized too soon, for so long as they are changing, they are all the time being softened and perfected.

The only cause of change in languages which are not being mixed at all with others is the establishment of metaphors, which become familiar and allow their metaphorical sense to be forgotten when they are used frequently and over a long period by writers. We know that the majority of the words which express objects which do not come directly within the purview of our senses are really metaphors derived from sensible things: for example, *penser*, *délibérer*, *contrition*, etc. Yet these words, when we hear them spoken today, no longer constitute metaphors. They appear to us only as the direct signs of some of our abstract ideas. Several of them have lost all the connections which they originally had with objects of the senses.

It is certain that those who heard a similar expression from the lips of its inventor were necessarily aware of the metaphor which it involved. Their minds, accustomed as they were to link expressions to ideas of sensible objects, must have needed to make a certain effort in order to give it a new meaning. But through its being repeated in the new sense which had been given to it, this sense became as it were appropriate to it; in order to understand it in its new meaning there was no longer any need to recall its old one. The use of the memory became all that was necessary in order to understand it; weak imaginations, which always constitute the majority, saw in it only the sign of a purely abstract idea, and passed it on to their successors on that footing.

I admit that this could lead us to fear that all those beautiful expressions which we admire in our poets may thus come to lose their charm, and that the flowers gathered by men of genius, as a result of passing through so many common hands, may one day wither. Then those who were born with the same talents would be obliged, in order to present their ideas with the same vigor, to invent new turns of phrase and new expressions, which would soon be subject to the same process of decline; and in the course of these revolutions the language of Corneille and that of Racine would become out of date, and people would no longer appreciate the charm of their poetry.

In spite of this reasoning, I think that the example of the Greek language ought to reassure us. From Homer to the fall of the Empire of Constantinople, during more than two thousand years, it did not appreciably change. Men have always been alive to the beauties of Homer and Demosthenes: the few Latin words which crept into the Greek language were far from altering it fundamentally. The critics, it is true, can tell roughly the century in which the works were written. But this is more or less solely by referring to this small number of foreign words, and still more often to the nature of the things concerned or the allusions made by the authors to different events.

I would say the same thing about Latin, in spite of the very common presumption that it was altered by the intermingling of the language of the Romans with those of the conquered nations. This is in fact so far from being true, that in the Latin authors who wrote while the Empire was in existence one can hardly find more than a few turns of phrase and a few words borrowed from barbarous languages; moreover, nearly all these words are terms relating to the arts, or names of dignities or new arms which never constitute the basic elements of a language. It all too often happens that the genius of a language is confused with the taste of those who speak it.

Claudian no doubt had very different tastes from *Virgil*, but their language was the same.

We are told that after the century of Leo X the *Cavalier Marin* substituted a puerile affectedness for the elegance of the Italian language. It is true that this is the character of his works, but it is quite false to say that he made it peculiar to his language; and I am sure that the Metastasios and Maffios, and so very many others who brought back good taste and the love of simplicity to Italy, found no obstacle in the genius of their language.

In general, a difference in style between authors who are separated from one another by several centuries no more proves that there is a difference in their languages than does the difference which is found between authors of the same period, and which is often just as great. It is not at all the difference in words and turns of phrase, but that in genius, which makes the writers of the dark ages so inferior.

The reasoning which gives rise to these reflections is valid only in the passing of the words of one language into another, and in the different revolutions undergone by a language which is a long way from being stabilized. It is then that the expressions which pass from mouth to mouth have for those who receive them only the sense given to them by those who transmit them, without their original and proper sense being preserved. But it is not the same when a language is stabilized. The books which have stabilized it always remain in existence, and, since the proper sense of the word is not lost, the metaphor is never deprived of its true meaning. Then it is not simply the ideas of the people of one generation which are passed to the following generation; the works of good authors are a storehouse in which they are preserved for ever, and to which all generations go in order to borrow them.

Languages may be stabilized so far as their analogy is concerned, and have great writers, a long time before they are enriched; for it is only the intermingling of languages which prevents them from being stabilized, and good writers resist this effect of the intermingling of languages, as happened in Greece in relation to Latin, and in relation to the oriental languages. The period of the stabilization of languages at a point more or less near to their perfection has a great influence on the genius of nations in relation to poetry and eloquence. All the peoples whose languages are poor, the ancient Germans, the Iroquois, and the Hebrews (proof that this is not the result of climate) express themselves in metaphors. In the absence of a fixed sign for an idea, people made use of the name of the idea which was nearest akin to it, in order to make what they wanted to say understandable. The imagination struggled to find resemblances between objects, guided by the clue of a more or less exact analogy. One finds in the most civilized languages traces of these unrefined metaphors which necessity, more ingenious than fastidious, introduced into them. When the mind becomes familiar with the new idea, the word loses its metaphorical sense. I have no doubt that we could find many metaphors in the oriental languages of which those who speak them are quite unaware, and that this would be reciprocal. It must be acknowledged that the ancient languages admit metaphors which are bolder, that is, in which the analogy is less perfect, at first through necessity and later through habit. Moreover, metaphors sown in a smaller field strike us more. We have as lively an imagination as the orientals; or at any rate it would not be disputed that the Greeks and the Romans had as lively a one as the ancient peoples of the north; but since the minds of the Greeks and the Romans, and our own, are filled with a host of abstract ideas, the languages of the Greeks and the Romans, and our own, are less burdened with figures.

It follows that these languages are also more fitted to express with greater exactitude a much greater number of truths. If a language which is stabilized too soon may retard the progress of the people which speaks it, a nation which attains stability too quickly may for a similar reason find that the progress of its sciences is arrested. The Chinese were stabilized too soon. They became like those trees whose trunk has been lopped and whose branches grow close to the ground; they never escape from mediocrity. There was so much respect among them for their barely sketched-out sciences, and they retained so much for the ancestors who had caused these first steps to be taken, that it was believed that nothing remained to be added, and that it was no longer a question of anything but preventing this wonderful knowledge from being lost. But to limit oneself to preserving the sciences in their existing state is equivalent to deciding to perpetuate all the errors they contain.

The manifold investigations of men of letters which the Chinese administration is pleased to undertake necessarily restrict their minds to the matters which are their object. No longer is anything learned; no longer is anything invented. To venture in this way to mark out the roads which genius must follow, it would have been necessary to know its course; and this is something which one can never ascertain exactly, since one knows only what has been discovered, and not what remains to be discovered. The protection given to the sciences in the kingdoms of the Orient is what has caused their ruin: by burdening them with rites and transforming them into dogmas, it has restricted their progress and even caused them to move backwards. Greece so greatly surpassed the Orientals in the sciences which it obtained from them only because it was not subject to a single despotic authority. If it had been constituted, like Egypt, as a single state body, a man like Lycurgus, in order to protect the sciences, would have claimed to regulate research by administrative means. The sectarian spirit, which was quite natural for the first philosophers, would have become the spirit of the nation. If the legislator had been a disciple of Pythagoras, the sciences of Greece would have been confined for ever to the knowledge of the dogmas of that philosopher, which would have been erected into articles of faith. He would have been what the celebrated Confucius was in China. Fortunately the situation in which Greece found itself, divided up as it was into an infinity of small republics, allowed genius all the freedom and all the competition of which it has need in its endeavors. The perspectives of men are always very narrow in comparison with those of nature. It is much better to be guided by the latter than by imperfect laws. If the sciences have made such great progress in Italy, and consequently in the rest of Europe, they undoubtedly owe this to the situation in which Italy found itself in the fourteenth century, which was rather similar to that of ancient Greece.

The sciences were always regarded as mysterious among the Asiatics; and wherever sciences are *mysteries* it is rare for them not to degenerate into superstitions. Genius is never attached exclusively to certain families, or to certain places; to concentrate the sciences there is to alienate them from almost all those who are capable of perfecting them. Moreover, it is very difficult for men, the majority of whom are second-rate, once they have received the truth or the sciences as an inheritance, not to regard them as if they were an estate, a capital from which they ought to draw interest. In their hands they become the object of a shameful traffic and a vile monopoly, a kind of commodity which they further corrupt by the absurd intermixture of the most ridiculous opinions. This was the fate of the early discoveries made in the Orient, which were put in the custody of the priests. There they were debased to the point where they were no longer anything but a monstrous collection of fables, of magic, and of the most extravagant superstitions.

All these absurdities, incorporated under Alexander's successors into the ancient philosophy of the Greeks, produced the modern Pythagorism of Iamblichus, Plotinus, and Porphyrius.

We see from this that a precocious maturity, whether in the sciences or in languages, is not an advantage to be envied. Europe, slower in its progress, has borne more nourishing and more fertile fruit. The instrument which the Greek and Latin languages, and our modern languages, have offered to it, and offer to us, is more difficult to handle. But it is capable of being applied to a much greater number of uses and tasks. The multiplicity of abstract ideas which our languages express, and which enter into our analogies, demand great dexterity in their employment. That is the disadvantage of perfected languages. There are more words which are not the bearers of images at all. Thus it needs more skill and talent to paint portraits in these languages, which have become so suitable for defining and demonstrating. But for the great geniuses this very difficulty, which exercises their talent and obliges them to put forth their strength, leads them to successes of which the infancy of languages and nations was not capable. The first painters in Greece used only three colors: their pictures were able to show feeling. But Raphael could draw as well as they could, and Guido Reni, Titian, and Rubens, with the thousand colors with which they loaded their palettes, achieved a fidelity to nature of which the Ancients could have no idea. In the same way

Greek and Latin, by giving sonorous terminations to the old, hard roots of the Asiatic languages, and our modern languages by giving them to those of the peoples of the north, have promoted harmony; and the multiplicity of analogies has given birth to happy turns of phrase which have afforded number and variety to style.

From this arises the beauty especially of Greek and Latin poetry, which were able, owing to the particular constitution of their analogy, to look after inversions and to make use of the quantity of syllables in order to create their rhythm, while almost all other nations were reduced, in order to mark out the meter perceptibly, to have recourse to rhyme. Poetry, once brought to perfection in these languages, became truly a kind of painting, although one would have believed at first sight that the metaphorical languages of the Orient would have painted with more brilliance and force. Nothing of the kind: these languages paint readily, but crudely and badly, without propriety and without taste.

The sciences, which are based on the combination or the knowledge of objects, are as boundless as nature. The arts, which are only relations to ourselves, are as limited as we are; in general all those which are carried on to give pleasure to the senses have a point which they are unable to pass, determined by the limited sensibility of our organs. They are a long time in reaching this point. For example, it is only lately that music has reached its perfection, and, indeed, perhaps it has not yet done so. Moreover, it is wrong to criticize those who want to advance further: if they go beyond the mark, our senses are bound to give us warning of this. Poetry, indeed, in so far as it harmoniously renders images which are full of elegance, will go no further than Virgil. But although perfect in this respect and in relation to style, it is capable of continuous progress in many other respects. The passions will not be painted more effectively, but variations in circumstances will mean that their activity has new effects. The art of combining all the circumstances and directing them to our interest, the verisimilitude and choice of characters, and everything which pertains to the composition of the works, will be capable of being perfected. Ever more dexterity will be acquired as the result of experience. By means of a great amount of subtle reflection, men will learn the way in which one should go about giving pleasure. They will know how to make pleasing garlands from those flowers which nature gave to all the Ancients and which she has not denied to us. In the long run the unceasing imitation of the great models, even their faults, will often preserve their successors from the lapses which sometimes mar the most sublime writings. The progress of philosophy, of all branches of physical knowledge, and of history, which at every moment brings new events on to the world scene, will provide writers with those new subjects which are the food of genius.

There is another cause of variations in taste: manners have a powerful influence on the choice of ideas, and it would consequently appear that the peoples whose society was in the most flourishing condition must have had a more exquisite taste. Taste consists in properly expressing graceful or powerful ideas. Everything which is neither fact, nor feeling, nor image, languishes. Hence in part the disadvantage of languages which are advanced and rich in abstract ideas; it is easier to chatter in them, if I may put it like that, and less easy to paint in them. Reflection is the remedy for this defect, for whatever our pedants say about it, we have become more simple in our century. Transportation is now despised: a strange difference between our progress and that of the Ancients! The leading men among them were too unrefined; among us they are too subtle. This arises from the fact that their taste was formed at the same time as their ideas, but we had ideas before we had any taste.

In general, taste may be bad either as a result of the choice of vile, base, and tedious ideas—and wealthy peoples, to the extent that their society is more cultivated, learn to avoid these; or else as a result of images which are not sensible enough. Let me explain. In the pleasure which comparisons give us there are two pleasures: one is that of the mind which connects two ideas; the other, and unquestionably the greater, is that which arises from the very agreeableness of the images which are presented to it. All the images of things which speak to the imagination and the heart, and which give pleasure to the senses, beautify style and imbue it with that charm with which nature has endowed the things which surround us and which constitute the source of our wellbeing; the sensitive soul is moved by them. But mathematical images, those figures which are indeed in nature, but do not form part of that living nature which alone is connected with us through the bond of pleasure—these images do not bear anything with them except barrenness. The relations may be just as true, but they are more difficult to grasp and say nothing to the heart. This is one of the great differences between intellect and genius. The latter, based as it is on sensibility, is able to choose images capable of putting the soul into that state of happy perturbation which affords visions of the beauties of nature. That is why so many new combinations of matter which our modern discoveries have put before our eyes have so little enriched our poetry: it is because all these ideas, although sensible, give no pleasure to our senses, or at any rate there are very few which have this advantage. Thus it is an effect of the progress of philosophy to put more intellect into style and to render it colder. One must also avoid pushing even the most graceful ideas of nature to the point of anatomical detail where their pleasure is lost; it is in this way alone that intellect can displease. I believe that the language of a people, once it has been formed and stabilized by great writers, no longer changes. Thus I think that the decline of letters in Italy and in Greece came only after a period much longer than we are told, and that poetry then fell into the same state of decline as all other studies, this being the result of the very decline of manners in the Empire. So far as eloquence is concerned, I have given the reason elsewhere.

The Ancients, because they were ancients, were sheltered from pedantry. We know how harmful to taste the vain display of erudition has at all times been.

To want to preserve admiration for the great models by establishing a taste which excludes new forms—that is to behave like the Turks, who did not know how to preserve the virtue of their women except by keeping them in prison. Must one always admire, without producing anything? Pedantry of this kind destroyed Greek literature under the Roman Empire.

There are minds which nature has endowed with a memory capable of assembling together a large number of pieces of knowledge, and a power of exact reasoning capable of comparing them and arranging them in a manner which puts them in their full light; but to whom at the same time she has denied that fire of genius which invents and which opens up new paths for itself. Created to unite the discoveries of others under a point of view fitted to clarify and perfect them, if they are never torches which shine with their own light, they are diamonds which brilliantly reflect a borrowed light, but which in total darkness would be confounded with the meanest stones. These minds are necessarily the last to arrive.

It is not necessary to believe that in times of weakness and decline, or even in those of barbarism and darkness which sometimes succeeded centuries of the greatest brilliance, the human mind made no progress. The mechanical arts, commerce, and the usages of civil life gave birth to a host of reflections which were diffused among men, which were mingled with education, and which constantly grew in quantity as they passed from generation to generation. They pave the way slowly, but profitably and surely, for happier times: like those rivers which are hidden beneath the ground during a part of their course, but which reappear further down, swollen by large quantities of water which have seeped through all those parts of the soil which the current, as determined by the natural gradient, has passed through without showing itself.

The mechanical arts have never suffered the same eclipse as letters and the speculative sciences. An art, once it has been invented, becomes an object of commerce which is self-sustained. There is no need to fear that the art of making velvet will be lost so long as there are people to buy it. The mechanical arts thus continue to exist when letters and taste have fallen, and if they continue to exist, they are perfected. No art whatever can be cultivated during a long succession of centuries without passing through the hands of several inventive minds. We also see that in spite of the ignorance which prevailed in Europe and in the Greek empire after the fifth century, the arts were enriched by a thousand new discoveries without any of the slightest importance being lost.

The art of navigation was perfected, and also the art of commerce. To these centuries we owe the habitual use of bills of exchange, the science of keeping commercial books which is the most perfect form of accounting, the cotton paper invented in Constantinople and the rag paper invented in the west, window glass, plate glass and the art of making mirrors, spectacles, the compass, gunpowder, windmills and water-mills, clocks, and an infinite number of other arts unknown to antiquity.

Architecture offers us an example of the reciprocal independence of taste and mechanical operations in the arts. There are no buildings at all which are in worse taste than Gothic structures; and there are none at all which are more durable, or whose construction demanded more vigor and more practical knowledge of the methods of carrying it out, although these methods could only be the result of a multitude of tentative attempts, since the mathematical sciences were then in their infancy, and the thrust of the arches and roofs could not be calculated with precision.

It was necessary that these arts should be cultivated and perfected in order that real physics and the higher philosophy could be born. They brought the carrying out of exact and conclusive experiments within reach. Without the invention of the telescope, we would never have been able to work out the causes of the movements of the heavenly bodies. Without that of the suction-pump, we would never have been able to discover the heaviness of air.

Let us be careful, therefore, not to confuse success in the mechanical arts with artistic taste, or even with the speculative sciences.

Artistic taste can be lost as the result of a multitude of purely moral causes. The diffusion of a spirit of apathy and softness in a nation, pedantry, contempt for men of letters, eccentricity in the taste of princes, tyranny, and anarchy can corrupt it.

It is not the same with the speculative sciences. So long as the language in which books are written continues to exist, and so long as a certain number of men of letters still remain, nothing that is known is forgotten. It is true that the sciences are then not perfected, because there are few men and consequently few geniuses who apply themselves to them; but they are not completely lost.[2] Also, the Greek teachers of rhetoric who went to Italy after the taking of Constantinople knew everything which had been known in ancient Greece. All that they lacked was taste and the critical faculty. They were simply scholars.

The inundations of the barbarians in the east had a more fatal effect. By destroying the Latin language, they caused the knowledge of the books written in that language to be lost. We would no longer have them, if the monks had not preserved a part of them.

The arts continued to exist in spite of this general calamity. Blows more violent than this are needed in order to overthrow them. It was only the Turks who, in the ferocity of their conquests, were able to cause them to retreat. This must be attributed less to their religion, which did not prevent the Moors of Spain from being very enlightened for their time, than to the nature of their despotism of which we have spoken above, and to the complete separation of the nations made subject to their empire—a separation which kept up a war of hatred in the state, and a balance of oppression and revolt. Brought up in *harems*, abodes of softness and of an authority at the same time ignorant and absolute which could only degenerate into habitual cruelty, the Turks had no industry and knew nothing but violence. The Greeks, bent under a yoke of the harshest kind, lived in fear of it all the time. The enervated Turks, and the oppressed Greeks, both in a state of uncertainty as regards their position, their goods, and their lives, could not think of easing an existence which was so disturbed and so little theirs. Consequently there were no arts at all, apart from those which were absolutely indispensable; and among the others, the few which had been preserved in the seraglio were reduced to techniques without any taste.

The invention of printing spread not only the knowledge of books, but also that of the modern arts, and it has greatly perfected

---

[2] The revolutions which bring about the fall of eloquence and taste in the fine arts, without wiping out the memory of the sciences or preventing a certain amount of cultivation of them, are like the fires which sometimes devastate forests. One can still find a few half-formed trunks remaining alive, but stripped of their branches and their leaves, without flowers and without adornment. (Note by Turgot.)

them. Before its invention, a host of admirable techniques, which tradition alone passed on from one craftsman to the other, excited no curiosity at all among the philosophers. When printing had facilitated their communication, men began to describe them for the use of the craftsmen. Through this, men of letters became aware of a thousand ingenious operations of which they had been ignorant, and they found themselves led toward an infinity of notions which were full of interest for physics. It was like a new world, in which everything pricked their curiosity. Thus was born a taste for experimental physics, in which great progress could never have been made without the help of inventions and technical processes....

Afterword by du Pont

It would seem that this work was never completed. M. Turgot regarded it only as a *sketch*. But although he did not put the finishing touches to it, in which he would perhaps have extended or contracted part of the metaphysical observations, subtle and profound as they are, which are mixed up with his historical views, we have thought fit neither to suppress nor to mutilate an essay which contains such a large number of philosophical truths, often expressed with so much elegance and genius.

PART III

Social Questions

On Some Social Questions, Including the Education of the Young

In a letter to Madame de Graffigny, a popular fiction writer, Turgot strongly defends inequality. People have different abilities, and people need to develop these abilities in order to achieve economic progress. This cannot be done unless people are free to engage in unequal bargains. Equality is an enemy of liberty and economic progress. In our efforts to improve on nature, however, we should not disregard the lessons we can learn from nature. Turgot contends that marriage should be founded on natural affection, not arranged by families on social and financial considerations. Children need to be encouraged to be virtuous, not constantly watched and repressed. Education should lead children to be virtuous and should avoid the accumulation of useless knowledge.

CHAPTER 16

On Some Social Questions, Including the Education of the Young

Addressed to Madame de Graffigny

I have again read the *Lettres péruviennes*.[1] Zilia is a quite worthy sister of Cénie. I am like Henri Quatre, for the last one I have heard. I would indeed prefer the constantly discovering new beauties (which I am always astonished not to have already admired) to amusing myself by making poor criticisms. But you do not wish praise, and I must renounce gratifying myself.

In obedience to the request you have honored me by making, I begin by suggesting the additions which I imagine might be made to the work. You seem to me to approve of the principal of these, which would be to show Zilia as Frenchwoman, after having shown her as Peruvian; to show Zilia judging no longer according to her prejudices, but comparing her prejudices with our own, making her regard objects from a new point of view, making her remark how far she has *been* wrong in being astonished at so many things, and making her search out the causes of those arrangements, derived from the ancient constitution of government, bearing upon the distribution of social conditions as well as on the progress of knowledge.

The distribution of conditions is a very important feature in the social state, and one very easy to justify by showing its necessity and

---

Written 1751.

[1] Madame de Graffigny, born 1695, published between 1745 and 1758, the year of her death, several romances and plays. The *Lettres d'une Péruvienne,* of 1747, was her greatest success, and went through many editions.

its utility. Its necessity, because men are not born equal, because their strength, their mind, their passions, would constantly disturb the equilibrium which laws might attempt to set, because all men are born in a state of feebleness, which renders them dependent on their parents, and which forms between them indissoluble ties. Families unequal in capacity and in strength redoubled the causes of inequality; the wars of savages required a chief. What would society have been without this inequality of conditions? Each would have been reduced to a life concerning itself merely with necessities, and there would be many to whom even these would not be assured. One cannot labor at the soil without having utensils and the means of sustenance until the harvest. Those who have not had the intelligence or the opportunity to acquire these means have not the right to deprive of them him who has earned and won them by his work. If the idle and the ignorant robbed the laborious and the skilful, all work would be discouraged, misery would become general. It is more just and more useful for all that those who are deficient in mind or in good fortune should lend their strength to others who can employ them, who can, in advance, give them wages, and thus guarantee them a share of the future products. Their subsistence then is assured, but so is their dependence. It is not unjust that he who has invented a productive work, and who has supplied to his co-operators the sustenance and the instruments necessary to execute it, who has made with them, in that, only a free contract, should reserve for himself the better part, and, for the price of his advances, should have less hard work and more leisure. This leisure enables him to reflect more, and still further to increase his mental resources. What he can save from the portion, equitably greater, which he will have of the products, increases his capital and his power to undertake new enterprises. Thus inequality will arise, and will increase, even among the most capable and most moral peoples.... It is not an evil, it is a blessing for mankind: where would society be if every man labored only at his own little field? It would be necessary for him also to build his own house, to make his own clothes. The work of each would be limited to himself and to the productions of the little piece of ground surrounding him. How would the inhabitant of the land which did not produce wheat manage to live? Who would transport the products of one country to another? The humblest peasant now enjoys many commodities gathered often from distant countries. A thousand hands, perhaps a hundred thousand hands, have worked for him. The distribution of employments necessarily leads to the inequality of conditions. Without it who would perfect the useful arts? Who would succour the infirm? Who would spread the light of the miner? Who would give to men and to nations that education, particular as well as general, which forms their manners? Who would decide peacefully men's quarrels? Who would check the ferocity of some men, or support the feebleness of others? Liberty! I say it in a sigh, men are perhaps not worthy of thee! Equality! they desire thee, but they cannot attain to thee!

Let your Zilia weigh again the relative advantages of the savage and of the civilized man. To prefer the condition of the savage is a ridiculous declamation. Let her refute it, let her show that the vices which we regard as produced by civilization are the appanage of the human heart; that he who has no gold may be as avaricious as he who has it, because, in all circumstances, men have the hunger for property, the right to preserve it, the avidity which actuates them to accumulate its products. But let not Zilia be unjust; let her, at the same time, unfold the compensations, unequal indeed but still real, belonging to the condition of uncivilized people. Let her show that our arbitrary institutions too often lead us away from Nature; that we have been the dupes of our own progress, that the savage, without knowing how to consult Nature, knows often how to follow her.

Let Zilia criticize, above all, the method of our education; let her criticize our pedantry, for it is in that today that our education consists. Our teaching is applied quite against the grain of Nature. See the "Rudiments." We begin by wishing to cram into the heads of children a perfect crowd of the most abstract ideas. We deluge them with words which can offer to them no meaning, because the meaning of words can only be presented along with ideas, and these ideas can come only by degrees, by proceeding from sensible objects. Then we suppress their imagination, we keep from their view the objects by which Nature gives to the savage the first notion of all things, of all the sciences, even of astronomy, of geometry, of natural history. A man, after a very long education, is still ignorant of the cause of the seasons, cannot fix the cardinal points, does not know the most common animals and the most common plants. We have not an eye for Nature. It is the same with us in morals; general ideas again spoil everything. We take enough care to say to a child that he must be just, temperate, virtuous, but has he the least idea of virtue? Do not say to your son, *Be virtuous*, but make him find pleasure in being so. Develope in his heart the germ of the sentiments which Nature has put there. We often need more barriers against our education than against Nature. Place the child in the opportunities to be true, liberal, compassionate, rely upon the heart of man, let the precious seeds of virtue expand in the air that surrounds them. Do not smother them under a load of straw-mattings and wooden frames.

Another point in our education which seems to me to be bad and ridiculous is our severity in respect to these poor children. They have done some mere foolishness, and we reprehend them as if it were a most important fault. There are many of these childish follies which age itself will correct, but we do not think of that. We wish our son to be "well brought up," and we overwhelm him with petty rules of civility, often frivolous, which cannot but annoy him, for he does not see the reasons for them. It would be quite sufficient to prevent him from being troublesome to those he meets. The rest will follow by degrees. Inspire in him the desire to please, he will soon know more in that respect than all that masters could teach him. We wish our child to be serious, we make it a virtue in him not to run about; we fear every instant that he is going to fall. What happens? We weary and vex him, and we enfeeble him. We have forgotten that above all it is a part of education to form the body. We can trace the cause of this to our ancient manners and our old government. Our ignorant nobility indeed knew nothing but the body; it was men of the people who studied, and that only in order to become priests or monks. Latin was then the whole education, because it was not men who were to be formed, but priests, capable of passing an examination required of them. And again, today we study philosophy, not to be a philosopher, but to pass Master of Arts. What has followed from this? When the nobility have desired to study they have studied according to the forms of colleges established for ecclesiastical objects, and this has often had the effect of disgusting them with study altogether.

I know that you wish to take the conceit out of men by placing woman's constancy above man's. This reminds me of the lion in the fable, who, seeing a picture in which a man had overcome a lion, observed, "If lions could paint, they would show another story." You, who can paint, wish to abase them too. But, candidly, I advise you not to blemish your romance for the glory of women—you have no need to do so.

I have long thought that our nation has need to have marriage preached to her—good marriage. We make our marriages with sordidness, from views of ambition or self-interest, and for this reason many of them are unhappy. We see becoming stronger day by day a fashion of thinking which is hurtful to the State, to manners, to the duration of families, to happiness and the domestic virtues. We dread the ties of marriage, we dread the care and the expense of children. There are many causes of this mode of thinking, but this is not the place to detail them. It will be useful to the State and to manners that we set ourselves in this to reform our opinions less by reasoning than by sentiment. Assuredly there is no lack of matter to be urged; it is Nature that brings about marriage, it is she who adds to the attraction of pleasure the still more delightful attraction of love, because, man having a longer need of help than other young beings, it is necessary for the father and the mother to be united by a durable tie in order to guide the education of their children. It is this same Nature which, by the wise providence of the Supreme Being, endows animals with a maternal tenderness, which endures precisely to the time when the little ones cease to need it. It is Nature that renders the caresses of the little ones so agreeable to their parents. You might introduce this topic by making Zïlia dilate upon the happiness she promises herself with Aza. She might see Céline playing with her young children, might envy the sweetness of those pleasures so little tasted by people of the world; she could—and this is still a point in the comparison between man civilized and man uncivilized—she could reprehend this blot on our manners. We blush at our children, we regard them as an embarrassment, we keep them away from us, we send them to some college or convent, in order to be troubled with them as little as possible. It is a true reflection that the ties of the natural society of the family have lost their strength proportionally as society in general has expanded. General society has jostled out Nature; we have taken away society from the family to give it to the public. It is true that this general society is advantageous in many respects, and will some day destroy the prejudices it has established; for although the first effect of society is to render individuals slaves to public opinion, the second, but more distant effect is to embolden everyone to judge for himself.... The most courageous venture to say aloud what others think only in secret, and, in the long run, the voice of the public becomes the voice of Nature and of truth, because in the long run it becomes the judgment of the greatest number.

Returning to the question of marriage, I would that Zilia should dwell a little on the abuse of which I have already spoken—the manner in which we make marriages without the two parties we join together for life being known to each other, merely by the authority of the parents who determine their own choice only by the fortune of rank or of money, or of rank which it is hoped will one day be translated into money, and who give point to their ideas by the saying we hear every day, "He has done a foolish thing—*married for love*...." I believe it will take a long time to correct society on this matter. I know that even marriages of inclination are not always happy; but because in choosing we are sometimes deceived, it is concluded that we must never choose. The consequence drawn is amusing.

And this leads me to another matter very important for our happiness, of which I would like your Zilia to speak. I would examine closely into the causes of the inconstancies, and even occasional dislikes, that occur between those who at heart love each other. I believe that as we live longer in the world we see that the bothers, the teasings, and the bad temper, brought about by trifles, place more trouble and divisions between people than serious things do. It is deplorable to see so many quarrels, and so many people made unhappy actually on account of mere nothings. How much acrimony rises on the foundation of a word, or on some presumed forgetfulness of respect! If we only put ourselves in the place of others, if we were only to think of the many times we ourselves have had movements of temper, how often we ourselves have forgotten things! A word spoken in depreciation of our judgment is enough to render us irreconcilable, and yet how many times *we* have found ourselves wrong in forming opinions!—how many men of mind we have sometimes taken for fools!—and why should not others have the same right to err as we? But *their* self-love, it is said, makes them find pleasure in preferring themselves to us. Honestly, without our own self-love being concerned, should *we* be thus shocked? Pride is the greatest enemy of pride: they are two inflated balloons which mutually repel each other. Let us pardon the pride of others and let us fear our own. Nature, by forming men so subject to error, has given them but so many claims to tolerance. Why should we refuse it because it is ourselves who are concerned? It is here the evil is; because it is so rare for us to judge fairly, because almost no one weighs truly himself with others.... How much tact is needed in those living together to be compliant without lowering one's self, to blame another without harshness, to correct without dominating, to complain without ill-temper! Women, above all, whom we train up to believe that every deference is due to them, are not able to bear contradiction. This is of all the dispositions the most liable to render them unhappy and all those surrounding them. Nothing is more miserable for us than to be ever dwelling on the respect we think due to us; it is the sure way to our becoming insufferable, it is to make for others a burden of that respect we desire. Respect is tendered with pleasure only where it is not exacted. The best advice that can be given to persons living together is to be quite frank with each other in dealing with any serious difference as soon as it appears; this arrests at their source many of the annoyances often proceeding from mere prejudiced dislikes. But this must be done with full sincerity; we must habituate ourselves to criticise, to examine, and to judge others with a perfect impartiality. I do not speak of tempering our criticisms by giving to them some agreeable turns, and of seasoning them with some mixture of praise and tenderness. How difficult this art is! ... It is true that, even with the best tact used by us to soften reproaches, there are persons who do not know how to receive them; advice they mistake for scolding, they imagine always to see in him who gives it them an assumption of superiority and authority which repels them. It must be admitted that this is a defect belonging to many givers of advice. I have often met with persons who say in self-defense: "I am so made, and I cannot help it." These are persons whose self-love embraces even their defects. This bad disposition proceeds, perhaps, from the manner in which we have had advice given us in childhood, always under the form of reproach, of correction, with the tone of authority, often of threatening. Hence a youth when once free from the hands of his masters or his parents places all his happiness in having no longer to give account of his conduct to anyone, and the most friendly advice appears to him an act of domination, a yoke, a continuance of childhood. Ah! why not accustom children to listen to advice with sweetness by our giving it to them without bitterness? Why exercise authority? I would that children really felt that it is from our affection for them that we reprehend them; but how can we make them feel this if we do not express it in our own softness with them? I have no sympathy with Montaigne when he censures the caresses given by mothers to their children. Who can know better than mothers themselves? It is the instinct that Providence has given them. It is the seasoning which reason teaches should be added to instruction in order to give it genial growth. We forget that it is the caresses of a courageous mother that inspire courage, that they are the most powerful medium of opening the young soul to the inlet of all fine and pure feelings.

I complain above all that our system of educating the young is, for the most part, a mass of most frivolous rules for the teaching of most frivolous things. Why should not children be taught, instead, the art to know themselves, to acquire that fairness of mind which would in time banish from society, if not ill temper, at least the quarrels which ill-temper occasions? How many men would have been happier had they but learnt earlier that tact in giving advice, that docility to receive it and to follow it, of which I have spoken! It is supposed that such quiet impartiality as this is only a gift of Nature, the result of a fortunate temperament, and that education is powerless to effect this constant attention to oneself. We little know the power of education. I will mention one of the reasons of its failure; it is that we content ourselves with giving *rules* where it is necessary to create *habits*.... I believe that Nature has sown in all hearts the seeds of all the virtues, that they require only to be developed; that education (but indeed only a skilful education) can render virtuous the most of men. I know that human progress cannot be rapid; man slowly trails himself along step by step. We must commence by teaching parents to feel the necessity of this true education and to know how to impart it. Each generation will learn a little from the preceding one, and books will thus become the preceptors of nations. And you, Madame, who are so zealous for the good of humanity, who can work better than yourself to spread these principles? They are not quite unrecognized. We have already begun in our time to have a glimpse of them, to render justice to them, even to favor them. But we do not yet know how to instill them. What slovenliness there is in home education, and how easy it would be to penetrate the hearts of children with the sentiments of compassion and of good-will! I have seen parents who taught their children that "nothing is so beautiful as to make people happy." And I have seen the same rebuff their children when they wish to invite some young friends. These, perhaps, might not be quite suitable, but the parents should be careful not to intimidate the rising sensibility of their children, they should rather encourage it, and should make evident the pain they feel in refusing their children's request and the necessity there is for refusing it. But only the present moment is thought of. Again, we reproach children for having been foolish in making some generous gift, as if they would not be corrected of that soon enough!... Thus we contract the heart and mind of a child. I wish, too, that we could avoid exciting in them a shyness when doing a good action, and that we did not believe in inducing them to do it by praises. These repel a timid child; they cause him to feel that we are watching him, and they throw him back upon himself. It is the perfection of tact to bestow praise appropriately. We should teach our children to seek out and to seize occasions of being helpful to others, for this is an art which can and ought to be taught. I do not speak of the delicacy to be used with the unfortunate while we relieve them, for which natural benevolence, without some knowledge of the world, is not sufficient. But above all the great point in home education is to preach by example. Morality in the general is well enough known by men, but the particular refinements of virtue are unknown by most persons; thus the majority of parents, without knowing it and without intending it, give very bad examples to their children....

You might also have alluded in your work to the abuse in the capital absorbing the provinces, etc.

Local Government and National Education

Turgot, illustrating one strand of French Enlightenment thought, argues in a memorial to the king that rights rest on principles of natural justice, not on history. There is then no need for the king to respect tradition in promulgating new laws. One deficiency of the contemporary situation (Turgot wrote in 1775) was that people lack public spirit. The divisions of France lack any rational basis, and local particularism leads people to view others of their countrymen as enemies. To remedy this, a Council of National Education should be established to unify the schools. A common curriculum would stress virtue, public spirit, and the principles of justice.

CHAPTER 17

Local Government and National Education

Introduction to the Memorial to the King "sur les Municipalités"

Sire,—In order to judge whether it be expedient to establish municipalities in France in the cantons where they do not exist, and whether we should improve or should modify those that already exist, and how we should constitute those which we may believe to be necessary, there is no need for us to go back to the origin of municipal administrations, to make an historical relation of the vicissitudes which they have undergone, nor even to enter with much detail on the different forms they assume today. We have been too much in the habit, when dealing with seriously urgent questions, of deciding what is to be done by the examination into, and by the example of, what our ancestors have done in times which we ourselves confess to have been times of ignorance and barbarism. This method is only fit to lead justice astray through the multiplicity of facts presented to us as authorities. It tends to disgust rulers with their most important functions when they are told that in order to acquit themselves with effect and with honor it is necessary to be prodigiously learned. All that is necessary is to thoroughly understand and to correctly weigh the rights and the interests of men. These rights and these interests are not very numerous, so that the science which embraces them, being founded on the principles of justice which every one of us carries in his heart, has a great degree of certitude without having

---

Written 1775.

any great complexity. It does not exact a very deep study, and is not beyond the powers of any straightforward man.

The rights of men gathered in society are not founded on their history as men, but in, their nature. There can be no reason to perpetuate establishments which were made without reason. The kings, your Majesty's predecessors, pronounced, in the circumstances in which they found themselves, laws which they judged to be expedient. They were sometimes wrong. They were often led by the ignorance of their age, and still oftener their views were obstructed by the very powerful self-interests of parties whom they were not strong enough to conquer, and with whom they judged it wiser to compromise. There is nothing in that to subject you to retain the ordinances your ancestors made or the institutions they supported, when you come to recognize that a change is now just, useful, and possible. None of your courts, the most accustomed to make complaints, would venture to contest your Majesty's right, in order to reform abuses, to a legislative power as extensive as that of the princes who created or permitted the abuses we now deplore. The greatest of all powers is a pure and enlightened conscience in those to whom Providence has entrusted authority, shown in their governing for the good of all. So long as your Majesty does not stray beyond the lines of justice, you may regard yourself as an absolute legislator, and may depend on your well-affected subjects for the execution of your decrees.

Your nation is large, it is necessary to have some confidence in the means of well governing it, and for this end it is necessary to know its situation, its needs, its possibilities, and these even in some detail. This will be much more useful than the history of past positions. But it is a knowledge to which your Majesty cannot hope to arrive in the present state of things, a knowledge which your ministers cannot furnish, or the intendants themselves, and which the sub-delegates appointed by the intendants can gather only very imperfectly, owing to the limited duties confided to their care. Hence arise in the assessment and division of the taxes, in the means of levying them and in the administration connected with them, an infinity of errors which excite as many murmurs, and which, bearing most upon the lower classes of people, contribute so effectively to keep their condition unhappy....

The cause of the evil, Sire, lies in the fact that your nation has no constitution. It is a society composed of different orders ill-united, and of a people the members of which have between them very few social ties, where consequently each is concerned almost exclusively with his own private interest, since there is no opportunity for anyone to fulfil his social duties, or even to know what his relations are to his fellow-citizens; so that in this continual war of individual pretensions and violations, reason and enlightenment bearing upon the circumstances have no regulating effect. Your Majesty is obliged to decide everything by yourself or by your mandatories. The issue of your special orders is waited for before the public good can be served, before the rights of others can be respected, sometimes even before one's own rights can be exercised. You are compelled to decree upon everything (and very often through private importunities), while you would govern as God does, by general laws, if the integrant parts of your empire had a regular organisation and had recognized connections.

Your kingdom is composed of provinces; these provinces of cantons or of *arrondissements*, which are named, according to the provinces, *bailliages*, *élections*, *sénéchaussées*, or some such other name. These arrondissements are formed of a certain number of villages and towns. These towns and villages are inhabited by families. These families are composed of individuals who have many duties to fulfil toward each other and toward society, duties founded on the benefits which they have received in the past from these others, and which they every day continue to receive. But the individuals are very ill-instructed upon the duties in the family, and they are not instructed at all upon the duties that bind them to the State. The families themselves scarcely know that they belong to the State of which they form part; they are ignorant by what title. They regard the exercise of authority in requiring contributions to serve to maintain public order as merely the law of the stronger party, to which there is no other reason to yield than the powerlessness to resist it, and which one ought to elude whenever the means can be found.

Hence everyone seeks to deceive you and to escape his social obligations. His income is concealed, and can be discovered very imperfectly by a sort of inquisition, in which, we might say, your Majesty is at war with your own people, and in this kind of war no one has any interest in taking part with the Government; the man doing so would be regarded with an evil eye. There is no public spirit, because there is no point of common interest visible and recognized. The villages and the towns, the members of which are thus disunited, have no connection between themselves in the arrondissements to which they are attributed. They cannot come to an arrangement for any of the public works which are necessary. The different districts are in the same case, and the provinces themselves find themselves in the same toward the kingdom.

In order to dissipate this spirit of disunion (by which the work of your adminstrators and of your Majesty is ten times multiplied, and which necessarily and increasingly diminishes your power), in order to substitute for it a spirit of order and of union, by which the strength and the resources of your nation may concur toward the common good, we must devise a plan which shall link, one to the other, all the parts of the kingdom by an education which we must see to be nowhere neglected, by a common interest made clearly evident. The individuals must be attached to their families; the families to the village or town to which they belong; the towns and the villages to the arrondissement in which they are comprised; the arrondissements to the provinces of which they form part; finally, the provinces to the State.

The first and the most important of all the institutions which I believe to be necessary, the one most fit to immortalize your Majesty's reign, to have the most influence over the whole extent of the kingdom, is, Sire, the formation of a Council of National Education, under whose direction will be placed the academies, the universities, the colleges, and all the smaller schools. The backbone of a nation is its morality; the first basis of morality is the instruction imbibed from the time of childhood on all the duties of man in society. It is astonishing that this science is so little advanced. There are schemes and establishments for forming geometers, physicians, painters. There is not one devised for forming citizens.

It would be the duty of one of the Councils to get composed a series of classic books, according to a regular plan, so that one would lead on to another, and that the study of the duties of the citizen, member of a family and of the State, might be the foundation of all other studies, which would be graduated in the order of utility they have for the State.

The Council of National Education should supervise the whole machinery of education. It should endeavor to render all literary bodies really useful. The efforts of these at present tend only to form savants, men of intellect and of taste; those who cannot arrive at this eminence remain abandoned and come to nothing. A new system of education which can only be established by the authority of your Majesty, seconded by a well-chosen council, would conduce to form in *all* the classes of society men virtuous and useful, just souls, pure hearts, zealous citizens. Those among them whom time could and would give themselves specially to science and literature, being drawn away from frivolous things by the importance of the principles instilled into them during their early education, would display in their subsequent work a character more manly and more coherent. Taste itself would gain by this, and so would the national moral tone; it would become less frivolous and more elevated, and would above all be more concerned with things praiseworthy.

There is at present only one kind of instruction possessing any uniformity—that is religious instruction. But religious instruction is particularly limited to things of heaven. Your kingdom, Sire, is of this world, and it is with the conduct due from your subjects toward each other and toward the State that your Majesty is bound to concern yourself. Without placing any obstacle in the way of instructions whose object is higher, and which already have their regulation and their ministers, I can propose nothing to you more advantageous for your people, more fit to maintain peace and good order, to give activity to all useful works, to make your authority to be cherished, to attach to you each day more and more the affections of your subjects, than to give to all of them an instruction which opens their mind to the obligations they have to society and to your power that protects them, the duty which these obligations impose, the self-interest that all have to fulfil these duties, for the public good and for their own. This moral and social instruction requires books made for the purpose, by competition, selected with great care. It requires a schoolmaster in each parish who will teach these books to the children, with the arts of reading, writing, counting, weighing, and with the principles of mechanics. A higher instruction, embracing progressively the knowledge necessary to citizens from whom the State requires more scientific training, would be given in the colleges.

If your Majesty approves of this scheme, I will place before you the details of it in a special memorial. I venture to promise that in ten years your people will not be ungrateful for it, and that by their enlightenment, their higher moral life, their sincere zeal for your service and for that of the nation, your people will stand above all other peoples. The children who are now of ten years will then find themselves men of twenty, prepared for the State, attached to our country, submitting, not by fear but by reason, to authority; assisting their fellow-citizens, accustomed to recognize and to respect justice, which is the permanent foundation of societies. Such men would fulfil all the duties toward their families which Nature lays upon them, and would form in time families which would well conduct themselves in the village to which they would belong.

But in order to interest existing families in the public good and your Majesty's service, it is not necessary to wait for the fruits appearing of this good education. There is nothing to prevent our employing families, such as they are, toward the constitution of regular villages, which would be something quite different from the present mere assemblage of houses, and cottages, and of inhabitants not less passive.

[Turgot then proceeds to develop in great detail his scheme of the representative bodies for the villages, the towns, the arrondissements, and the provinces, and he concludes with another appeal to the king's heart, picturing in enthusiasm the future fruits of the beneficent policy suggested.]

The civic education which the Council of Education would promote through the whole extent of the kingdom, the appropriate books it would introduce and direct to be taught, would contribute still more to form an instructed and virtuous people. There would be sown in the heart of the young the principles of humanity, of justice, of benevolence, of love for the State; these principles, finding their application as the young advanced in age, would grow more and more. In time your Majesty would have a people renovated, and the first of peoples. Instead of corruption, meanness, intrigue, and greed, which are found everywhere, we should find virtue, disinterestedness, honor, and zeal. It would be common to be a man of probity. Your kingdom, connected in all its parts, each part acting as a support to the rest, would appear to be (and indeed would be) increased in its strength beyond measure. Your kingdom would flourish each day as a fertile garden. Europe would regard you with admiration and respect, and your loving people with a felt devotion.

Religious Liberty
"Le conciliateur"

Turgot, in his first published writing, makes clear his belief in the complete separation of Church and State. He comments on a dispute that involved Protestants, the French bishops, Jansenists, and the Parlement of Paris. The Jansenists were a party within the French Church who insisted on severe moral requirements as a prerequisite to taking Communion. They had been condemned by Rome in the bull Unigenitus (1713), but they had not been eradicated even in the 1750s. The French bishops wanted to deny them admission to Communion. The Parlement forbade the bishops from doing this. At the same time, the Parlement wanted to impose disabilities on the Protestants, reminiscent of Louis XIV's Revocation of the Edict of Nantes in 1685.

Turgot argues that everyone should be free to believe as he wishes. No civil disabilities could rightfully be imposed on the Protestants and Jansenists. On the other hand, the Parlement should leave it up to the Church to determine who has access to Communion. Turgot appeals to the renunciation of force by Jesus and the practice of the pre-Constantinian Church in support of his views. An abundance of competing sects will promote peace, not social unrest, so long as no one uses coercion.

CHAPTER 18

Religious Liberty
"Le conciliateur"

LETTER I

1 May 1754

Can it be true what I heard, as I was leaving Paris, that the king intends to renew the old laws against the Protestants, and at the same time to support the Parliament in its cause against the clergy? It seems to me impossible that, by so astounding an inconsistency, the Council should propose to adopt, at the same time, two such opposite extremes, and to take toward both matters in dispute the course which is the least just and the least reasonable. What next? While the bishops are to be permitted to exclude protestants from the rank of citizens, they themselves are to be ordered to dispense divine grace to those whom they consider unworthy of it...!

The king has four parties to content—the Protestants, the Jansenists, the Bishops, and the Parliament. Each party has its prejudices;

Written 1754. Of Turgot's writings this was the first that was published. It is noteworthy for having exercised a real influence on the settlement of the question in dispute. Its length is about equal to an octavo pamphlet of forty pages. The extracts we give are sufficient to show the nature of his argument and the spirited manner in which it was developed. The form is that of "Letters of an Ecclesiastic to a Magistrate." "In 1754," says du Pont, "after prolonged quarrels between the parliaments and the bishops on the subject of tickets of confession and the refusal of sacraments, it was proposed to the king as a means of contenting both parties to grant to the parliaments the right to compel the bishops to administer the Communion to the Jansenists, and to console the clergy by restoring to them the power of persecuting the Protestants; thus withdrawing from the latter the actual half-tolerance which the Government, now become milder than the law, had been allowing them to enjoy."

but it is not prejudices which we have to consider. Favour ought to form no part in the act of our deliberations; justice alone ought to decide. The king should act exactly as he has a right to do. Each party may complain at first that it has not gained more for its own side, but in time each party will bless a settlement which has done equal justice to all.

Now this is what the king would be in the right to do; he ought to say to the Protestants: "I grieve, and shall always grieve, to see you separated from Unity. With the belief in which I rest, that the truth can be found only in the bosom of the Catholic Church, and with the affection I have for you, I cannot see your condition without feeling pain. But, in error though you be, I shall not the less treat you as my children. Submit yourselves to the laws; continue to be useful to the State of which you are members, and you will receive from me the same protection as my other subjects enjoy. My mission is to render justice and happiness to all."

He ought to say to the Jansenists: "I would that the Church should be without divisions, but it does not belong to me to end them. I would that no one should pronounce anathema against you, but it belongs to me neither to pronounce it nor to suspend it. I am faithful, but I judge not. All that concerns me is to see you tranquilly enjoying your life as citizens. It is only in this connection that I am interested in you. Fear then neither exile, penalty, nor prison. Pray to Heaven that peace be restored to the Church. But evil be to me if these divisions are dragged into the State."

He ought to say to the bishops: "No one respects your judgments more than I do. I submit myself to your decision; I have no other faith than yours; but I shall never meddle with the affairs of religion, I have no right to exact that all my subjects should believe as I do. Use your example, your exhortations, to convert them, but do not count on my authority. Had I been unfortunate enough not to have been a Christian, should I have had the right to compel you to cease to be so? You have your own laws in dealing with divisions; I leave to you the control of them. But I shall not lend the temporal arm to the spiritual authority. Needlessly will you press me to molest the Protestants and the Jansenists, to exile the one body, to imprison the other, or to deprive them of their charges. I shall reply to you in the same spirit which you admire in Gamaliel: 'If their doctrine be undoubtedly the work of men, it will, in God's time, be overthrown.' Count upon my personal submission as a faithful son of the Church, but, as king, count only on receiving from me the same justice which I owe to all my subjects."

He ought to say to the Parliament: "My authority and yours should harmonize. I have endowed you with my power, and I have no thought of withdrawing it. But you cannot use it beyond its province. I have myself no power in the spiritual order, my kingdom is not established to save souls. Your own jurisdiction, then, cannot have greater extent. Leave to the bishops the care of terminating the divisions in the Church; make it your care only that my subjects be not troubled in their honor, in their estate, in their life; preserve for them all that belongs to them as citizens. Leave to the Church all that belongs to itself."

LETTER II

8 May 1764

All that I have said in my first letter was founded on the principle of civil tolerance. Although all men seem disposed to admit it, we are so accustomed to hear civil tolerance proscribed, that one almost fears, in defending it, to be thought guilty of religious indifference. We have our heart tolerant, but custom has rendered our mind fanatical. This fashion of thinking, too common in France, is perhaps the effect of the approbation lavished on the revocation of the Edict of Nantes. We have dishonored religion in order to flatter Louis XIV. It is necessary for me to show, then, that ecclesiastical tolerance is the only one which [the Catholic] religion excludes, and that religion itself proscribes civil intolerance. To prove this I shall not draw upon any reasons, purely human, which, while enlightening the faith of a Christian, are not accepted for guiding it; I shall give as authorities for my statement Jesus Christ and the fathers of the Church.

I have already alluded to Jesus Christ reprehending his apostles, who desired that the fire of heaven should fall upon the Samaritans. Every incident in his recorded life is marked by the same spirit. He does not instruct his disciples to implore the assistance of kings to constrain unbelievers, to employ human authority in order to make converts. He tells them to let grow the tares along with the good grain until the time of harvest, when the master himself will discern them. He performs miracles in order to influence minds, not to subjugate bodies. When his apostles propose to Him to repulse the soldiers coming to seize Him, he replies to them that a legion of angels would be at his command to exterminate his persecutors, but that his "kingdom is not of this world." He performs a miracle that He may teach them not to confound the rights of God with those of Caesar, the things of heaven with the things of earth…. It was less exterior homage that He demanded than the sacrifice of the heart and the adhesion of the mind. A consent due to fear and self-interest does not make a Christian; it is not by such means that Jesus Christ desired his religion to be spread….

But, it is said, it is not the prince who interferes to decide—he only follows and executes the decisions of the Church. The Council of Trent proscribes the Protestants, the Constitution proscribes the Jansenists; the prince has made these decisions into laws of the State, persons who contravene them infringe the laws of the kingdom and they can be punished, without its being held that the prince has meddled in the affairs of religion. But has the king a right to make a law of the State of the decision of the Council of Trent, or of the Constitution? The first fathers of the Church did not require of the pagan princes to make the gospel a law of the empire. They demanded only the liberty to profess their religion, and they were grateful to the emperors when they had the happiness to obtain that liberty. It is to those early times that we must go back in order to fix the limits of the two powers. When the princes became Christians, the bishops, in order to concern themselves in matters of State, demanded that their decisions should be made laws of the kingdom. The princes, either through zeal or through self-interest, complied with this, imagining to have thereby a greater authority over their subjects. The step was prejudicial to both parties....

But let us go back to the origin of things. We shall see Religion, as she should be, separated from the Government; the Church occupied with the salvation of souls; the empire occupied with the welfare of the people; the one and the other having its laws distinct, as the things of heaven ought to be from the things of earth.

To make an edict of a decision of the Church . . . is to compel the people to adopt an opinion because it appears truth to us. Is not this overruling consciences? . . . If the King of France can make of the Council of Trent and of the Constitution laws of his State, has not the King of England the right to establish for himself the supremacy, the Turk the right to establish the Koran, each prince his own religion? This idea revolts us, because in foreign countries *we* should be the persecuted. Ought it not to revolt us all the same when we would be the persecutors?

"But," it is said, "the prince would thus be obliged to tolerate in his states all sorts of religion, even those contrary to social good, as human sacrifices, etc." God forbid that I should advance such a principle! *Actions* are the only things that interest the State in respect to religion. As for doctrine, or even morals, in the objects of pure speculation, the State ought to be indifferent to them. Actions are either contrary to social welfare or they are not. If they are not contrary, why forbid them to be made acts of religion? If they are contrary they are already proscribed and cannot be authorized. It is indifferent to the State that each day I purify my body by different ablutions; the practice may be superfluous, but it is not dangerous. Kings have no right to hinder it from being made a religious ceremony. But it is another thing to shed human blood. If I preach a religion which permits it, the prince has a right to proscribe me; it is less the religious action than the criminal action that is forbidden. It would be a crime to immolate, because it is already a crime to kill....

Then it is said, "if the king is to permit all religions whose doctrine is not contrary to the good of the State, what a monstrous assemblage of sentiments you would introduce! Do you believe that peace could exist between minds filled with principles so opposed?

Is not unity in religion necessary in a government? The fields of our country reek yet with the blood shed in the wars of religion." I know of how many wars heresies have been the source, but is not this because we have persisted in persecuting them? The man who believes earnestly believes with still more firmness if we would force him to change his belief without convincing him; he then becomes obstinate, his obstinacy kindles his zeal, his zeal inflames him; we wish to convert him, we have made of him a fanatic, a madman. Men, for their opinions, demand only liberty; if you deprive them of it, you place arms in their hand. Give them liberty, they remain quiet, as the Lutherans were at Strasburg. It is then the very unity in religion we would enforce, and not the different opinions we tolerate, that produces trouble and civil wars....

[After a further vindication of the principle of tolerance in all its applications, Turgot sums up the anticipated results from the policy of neutrality he recommends.]

I can easily imagine that each party will at first be ill-pleased at being denied the rights it would usurp, but as it is still gratifying not to lose those rights it possesses, and ought to possess, each party will in time be grateful to the Government for having preserved these.... The bishops will thank the king for having left them masters in the affairs of religion; the Parliament for having confided to it his authority; the Jansenists for having no longer to fear punishment, exile, imprisonment; and, finally, the general public will bless a government so wise, whose authority will be exercised only in allowing each party to enjoy tranquilly its own rights, this being the end for which government is established.

I should finish, but as there have occurred to me some reflections that tend to make these principles more sensibly felt, I feel I ought not to omit them.

First Reflection.—In France we have always proscribed the Inquisition, that odious power which has carried sword and fire into the world of the God of peace and charity. Now, odious as this tribunal is, he who establishes intolerance would not be less odious. If the prisons of the Inquisition were terrible, France itself has had only too many which have echoed the cries of the oppressed conscience.

If the former were unjust, why should the latter be authorized? We who condemn with horror the minister of the Church who, by torture, compelled the mind, should we give to our king the right still to subjugate it? We regard with indignation the inflictions which, in Italy and in Spain, obstruct the rights of conscience; the least reflection should prevent our feeling less for the conscience of our own citizens.

Second Reflection.—To justify what I have advanced, let us suppose that these actual disputes had occurred in a country where the prince was neither Jansenist nor *constitutionnaire*; at Berlin, for example, the King of Prussia, although Protestant, has permitted the Catholics to build a church in his capital. If among them were found some Jansenists to whom the sacraments were refused, should we not be astonished to see that prince entering into their disputes and pretending to dictate their laws to them? We should feel shocked to see the Protestant prince meddling with Catholic affairs. Does the faith of the prince, then, make all the difference? . . . What we consider the King of Prussia ought to do, is that not the principle for our own kings to follow?

Third Reflection.—It has been usual to compare the salvation of the soul to the health of the body. The bishops themselves style themselves spiritual physicians. Errors are the maladies that affect the mind; those who rule the consciences are established in order to apply the remedies. Let us judge then of the liberty that ought to reign in the sphere of salvation by that liberty which every one must have in order to govern his own health. However excellent a remedy may be, should we not find it rather hard if a prince compelled his subjects to make use of this particular one in preference to all others? Should we not say to him that confidence cannot be prescribed, that each is master of his health, that we cannot cure a man in spite of himself? If the king did more and if the confidence he had in his remedy induced him to order that all physicians in his kingdom should use that remedy on all occasions, would they not have the right to represent to him that no one could better know the utility of a remedy than they could, that its application varies according to different temperaments and conditions, of which they are the best judges, that they cannot all be kept within the same fixed lines, that they would rather suffer a thousand penalties than administer a remedy that they knew might be dangerous? . . . If, in spite of these just representations, the king persisted in compelling all his subjects to take this remedy, and all the physicians to administer it, even when they believed it dangerous, what should we think of such conduct? I leave to you to make the application of this comparison; I avoid for myself the mixing overmuch things profane with things sacred.

I believe, Sir, that I have thus justified Toleration. There was a time when these principles would have shocked many persons, but we become every day more enlightened, and we learn to distinguish in religion what is essential to it and what men have added. We detest more than ever the Inquisition, we admire the edict of tolerance of the empress-queen. The King of Prussia appears to us wise in having, although a Protestant, accorded to Catholics the free exercise of their religion. The revocation of the Edict of Nantes revolts us; our soldiers murmur when they are employed against the Protestants. The cause of Civil Toleration has been sustained even in some theses of the Faculty of Theology, it is being advocated in many writings; everywhere discussion is tending to establish it. Let us, the one and the other, be happy if we can help toward this end.

Religious Equality

In a memorial to King Louis XVI before his coronation, Turgot continues his argument for religious freedom. He points out that if the government demands that someone profess a religion he does not really believe, this imposes a tremendous burden on his conscience. Suppose that the person believes that his eternal salvation depends on accepting a certain religion. (Turgot notes that most religions do teach exclusivism of this type.) Then, persecution is likely to be ineffective, since whatever penalty the state can impose will be much less significant than the loss of salvation. If it is argued that the king simply acts as the servant of the Church in suppressing heresy, Turgot answers that the Church has no power over temporal matters. Further, the king has no special knowledge of theology that would justify him in claiming to determine the true religion, and Turgot does not hesitate to criticize Louis XIV for persecuting Protestants, even though he was ignorant in theology. Even if persecution were successful, it would induce sin. People who professed a religion they did not really believe would be guilty of perjury.

CHAPTER 19

Religious Equality

Memorial to the King "on Toleration"

Sire,—When I proposed to your Majesty to alter the form of the oaths to be pronounced at your consecration, I could only indicate to you, summarily, the reasons which I considered warranted my proposals. I undertook to develop to you, in more detail, the principles pertaining to the most essential object of the alterations proposed, that is to say, to the use of the prince's power in matters of religion. Your Majesty, while rendering justice to my views, dreaded the explosion which might result, in certain quarters, from the step I recommended. You know how deeply I have regretted your submission to formulas of obligation drawn up in times so deficient in enlightenment. But all is not lost, for your Majesty cannot hold yourself bound to take any action that would be unjust.

Your oaths, Sire, have been pronounced in presence of God and your subjects. Your subjects have an interest in, have a right to your justice; God has given you a law. To commit an injustice in order to execute the formulas which you have been induced to pronounce would be to violate the duty you owe to God, to your people, to yourself. You must, therefore, Sire, examine if the engagements included in the formulas of consecration with respect to heretics are

---

Written 1775. To appreciate the style of thought and of composition adopted in the following Memorial, the reader must be reminded of two things: first, that it was written for the purpose of instructing the young king in the very elements of religious liberty; and, second, that at that time the doctrine of toleration was, by the religious classes, still deemed a *heresy*.

just in themselves; and if they are unjust, it cannot be your duty to fulfil them....

I have never concealed from your Majesty my own way of thinking. You saw it in a letter with which I accompanied the new forms of oath which I proposed to you. I venture to repeat today that your Majesty is bound, as a Christian, as a just man, to leave to all your subjects the liberty of following and of professing the religion which in their conscience they believe to be true. I add, Sire, that your own political interests on this point are entirely conformable with what Christianity and justice prescribe. These three points of view form the natural division of this Memorial. I shall examine first the rights of conscience according to the principles of religion; I shall next establish these rights according to the principles of natural law; in the third place, I shall discuss the question of this liberty of conscience in its connection with the political liberty of the State.

1. What, Sire, is religion? It is the binding together of the several duties of man toward God; duties of worship to be rendered to the Supreme Being, duties of justice and of benevolence to men; those duties known by the simple light of reason which constitute what we call Natural Religion, and those which the Divinity Himself has taught to men by a supernatural revelation which constitute Revealed Religion.

All men do not agree in acknowledging divine Revelation, and those who do acknowledge it do not agree in interpreting alike particular revelations. It is notorious that there are on the surface of the earth a multitude of religions, the votaries of which believe that the one they profess is the only one that is the work of the Divinity, and which is agreeable to Him.

The principal religions, such as Mahommedanism and even Christianity, are divided into a multitude of sects, each of which believes itself to hold exclusively the true religion. All, or almost all religions, in exacting from man certain beliefs and the accomplishment of certain duties, add to this obligation the sanction of rewards and punishments in the life to come. A great number of religions teach that these punishments and these rewards are eternal. This is the doctrine of nearly all the Christian communities, and in particular of the Roman Catholic Church, whose doctrine your Majesty professes. So that on the belief and on the practice of a true or a false religion depends for man an eternity of happiness or of misery.

I can conceive that the men who believe all religions to be equally false, and who regard them as inventions of policy in order to govern more easily the people, can make no scruple about compelling them to follow the religion which it is thought most expedient to prescribe for them.... But if there is a true religion, if God is to demand account from each man of what he has believed and practiced, if an eternity of punishment must be the portion of him who shall reject the true religion, how can we imagine that any power on earth can have the right to order a man to follow another religion than the one which he believes true in his soul and conscience?

If there is a true religion a man must follow it, and profess it in spite of all the powers of the earth, in spite of the edicts of emperors and kings, in spite of the judgment of proconsuls and of the executioner's sword. It is for having had this courage, for having fulfilled this sacred duty, that we have had held up to our veneration the martyrs of the primitive Church. If the martyrs were right in resisting the civil power, and following the voice of their conscience, their conscience, by that fact, did not recognize the civil power as judge.

All sovereigns have not the same religion, and each religious man feels himself, in his conscience, by his duty and for his salvation, obliged to follow that religion which he believes to be the truth. Sovereigns have not the right to order their subjects to disobey their conscience. God, in judging men, will demand of them whether they have believed and practiced true religion; not whether they have believed and practiced the religion of their sovereign. How could He demand that of them if all the sovereigns have not the true religion? Cast your eyes, Sire, on the map of the world; and see how few countries there are of which the sovereigns are Catholics. How can it be that with the greatest number of sovereigns of the world existing in error, they have received from God the right to judge of the true religion? If they have not the right, if they have neither infallibility nor the divine mission which alone could give it them, how dare they take upon themselves to decide the fate of their subjects, of their happiness or their misery during eternity? Every man, by the principles of religion, has his soul to save; he has all the light of reason and of revelation in order to find the way of salvation; he has his conscience in order to apply these lights—but this conscience is for himself alone. To follow his own conscience is the right and duty of every man, and no man has the right to make his conscience a rule for another. Each one is in this responsible for himself to God, none is responsible for another.

This principle is so clearly evident, that it would seem a waste of time to prove it, if the illusions opposed to it had not blinded the greater part of the human race, if they had not inundated the earth with blood, if even today they did not make millions unhappy.

Will the defenders of intolerance say that the prince has only the right to command when his religion is true and that then he ought to be obeyed? No, even then we cannot and ought not to obey him, for if we ought to follow the religion he prescribes, it is not because he commands it but because it is true, and it is not and it cannot be because the prince commands it that it is true. There is no man so irrational as to believe a religion true for such a reason. The man who submits himself to it in good faith does not obey the prince, he obeys only his conscience, and the order of the prince does not add, and cannot add, any weight to the obligation which, conscience alone imposes. Let the prince believe or not believe a certain religion, let him command or not command his subjects to follow it, it is neither more nor less than it is—either true or false. The opinion of the prince is thus absolutely foreign to the truth of a religion, and consequently to the obligation to follow it; the prince then has, as prince, no right to judge, no right to command in this respect; his incompetence is absolute on things of this order, which are beyond his jurisdiction, and in which the conscience of each individual has only, and can have only, God Himself for Judge.

Some theologians say: "We admit that the prince has not the right to judge of religion, but the Church has this right, and the prince, in submission to the Church, ordains in conformity with its judgments.... He himself does not judge, but orders his subjects to submit themselves to a legitimate judgment." As this reasoning has been used and is still used seriously, it has to be answered seriously.

The Church has the right to judge of the things of religion—yes, without doubt; it has the right to exclude from its body, to anathematize, those who refuse to submit to its decisions, its decisions are obligatory [upon those who belong to it, and who believe that] what the Church binds and looses shall be bound and loosed in heaven. But the Church is not a temporal power, it has neither the right nor the power to punish in this world; its anathemas affect only the penalties which God reserves in the future life for the obstinately refractory. The prince, if he is a Catholic, is the child of the Church; he is subject to her, but only as a man concerned with his personal salvation; as a prince he is independent of the ecclesiastical power. The Church, then, can order him in nothing so far as he is prince, but only so far as he is a man; and as it is only in quality of prince that he could compel his subjects to submit to the judgment of the Church, it follows that the Church cannot make it a duty for him to use his authority to compel his subjects against their conscience. The Church cannot give him the right to do so, because she has it not herself, and besides, because the prince, as prince, not only does not acknowledge the superiority of the Church, but is not competent to judge for others what are the rights of the Church, or whether such a society is the true Church.

Is there an infallible Church? Is the society of Christians united with the Pope that Church? This is precisely the question that divides all Europe into two parties nearly equal—the question of judgment between the Protestants and the Catholics. There is even another question to be judged on before that. The Protestants and the Catholics both recognize the truth of Christianity and the divinity of the Scriptures, on which all Christian Communions profess to found their beliefs. But the Jews do not accept all the Scriptures; a great part of Asia follows the religion of Mahommed and rejects that of Jesus Christ. The Mussulman countries are as extensive as those where Christianity is established; the rest of the earth, still vaster, recognizes neither Mahommed nor Jesus Christ, and follows different religions.

[This doctrine of making the prince the creature of the Church is] the same doctrine, the same spirit, which produced the infernal St. Bartholomew and the detestable League, placing alternately the sword in the king's hand to massacre the people, and in the people's hands to assassinate their kings. This, Sire, is a subject of meditation which should ever be kept in princes' minds. But, without ascending to those high principles, would the simplest common sense allow it to be imagined that princes could have any right over the conscience and the salvation of their subjects? If the fate of men during eternity could depend upon other men, should there not be a reasonable certitude that these other men should be endowed with natural or acquired enlightenment, superior to those of common men? Without such light—or even with it, without an express mission from the Deity, what man could dare to take upon him the eternal happiness or misery of other men?

The mission of kings is to make the happiness of their people on earth. This mission is noble enough, beautiful enough, and the work it involves is weighty enough for the strength of anyone, whoever he may be. He who has fulfilled with success this sublime and laborious career can die content with himself, and need not fear to render an account of his life. With attention, straightforwardness, and diligence, a prince has every enlightenment and assistance to discover what is really just and truly useful; he has no need to know anything else. He may make mistakes; this is an evil no doubt, but it is an inevitable result of the nature of things.

Sire, I speak to a king, but to a king just and true; let him ask himself what he thinks on this matter, and let him answer himself. There are in the different universities and among the ministers of the different Protestant sects, men who, endowed with great mind, have grown white-haired in the study of religion, have all their life read the Holy Scriptures, have researched thoroughly into all ecclesiastical antiquity; and although in all religions there are men who concern themselves less to discover truth than to find means to prop up the doctrine they are interested to maintain, yet one cannot doubt that a great number of these learned men are quite sincerely convinced that the doctrine of which they make profession is the only true one. Who among Catholic princes would feel himself fit to convince these men, fit even to defend himself against their objections? Doubtless the Protestant princes would not be less embarrassed if their turn came to dispute against the learned Catholic doctors. Princes, to whatever religion they may belong, are not made to fathom theology. I recollect only one king who had this fancy, and he was a Protestant—James I of England. It did not succeed with him, and Europe felt that he would better have employed his time to become a great king than to be a middling theologian. Too many are given up only to pleasure and dissipation. Those who reflect apply themselves to the affairs of their state and to do good. I venture to ask you, Sire, if among the princes of different times and of different countries of whom you have read in history, there is a single one whom you would have taken as authority in the choice of a religion. And yet all those princes were believed to have the right to ordain the religion of their subjects, to render religion's laws, to pronounce its penalties, and to subject to torture men whose only crime was having religious opinions different from those of the prince, and desiring to follow the dictates of their own conscience. What increases our astonishment is that the most of these princes, at the very time of issuing these orders, were violating in a thousand ways the precepts of their own religion, and were allying the scandal of debauch with the barbarity of persecution. Louis XIV, deservedly thought a great prince because he had probity, honor, character (although somewhat spoiled perhaps, being inflated by an excessive love of glory), but above all because he possessed that firm will without which kings can neither do good nor prevent evil, even Louis XIV knew very little. He candidly confessed that his education had been neglected. He made that confession, and he dared to judge what the religion of his subjects should be; he believed he had the right to deprive the Protestants of the liberty of conscience solemnly insured to them by Henry IV, whose succession to the crown had been cemented with their blood. Louis XIV reduced the Protestants to despair by a continued vexatious persecution, the details of which make us shudder while we read of them in the memoirs of the time, and the errors into which this despair drove them he punished with the most relentless cruelty. He believed himself to be doing a praiseworthy and pious action. This was a deplorable blindness in a prince otherwise well-intentioned, who knew not how to distinguish his duties as man from his rights as prince.... But the interest of the priests about the Court has always been to confound these two things, and, in order to support their credit and serve their ambition, to misuse the prince's ignorance on these matters. That was not the only fault of the kind they caused Louis XIV to commit. The miserable disputes of Jansenism and Molinism, which have been the rain of so many and which served as pretexts for commotions dangerous to the royal authority, existed only as a consequence of the passion of the clergy to force the Government to interfere in questions with which it has neither interest nor right to meddle.

How can religion command sovereigns to use their power to constrain their subjects in matters of religion? Can religion then command, can it permit, crimes? To order a crime is to commit one; he who orders to assassinate is regarded by all the world as an assassin. Now the prince who orders some of his subjects to profess a religion they do not believe, or to renounce one they do believe, commands a crime; the subjects who obey act a lie, they betray their conscience, they do an act which they believe God forbids. The Protestant who through self-interest or fear makes himself a Catholic, and the Catholic who by the same motives makes himself a Protestant, are both guilty of the same sin, For it is not the truth or the falsity of an assertion that constitutes a perjury; the man who affirms on oath a true thing, but which he does not believe, is as much a liar, as much a perjurer, as if the matter were really false. The lie or the perjury consists in the contradiction between the assertion and the real belief of him who affirms or makes the oath....

[The remainder of the Memorial has unfortunately been lost.]

Endowments

Turgot, in his article on "Endowments" for the famous French Encyclopedia of Diderot and D'Alembert, strongly opposes a certain type of private foundation, one that establishes a perpetual endowment devoted to some purpose, e.g., a home for women who repent a dissolute life. He suggests that no one has the wisdom to anticipate the consequences of a policy for the remote future. Even if one considers less remote times, foundations often have unanticipated effects. A foundation to relieve poverty will increase the number of poor people, because it will reduce the incentive for people to work. "To enable a large number of men to live gratuitously is to subsidize idleness and all the disorders which are its consequences; it is to render the condition of the ne'er-do-well preferable to that of the honest working-man." Further, even if the purpose of the foundation is a good one, later administrators will, lacking the zeal of the founder, act in a way that leads to poor results. Even foundations that are well run and have good purposes eventually lose their usefulness. Instead, social problems should be solved by individuals acting to promote their own interests. Emergencies should be dealt with by voluntary subscription. Corporations can properly be suppressed, because only individuals have rights.

CHAPTER 20

Endowments

Article "Fondation" in the "Encyclopédie"

To found, in the sense in which we are now using the word, is to assign a fund or a sum of money in order to its being employed in perpetuity for fulfilling the purpose the founder had in view, whether that purpose regards divine worship, or public utility, or the vanity of the founder—often the only real one, even while the two others serve to veil it....

Our intention in this article is limited to examining the utility of *foundations* in general, in respect to the public good, and chiefly to demonstrating their impropriety. May the following considerations concur with the philosophic spirit of the age, in discouraging new foundations and in destroying all remains of superstitious respect for the old ones!

1. A founder is a man who desires the effect of his own will to endure for ever. Now, even if we suppose him to be actuated by the purest motives, how many reasons are there to question his enlightenment! How easy it is to do harm in wishing to do good! To foresee with certainty that an establishment will produce only the effect desired from it, and no effect at variance with its object; to discern, beyond the illusion of a near and apparent good, the real evils which

---

Written in 1756. Much has been done since Turgot's time, and much in the direction he has indicated. But we give the article as written, nearly *verbatim*. It is still not without some application to present-day discussions.

a long series of unseen causes may bring about; to know what are the real sores of society, to arrive at their causes, to distinguish remedies from palliatives; to defend oneself against the prestige of a seductive project, to take a severe and tranquil view of it amidst that dazzling atmosphere in which the praises of a blind public, and our own enthusiasm, show it us surrounded; this would need the effort of the most profound genius, and perhaps the political sciences of our time are not yet sufficiently advanced to enable the best genius here to succeed.

By these institutions support is often given to a few individuals against an evil the cause of which is general, and sometimes the very remedy opposed to the effect increases the influence of the cause. We have a striking example of this kind of abuse in the establishment of houses designed as asylums for repentant women. In order to obtain entrance, proof of a debauched life must be made.... I know well that this precaution has been made in order to prevent the foundation being diverted to other objects; but that only proves that it is not by such establishments, powerless against the true causes of libertinage, that it can be combated. What I have said of libertinage is true of poverty. The poor have incontestable claims on the abundance of the rich; humanity and religion alike make it a duty on us to relieve our fellow-creatures when under misfortune. It is in order to accomplish these indispensable duties that so many charitable establishments have been raised in the Christian world to relieve necessities of every kind, that so many poor are gathered together in hospitals and are fed at the gates of convents by daily distributions. What is the result? It is that precisely in those countries where gratuitous resources are most abundant, as in Spain and some parts of Italy, there misery is more common and more widely spread than elsewhere. The reason is very simple, and a thousand travellers have observed it. To enable a large number of men to live gratuitously is to subsidize idleness and all the disorders which are its consequences; it is to render the condition of the ne'er-do-well preferable to that of the honest working-man. Consequently it diminishes for the State the sum of labor and of the productions of the earth, a large part of which is thus left necessarily uncultivated.

Hence frequent scarcities, the increase of misery, and depopulation. The race of industrious citizens is displaced by a vile populace, composed of vagrant beggars given up to all sorts of crime.... From this loss of the labor and wealth of the State there results a great increase of public burdens, thrown on the shoulders of the industrious man, and an increase of all the disorders we see in the present constitution of society. It is thus that the purest virtues can deceive those who surrender themselves without precaution to all suggestions that they inspire. But if these pious and respectable designs contradict in practice the hopes that were conceived for them, what must we think of those endowments (undoubtedly numerous) whose only motive and object is the satisfaction of a frivolous vanity? I do not fear to say that were we to weigh the advantages and the disadvantages of all the foundations in Europe, perhaps there would not be found one which would stand the test of an enlightened scrutiny.

2. But of whatever utility a foundation might be at its conception, it bears within itself an irremediable defect which belongs to its very nature—the impossibility of maintaining its fulfilment. Founders deceive themselves vastly if they imagine that their zeal can be communicated from age to age to persons employed to perpetuate its effects. There is no body that has not in the long ran lost the spirit of its first origin. There is no sentiment that does not become weakened, by mere habit and by familiarity with the objects which excite it. What confused emotions of horror, of sadness, of deep feeling for humanity, of pity for the unfortunates who are suffering, does that man experience who for the first time enters the ward of a hospital! Well, let him open his eyes and look around. In this very place, in the midst of these assembled human miseries, the ministers provided to relieve them walk about with an air careless and expressionless; they mechanically and without interest distribute from invalid to invalid the food and the remedies prescribed, and sometimes do so even with a brutal callousness; they give way to heedless conversation, and sometimes to ideas of the silliest and the grossest; vanity, envy, hatred, all the passions reigning there, as elsewhere, do their work, and the groans from the sick-bed, the cries of acute pain, do not disturb the *habitués* any more than the murmur of a rivulet

interrupts an animated conversation. Such are the effects of habit in relation to objects the most capable of moving the human heart. Thus it is that no enthusiasm can be constantly sustained. And how without enthusiasm can ministers of a foundation fulfil its purpose always and with precision? What interest, in their case, can counteract idleness, that weight attached to human nature which tends constantly to retain us in inaction? The very precautions which the founder has taken in order to insure for them a constant revenue dispenses them from meriting it by exertion. Are there superintendents, inspectors, appointed to see the work of the foundation carried out? It will be the same with these inspectors. If the obstacle to the right working comes from idleness, the same idleness on their part will prevent them from exposing it; if the abuse proceeds from pecuniary interest, they will too readily share in it. Supervisors themselves would need to be supervised…. Thus almost all old foundations have degenerated from their primitive institution. Then the same spirit which had devised the first has created new ones on the same plan, or a different plan, which, after having degenerated in their turn, are displaced in the same manner. Measures are ordinarily so well taken by the founders to protect their establishments from exterior innovations, that generally it is found to be easier to found new establishments than to reform the old; but, through these double and triple renovations, the number of useless mouths in society and the sum of wealth kept from general circulation are continually increased. [After having alluded to the case of foundations being affected, and often prevented, by changes in the value of money, he proceeds:—]

3. I will suppose that a foundation has had at its origin an incontestable utility, that sufficient precautions have been taken against its degeneration through idleness and negligence, that the nature of its funds has sheltered it from the revolutions of monetary changes, then I say that the very immutability which the founders have succeeded in giving it is still a great public impropriety, because time brings about new revolutions which will sweep away the utility, the foundation once fulfilled, and will render its continued operation even injurious. Society has not always the same needs; the nature and dispositions of properties, the divisions

between different orders of the people, opinions, manners, the general occupations of the nation or of its different sections, the climate even, the maladies and the other accidents of human life—all experience a continual variation. New needs arise, others cease to be felt. The proportion of those remaining declines from day to day, and along with them the utility of the foundations designed to relieve them diminishes or disappears. The wars of Palestine gave rise to innumerable foundations whose utility ceased with the wars. Without speaking of the military religious orders, Europe is still covered with leper hospitals (*maladreries*), although for long leprosy has been almost unknown. The greater number of foundations long survive their utility: first, because there are always men who profit by them, and who are interested in maintaining them; secondly, because even when we become convinced of their inutility, we make long delays before deciding either upon the measures or the formalities necessary to overthrow establishments consolidated for many centuries, or deciding upon the use or the distribution we should make of their property.

4. I have said nothing of the splendor of the buildings and of the pomp connected with some of the grand foundations. It would be perhaps to value very favorably the utility of these objects if we estimated them at one hundredth part of the whole cost.

5. Woe to me if my object be, in presenting these considerations, to concentrate man's motives in his mere self-interest, and to render him insensible to the sufferings or the happiness of his fellow-creatures, to extinguish in him the spirit of a citizen, and to substitute an indolent and base prudence for the noble passion of being useful to mankind. In place of the vanity of founders, I desire that humanity, that the passion of the public good, should procure for men the same benefits, but more surely, more completely, and at less cost, and without the drawbacks of which I have complained.

Among the different needs of society intended to be fulfilled by means of durable establishments or foundations, let us distinguish two kinds. One belongs to society as a whole, and is just the result of the interest of each of its members, such as the general needs of humanity, sustenance for everyone, the good manners and education of children, for all families.... It does not require much reflection to be convinced that the first kind of social needs is not of a nature that can be fulfilled by foundations, or by any other gratuitous means, and that, in this respect, the general good ought to be the result of the efforts of each individual for his own interests. Every able-bodied man ought to procure his subsistence by his work, because if he were fed without working, it would be so at the cost of those who work. What the State owes to all its members is the destruction of the obstacles which impede them in their industry, or which trouble them in the enjoyment of the product which is its recompense. While these obstacles subsist, particular benefits will not diminish the general poverty, for the cause will remain untouched. For the same reason every family owes education to the children who are born to it, and it is only from the efforts of each in particular that the general perfection of education can arise. If you amuse yourself to endow masters and bursaries in colleges, the utility of which will be felt only by a small number of scholars, favored by chance, who have not perhaps the necessary talents to profit by them, that will be, for the whole nation, but a drop of water spread on a vast sea, and you will have procured, at very great expense, very small results. And then you have accustomed people to be ever applying for these endowments, and (not always) receiving them, and to owe nothing to themselves. This sort of mendicity spread over all conditions of men degrades a people and substitutes for the high impulses a character of lowness and intrigue. Are men powerfully interested in that good which you would procure for them? Leave them free to attain it; this is the great, the only principle. Do they appear to you to be actuated by less ardour toward it than you would desire to see? Increase their interest in it. You wish to perfect education—propose. prizes for the emulation of parents and children, but let these prizes be offered to whosoever can *merit* them, offered at least to every order of citizens; let employments and places become the recompense of merit, and the sure prospect of work, and you will see emulation struck up at once in the heart of all families. Your nation will soon be raised above its old level, you will have enlightened its spirit, you will have given it character, you will have done great things, and you will have done all at less expense than founding one college.

The other class of public needs intended to be provided for by foundations comprise those regarded as accidental, which, limited to particular places and particular times, enter less into the system of general administration, and may demand particular relief. It is desired to remedy the hardships of a scarcity, or of an epidemic, to provide for the support of some old men, or of some orphans, for the rescue of infants exposed, for the working or maintaining works to improve the amenity or the salubrity of a town, for the improving of agriculture or some arts in a backward condition in a locality, for rewarding the services rendered by a citizen to the town of which he is a member, to attract to it men celebrated for their talents. Now, it is before all necessary that the means taken by public establishments or foundations should be the best in order to procure for their subjects all these benefits as fully as possible. The free employment of a part of the revenues of a community, some contribution of all its members in the case of the need being pressing and general, with a free association of, and voluntary subscriptions of some generous citizens, in the case of the need being less urgent and less generally felt—here is the true means of fulfilling all kinds of schemes really useful, and this method will have the inestimable advantage over foundations, that it is subject to no great abuse. As the contribution of each is entirely voluntary, it is impossible for the funds to be diverted from their destination. If they were, their source would be soon dried up. There would be no money sank in useless expenses, in luxury, or in building. It is a partnership of the same kind as those made for business, with the difference that its object is only the public good; and as the funds are employed only under the eyes of the shareholders, these are able to see them employed in the most advantageous manner. Resources would not be permanent for needs that are temporary; succour would be given only to the portion of society that suffered, to the branch of commerce that languished. If the need ceased, the liberality would cease, and its course would be directed to other needs. There would never be useless repetitions of schemes, because the generosity of the public benefactors would be determined only by the actual utility recognized. In fine, this method would withdraw no funds from general circulation, the lands would not be irrevocably possessed by idle hands, and their productions under the hands of an active proprietor would have no limit except that of their fecundity. Is it said that these ideas are chimerical? England, Scotland, Ireland are full of such voluntary associations, and they have experienced from them, for many years, the happiest effects. What has taken place in England can take place in France, and the English have not the exclusive right to be citizens. We have already in some provinces examples of such associations, which prove their possibility. I would cite in particular the city of Bayeux, whose inhabitants are associated in order to banish begging entirely from their town, and have succeeded in providing work for all able-bodied mendicants, and alms for all those unfit for work. This fine example deserves to be proposed for the emulation of all our towns. Nothing would be so easy, if we really willed it, as to direct to objects of certain and general utility the emulation and the tastes of a nation so sensible to honor as ours is, and so easy to lend itself to all the impressions which the Government might know how to give.

6. These reflections ought to strengthen our approval of the wise restrictions which the king, by his edict of 1749, has made to the liberty of creating new foundations. Let us add that they ought to leave no doubt on the incontestable right possessed by the Government—in the first place, in the civil order, next, by the Government and the Church, in the order of religion—to dispose of old foundations, to extend their funds to new objects, or, better still, to suppress them altogether. Public utility is the supreme law, and it ought not to be nullified by any superstitious respect for what we call the *intention of the founder*—as if ignorant and shortsighted individuals had the right to chain to their capricious wills the generations that had still to be born. Neither should we be deterred by the fear to infringe upon the pretended rights of certain bodies—as if private bodies had any rights opposed to those of the State. Citizens have rights, and rights to be held sacred, even by society—they exist independently of society, they enter into it with all their rights, only that they may place themselves under the protection of these

same laws which assure their property and their liberty. But private *bodies* do not exist of themselves, nor for themselves; they have been formed by society, and they ought not to exist a moment after they have ceased to be useful.

We conclude. No work of man is made for immortality; and since *foundations*, always multiplied by vanity, would in the long run, if uninterfered with, absorb all funds and all private properties, it would be absolutely necessary at last to destroy them. If all the men who have lived had had a tombstone erected for them, it would have been necessary, in order to find ground to cultivate, to overthrow the sterile monuments and to stir up the ashes of the dead to nourish the living.

PART IV

Correspondence

To Voltaire

Turgot corresponded with many of leading thinkers of the Enlightenment, including Voltaire, Condorcet, and Hume, and these letters disclose important aspects of his thought. He strongly condemns the French utilitarian philosopher Helvétius for reducing all human motives to self-interest. To the contrary, human beings display strong sympathy for others. Although morality helps people achieve happiness, it must be based on justice, not a narrow conception of self-interest. Turgot left no doubt about the contents of morality founded on this basis. It requires equal rights for everyone. He warns against confusing this conception with rule by the majority, which can, in his view, lead to a destruction of liberty worse, because less easily changed, than despotism. A prime mistake in thinking about morality is to suppose that nations have interests apart from the individuals who live in them. If one correctly considers the interests of individuals, it is clear that absolute freedom of commerce and avoidance of war are required. Turgot strongly supported independence for all European colonies; and in a letter to Richard Price, he offers criticisms and suggestion for the newly independent United States.

To Voltaire

Paris, 24 August 1761

Since I received the letter which you did me the honor of writing to me, a change that concerns me has taken place: I have had the misfortune to be made intendant. I say the misfortune, for in this age of troubles there is no happiness except in living philosophically among our studies and our friends.

It is to Limoges that I am to be sent. I should have much preferred Grenoble, which would have enabled me to make little pilgrimages to the chapel of Confucius and to sit at the feet of the high priest. But your friend M. de Choiseul has judged that to fill a place so important I have still need of some years of training. Thus I cannot hope to see you for a long time, unless indeed you come to fix your tent in Paris—an event I desire more than I dare to advise.

You would find there certainly nothing so good as your present repose—*rem prorsus substantialem*, said the truly wise Newton. You already enjoy as much glory as if you were dead, while you delight yourself as a man in every sense alive; without being in Paris you amuse it, you instruct it, you make it laugh or weep according to your own good pleasure. It is Paris that ought to visit you.

I thank you for having thought of me in proposing the subscription to the edition you are preparing of the works of the great Corneille, and I have to apologize for having so long delayed in replying to you. My desire to see gathered, first, a greater number of subscriptions, then the duties connected with my entrance into the intendancy, and above all, some degree of indolence in writing letters, have been the cause of this delay. I am the more ill-pleased with myself in now being able to ask of you only a small number of copies, the most of my friends having already subscribed on their own account.

But you need not doubt that the public will speedily concur in your enterprise. Independently of the interest which the name of the great Corneille must excite in the nation, the notes and reflections which you promise will render your edition infinitely precious. I have, however, learned from M. d'Argental that you intend to limit these to the pieces which have kept possession of the theatre. I feel that you have in this wished to avoid occasions of criticizing Corneille too hardly, while raising a monument to his glory. But I believe that you would have been able to trace with nicety his beauties and his defects, without deviating from the respect due to his memory. You have left things less complete, and I think that an adequate criticism of the very pieces which we no longer act would be really useful to literature, and above all to young men who destine themselves to art. Your analysis would teach them to distinguish the defects springing from the subject, from those belonging to the manner in, which it is treated. You would indicate the means of their avoiding some of these defects and of modifying others. You would lead them to regard essays which have failed under new aspects which would display the conditions of success.

The Court is in difficulty which side to take [in the decree of the Parliament against the Jesuits]. For myself, I would wish that we did these poor fathers the good turn of sending each of them back to his family, leaving him a reasonable pension and the distinction of the *petit collet*. The college finances would not be overburdened, the individuals would be made happy, the body would no longer exist, and the State would be tranquil.

Adieu, Monsieur; I repeat all my excuses and I pray you to be assured that nobody is, with a more real attachment, etc., etc.

To Condorcet

[Condorcet had written to Turgot (June 14, 1773): "You are very fortunate in being possessed by the passion for the public good and in having the ability to satisfy it; this is a great consolation and of a kind superior to any afforded by literature." Turgot replies to this:]

Ussel, 21 June 1772

WHATEVER YOU MAY SAY, I believe that the satisfaction resulting from literary studies is deeper than any other satisfaction. I am quite convinced that by literature we may be a thousand times more useful to mankind than we can be in any official position, in which we strain ourselves, and often without succeeding, to effect some small benefits, while we are made the unwilling instruments of very great evils. All these small benefits are transient, but the light that a man of letters can shed must, sooner or later, destroy all the artificial evils of mankind, and enable men to enjoy all the good offered them by Nature. I know well that in spite of this there will still remain physical evils and moral disappointments which must be endured by bowing the head under the yoke of necessity. But enduring, and yet fighting against these, the human race is strengthened in moral character. I confess to you that my gout has not prevented me from still believing in final causes. I know well that no individual, or even world of individuals, is the centre of the system of final causes, and that the bounds of this system are not and cannot be known by us. To burst blood, to cough, to have the gout, to lose our friends, all these are but in detail the execution of the decree of death pronounced against everything that is born: and if we die only to be born again, it will still be true that the sum of good will be greater than that of evil (always of course setting aside those evils which men bring upon themselves), transient evils, as I believe they are, for the species, and transient also for the individual, if the thinking and feeling individual has successive careers to fulfil.

[Alluding to a reported commentary on the Bible, written by "Émilie" (Madame du Châtelet, Voltaire's friend), Turgot in the same letter remarks:]

Such a commentary will be an interesting work, but I would wish it written without passion, and in a design to gather from the text commented on all that can be gathered of what is useful as an historical monument precious in many respects. The indulged desire to discover absurdities and things to ridicule, which sometimes are not there, lessens the effect of the incongruities which really are there.

[In reply to some remarks of Condorcet on Helvétius, Turgot writes:]

Limoges, 28 December 1773

I DO NOT THINK that morality in itself should be regarded as *local*. Its principles everywhere spring from the nature of man and from his relations with his fellow-creatures, which do not vary, except in very extraordinary circumstances. But the *judgment* to be passed on the actions of individuals is a problem much more complicated, and infinitely variable, by reason of local opinions and the prejudices of education. In respect to moral judgments, I am a great enemy to indifference, and yet a great friend to indulgence, of which I have often as great need as any other man.

[On this and other questions in moral philosophy connected with it we have a longer letter by Turgot, the date of which is uncertain. du Pont considered it to belong to the pre-Limoges period. But Charles Henry relegates it, we think with more reason, to the period of correspondence marked by the previous letter—December 1773.]

As I do not believe that you yourself could ever write a work in philosophy without logic, in pure literature without taste, and in morals without honesty, I do not see that the severity of my judgment on the book "De l'Esprit" by Helvétius need displease you.... I agree with you that the book is the portrait of the author. But apart from this merit, and that of some passages, written in a kind of poetic eloquence brilliant enough, although usually ill-introduced and also spoiled by some features of bad taste, I confess I cannot see any more in it. It appears to be made and written with the same incoherence that existed in the head of the author. In spite of a pretentious apparatus of definitions and divisions, one finds scarcely an idea analysed with justice, scarcely a word defined with precision. Even with the good maxims which he has stuffed into his work, it is seldom that their effect is not missed or is not spoiled by false applications and by paraphrases which take away all their sharpness or their energy....

I know that there are many good men who are so according to the principles of the book "De l'Esprit"—that is to say from a calculation of self-interest. To make the work one of merit the author might have concerned himself in proving that men have a real interest in being virtuous. But he seems continually occupied in proving the contrary. He pours floods of contempt and ridicule on all honest sentiments, and on all the private virtues; by the grossest and most absurd errors in viewing morals and politics, he would regard these virtues as worthless in order that he may laud presumed public virtues, much more fatal to men than useful to them. Everywhere he seeks to exclude the idea of justice and morality. Those who concern themselves with these *minutæ* he confounds with the bigots in religion and hypocrites in morals. Never do we find him founding his morality on justice, and he has not a word tending to prove that justice toward all is the interest of all, that it is the interest of every individual as well as of every society. According to his false method and very false principles, he lays it down that there is no foundation for probity between nations, from which it would follow that the world must be for ever a den of robbers. On no side does he see that the interest of a nation is nothing else than the interests of the individuals who compose it. Nowhere does he rest himself upon any deep knowledge of the human heart; nowhere does he analyze the real needs of men—which appear to him to consist only in their having wives. He has no idea that man may have need to love. But indeed a man who could have felt this need could not have said that *self-interest is the only principle that actuates men.* He would have understood that, in the sense in which this proposition is true, it is a puerility and a metaphysical abstraction from which there is no practical result to be drawn, since it is just equivalent to saying that *men only desire what they desire.* If he alludes to self-interest, reflected upon, calculated upon, by which a man compares himself with others, and prefers himself, it is false to say that men, even the most corrupt, conduct themselves always by this principle. It is false to say that the moral sentiments do not influence men in their judgments, in their actions, in their affections. A proof that they do influence is that men have to make an effort to overcome their sentiment when it is in opposition to their interests. A proof is that they have remorse. A proof is that this interest, which they pursue at the expense of integrity, is often founded on a sentiment honest in itself and only ill-directed. A proof is that they are deeply touched by romances and by tragedies; a romance whose hero acted according to the principles of Helvétius—I mean to those he teaches—would displease readers much. Neither our ideas nor our sentiments are innate, but they are natural, they are founded in the constitution of our mind and of our soul, and on our relations with everything that surrounds us.

I know that there are some deficient in moral sensibility who are at the same time virtuous men, such as Hume, Fontenelle, etc., but all take for the foundation of their virtue *justice*, and even a certain degree of kindness. Thus I make it less a reproach to Helvétius for his having little sensibility than for his representing the quality as a ridiculous folly, or as a piece of hypocrisy, and for his exalting only the passions without fixing the definition of any duty, and without acknowledging any principle of justice....

I forgot to mention the affectation with which he recounts to you the greatest horrors of every kind, the most horrible barbarities, and all the infamies of all the vilest debauchery, in order to declaim against hypocritical or imbecile moralists, who make them, he says, the object of their preachings, without seeing that they are the necessary effects of such or such stated legislation. As regards the most sensual vices of mankind, he reflects complacently on the debaucheries of great men.... Doubtless a debauchee, a brigand, a murderer may be a Nadir-Shah, a Cromwell, or a Cardinal de Richelieu—but is that the destination of man? Is it desirable that there should be such men? Everywhere Helvétius finds grandeur only in startling and stunning actions; certainly it is not by this fashion of judging that we can arrive at just ideas of morality and happiness.

I cannot side with his declamations against the intolerance of the clergy, nor with those against despotism. 1. Because I do not love declamations; 2. Because I see in his book, everywhere, the question of intolerance is treated not in a manner that could improve either clergy or princes, but only in a manner to irritate them; 3. Because in his declamations against despotism he confounds all ideas, and adopts the style of an enemy of all government.... When we would attack intolerance and despotism, it is before all necessary to stand on just ideas, for the inquisitors have their self-interest in being intolerant, and the viziers and sub-viziers have a self-interest in maintaining all the abuses of government. As they are the stronger, we should not add right to their might. I hate despotism as much as any man does, but it is not by declamations that we ought to attack it; it is by establishing, in an unanswerable manner, the rights of man. And besides, we must distinguish despotism in its degrees; there are a crowd of abuses of despotism in which the princes themselves have no real interest; there are other abuses which they permit only because public opinion has not decided upon their injustice and their evil effects. We should win a better hearing from nations by attacking these abuses with discernment, with courage, and above all by interesting humanity against them, than by indulging in mere eloquent invective. When we do not insult we rarely offend. Men in place are justly shocked by violent expressions which everyone seizes upon, and they attach only a minor importance to the cause provoking the outburst, and to the uncertain or far-distant consequences of philosophic truths, often con-tested and regarded by most men as problems. There is no form of government without some anomalies to which the governments themselves would not willingly apply a remedy, and without some abuses which they intend to reform sooner or later. We should therefore assist them by treating questions of public good solidly, calmly; not coldly, yet not passionately, but with that touching warmth which arises from a deep feeling of justice and the love of order. It is not necessary to believe that to persecute is a pleasure. See what an interest J.-J. Rousseau has inspired in spite of his follies, and how highly he would have been respected if his self-love had only been reasonable. He has been condemned, it is true, by the Parliament; but, 1, because he had the madness to put his name to "Émile"; 2, the Parliament was sorry enough to take it up, and if Rousseau had wished he could easily have avoided the storm by concealing himself two or three months.... By adopting a proper tone, we may say almost anything, and still more effectively when we add to it the weight of solid reason, along with some slight precautions not difficult to take.

I have a leaning to Rousseau in almost all his works, but what case can I make for a declaimer such as Helvétius, who pours vehement insults and scatters bitter sarcasms on all government, and who undertakes to send to Frederick a company of finance-mongers, and who, while deploring the misfortunes of his country, in which he says that despotism has arrived at the last degree of oppression, and the nation at the last degree of corruption and of baseness (which is not true), holds up as his heroes the King of Prussia and the Empress of Russia? I see in all that nothing but vanity, the spirit of party, an excited brain; I see neither the love of humanity nor of philosophy.... I am, I confess, indignant at hearing him praised with a kind of fervor which seems to me an enigma which party-spirit only can explain...

I have received news to the effect that my return is not urgent. I will, therefore, stay here all the month. It is not for any pleasure, nor even for "interest" for I should greatly prefer to be with you, my friends. I find there is more substance in this verse of La Fontaine.

"Qu'un ami véritable est une douce chose!"

than in the whole book "De l'Esprit." I hope that this will obtain my pardon from you for all the ill I have said of the hero whose glory I have attacked. You know well that it is like trying to obscure the sun by throwing dust into the air.

[Condorcet writes in January 1774: "There is a degree of character being below which a man is a fool; but, that aside, we can scarcely cultivate one talent except at the expense of another; in like manner in morality we cannot absolutely avoid certain vices of some danger without the risk of losing some great virtues. In general, scrupulous persons are not fit for great things; a Christian will, while subduing the motions of the flesh, lose the time which he might have employed on things useful to humanity. He will not dare to rouse himself against tyrants, fearing that he may have formed a rash judgment, etc." Turgot replies:]

Limoges, 14 January 1774

I DO NOT LEAN much to the opinion that virtues may be opposed, one kind to another, unless in the case where by virtues we mean certain active qualities which are perhaps as much talents as virtues. Besides, all these words are taken in different senses, and are almost always so ill-defined that we may easily dispute for ages on those matters without coming to an agreement. Morality turns much more on duties than on these active virtues, which, belonging to characters and to passions, are in fact rarely combined in a high degree in the same individual. But all duties are in accord with themselves. No virtue, in whatever sense we take this word, dispenses with justice, and I do not set much value on the men who do "great things" at the expense of justice, or on poets who think that they can produce great beauties of imagination without justness. I allow that excessive exactitude dulls in some degree the fire of composition and that of action, but there is a middle point with everything. We have nothing to do in our argument with a monk who loses his time in subduing the movements of the flesh (although, by parenthesis, the time lost in satisfying them might have been really much greater). Nor has our argument anything to do with the case of a blockhead who hesitates to reprobate a tyrant from fear to form a rash judgment.

To David Hume

23 July 1766

I AM TEMPTED TO send you at the same time a trifle of a very different sort,—the program of an academic prize I think of offering, on a subject we have sometimes discussed. The best means of deciding this, like all other questions, is to get it discussed by the public. I have tried to set forth the state of the question in a clear fashion, as well as the different aspects under which it may be considered. I very much wish you could have the time to give us your ideas. We should take essays on the subject even in English. Our economic philosophers, who belong to Quesnay's sect, will strongly maintain the system of their master. This is a system from which the English writers have been far removed, up to the present, and it is too hard to reconcile its principles with the ambition to monopolize the commerce of the universe for one to expect that they will adopt it from this side for a long time to come. It would, however, be very desirable that Mr. Pitt, and all those who lead the nations, should think as Quesnay does upon all these points. I fear greatly lest your famous demagogue should follow altogether different principles, and think himself interested in keeping up in your nation the prejudice you have called "The Jealousy of Trade." It would be a great misfortune for the two nations. I believe, however, the almost equal exhaustion on both sides will prevent this folly from being long maintained.

7 September 1766

I DON'T KNOW WHY you have thought that those who would like to maintain that indirect taxation is favorable to the proprietors of landed estates will be excluded from competing for my prize. I assure you that if you will give us an essay looking at the question from that point of view, it will be very well received. It is true that the instructions seem to direct authors to look at it from another. But the fact is I have offered the prize rather to get people to see what they can do in the way of estimating the effects of indirect taxation,—for I am still uncertain how the exact share should be reckoned,—than to get a discussion of the general question, as to which my mind is entirely made up.

I have said it was agreed that indirect taxation fell back altogether on the proprietors, since as a matter of fact I have supposed that most of those who defended indirect taxation for other reasons have agreed as to this, especially during the last fifteen or twenty years; and because most of the people agreed with it with whom I have had occasion to talk on the matter. I well know that the practice of no government at all conforms to the principle; but, in the first place, you know, as well as I do, that the principles put into practice by all the governments do not change as easily as speculative principles. The financial system of all the peoples was formed in periods when men gave little thought to these matters; and, although people might be quite convinced that it was established on weak foundations, it would still be a good deal of trouble, and take a good deal of time, to remove a machine in full working and substitute another for it. You know, also, as well as I do, what is the great aim of all the governments of the earth: obedience and money. The object is, as the saying goes, to pluck the hen without making it cry out; but it is the proprietors who cry out, and the government has always preferred to attack them indirectly, because then they do not perceive the harm until after the matter has become law; and, moreover, intelligence is not widely enough distributed, and the principles involved are not clearly enough proved, for them to attribute the evil they suffer to its true cause. I am always sorry not to find myself in accord with you. But I rely upon your tolerance....

25 March 1767

I SHOULD VERY MUCH have liked to enter into some detail on the subject of taxation; but to reply to your objections it would have been necessary, so to speak, to write a book and earn my own prize. I will only indicate to you the principle from which I set out, and which I believe incontestable: it is, that there is no other revenue possible in a State than the sum of the annual productions of the land; that the total mass of these productions falls into two parts: one set aside for the reproduction of the following year, which comprises not only the portion of the crops that the undertakers of agriculture consume in kind, but also all they use to pay the wages of the workmen of every kind who labor for them: blacksmiths, wheelwrights, saddlers, weavers, tailors, etc., it includes, also, their profits and the interests upon their advances. The other part is the net produce, which the farmer pays over to the proprietor, when the person of the latter is distinguished from that of the cultivator,—which is not always the case; the proprietor employs it to pay all that labor for him. If this is granted, it necessarily follows that that taxation which does not bear directly upon the proprietor, falls either upon the wage-earners who live upon the net produce, or upon those whose labor is paid on the part of the cultivator. If wages have been reduced by competition to their just price, they cannot go up; and as they cannot go up except at the expense of those who pay them, one part falls ultimately upon the proprietor for the expenditure he engages in with his net product, the other part increases the expenditure of the cultivators, who are consequently obliged to give less to the proprietor. It is, therefore, in all cases the proprietor who pays.

You remark that I am supposing that wages increase in proportion to taxes, and that experience proves the falsity of this principle: and you justly observe that it is not taxes, high or low, which determine the price of wages, but simply the relation of supply and demand.

This principle has certainly never been disputed; it is the only principle which fixes at the time the price of all the things which have a value in commerce. But one must distinguish two prices, the current price, which is established by the relation of supply to demand, and the fundamental price, which, in the case of a commodity, is what the thing costs the workman. In the case of the workman's wages, the fundamental price is what his subsistence costs the workman. You cannot tax the man who receives wages without increasing the price of his subsistence, since he has to add to his old expenditure that involved by the tax. You thus increase the fundamental price of labor. But although the fundamental price be not the immediate principle of the current value, it is nevertheless a minimum below which it cannot fall. For if a merchant loses by his trade, he ceases to sell or manufacture; if a workman cannot live by his labor, he becomes a mendicant or leaves the country. That is not all: it is necessary that the workman obtain a certain profit, to provide for accidents, to bring up his family. In a nation where trade and industry are free and vigorous, competition fixes this profit at the lowest possible rate. A kind of equilibrium establishes itself between the value of all the productions of the land, the consumption of the different kinds of commodities, the different sorts of works, the number of men employed, at them, and the price of their wages.

Wages can be fixed and remain constantly at a definite point only in virtue of this equilibrium, and of the influence which all the parts of the society, all the branches of production and commerce, exercise upon one another. This granted, if you change one of the weights, a movement cannot but result from it in the whole of the machine which tends to restore the old equilibrium. The proportion which the current value of wages bears to their fundamental value was established by the laws of this equilibrium and by the combination of all the circumstances under which all the parts of the society are placed.

You augment the fundamental value: the circumstances which have before fixed the proportion which the current value bears to this fundamental value cannot but cause the current value to rise until the proportion is reestablished. I am aware that this result will not be sudden; and that in every complicated machine there are frictions which delay the results most infallibly demonstrated by theory. Even in the case of a fluid perfectly homogeneous, it takes time for the level to be restored; but with time it always is restored. It is the same with the equilibrium of the values which we are examining. The workman, as you say, taxes his ingenuity to work more or consume less; but all this is only temporary. Doubtless there is no man who works as much as he could. But it is no more natural for men to work as much as they can than for a cord to be stretched as much as it can be. There is a degree of relaxation necessary in every machine, without which it would run the risk of breaking at any moment. This degree of relaxation in the case of labor is fixed by a thousand causes which continue to operate after the tax is imposed; and consequently, even if by a first effort the tension had increased, things would not be long in regaining their natural shape.

What I have said about the augmentation of labor I also say about the diminution of consumption. Wants are always the same. That kind of superfluity out of which retrenchment can, strictly speaking, be made, is nevertheless a necessary element in the usual subsistence of the workmen and their families. Molière's miser says that when dinner is laid for five, a sixth can always make a meal; but by pushing this reasoning a little further one would quickly fall into absurdity. I add that the diminution of consumption has another effect upon the revenue of the proprietor which is very serious,— through the diminution of the value of commodities and of the products of his land.

I do not enter into the details of the objection drawn from foreign trade, which I cannot regard as a very important matter in any nation, save in so far as it contributes to augment the revenue from lands; and which, moreover, you cannot tax without causing it to diminish. But the time fails me, and I am forced to conclude, although I should have a good deal to say as to the inconveniences caused to the consumers by a tax whereof the very collection involves a perpetual assault on the liberty of the citizens: they have to be searched in custom-houses, their houses have to be entered for *aides* and excises; not to mention the horrors of smuggling, and of the sacrifice of human life to the pecuniary interest of the treasury,— a fine sermon legislation preaches to highwaymen!

Paris, 25 March 1767

I PROFIT BY THE opportunity, through Mr. Francis, to acquit myself of the reply I have so long been owing you, and at the same time to give you my congratulations on the place which you now occupy in the Ministry, so far as there can be a congratulation made to a man of letters upon finding himself thrown into the whirlpool of affairs. As for myself, I should receive much more heartily a congratulation on an event which would set me free from affairs, and would restore me to letters and to liberty. Whatever may be your sentiments on this event, I share them, and I take in it the interest which I shall always take in everything concerning you.... I hesitate to allude to the subject again [the quarrel between Hume and Rousseau], at which you have, with reason, been so much annoyed. Besides, in order to explain oneself at this distance volumes would need to be written, and even after these we might not succeed in understanding each other perfectly, because the slightest circumstance, differently looked upon, suggests interpretations quite contrary to the intention of the writer. I see, for example, by the details into which you enter, and by the pains you take to defend yourself, that you have believed my reflections to be dictated by my attachment for Rousseau, of whom you call me a zealous friend, and of whom you say elsewhere, I am so fond (*engoué*).... I can well assure you that no other motive has dictated what I wrote to you than my attachment for you—attachment very real, and founded on personal knowledge, while of Rousseau I have no knowledge personally, for I met him only for half an hour at Baron d'Holbach's more than twelve years ago. I know Rousseau only as an author. Unfortunately experience has dispelled in me the illusion that the man himself is to be loved merely from faith in his writings. I say unfortunately, because this illusion is very sweet, and I have lost it only with much regret. I do not, however, less esteem, and love greatly, the works of Rousseau. Quite independent of the beauty of his language, the eloquence of Rousseau in his moral writings has a charm of peculiar power. I believe that he is one of the authors who have best served morality and humanity. Very far from reproaching him for having in this respect wandered from common ideas, I believe, on the contrary, that he has respected still too many prejudices. I believe that he has not gone far enough forward on his road; but it is by following his path that we shall arrive at the end which is to draw men together into equality, into justice and happiness. You must understand me. You will do me the honor of believing that I do not adopt his ridiculous paradoxes on the danger of literature, and on the destination of man to the savage life. Like yourself, I regard them as a display, a kind of "feat of strength" of eloquence. Rousseau was not yet known when he set himself on this false track; the body of his ideas was not yet formed. He imagined himself as gaining an advertisement by seizing on the paradoxical sides of the subjects proposed by the Academy of Dijon. This unfortunate pride, which I do not pretend to justify, has led him constantly to heap up paradoxes in order not to have to retract those first made; and his "Émile" is still spoiled by the twists he sometimes gives in it to truths placed there merely in order to connect them with his crack-brained fads. I believe that in this he is a victim of the charlatanism produced by an ill-conceived self-love. Moreover, I do not believe much in his pretended Christianity. But, in spite of these defects, how many potent truths there are in "Émile," how closely the path which he presents to education is drawn from Nature, what fine and original observations there are on the successive developments of the human mind and human heart! He prolongs rather much this development. Nature moves faster than he thinks; but she follows the route which he traces, and he is the first who has known to quicken and advance Nature without hampering her, and for this assuredly the human race is to him under an eternal obligation. And do you count for nothing the *contrat social*? At all events it presents a very luminous truth, which appears to me to fix for ever our ideas on the inalienability of the sovereignty of the people under whatever government may exist. "Émile" appears to me everywhere to exhale the purest moral lessons ever yet taught, and they might in my opinion be carried into further application; but I guard myself against giving you more of my ideas on this because you would think me perhaps to be still madder than Rousseau. I will not say to you, then, that I find true morality in no book on morals, and that all I recognize of it is scattered here and there *in romances*. I will not say to you that it is precisely because the morality in the writings of Rousseau approaches nearest to that of romances, that I so much esteem it, for I should thus give you too ill an opinion of myself. After this profession of faith in Rousseau considered as author, I confess freely, but not without regret, that there are defects which render his person intolerable in society and which have caused him to fall into odious improprieties. There is no one in the world who can be more indignant than I am at his suspicions against you. Although I have regarded them quite in the same light as you have, and although I have not believed them to be a mere pretext suggested in bad faith, and deliberately, in order to shake off the obligations which he received from you; although I have regarded them only as the fruit of an imagination excited by pride and by melancholy, I do not the less feel that no honest soul could conceive such suspicions against a benefactor, and that a misbelief so evil-minded proclaims a man in whom we can have no confidence. I believe that at present Rousseau is quite convinced of the falsity of his suspicions, and I hold him to be inexcusable for not having retraced his steps. However, I am less surprised at this second fault than at the first, considering that the excess of his pride and the horror he would doubtless feel to see himself humiliated before you after the manner in which you have treated him. If I have differed from your view of the matter, it was not that I might justify Rousseau, because no one in the world can justify him, but I believed—and I confess to you that I still think the same—that you are mistaken in the manner of regarding his conduct; and I see with pain that in defending yourself on the subject of Rousseau's accusation—on which assuredly you have no need of defense, and which falls by its own atrocity—you have put yourself slightly in the wrong toward him by attributing to him views which I believe he did not hold, and you have given him, so to speak, a means of setting him on his feet again in the fight. It seems to me that by confining yourself to making public the two letters without comment he would have been confounded in the most overwhelming manner. I know well that he is so already; but the partisans of Rousseau still say: "Mr. Hume has taken this affair too seriously"; besides I think all this ought to disquiet you very little. Men who know you the least of the world have rendered you full justice, in France as well as in England, and I am sure that even among Rousseau's partisans who know you the least no one has been tempted to give the least credence to the absurdities of his letters. If in order to lead Rousseau into England you shortened your stay in France, it is we who suffer the most by the whole affair, since we are deprived of the pleasure to possess you and to live with you. I am one of those who regret it the most. I have dwelt longer than I intended upon this affair, but it shall be certainly the last time of my mentioning it to you, [The remainder of Turgot's letter is given to an argumentative defense of his "agricultural" doctrine.]

Paris, 1 June 1767

I AM NOT SURPRISED at your ways of thinking on literature and public affairs, although they are quite opposed to my own. Your passion for Letters is a love used up by long enjoyment, and public affairs are to you a new taste. As to me, on the contrary, I am more than satiated with affairs, and circumstances have never permitted me to give myself up to my taste for literature. It may possibly be that my career will thus become the inverse of yours, and that I shall yet find my relaxation in study as you find yours in affairs.

It is right to say that the affairs with which you meddle are probably less irksome than those occupying me. With us the interior administration is complicated with a multitude of details repulsive and trivial, entangled with the spirit of pettifogging, by the multiplicity and perplexity of forms, etc.... However, literature and public life are both *means*—the end is happiness. But it happens too often that the equipments embarrass the march, and prevent the end being reached. I wish very earnestly that you may find everywhere the happiness of which you are so worthy. It will ever be a happiness for me to be counted one of your friends.

Paris, 3 July 1768

THE GOOD GOVERNMENT [hoped for in the future] cannot establish itself without creating a crisis, and crises are accompanied by disorder. Must we accuse on that account the light and liberty which force us to pass through these disorders in order to bring about a happier condition? No, certainly no. They make evil on the way to good; but after all do they make more evil than the tyranny and the superstition which would suppress them? You do not think so, I am sure, any more than I do. The people occupied with their necessities, the great occupied with their pleasures, have no time to be wise and to extricate themselves from their prejudices. But in the progress of knowledge it will come about that we need not be so learnedly wise in order to have good sense and to be able to render truths easily popular which today exact labor before they carry conviction.

To Mlle. de Lespinasse

Limoges, 26 January 1770

YOU SEEM TO BELIEVE that I think the Abbé Gialiani's work (*"Dialogues sur le commerce desbBlés"*) to be a good one; I only find it to be full of wit, of genius, of tact, of depth, of good temper, etc., but I am far from finding it to be good. I think that, on the whole, it is intellect infinitely ill employed, all the worse for its greater success, for it will be a welcome support to all the fools and knaves attached to the old system, which after all the Abbé himself surrenders in his conclusions. He has the art of all those who set themselves to darken things that are clear to the open mind, of the Nollets disputing against Franklin on electricity, of the Montarans against Gournay on the freedom of commerce, of the Caveyracs attacking tolerance. This art consists in never commencing at the commencement, but by rushing into the subject in all its complications, or with some fact which is only an exception, or some circumstance isolated, far-fetched, or merely collateral, which does not belong to the essence of the question and goes for nothing in its solution. The Abbé Galiani, commencing with the case of Geneva to treat of the question of the freedom of the corn-trade, is like the man who, writing a book on the means men employ to procure themselves subsistence, should make his first chapter on "culs-de-jatte"; or like a geometer who, treating of the property of triangles, should commence by white triangles as the most simple, in order to treat after of blue triangles, then of red triangles, etc. I would state generally that whoever overlooks the fact of political States being separated from each other and being differently constituted will never treat properly any question of Political Economy. Besides, I do not like to see him always so prudent, so much an enemy to enthusiasm, so much in accord with all the *ne quid nimis*, and with all men who simply enjoy the present and are quite satisfied that the world should go on as it does, because it goes on well enough for them, and who, as Gournay said, having their own bed well made, do not wish to be disturbed. These indeed are not the men to love enthusiasm, and they like to call "enthusiasm" all that attacks the infallibility of men in office....

I believe it possible for a very good reply to Galiani to be made, but it would demand much study and tact. The Economists are too confident in their science to fight against one they consider a merely adroit dealer in old wares. As for the Abbé Morellet, he must not think of it; he would do himself a real wrong by turning again from the work of his dictionary.

To Abbé Morellet

Limoges, 17 January 1770

YOU HAVE BEEN VERY severe. Galiani's "Dialogues" is not a book to be called bad, although it sustains a very bad cause, but it could not sustain it with more spirit, more charm, more tact in the exercise of its frank pleasantry and of its subtlety in discussion of details. A book written with this elegance, this airiness of tone, this correctness and originality of expression, and by a foreigner, is a phenomenon. The work is very amusing, and unfortunately it will be very difficult to reply to it in such a manner as to dissipate the seduction induced by the speciousness of its reasonings and the piquancy of its style, I wish I had the time, but I have it not. Neither have you. du Pont is absorbed in his paper. The Abbé Baudeau would reply too much as an economist, etc.

[To same, some time later, same year.]

I AM CURIOUS TO know what the English have thought about "L'Histoire des deux Indes" [by the Abbé Raynal]. I confess that while admiring the talent of the author and his work, I have been somewhat shocked by the incoherence of his ideas, and by seeing paradoxes the most opposite brought forward or defended with the same warmth of argument, the same eloquence, the same fanaticism. He is sometimes puritanic like Richardson, at other times immoral like Helvétius . . . irrational in science, irrational in metaphysics, and often in politics. His book brings out no result, except in showing the author to be a man full of thought, well instructed, but without one idea in him properly determined, such a man as would allow himself to be carried away by the enthusiasm of a jejune rhetorician.

He seems to have put himself to the task of sustaining successively all the paradoxes which have presented themselves to him in the course of his readings or of his dreams. He has more learning, more sense, and more natural eloquence than Helvétius, but he is in fact as incoherent in his ideas, and as ignorant of the true nature of man.

To Dr. Josiah Tucker

Paris, 12 September 1770

I HAVE NOT THE honor to be personally known to you, but I know that you were pleased with the translation I made, fifteen years ago, of your. Questions on the Naturalisation of Foreign Protestants.' I have since translated your pamphlet on the wars of commerce ["On going to War for the sake of Trade." London, 1763]. I have delayed its publication purposing to add some notes, which my occupations have not yet left me time to complete. A translator owes to his author every kind of homage, and I now request of you to accept as such a pamphlet which, while certainly conveying to yourself nothing new, may, I have been told, prove useful in spreading elementary ideas on subjects with which we desire to see the public better acquainted.[1] This little piece was written for the instruction of two Chinese whom I met in this country, in order to let them better understand questions I had put to them on the state and the economical constitution of their empire.

These questions reminded me of others which you had the goodness to send to me by Mr. Hume, but which I never received; for the packet put into the post-office at Paris for Limoges was lost. Mr. Hume no doubt informed you of this accident and of my regrets. I owe you not the less my deep thanks. If a copy should remain to you and you are disposed to repair my loss, the surest way would be simply to put it into the London post-office, to the address of M. Turgot, Intendant of Limoges, Paris.

---

[1] The work thus modestly referred to is the *Réflexions sur la formation des richesses*.

I have a regret very much greater, that of not having been able to profit by the visit you made some years ago to Paris, in obtaining the honor of personal acquaintance with you. I should have been all the more flattered by it, for I find by your works that our principles on liberty and on the main objects of political economy are much in accord. I confess I cannot help being astonished that, in a nation enjoying the liberty of the press, you should be almost the only author who has known and felt the advantages of a free commerce, and who has not been seduced by the puerile and suicidal illusion of a commerce fettered and exclusive. May the efforts of enlightened and public-spirited politicians destroy this abominable idol, which still remains after the mania of conquests and of religious intolerance of which the world begins to be undeceived! Think of the millions of men who have been immolated to these three monsters! I see with joy, as citizen of the world, an event approaching, which more than all the books of philosophers will dissipate the phantom of the jealousy of commerce. I allude to the separation of your colonies from the mother country, which will soon be followed by that of all America from mother Europe. Then the discovery of that part of the world will become really useful. Then will it multiply our commercial enjoyments much more abundantly than when we purchased them with streams of blood. The English, the French, the Spaniards, etc., will consume the sugar, the coffee, etc., etc. and will sell their commodities just as the Swiss sell theirs today, and these nations will also have, like the Swiss people, the advantage that this sugar, coffee, etc., will no longer serve as pretexts to intriguers to involve their nation in ruinous wars and to burden it with accumulated taxes.

I have the honor to be, etc.

Limoges, 10 December 1778

I HAVE MANY EXCUSES to make to you for having so long-delayed the thanks I owe you for all the particulars you have been kind enough to send to me at the request of my friend M. Bostock, relating to the production of cereals and their commerce.

To Dr. Josiah Tucker

I intended to reply to you in English, but at the time I found myself just convalescent from an attack of gout; and as it is to me somewhat of a task to write in your language, I delayed my answer until another time. Since I returned to the province, I have had quite a pressure of occupations, and I take advantage now of my first moment of liberty. But as Mr. Bostock is now in London, he can translate my letter to you, and thus it is I write it in French.

I begin by thanking you for the different pamphlets you have forwarded to me, of your own composition, on this interesting subject. I am entirely of your opinion on the inutility of the bounty which your Government have so long granted on the export of corn. My principles on this matter are: absolute liberty to import, without distinction of vessels of this or that nation, and without any duties on import; similarly, absolute liberty to export in all kinds of vessels without any duties on export and without limitation even in times of scarcity; liberty in the interior to sell to whomsoever we wish, when and where we wish, without being obliged to carry to the public market, and without any authority interfering to fix the price of corn or of bread. And I would extend these principles to commerce in all kinds of merchandise. This policy is, as you know, far distant from the practice of your Government and of our own.

[Turgot then, at considerable length, dwells on the desirability of obtaining reliable statistics on the price of wheat, etc., in France and England, with various suggestions, and then replies to an inquiry by Dr. Tucker on a minor matter.]

I have made several inquiries relative to the question you have put to me on the opportunities which an English farmer would have to establish himself in one of our provinces. To work a farm it would be necessary to have a capital sufficient to develop it in value, and I doubt if capital would return as much in a French farm as in an English one. The reason is that our Government is still very undecided on the principles of the liberty of the corn-trade. It is even still extremely prepossessed against the exportation, and if it does not change its way of thinking by permanently establishing liberty of transit, there is reason to fear that our agriculture will become very slightly profitable. Besides, in the greatest part of our provinces, the land-tax is imposed on the farmer and not on the proprietor, which renders the condition of the farmer much less advantageous. I add that a Protestant would, in certain provinces, often have many disagreeable experiences to endure.

To Dr. Richard Price

Paris, 22 March 1778

Mr. Franklin has forwarded to me, on your part, the new edition of your "Observations on Civil Liberty, etc." I owe you a doubly grateful acknowledgment. 1. For your work, of which I have long known the value, and which I had read with avidity at the time of its first appearance, in spite of the onerous duties that then pressed upon me; 2. For the kindness and sincerity in which you have withdrawn the imputation of "awkwardness" (*maladresse*) which you had mingled with the good you had said of me elsewhere in your "Observations." I should indeed have deserved the imputation if you had had in view no other *maladresse* than that of my being unable to untwist the secret springs of the intrigues directed against me by men much more adroit in this kind of work than I am—than I shall ever be, or ever wish to be. But at first it seemed to me that you imputed to me the *maladresse* of having rudely offended the general opinion of my nation, and in this respect I believe that you did justice neither to me nor to my nation, where there is much more enlightenment than your countrymen generally suppose, and where, perhaps, it is easier to lead the public to reasonable ideas than it is with yourselves. I judge thus by the infatuation of your nation on the absurd project of subjugating America which so long endured, until the result of Burgoyne's adventure began to open its eyes. I judge thus by the spirit of monopoly and exclusion which prevails among all your political writers on commerce (I except Mr. Adam Smith and Dean Tucker), a spirit involving the very principle on which your separation from your colonies took effect. I judge thus by all your polemical writings on questions which have agitated your nation for the last twenty years, and among which, until your own appeared, I can scarcely recollect to have read one in which the real point of the question was seized.

I cannot conceive how a nation which has cultivated with so much success all the branches of natural science, should remain so completely below itself in the science the most interesting of all, that of public happiness; in a science in which the liberty of the press, which your nation alone enjoys, would give to it prodigious advantage over all the other nations of Europe. Is it national pride that has prevented you from turning these advantages to account? Is it because you are somewhat less ill than others that you have employed all your speculations to persuade yourselves that you are perfectly well? Is it the spirit of party, the desire to find a support in [uneducated] popular opinions, which has retarded your progress by inducing your politicians to treat as vain metaphysics all those speculations which tend to establish fixed principles on the rights and the true interests of individuals and of nations? How has it happened that you are almost the first among your men of letters who has advanced just notions of liberty and who has exposed the falseness of the idea, again and again pronounced by almost all public writers, that liberty is secured if men are only subject to *laws*—as if a man oppressed by an unjust law could be free? This would not be true, even supposing all the laws were the work of the assembled nation; for beyond all, the individual has also his rights, and the nation cannot deprive him of them, except by violence and by an illegitimate use of the general power. Although you have, indeed, yourself dwelt upon this truth, perhaps it still merits from you a fuller development, considering the little attention that has been given to it, even by the most zealous advocates of liberty.

Again, it is a strange thing that in England it should not be held as a common truth that one nation has never any right to govern another nation; that such a government can have no other foundation than physical force, which is also the foundation of brigandage and of tyranny; that the tyranny of a people is of all tyrannies the most cruel and the most intolerable, and the one which leaves the fewest resources to the oppressed nation; for after all a despot is limited by his own interest, he is checked by conscience or by public opinion, but a multitude [in a fit of ascendency] never calculates, is checked by no conscience, and awards to itself glory while it more deserves disgrace.

Events are, for the English nation, a terrible commentary on your book. For some months they have rushed on with an accelerated rapidity. The end is reached in respect to America. She is independent now for ever. Will she be free and happy? Is this new people, placed so advantageously to give to the world the example of a constitution by which man may enjoy all his rights, freely exercise all his faculties, to be governed only by nature, reason, and justice?—will this people be able to form such a constitution? Will they be able to establish it on permanent foundations, and to ward off all the causes of division and of corruption which can undermine it, little by little, and destroy it?

I confess that I am not pleased with the constitutions that have been drawn out by the different American States up to this time. You reproach with reason that of Pennsylvania for the religious oath exacted from members of the representative body. The case is even worse in other States; there are several which exact, by oath, specified belief in certain dogmas. I observe in a great many instances an imitation, without any real necessity, of the usages of England. Instead of radiating all the authorities to one centre, that of the nation, different bodies have been established, a body of representatives, a council, a governor, just because England has a House of Commons, a higher chamber, and a king. They think of balancing the different powers; as if this equilibrium of forces, which was believed to be necessary to balance the great preponderance of royalty, could be of any use in republics founded on the equality of all the citizens, and as if the establishment of so many different bodies would not be a source of so many divisions! In wishing to prevent chimerical dangers, they have created real ones. It was desirable to have nothing to fear from the clergy; they have united them under their banner of a common proscription. By excluding them from the right of eligibility [to the representative body], they have made of them a body by themselves, a body foreign to the State. Why should a citizen, who has the same interests as others in the common defense of liberty and its possessions, be excluded from contributing to the State his enlightenment and his virtues, because he belongs to a profession which itself exacts these virtues and this enlightenment? The clergy is dangerous only when it exists as an organized body in the State, when we attribute to this body special rights and private interests, and when we attempt to have a religion established by law—as if men could have any right or any interest in regulating the conscience of others; as if the individual man should sacrifice, for the advantages of civil society, the principles to which he believes his eternal salvation to be attached—as if a people were to be saved or to be damned *in a lot*! Wherever tolerance, that is to say the absolute neutrality of the Government in dealing with the conscience of individuals, is established, there the ecclesiastic, in the midst of the national assembly, when he is admitted, is but a citizen; he becomes an ecclesiastic only when he is excluded.

The framers of American constitutions cannot study enough to reduce to the smallest number possible the kinds of affairs of which the Government of each State should take charge; to separate the objects of legislation from those of general administration and from those of local administration, and to constitute minor local assemblies which by fulfilling the functions of Government in local matters would exclude these from the general assemblies, and remove from their members every opportunity, means, and desire of abusing an authority which should be confined to general interests, and kept free from the petty local passions which agitate people....

No fixed principle is established in respect to taxation; it would seem that each province could tax itself according to its fancy, could establish personal taxes, taxes on consumption, and on importation—that is to say, would maintain an interest of its own, contrary to the interest of the other provinces.

The right to control commerce is everywhere taken for granted; exclusive bodies, or the governors, are even authorized to prohibit the exportation of certain commodities in certain circumstances. So far are people yet from realizing that the law of complete freedom of all commerce is a corollary of the right of property—so deep are they still immersed in the fog of European illusions.

In the general union of the provinces with each other I do not see a coalition, a fusion of all parties, in order to make a body one and homogeneous. It is only an aggregation of parties, always too separated, and which will always maintain a tendency to separate, by the diversity of their laws, of their manners, of their opinions, by the inequality of their actual forces, and still more by the inequality of their eventual progress. It is only a copy of the Dutch Republic, which had not to guard, like the American Republic, the possible extension of some of their provinces. The whole edifice at present rests on the false basis of a very ancient and very vulgar policy, on the prejudice that nations and provinces have an *interest*, as nations and provinces, other than the interest of the individuals composing them, which is to be free and to defend their property against invaders; that they have an interest, not in buying merchandise from the foreigner, but in compelling the foreigner to consume their productions and the works of their manufactures; an interest in having a vaster territory, in acquiring such and such a province, such an island, such a village; an interest in gaining an ascendency over other peoples.... Some of these prejudices are fostered in Europe, because the ancient, rivalry of nations and the ambition of princes obliged all States to hold themselves armed to defend themselves against their armed neighbors, and to regard the military force as the principal object of Government. But America has the happiness to have no enemy to fear (unless she creates a division within herself); thus she can and should appreciate at their real value those presumed interests, those subjects of discord which would threaten her liberty. By the sacred principle of the freedom of commerce, regarded as a consequence of the right of property, all the presumed interests of national commerce disappear, also the interest to possess more or less territory will vanish, by the principle that the territory belongs not to the nations but to the individual proprietors of the land [and other inhabitants]; that the question whether such a canton, such a village ought to belong to such a province, to such a State, ought not to be decided by the presumed interest of that province or that State, but by the interest of the inhabitants of that canton or village themselves.

To Dr. Richard Price

I imagine that the Americans are yet far from feeling the force of these truths to the degree necessary to insure the happiness of their posterity. I do not blame their leaders. They had to provide for the necessity of the moment by a Union, such as it is, against a present and formidable enemy; there was no time to think of correcting the vices of constitutions and deciding upon the composition of the different States. But they ought to beware of making these defects permanent. They ought to set about uniting opinions and interests, and placing them under uniform principles in all the provinces. They have in this respect great obstacles to overcome....

In the Southern colonies there is a too great inequality of conditions, and above all, the great number of black servants, whose slavery is incompatible with a good political constitution, and who, even when their liberty is granted, will cause embarrassment by forming almost a second nation in the same State.

In all the States there prevail prejudices, an attachment to established forms, the use and wont of certain taxes, the fear of taxes of a better kind that should be substituted for them, the vanity of those colonies which think themselves to be the most powerful, and most unhappy symptoms beginning of national pride. I believe that the Americans are bound to become great, not by war but by culture.... If they leave neglected the immense fields that stretch to the sea on the west, there might be formed there a mingling of their outlaws, of their scamps escaped from the severity of the law, with the savages there, from which would rise hordes of brigands to ravage America as the barbarians of the North ravaged the Roman Empire; hence another danger, the necessity of holding themselves armed on the frontier and of being there in a state of continual war. The colonies on the frontier will in consequence become more inured to war than the others, and this inequality in military strength may become a terrible spur to ambition. The remedy for this possible inequality would be to maintain a standing military force, to which all the colonies will contribute in proportion to their population. The Americans, who harbor still all the fears that prevailed in England, dread more than anything a permanent army. They are wrong. Nothing is easier than to connect the constitution of a standing army with the militia, in such a manner as to improve the militia and to make liberty even more assured.... There are thus many difficulties for the future, and perhaps the secret self-interest of powerful individuals will be joined to the prejudices of the multitude to frustrate the efforts of the truly wise and good citizens.

All right-thinking men must pray that this people may arrive at all the prosperity of which they are capable. They are the hope of the human race. They should be the model. They must prove to the world, as a fact, that men can be both free and peaceful and can dispense with the trammels of all sorts which tyrants and charlatans of every costume have presumed to impose under the pretext of public safety. They must give the example of political liberty, of religious liberty, of commercial and industrial liberty. The asylum which America affords to the oppressed of all nations will console the world. The facility of profiting by it, in making escape from the consequences of bad governments, will compel the European powers to be just, and to see things as they are. The rest of the world will, by degrees, have its eyes opened to the dispersion of the illusions amidst which politicians have been cradled. But, for that end, America herself must guarantee that she will never become (as so many of your ministerial writers have preached) an image of our Europe, a mass of divided powers disputing about territories or the profits of commerce, and continually cementing the slavery of peoples by their own blood.

All enlightened men, all the friends of humanity, should at this moment contribute their lights and join their reflections to those of wise Americans, in order to concur in the great work of their legislation. This would be well worthy of you, Sir; it has been my desire to excite your zeal; and if in this letter I have given myself up, perhaps too much, to the expression of my own ideas, this desire has been my only motive, and will excuse me, I hope, for the weariness I may have inflicted on you.

I would that the blood which has been shed and which will yet be shed in this quarrel, should not prove useless for the happiness of mankind.

Our two nations have done each other much evil, without either of them probably having gained any real profit. The increase of national debts and expenditure, and the loss of many lives, are perhaps the only result. England, it seems to me, has incurred that even more than France. If, instead of pursuing this war, you had only acted with a good grace at the beginning, if you had allowed policy to dictate then what it was inevitably compelled to do later, if national opinion had permitted your Government to have been beforehand with events, and to have consented at first to the independence of America, without making war on anyone, I firmly believe that your nation would have lost nothing by such a policy. She will lose now all that she has spent, and she will spend more; she will suffer for some time a great falling off in her commerce, and suffer many internal troubles, if she is forced to bankruptcy; and whatever happens, she must suffer a great loss in her influence abroad. But this last point is of very little importance for the real good of a people.... Your present misfortunes are the effect of a necessary amputation, which will make for your future happiness; it was perhaps the only means of saving you from the grangrene of luxury and corruption.

If in your political agitations you could reform your Constitution by making elections annual, by granting the right of representation in a more equal manner and one more proportionate to the interests of the represented, you would gain as much perhaps as America herself by this Revolution; for your liberty would remain to you, and your other losses would be soon repaired with that and by that.

You can judge, Sir, by the frankness with which I have expressed myself on these delicate points, of the esteem with which you have inspired me, of the satisfaction I have in feeling that there is some resemblance between our ways of thought. I need not remind you that this confidence is intended only for yourself. I must request of you not to reply to me in detail, *by the post*, for your letter would certainly be opened at the office, and they would find me much too great a friend of liberty for a minister—even for a disgraced minister—to be!

I have the honor, etc.

To du Pont

9 December 1766

I HAVE DRAWN UP some questions for the two Chinese I have mentioned to you; and to enable them to see their object and meaning, I have prefaced them by a sketchy sort of analysis of the labors of Society and of the distribution of riches. I have put no algebra into it, and there is nothing of the *Tableau économique* but the metaphysical part; moreover I have left a good many questions on one side which one would have to treat to make the work complete. But I have gone pretty thoroughly into what concerns the formation and the movement of capitals, the interest of money &c ...

2 February 1770

THE PASSAGE ABOUT THE original agricultural advances has especially troubled me; you know how I have argued on this point with the abbé Baudeau in your presence. I may be wrong, but everybody likes to be himself and not somebody else.... These additions all tend to make me out an economist, which I don't wish to be any more than an encyclopedist.

20 February 1770

ALTHOUGH THE ADVANCES WHICH you call *foncières* contribute their share to the production of the crops,—as I should have said if my object had been to expound the principles of the *Tableau économique*, yet it is false that the *avances foncières* are the principle of property. It is this alteration which has given me most annoyance.

I will content myself with simply telling you this: that no one can argue from what I have said that slavery was good for any society, even in its infancy. As to individuals who have slaves, that is another matter. I should be glad to think you are right in maintaining that slavery is for no one's advantage, for it is an abominable and barbarous injustice; but I very much fear that you are mistaken, and that this injustice may sometimes be useful to the man that perpetrates it.

23 March 1770

TO SUPPOSE THAT SAVING and hoarding are synonymous, what a confusion of ideas, or rather of language! and that to cover certain mistaken expressions which fell from the good doctor[2] in his earlier writings. Oh, this sectarian spirit!

---

[2] I.e., Quesnay.

Appendix:
Miscellaneous Extracts

Great Questions to be Discussed Philosophically.—It seems to me that it is only by treating the matter in its whole length and breadth, and by developing in their natural order all the principles involved, that we can determine what is the best; for it is always with the *best* that we must concern ourselves in theory. To neglect this research, under the pretext that the best is not practicable in existing circumstances, is attempting to solve two questions at one operation; it is to miss the advantage of placing the questions in the simplicity that can alone render them susceptible of demonstration; it is to throw ourselves without a clue into an inextricable labyrinth, or rather it is to shut our eyes wilfully to the light, by placing ourselves in the impossibility of finding it. (Memoir "*Sur les impositions*," 1764.)

* * *

Freedom of Thought.—In directing the forces of your mind to the discovery of new truths, you fear to go astray. You prefer to remain quietly in the opinions most generally received, whatever they may be. That is as much as to say that you should not walk beyond doors, for fear that you might stumble and break your legs. But in that case you are in the position of him whose legs are *already* lamed, for yours are useless to you. And for what has God given limbs to man, if not to walk with them; or given him reason, if *not* to make use of it?

It is not error that opposes so much the progress of truth; it is indolence, obstinacy, the spirit of routine, everything that favors inaction.

I do not admire Columbus merely for having said: "The earth is round; then in advancing toward the west I shall meet the land again," because the most simple things are often the most difficult to find. But what characterizes a great soul is the confidence in which it abandons itself to an unknown sea on the faith of a reasoning. What genius and enthusiasm there would be in that man to whom a recognized truth gave such courage! In many other careers the tour of the world is still to be made. Truth is for us everywhere, in like manner, on our road; glory and the happiness of being useful are at the end.

Political Doctrines Subject to Modification.—Every kind of light comes to us only through time. The slower its progress is, the further the object (carried along by the rapid movement that distances or approaches all existing things) is already distant from the place in which we think we see it. Before we have learned to deal with things in a fixed position, they have already changed several times. Thus we always perceive events too late, and policy has always the necessity to foresee, so to speak, the present.

Discoveries Made by Accident.—The observation, by a thinking man, of a fact which strikes him, and from which he knows how to draw the useful consequences—this is what produces discoveries. We call the meeting of this fact with this man a *chance*. It is evident that these chances would be always more frequent if men were better instructed and had their reasoning powers more cultivated…. It is 2,500 years since medals were struck by first engraving, the reverse way, the inscriptions desired to be made on them, and it is only three hundred years since it was thought of to print on *paper*, with characters engraved, in the same way. The step seems very short; it took twenty-two centuries.

The End of Government.—Since it is admitted that the interests of nations and the success of a good government reduce themselves to a sacred respect for the liberty of persons and of labor, to the inviolable maintenance of the rights of property, to justice between all, from which conditions necessarily result a greater production of things useful to man, the increase of wealth, and of enjoyments, and of enlightenment and all the means of happiness, may we not hope that some day all the present chaos will evolve into some distinct cosmos, in which the elements will have become co-ordinated, and that the science of government will then become easy, and will cease to be beyond the reach of men endowed with only ordinary good sense? This is the term to which we should arrive. (*"Pensées et fragments,"* 1750.)

* * *

Mere Physical Courage.—We err in judging the merit of actions by their apparent difficulty, and in preferring the courage of a soldier, who exposes his life, to that of a man who follows reason in spite of prejudice. We do not realize that the effort of the latter comes entirely from himself. He walks, and often alone; the former is carried, and along with others. Men are children, who cannot take a step quite alone on the smoothest road. And whither may they not be led, through what dangerous paths, to what precipices, by the leading-strings of fashion and of public opinion! One may have sufficient courage of mind, and yet not desire to expose himself to a useless death. And those who have enough good sense not to desire a useless death for themselves, and enough virtue not to inflict it on other innocent people, are generally the most fit to brave death and to receive it nobly when the service of their fellow-creatures and the defense of their country are really concerned.

Certainty Attainable in all Sciences.—We are never deceived in mathematics. If by inadvertence a geometer falls into an error, it is easy to convince him of it, or at least no one will be deceived after him. I venture to believe that, with more pains taken, we may arrive at the same point in the other sciences; that there is no dispute on which, in time, men cannot come to an agreement—for a dispute would be at an end when demonstrated to be incapable of decision.... There is no reason to doubt that new discoveries or further advancement of the human mind will some day render very clear the contested points and will, over them, arrive at evident and irresistible science. (*"Observations et pensées diverses,"* n.d.)

* * *

Study of Languages the Best Lesson in Logic.—The study of languages, well carried out, would be perhaps the best of logics. In analyzing, in comparing the words of which they are composed, in following them from their formation up to the different significations which have been afterward attributed to them, we recognize the thread of ideas, we see by what degrees, by what shades of meaning, men have passed from one to the other; we seize the connection and analogy which exist between them, we succeed in discovering which of them were presented first to man's thought, and what order they kept in the combination of the primitive ideas. This kind of experimental metaphysics is at the same time the history of the mind of the human race and of the progress of its ideas, always proportioned to the needs which have called them forth. ("*Réflexions sur les langues*," 1756.)

* * *

Geography and History.—If we include in geography the state of nations, as the title of political geography seems to require, there is very little to add to geography of the different epochs, to form from them universal history, beyond the names and actions of some special men. In a word, history and geography place men in their different distances. The one expresses the distances of space, the other those of time. The bare description of a country on the one side, and the dry record of successive years on the other, are as the canvas on which objects are to be represented. Ordinary geography and chronology determine their situation; history and political geography paint them in their true colours. Political geography is, if I may call it so, the *coupe* of history. ("*Géographie politique*," 1750.)

* * *

Paternal Government.—The comparison between the magistrate and the father of a family, legitimate in some respects, ought not to be pushed too far. The father is necessarily the tutor of his children, he ought not only to direct them in all things belonging to social duties, but in those things which belong to private life. The magistrate leaves, and ought to leave, to private individuals the choice of the advantages personal to them. They have no need of him, and it would be impossible for him rightly to direct them there; the exercise of his authority is limited [to checking the encroachments of the individual upon the rights of others]. Besides, in those things having no relation to general society, where the private happiness of children is concerned, I shall always maintain that the duty of parents is limited to simple advice. It is the fashion of thinking otherwise which has made the young so unhappy for the rest of their life, which has brought about so many forced marriages, without reckoning the many unsuitable vocations. Every exercise of authority that goes beyond what is really necessary is a tyranny.

Clerical Intolerance.—The dogma of infallibility is certainly false, or inapplicable, when the exercise of infallibility is conferred on those who are certainly not infallible, that is to say, on princes or on governments, for then spring forth two necessary consequences, intolerance and the oppression of the people by the clergy, and the oppression of the clergy by the Crown. The Albigensian wars and the Inquisition established in Languedoc, the St. Bartholomew, the League, the Revocation of the Edict of Nantes, the raid against the Jansenists,—see what has come from that maxim: one law, one faith, one king. I acknowledge the good that Christianity has given to the world, but the greatest of its benefits has been in having enlightened and propagated natural religion. Besides, the greatest number of Christians maintain that Christianity is not Catholicism, and the most enlightened, the best Catholics, admit that it is still less intolerance. They are in this in accord with other sects truly Christian, for the characteristic signs of Christianity are, and are bound to be, gentleness and love.

Church and State.—You ask me to what I reduce *protection* which the State ought to accord to the dominant religion. I reply that, to speak accurately, no religion has any right to exact any other protection than liberty. It follows from the principle of tolerance that no religion has any right except on the submission of the [individual] conscience. The interest of each man is isolated with regard to salvation, he has in his conscience only God for witness and for judge. The laws of society have no relation but to those interests in pursuit of which men can help each other, where they can balance one interest against another. But in [actually determining one's own] religion the help of other men is impossible, and the sacrifice of one's own interest in this respect is a crime. The State, society, men incorporated, have as such no right to adopt arbitrarily a religion, for a religion is founded only on a personal conviction.

The Religion of Humanity.—Natural religion formed into a system and accompanied by a worship.

Individual Freedom.—Laws (according to some thinkers) are the articles of a treaty by which the parties who form it are united. The laws are the result of the interest of the greater or the stronger number, who compel the smaller or the weaker number to observe these laws, that is to surrender themselves to the will of the stronger. Laws, they say, approach the nearer to perfection by the degree in which they embrace the interests of the greater number of men, and in which they favor all more equally, because it is only then that the equilibrium is established between all the interests and all the forces. According to this system, to say that a man has not the right to oppress another man is to say that this other has the strength to resist the oppression. True morality knows other principles. It regards all men with the same eye. It recognizes in all an equal right to happiness, and recognizes this equality of right, not as founded on the struggle of forces between different individuals, but as founded on the destination of the nature of man and on the goodness of Him who has formed man. Hence, whoever oppresses another opposes himself to the divine order. The use he makes of his power is but an abuse. Hence the distinction between might and right—in a word, all intelligent beings have been created for an end; this end is happiness, and on this is founded the right of everyone to the heritage. It is according to the exercise of these divine rights to fulfil man's destiny that God judges men, and not according to their powers.... Thus the strong has no right over the weak.... Every convention contrary to these natural rights has no other authority than the right of the stronger; it is a real tyranny. We may be oppressed by a single tyrant, but we may, quite as much and as unjustly, be oppressed by a multitude. Liberties, like properties, are limited, the one by the others. The liberty to injure has never been sanctioned by conscience. The law ought to interdict it, because the conscience of mankind condemns it. On the other side, the liberty to act while not injuring can be restrained only by laws really tyrannical.

In matters of government we are too much given to sacrifice the happiness of individuals to the presumed rights of society. We forget that society is made up of individuals, that it is instituted to protect the rights of *all*, by insuring the fulfilment of all the relative duties. ("*Lettres sur la tolérance*," 1753.)

* * *

Free Trade.—The idea that the duties we put, either on our own commodities exported, or on foreign commodities imported, are paid by the foreigner is a chimera, for the foreigner sells his merchandise to any one nation at the same price he gets for it from other nations, the duty of import resting necessarily at the charge of the nation establishing it. A government intending to establish certain national manufactures by laying duties on merchandise or raw materials imported, favors these manufactures only at the expense of all others of the nation [and of all consumers]. The manufacturing interest in general is not promoted, because, by placing obstructions to commerce, the development of manufactures is restrained.... All the presumed advantages of these combinations of duties in favor of national commerce against foreign commerce are illusory; all their disadvantages are reciprocal and are increased, the one side by the other. Foreigners employ the same means against our commerce. This "mercantile" and jealous policy is injurious to all States, without being useful to any; it makes of commerce, which should be a tie between nations, a new source of divisions and of wars. It is the interest of all peoples that commerce should be everywhere free and exempt from duties. The first nation giving to others the example of this enlightened and humane policy, by liberating its productions, its industry, its commerce from all prohibitions and all duties, will raise herself rapidly to the very highest prosperity, and will soon compel other nations to imitate her, to the great advantage of the whole world.

The American War.—M. de Vergennes places the problem before us, whether France and Spain should desire to see the subjection or the independence of the English colonies, and he observes that it is not within ordinary human foresight to prevent or to divert the dangers that must result from either event. This remark appears to me to be very just, because I believe that whatever may be, in this respect, the desire of the two crowns, nothing can hinder the course of events which must certainly lead, sooner or later, to the absolute independence of the English colonies, and by an inevitable consequence to a total revolution in the relations of Europe and America.

All Colonies Must Sooner or Later Make their own Laws.—To this all European nations with colonies must come, sooner or later, by agreement or by force. The independence of the English colonies will precipitate this inevitably. Then that delusion, which for two centuries has rocked the cradle of our politicians, will be dissipated. It is then we shall appreciate the exact value of colonies, called *par excellence* "Colonies of Commerce," all the wealth of which European nations believed they would appropriate by reserving for themselves the selling to them and buying from them exclusively. We shall see how precarious and how fragile was the power founded on this system of monopoly.... Wise and happy will be that nation the first to bend its policy to the new circumstances, to see in its colonies only allied provinces, and no longer subject to the mother-country. Wise and happy the nation the first to be convinced that all policy in point of commerce consists in employing all lands in the ways most advantageous for the possessors of the land, all hands in the way the most useful to the individual who works—that is to say, the way in which each man, guided by his own interest, would employ them if let alone—and that all else is illusion and vanity. When the total separation of America shall have compelled all the world to recognize this truth, and shall have corrected European nations of the jealousy of commerce, there will exist among men one great cause of war the less, and it is dù¾difficult not to desire an event [the independence] which must bring about this benefit for the human race.

The Future of Colonies.—I firmly believe that all the mother-countries will be forced to abandon all empire over their colonies, to leave to them entire freedom of commerce with all nations, to content themselves in partaking along with the others this liberty, and in maintaining with their colonies the ties of friendship and fraternity. If it be an evil, I believe there exists, at all events, no means of preventing it, and that the only part to take is to submit to absolute necessity and to make the best of it. For those powers who should be so obstinate as to resist the course of events, there would be the very great danger that, after having been ruined by efforts beyond their means, they would see their colonies escape them all the same, and become their enemies instead of remaining their allies.

A Warning for Spain.—Unhappily there is reason to fear that Spain has less facility than any other power to abandon a road which she has followed for two centuries, and now to form a new system, adapted to a new order of things. Until now she has given her whole policy to maintain the multiplied prohibitions with which she has harassed her commerce.... Neither the ideas of her ministers, nor the opinions of the nation, nor the actual condition of her agriculture and her commerce, nor the constitution and administration of her colonies, nothing, in short, is prepared in advance in order to seize upon that opportunity of power of resolving to change, while change can be made, and of modifying the shock of change, and of the consequences it entails.... Nothing would be worthier the wisdom of the King of Spain and his council than to fix at present their attention on the possibility of this forced separation and on the measures to be taken to prepare for it.

Confidence in the Public Spirit of British America.—It is possible, if the war is prolonged, that the generals may take too much ascendancy by the glory they have acquired, by the enthusiasm they have inspired in their army. It is possible that, not daring to form projects to master a people intoxicated with liberty, recently gained through their courage, the leaders may still try to perpetuate their power and to prepare for a higher fortune at a future time, by insinuating the taste for conquests into their young republic.... We can, however, predict from the prudence that has as yet presided at the conduct of the Americans, from the courage and enlightenment diffused among them, and from their confidence in the wise counsels of the celebrated Franklin, that they have foreseen that danger, that they mean to protect themselves against it, and that they have decided, before all, to give a solid form to their government, and that consequently they will love peace and will seek to preserve it.

Reform for France Depends, "Perhaps For Ever," on War Being Now Avoided.—The king knows the situation of his finances. He knows that in spite of the economies and the ameliorations already made since the commencement of his reign, there is between the revenue and the expenditure a deficiency of twenty millions.... There are three means of clearing off this deficit: an increase of taxes; a bankruptcy, more or less decided, more or less disguised; and a considerable economy in the expenditure as well as in the cost of tax-collection. The first economy ought to be that of expenditure.... While the king finds his finances involved and in disorder, his military and his marine are in a state of weakness difficult to be imagined....

By making a premature use of our strength we risk the perpetuating of our weakness.... War we ought to shun as the greatest of evils, since it will render impossible for a very long time, and perhaps for ever; the reform which is absolutely necessary for the prosperity of the State and for the relief of the people. ("Turgot's last written State Paper," 1776.)

Sources

"Reflections on the Formation and Distribution of Wealth." 1766. In *The Economics of A.R.J. Turgot*, translated and edited by P.D. Groenewegen, pp. 43–95. The Hague: Martinus Nijhoff, 1977.

"Letter to M. l'Abbé de Cicé on the Replacing of Money by Paper, Also Known as the 'Letter on Paper Money.'" 1749. In *The Economics of A.R.J. Turgot*, translated and edited by P.D. Groenewegen, pp. 1–8. The Hague: Martinus Nijhoff, 1977.

"Remarks on the Notes to the Translation of Josiah Child." 1753–1754. In *The Economics of A.R.J. Turgot*, translated and edited by P.D. Groenewegen, pp. 9–13. The Hague: Martinus Nijhoff, 1977.

"Fairs and Markets." 1757. In *The Economics of A.R.J. Turgot*, translated and edited by P.D. Groenewegen, pp. 14–19. The Hague: Martinus Nijhoff, 1977.

"In Praise of Gournay." 1759. In *The Economics of A.R.J. Turgot*, translated and edited by P.D. Groenewegen, pp. 20–42. The Hague: Martinus Nijhoff, 1977.

"Plan for a Paper on Taxation in General." 1763. In *The Economics of A.R.J. Turgot*, translated and edited by P.D. Groenewegen, pp. 96–108. The Hague: Martinus Nijhoff, 1977.

"Observations on a Paper by Saint-Péravy." 1767. In *The Economics of A.R.J. Turgot*, translated and edited by P.D. Groenewegen, pp. 109–22. The Hague: Martinus Nijhoff, 1977.

"Observations on a Paper by Graslin." 1767. In *The Economics of A.R.J. Turgot*, translated and edited by P.D. Groenewegen, pp. 123–32. The Hague: Martinus Nijhoff, 1977.

"Value and Money." 1769. In *The Economics of A.R.J. Turgot*, translated and edited by P.D. Groenewegen, pp. 133–48. The Hague: Martinus Nijhoff, 1977.

"Extracts from 'Paper on Lending at Interest.'" In *The Economics of A.R.J. Turgot*, translated and edited by P.D. Groenewegen, pp. 149–63. The Hague: Martinus Nijhoff, 1977.

"Extracts from 'Letters on the Grain Trade.'" 1770. In *The Economics of A.R.J. Turgot*, translated and edited by P.D. Groenewegen, pp. 164–81. The Hague: Martinus Nijhoff, 1977.

"Letter to l'Abbé Terray on the 'Marque des Fers.'" 1773. In *The Economics of A.R.J. Turgot*, translated and edited by P.D. Groenewegen, pp. 182–88. The Hague: Martinus Nijhoff, 1977.

"A Philosophical Review of the *Successive Advances of the Human Mind*." 1750. In *Turgot: On Progress, Sociology and Economics*, translated and edited by Ronald L. Meeks, pp. 41–59. Cambridge: Cambridge University Press, 1973.

"On Universal History." 1750. In *Turgot: On Progress, Sociology and Economics*, translated and edited by Ronald L. Meeks, pp. 61–118. Cambridge: Cambridge University Press, 1973.

"Which Suppresses the Corvée." 1776. In *Turgot and the Six Edicts*, translated and edited by Robert P. Shepherd, pp. 147–61. Ph.D. diss. New York: Columbia University, 1903.

"Decreeing the Suppression of Craft-Guilds." 1776. In *Turgot and the Six Edicts*, translated and edited by Robert P. Shepherd, pp. 182–200. Ph.D. diss. New York: Columbia University, 1903.

"Which Repeals Certain Rules Concerning Grain Products." 1776. In *Turgot and the Six Edicts*, translated and edited by Robert P. Shepherd, pp. 162–75. Ph.D. diss. New York: Columbia University, 1903.

"Enacting the Suppression of the Exchange of Poissy." 1776. In *Turgot and the Six Edicts*, translated and edited by Robert P. Shepherd, pp. 201–06. Ph.D. diss. New York: Columbia University, 1903.

"Enacting a Change and Modification of Taxes on Suet." 1776. In *Turgot and the Six Edicts*, translated and edited by Robert P. Shepherd, pp. 207–09. Ph.D. diss. New York: Columbia University, 1903.

"Enacting the Suppression of Offices Connected with the Ports, Quays, Stalls and Markets of Paris." 1776. In *Turgot and the Six Edicts*, translated and edited by Robert P. Shepherd, pp. 176–81. Ph.D. diss. New York: Columbia University, 1903.

"On Some Social Questions, Including the Education of the Young." 1751. In *The Life and Writings of Turgot: Comptroller General of France 1774–76*, translated and edited by W. Walker Stephens, pp. 193–203. New York: Burt Franklin, 1895.

"Local Government and Education." 1775. In *The Life and Writings of Turgot: Comptroller General of France 1774–76*, translated and edited by W. Walker Stephens, pp. 265–72. New York: Burt Franklin, 1895.

"Religious Liberty." 1754. In *The Life and Writings of Turgot: Comptroller General of France 1774–76*, translated and edited by W. Walker Stephens, pp. 210–18. New York: Burt Franklin, 1895.

"Religious Equality." 1775. In *The Life and Writings of Turgot: Comptroller General of France 1774–76*, translated and edited by W. Walker Stephens, pp. 256–64. New York: Burt Franklin, 1895.

"Endowments." 1756. In *The Life and Writings of Turgot: Comptroller General of France 1774-6*, translated and edited by W. Walker Stephens, pp. 219–28. New York: Burt Franklin, 1895.

Correspondence to Voltaire, 24 August 1761. In *The Life and Writings of Turgot: Comptroller General of France 1774–76*, translated and edited by W. Walker Stephens, pp. 273–75. New York: Burt Franklin, 1895.

Correspondence to Condorcet, 21 June 1772–14 January 1774. In *The Life and Writings of Turgot: Comptroller General of France 1774–76*, translated and edited by W. Walker Stephens, pp. 275–83. New York: Burt Franklin, 1895.

Correspondence to David Hume, 23 July 1766–25 March 1767. In *Reflections on the Formation and the Distribution of Riches by Turgot, 1770*, translated and edited by W.J. Ashley, pp. 101–04, 106–10. New York: Macmillan Company, 1898. Reprinted, New York: Augustus M. Kelley, 1921, 1963, and 1971.

Correspondence to David Hume, 25 March 1767–3 July 1768. In *The Life and Writings of Turgot: Comptroller General of France 1774–76*, translated and edited by W. Walker Stephens, pp. 283–88. New York: Burt Franklin, 1895.

Correspondence to Mlle. de Lespinasse, 26 January 1770. In *The Life and Writings of Turgot: Comptroller General of France 1774–76*, translated and edited by W. Walker Stephens, pp. 288–89. New York: Burt Franklin, 1895.

Correspondence to Abbé Morellet, 17 January 1770. In *The Life and Writings of Turgot: Comptroller General of France 1774–76*, translated and edited by W. Walker Stephens, pp. 289–90. New York: Burt Franklin, 1895.

Correspondence to Dr. Josiah Tucker, 12 September 1770–10 December 1778. In *The Life and Writings of Turgot: Comptroller General of France*

1774–76, translated and edited by W. Walker Stephens, pp. 291–94. New York: Burt Franklin, 1895.

Correspondence to du Pont, 9 December 1766 – 23 March 1770. In *Reflections on the Formation and the Distribution of Riches*, translated and edited by William J. Ashley, pp. 110–12. New York: Macmillan Company, 1898. Reprinted, New York: Augustus M. Kelley, 1921, 1963, and 1971.

Miscellaneous Extracts. 1750–1776. In *The Life and Writings of Turgot: Comptroller General of France 1774-6*, translated and edited by W. Walker Stephens, pp. 309–25. New York: Burt Franklin, 1895.

Index

Abbé de Cicé, letter to, 67–78
Abbé Gialiani, 493
Abbé Morellet, correspondence with, 494
Abbé Terrasson, Turgot on letters by, 67–78
Abstract and incommunicable essences, 376
Agriculture. *See also* Farmers
    advances in, 31
    entrepreneurs, 152
    return and profits from capital, 37
    returns from, 55
    scale of and capital, 39
    slavery, 370
Alexandria, 333
Ambition, 356
America, savages, 352
American States, 500
American War, 515
Amplifications, 400
Ancient times, proprietors and farmers, 10
Angoulême, credit crisis in, 205
Appreciative value, 177
Architecture, 412
Aristotle, 385
Artisans
    in class structure, 12
    versus farmers, 9

Arts
    architecture, 412
    design, sculpture or painting, 384, 397
    development of, 332
    music, dance or poetry, 329, 381
Asia
    despotism, 367
    development and civilization, 330
    sciences, 406
Athens, 332
Average valuation, money, 23

Bacon, Francis, 385
Bankruptcies, risk of and interest rates, 206
Barbarians
    education and, 379
    and empires, 364
Beans. *See* Grain products
Bishops, 439–48
Böhm-Bawerk, Eugen von, xxv
Bondage to the soil, land cultivation by, 16
Borrowing
    by King or state, 71
    for spending, 145
Bossuet, Jacques-Bénigne, 347

Brandy trade, and interest rates, 205
British America, 517
Buyers, defined by money role, 29

Caesars, 366
Caligulas, 365
Capital
    advance in commercial enterprises, 39
    capital formation and circulation of money, 138
    cultivator's, 135
    equilibrium in use of, 56
    equivalence with land, 34
    free trade in grain, 235
    interest, 135
    return and profits from in agriculture, 37
    and scale of agriculture, 39
    scarcity of and interest, 57
    Turgot's theory of, xvii
    use of, 43
    value to State, 193
Capitalist-entrepreneur, xviii
Capitalists, in class system, 60
Capitalization, xxiii
Cattle
    Exchange of Poissy, 303–08
    as moveable wealth, 32
Cavalier Marin, 404
Charlemagne, 337
Child, Josiah, Turgot on, 79–85
Chinese, men of letters, 406
Church, separation of Church and State, 439–48
Circulation of money, 42
    capital formation, 138
    interest, 81
    savings, 144
City states, 360
Class system
    capitalists in, 60
    cultivators, artisans and proprietors, 12
    division of industry into capitalist entrepreneurs and workmen, 37
Clerical intolerance, 513
Colonies, 361
    independence, 473
    making own laws, 516
Commerce
    advantages from lending and interest, 220
    effect of rate of interest, 57
    effects of taxation on, 94, 191
    and general interest, 106
    importance of gold and silver for development of, 43
    valuations of money, 49–51
Commodities
    as a scale or common measure, 22
    equilibrium with labor, 239
    money qualities, 25
    as pledges on all other commodities, 25
    prices, 90, 135
    valuation and the exchange of, 21
    valuation of with regard to money, 52
    valuation with gold and silver, 28
Commodity money, gold and silver as, 161–82
Competition, just wages, 147

Condorcet, correspondence with, 476–83
Conquerors, 353
Constitution
  American, 501
  France, 433
Consumers, free trade in grain, 237
Consumption
  effect of taxation on, 229
  taxes on, 136
Corporations, rights, 461
Corruption, effects of taxation on, 183
Council of National Education, 429–37
Craft-guilds
  taxes attributed to, 314
  Turgot's recommendations about, 274–91
Credit, of merchants, 70
Crises, government, 492
Cultivators. *See* Farmers
Currencies
  defined, 167
  evaluation, 165
  gold and silver, 166
  value, 164
Cycle of life, 321

Dance, 381
Debts, craft-guilds, 281
Demosthenes, 399
Descartes, René, 385
Despotism
  Asia, 367
  women and, 371
Direct taxation, about, 189
Disposable revenue, 63

Disposable versus not disposable interest, 61
Distribution
  Turgot's theory of, xvi
  wealth, 3–66
Divinity, 385
Division of labor, money's role in facilitating, 29
Division of land, inequality of, 11
Du Pont, correspondence with, 506
Dutch. *See* Holland
Duties. *See* Taxation

Education
  Council of National Education, 429–37
  development of, 379
  government and, 368
  and inequality, 417–28
Empires, barbarians and, 364
Endowments, 461–69
England, right to govern other nations, 499
Entrepreneurs
  agricultural entrepreneurs, 152
  craft-guilds, 279
  origin of, 37
  road building, 263
Entrepreneurship, Turgot's theory of, xvii
Equal division of lands hypothesis, 5
Equal exchange value, xv
Equal value, defined, 175
Equality. *See also* Inequality
  and education, 417–28

Equality of exchange, valuation, 161
Equality of value, Turgot's interpretation of, 203
Equalization, prices, 242
Equilibrium
  gold and silver, 142
  prices of commodities and labor, 239
  in use of capital, 56
  wages, 487
  between wealth, revenue and wages, 152
Esteem value
  about, 172
  defined, 175
Evaluation, currencies, 165
Evasion, effects of taxation on, 183
Exchange
  of goods between people, 161
  role in the valuation of commodities, 21
  Turgot's contribution, xiii
  value of land relative to moveable wealth, 33
  and values, 173–178
Exchange of Poissy, 303–08
Exchange value, defined, 175

Fables, 383
Faculties, 395
Fairs and markets, 87–96
Farmers. *See also* Agriculture; Husbandman
  benefits from free trade, 227
  capital, 135
  division with proprietor, 12
  effect of taxation on, 231
  forced labor for construction of highways, 262
  free trade in grain, 234
  versus artisans, 9
  versus proprietors, 10
Farming. *See* Agriculture
Flour. *See* Grain products
Forced labor, for the construction of highways, 261–74
Foreign trade, 488
Foreigners, taxation of, 191
Foundations, 461–69
France
  constitution, 433
  free trade and industry, 147
  municipalities, 431
  philosophical development, 342
  provinces, 433
  reform for, 518
  Turgot's land taxation plan, 183–201
Fraud and malpractice, natural regulation of, 107
Free trade
  about, 515
  effect on French industries, 147
  iron, 247–57
  principles of, 150
  Turgot's background in, x
Freedom
  benefits from, 226
  of buying and selling, 107
  of commerce, 473
  Gourney on, 124
  individual, 514
  religious freedom, 449–58
  of thought, 509

French Enlightenment, 429–37
Frenicle, M., 387

General interest
　commerce and, 106
　defined, 97
Generality of Limonges, ironworks, 249–57
Genius, 325
Geography, study of, 512
God, law, 451
Gold and silver
　as commodity money, 161–82
　importance to the development of industry, 43
　mining, 140, 154
　role in commerce, 20
　suitability as money, 26–29
　Turgot on Law's ideas on gold and silver, 72–75
　valuation, 166
　valuation with commodities, 28
Goods, defined, 151
Gourney, Marquis de, Turgot on, 97–127
Government. *See also* Law; Monopolies; Regulation; State; Taxation
　borrowing for spending, 145
　correspondence with Condorcet, 478
　crises, 492
　and education, 368
　end of, 510
　formation of, 350
　municipalities in France, 431
　in nations, 359
　paternal, 512
　provinces in France, 433

Grain products, taxation, 291–303
Grain trade
　state power and interest rates, 82, 83
　Turgot's opposition to restrictions on, 223–46
Greece
　barbarism, 397
　development and civilization, 331, 363
　fall of eloquence, 398
　language, 403
Gross product, versus net product, 193
Guilds. *See* Craft-guilds

Helvétius, 473
Heresy, 449–58
Herodotus, 383
Highways, forced labor for construction of, 261–74
History
　fables, 383
　study of, 512
　on universal history, 345–414
Holland
　commercial environment, 94
　taxation, 159
Holy Writ, 322
Homer, 383
Houses, rent from, 136
Husbandman. *See also* Agriculture; Farmers
　about, 355
　pre-eminence of, 7
　wages of, 9

Import duties, who pays, 230
Imports, craft-guilds, 274–91
Independence, colonies, 473
Indirect taxation
  about, 190
  discussion of, 129–46, 147–61
  Turgot's criticisms of, 183–201
Individuals, rights, 461
Industry
  division into capitalist entrepreneurs and workmen, 37
  effect of rate of interest, 57
  free trade, 147
  importance of gold and silver for development of, 43
  money role in advancing, 35
  returns from, 55
Industry trade, 250
Inefficiencies, craft-guilds, 274–91
Inequality. *See also* Equality
  division of land, 11
  and education, 417–428
Inflation, process described, 76
Injustice
  basis of, 214
  craft-guilds, 278
Interest
  anti-usury laws, 203–21
  basis of in loans, 44–49
  capital, 135
  circulation of money, 81
  determination of in relation to moveable wealth, 52
  disposable versus not disposable, 61
  effect of rate of upon enterprises, 57
  free trade in grain, 235

interest rates and grain trade, 82
  laws against, 84
  legitimacy, 211
  risk, 203–21
  scarcity of capital, 57
  taxes, 136
  Turgot's theory of, xvii
Intolerance, 454
  clerical intolerance, 513
  correspondence with Condorcet, 481
Iron, free trade, 247–57

Jansenists, 439–48
Justice
  correspondence with Condorcet, 479
  morality, 473

King. *See* State
Kings, mission of, 456

L'Abbé Galiani, on value, 172
Labor
  equilibrium with commodities, 239
  exchange of for products, 7
  exchange of products for, 7
  forced construction of highways, 261–74
Laborer, wage laborer and land cultivation, 14
Land
  equal division of lands hypothesis, 5
  equivalence with capital, 34

exchange value relative to moveable wealth, 33
inequality in the division of, 11
ownership, 10
price of, 38
proprietor drawing revenue from, 14
returns from, 54
source of moveable wealth and capital, 64
source of taxation, 228
as source of wealth, 32
taxation and, 129–46
wage labor, 14
Landowners. *See* Proprietors
Language
  development and importance of languages, 330
  evolution of, 336
  Greece, 403
  intermingling, 401
  Latin, 403
  logic, 390, 511
  money as a type of, 163
  origin of, 374
  stabilization of, 404
Latin, 403
Law, John, monetary system, 70
Laws. *See also* Regulation
  God, 451
  interest rates, 84
Leases, land, 18
Legitimacy, interest, 211
Leibniz, Gottfried, 387
Lending money, business of, 139
Lentils. *See* Grain products
Leper hospitals, 465
Letter on Paper-Money, 67–78

Liberty. *See also* Freedom
  and equality, 421
Loans
  about, 44–49
  returns from, 55
Logic, language, 390, 511
Louis XIV, 457
Louis XVI, 449–58
Luxury, versus thrift, 53, 81
Lydia, 363

Madame de Graffigny, 419
Manufacturing. *See* Industry
Marginal utility, xiv
Markets. *See also* Fairs and markets
  in lending and interest, 213
  Paris, 311–15
  ports, 157
Marquis do Gourney, influence on Turgot, x
Marriage, 423
Mathematics, 389
Merchants
  credit of, 70
  political force of, 113
  role of profit, 41
Metals. *See* Gold and silver
Metaphysical decrees, 376
Metaphysics, 391
Military spending, usefulness of by small states, 79
Mining, gold and silver, 140, 154
Money. *See also* Commodity money; Currencies; Inflation
  as a type of language, 163
  average valuation, 23
  circulation of, 42

commodities and money qualities, 25
defined, 167
as merchandise, 26
price of, 219
revenue of, 19
role in advancing industry, 35
role in division of labor, 29
sterility of, 212
suitability of gold and silver as, 26–29
Turgot's theory of, xxiv
valuation of, 75
valuation of in commerce, 49–51
valuation with regard to commodities, 52
and value, 161–82
Monies of account, 161–82
Monopolies
as a form of taxation, 192
craft-guilds, 274–91
demands for, 251
Gourney on, 104
and prices, 251
and taxation, 137
Morality
correspondence with Condorcet, 478, 483
development of, 331
and education, 428
justice, 473
Moveable wealth
accumulation of money, 30
cattle as, 32
exchange value relative to land, 33
role in determining price of interest, 52
slaves as, 33
Municipalities, France, 431
Music, 381

Nations
customs and dialects, 354
defined, 155
governments in, 359
intermingling of, 350
origin of, 351
wealth of, 58–60
Natural justice, and rights, 429–37
Natural philosophers, 326
Navigation, 411
Neros, 365
Net product
agriculture, 38
effect of taxation on, 231
revenue and wealth, 149, 152
spending expenses of in the State, 154
taxation and, 134
versus gross product, 193
Newton, Isaac, 342, 387

Opinions, role in human development, 327
Original advances, 194
Ottoman Empire, 345
Ownership, land, 10

Painting, 384, 397
Paper currencies, defined, 167
Paper-Money, Letter on, 67–78
Paris
grain trade, 292–303

Parlement of Paris, 439
ports, quays, stalls, and markets, 311–15
suet trade, 309
Parlement of Paris, 439
Pastoral peoples, 352
slavery, 370
Peas. *See* Grain products
Penny of the price of land, defined, 34
Philosophy, 317–414
successive advances of the human mind, 321–43
Phoenicians, 329
Physics, 393
Poetry, 329, 381
Polygamy, 369
Ports
markets, 157
Paris, 311–15
Poverty, foundations for, 461–69
Price, Dr. Richard, correspondence with, 498–506
Prices. *See also* Valuation
and appreciative value, 177
commodities, 90, 135
effect of taxation on, 233
equalization, 242
equilibrium between commodities and labor, 239
land, 38
of money, 219
and monopolies, 251
Turgot's contribution, xiii
versus value, 178
Principle of value exchangeable objects, 20
Printing, 413
Prizes and gratuities, 114

Production
division between cultivator and proprietor, 12
effects of seizing wealth, 150
exchange of for labor, 7
time factor, 6
Turgot's theory of, xvi
Profits
about, 36
from capital in agriculture, 37
effect of taxation on, 232
free trade in grain, 238
government role in, 111
independence from interest, 211
merchants and, 41
Progress of the human mind, 373
Property, benefits from free trade, 227
Property rights, land, 10
Proprietors
benefits from free trade, 226
division with cultivator, 12
drawing revenue from lands, 14
effects of forced labor for constructing highways, 265
free trade in grain, 236
indirect taxation, 131
self-interest of, 108
source of taxation and, 228
versus farmers, 10
Protestants, 439–48, 449–58
Provinces, France, 433
Public interest. *See* General interest

Quays, Paris, 311–15
Quesnay, 484

Reason, 356
Receiver-General, taxation, 137
Reciprocal nature of transactions, 109
Regulation. *See also* Law
    effect of, 104
    effect on fairs and markets, 91
    grain trade, 83
Religion
    instruction in, 435
    religious freedom, 449–58
    separation of Church and State, 439–48
Rent
    from houses, 136
    ultimate source of taxation and, 228
Republics, women and, 371
Revenue
    about, 193
    compared to wealth, 151
    disposable, 63
    effects of taxation on, 183
    equilibrium with wealth and wages, 152
    of money, 19
    net product as wealth, 149
Revolutions, 324
Rice. *See* Grain products
Rights
    individuals and corporations, 461
    morality and justice, 473
    and natural justice, 429–37
Risk, interest, 203–21
Rome, 333
    fall of eloquence, 398
Rousseau, Jean-Jacques, 489

Rye. *See* Grain products

Saint-Péravey, Turgot's response to, 129–46
Salvianus, 400
Savages, America, 352
Savings
    circulation of money, 144
    Turgot's theory of, xvii
Scarcity of capital and effect on interest, 57
Sciences
    about, 511
    Asia, 406
    development of, 381
    principles, 392
Sculpture, 384, 397
Security, through generating wealth, 110
Seigneur censier, land revenue, 149
Seizing wealth, 150
Self-love, 425
Sellers, defined by money role, 29
Share cropping, land cultivation by, 17
Silver. *See* Gold and silver
Slaves
    land cultivation by, 15
    as moveable wealth, 33
    slavery, women and polygamy, 369
Smuggling, risk of, 136
Spain, a warning for, 517
St. Augustine, 400
Stalls, Paris, 311–15
State. *See also* Government; Regulation; Taxation
    borrowing by, 71

Index

defined, 156
effect of taxation on commerce, 94
separation of Church and State, 439–48
usefulness of military spending, 79
value of capital to, 193
Sterility of money, 212
Stimulating trade or industry, 250
Suet, taxation, 308–11
Systems, Gourney on, 122

Taille réelle, 198
Tariffs, intricacies of, 192
Taxation
  cattle trade, 305
  on consumption, 136
  craft-guilds, 281
  effect on fairs and markets, 91
  grain products, 291–303
  Holland, 159
  indirect taxation, 147–61
  interest, 136
  iron, 247–57
  and land, 129–46
  land tax, 183–201
  and monopolies, 137
  multiplicity of, 112
  origin of, 365
  preferred revenue source, 112
  principle of, 485
  ratio to wages, 486
  suet, 308–11
  ultimate source of, 223, 228
Tenants, land cultivation by, 17
Thrift, versus luxury, 53, 81
Time factor, in production, 6
Tithe, about, 197
Towns, taxes on, 191
Trade
  effects of taxation on, 183
  stimulating, 250
  wages from, 158
Transportation costs, location of fairs and markets, 91
Tucker, Dr. Josiah, correspondence with, 495
Turgot, Robert Jacques, biography, ix
Turks, despotism, 366

United States, 473
Usury laws, 203–21

Validation, of money, 75
Valuation. *See also* Prices
  equality of exchange, 161
  exchange of commodities, 21
  gold and silver, 166
  gold and silver with commodities, 28
  land in relation to moveable wealth, 33
  money and average valuation, 23
  money in commerce, 49–51
  money with regard to commodities, 52
  principle of value exchangeable objects, 20
Value
  currencies, 164
  defined, 151, 168–73
  equality of value, 203
  and exchange, 173–78

l'Abbé Galiani on, 172
in lending and interest, 213
and money, 161–82
Turgot's contribution, xiii
versus price, 178
Vassalage, land cultivation by, 16
Voltaire, correspondence with, 473

Wage laborer, land cultivation, 14
Wages
benefits from free trade, 227
competition and, 147
effect of taxation on, 232
equilibrium, 153, 487
freedom for workers to move and employers to hire, 153
of husbandman, 9
ratio to taxes, 486
from trading, 158
of workman, 8
Wealth. *See also* Moveable wealth
defined, 151
distribution of, 3–66
equilibrium with revenue and wages, 153
free trade in grain, 234
land as source of, 32
of nation, 58–60
net product as, 149
seizing, 150
Wheat. *See* Grain products
Women
enslavement of, 369
relationships, 425
Workman, wages of, 8